MAJOR PROBLEMS IN STATE CONSTITUTIONAL REVISION

Edited by

W. BROOKE GRAVES

Adjunct Professor of Political Science

The American University

Sponsored by

PI SIGMA ALPHA

THE NATIONAL POLITICAL SCIENCE HONOR SOCIETY

PUBLIC ADMINISTRATION SERVICE

1313 East 60th Street, Chicago 37, Illinois

Printed in United States of America
The Vermont Printing Company, Brattleboro

foreword

THE STATES IN THE FEDERAL SYSTEM

Half a century ago, in his famous address before the Pennsylvania Society of New York, Elihu Root said that "it is useless for the advocates of State rights to inveigh against the supremacy of the constitutional laws of the United States or against the extension of national authority in the field of necessary control where the States themselves fail in the performance of their duty."

This view has been echoed many times since by various authors and groups. More than two decades ago, one of the present writers asserted that the states had never lost a power of which they had made effective use. More recently, two important groups—one private, the other official—have given expression to similar views. In October, 1955, the Eighth American Assembly, meeting at Arden House, stated in the report of participants' findings, in *The Forty-eight States: Their Tasks as Policy Makers and Administrators:*

Some state governments are well geared to handle their responsibilities and have earned the confidence of their citizens; some have taken steps to qualify for confidence; but a large number are poorly prepared to meet the problems that press upon them. Unless these latter states make substantial improvement, they will not win the confidence of their citizens, and in the natural course of events power will gravitate to other levels that meet more nearly the standards of democratic and competent government.

Somewhat along the same line, the Commission on Intergovernmental Relations said in its *Report to the President,* also published in 1955:

The success of our federal system depends in large measure upon the performance of the States. They have the primary responsibility for all government below the National level. The States and their subdivisions bear directly more than two-thirds of the growing fiscal burdens of domestic government. In recent years their activities have been increasing faster than the nondefense activities of the National Government.

. . . . . .

The strengthening of State and local governments is essentially a task for the States themselves. Thomas Jefferson observed that the only way in which the States can erect a barrier against the extension of National power into areas within their proper sphere is "to strengthen the State governments, and as this cannot be done by any change in the Federal constitution . . . it must be done

iii

by the States themselves. . . ." He explained: "The only barrier in their power is a wise government. A weak one will lose ground in every contest."

There is a growing knowledge and understanding of the means available to strengthen State and local governments. For example, the Council of State Governments, an organization founded and supported by the States, has called upon them to revise their constitutions, to modernize their legislative processes and procedures, to reorganize their executive branches, to make more extensive use of interstate compacts and other methods of interstate cooperation, to reorganize their tax systems, to maintain adequate planning and resource agencies, and to extend home rule to their political subdivisions.

THE BALANCE SHEET

In his final report as executive director of the Council of State Governments for the year 1957, Frank Bane observed that there has been "an amazing rejuvenation and expansion of state government in the last decade." As specific illustrations, he cited what the states have done in education—elementary, secondary, and higher—, highways, and treatment of the mentally ill. They administer more programs, and administer them with a higher degree of competence and efficiency, than ever before. They employ more personnel, collect more revenue, and expend more money than ever before. Truly, they have made enormous progress.

But this is only half the story. There are many areas in which the states are not doing well the job that needs to be done, and in some they are not doing the job at all, or trying to do it. So far they have not made the progress that must be made in more fairly apportioning legislative representation or in modernizing legislative organization and procedures. Only a few have made more than a good start toward giving the governor the powers and the administrative tools that he must have if he is to discharge effectively the duties of administrative and political leadership that should be his in a modern democratic society. In many jurisdictions, the judicial system stands in urgent need of revision and modernization. The states are not yet showing much sign of willingness to make the necessary revisions of their tax systems to provide the additional revenues that are needed now and will be needed even more in the foreseeable future.

In the face of predictions of tremendous growth in population and resultant demands for more and better governmental services, the planning agencies of the states, which made such a promising start in the 1930's, in many jurisdictions have been permitted to degenerate into something "little more than fact-gatherers for industrial promotion units." The states also are showing little initiative or imagination in dealing with the tremendous problems of governmental organization and services in our "exploding metropolitan areas." And, if our population analysts are correct, "the metropolitan mushroom," still growing, is but a slight indication of the shape of things to come. The list of state inadequacies could be extended, but for the present purposes, the extension would not be particularly useful.

OUR ANTIQUATED CONSTITUTIONS

Why have the states failed, why are they failing now, in their efforts to deal with these and other important problems? There are, of course, almost as many reasons as there are states. No two states are alike, and there are many problems. Not the least important among these reasons, however, is the fact that, with few exceptions, our states are attempting to provide governmental services in twentieth century conditions under the outmoded and hampering restrictions which abound in eighteenth and nineteenth century constitutions. Worst offenders are the half of the constitutions now in effect which were drafted in the last 30 years of the nineteenth century, when the state of governmental affairs in this country was at an all-time low.

During this period, provisions reflecting ancient prejudices against the executive were carried over, and a multitude of new restrictive provisions upon the powers of the legislature made their appearance and found widespread acceptance. Distrust of elected representatives, then and since, and the inclusion of much material purely legislative in character, have resulted in an impressive growth in the size of state constitutions.

The extent and significance of this basic fact is just coming to be realized. The Eighth American Assembly and the Commission on Intergovernmental Relations both made cogent reference to the widespread need for constitutional revision, and it has been reported that the governors at their conference at Bal Harbour in 1958 indicated a serious interest in constitutional revision, realizing that existing constitutional limitations were among the basic reasons why they find it so difficult to get some things accomplished, and impossible to accomplish others.

The American Assembly recommended that "those states which have not already done so should take steps to secure a modernized, short, basic state constitution; further, that in every state citizens be given the right to call constitutional conventions at periodic intervals." The Commission on Intergovernmental Relations stated its position at somewhat greater length:

Early in its study, the Commission was confronted with the fact that many State constitutions restrict the scope, effectiveness, and adaptability of State and local action. These self-imposed constitutional limitations make it difficult for many States to perform all of the services their citizens require, and consequently have frequently been the underlying cause of State and municipal pleas for Federal assistance.

It is significant that the Constitution prepared by the Founding Fathers, with its broad grants of authority and avoidance of legislative detail, has withstood the test of time far better than the constitutions later adopted by the States. A due regard for the need for stability in government requires adherence to basic constitutional principles until strong and persistent public policy requires a change. A dynamic society requires a constant review of legislative detail to meet changing conditions and circumstances.

The Commission finds a very real and pressing need for the States to improve their constitutions. A number of States recently have taken energetic action to rewrite outmoded charters. In these States this action has been regarded as a first step in the program to achieve the flexibility required to meet the modern needs of their citizens.

Close observation of developments in this field over a period of many years justifies the assertion that there is perennially a good deal of interest in constitutional revision. At any given time, it appears to be true that in approximately one-third of the states serious consideration is being given to the problem.

But in the existing climate of opinion, constitutional revision, once relatively easy to achieve, has come to be a long-drawn-out and exceedingly difficult operation. In addition to psychological barriers, there exists an almost unbelievable number of constitutional and legal barriers that are well calculated to discourage all but the most devoted and determined supporter of revision.

Under these conditions, revision can be achieved only at the expense of tremendous time, effort, and money. It cannot be achieved at all unless there is able and courageous leadership, a strong citizens organization functioning with at least some appreciable financial support, on a continuing basis, and—above all—a determination to stay with the undertaking for an indefinite period of time, until the objective is finally achieved.

The problems of constitutional revision are not solved when a constitutional convention in a given state is assured. In a sense, it may be said that this is only the beginning. What shall the convention do? What should the new constitution contain? And what should it omit? These are fundamental questions and, unfortunately, they are questions regarding which adequate answers are difficult to find in the existing literature. Considering the fact that we have been in the business of making and revising state constitutions for close to 200 years, it is amazing to discover that the literature is so meager. The National Municipal League, to be sure, published the original edition of its Model State Constitution in 1920, and has revised it several times since, but the present edition is now much out of date and, in some respects at least, itself much in need of revision.

If the oft-quoted statement is true that a constitution is—or ought to be—a body of fundamental law, this, in itself, helps to delineate the field to be covered in such an instrument. There are at least four elements that should be included: the bill of rights, the framework of government, the powers of government, and provisions for amendment and revision. By the same token, it would follow that every effort should be made to exclude provisions regarding matters which can and should be handled by statute or provisions relating to problems of a temporary or transitory nature.

PURPOSE AND SCOPE OF THIS VOLUME

In the hope that it might be of service, both to the political science profession and to the cause of better government in the United States, the officers and Executive Committee of Pi Sigma Alpha, the National Political Science Honor Society, have decided to devote this, their first volume of essays in a projected series on major problems in American government, to the problem of constitutional revision in the states. In it, a distinguished group of political scientists, nearly all of them members of the Society, have cooperated in the effort to present a clear picture of the methods by which constitutional revision may be effected, what the provisions of our state constitutions now are, and what they could and should be if, in the years ahead, they are to serve the best interests of democratic government in the United States.

At the outset, two major objectives were established for this study. Since the major published works in the field were either long out of date or out of print, or both, it was our purpose to provide a new and, it was hoped, a significant statement regarding the essential characteristics and contents of a good state constitution. At the same time, it was our purpose to offer some guides for the benefit of those who as citizen leaders, members of constitutional commissions, or delegates to constitutional conventions might, at various times and in various places, be attempting to translate these principles and policies into terms of a new and vital constitution for one of our 50 states.

These two objectives are quite separate and distinct, but they are also very closely related. What is a good state constitution, and how does one go about getting one? The Introduction and Part II of this volume are concerned primarily with the first of these questions, Part I with the second. It is recognized full well that many volumes could be written on both of them—on content and on methods and procedure. We felt that the immediate need was for a treatment of both questions that was authoritative and reasonably comprehensive, yet of a size that would permit of convenient and widespread use. This is, to be sure, a large order! We can only hope that we may have succeeded, to some reasonable extent, in meeting it.

Being fully cognizant of the criticisms most frequently made of works pre-

pared by multiple authors—that they usually lack unity and coherence and
are marred by frequent and annoying repetition—the Editor and other members of the Society's Committee on Publications planned this work in detail
before a single invitation was issued. Topics to be included and the subject
matter coverage of each were determined clearly in advance, so that there
would be a minimum number of instances of repetition, duplication of effort,
and overlapping jurisdiction.

If the symposium form has weaknesses (which can be controlled by careful
planning and editing), it also has important elements of strength. There
may be great value in bringing to bear upon the central problem the minds of
many trained men, each a specialist in his field. Within limits, such repetition
as may occur may be valuable, in that it serves to emphasize points that are
generally agreed upon and recognized as of fundamental importance.

This, in fact, turned out to be the case in the present study, in the treatment
of such questions as the urgent need for constitutional revision, the essential
characteristics of a good constitution, the need for legislative reapportionment, and the need for reorganization of the executive branch of state government and the strengthening of the powers of the governor. Each of these
questions is discussed at length in the appropriate chapter, but various brief
references to them are found at other places, as the significance of one or
another of these problems appears in relation to other major problems in the
field of state government.

Thus, the symposium is not merely a series of separate papers, bound for
convenience between the covers of one book, but a unified whole in which
are pooled the breadth of knowledge, the insight and understanding of as
distinguished a company of scholars in the field of state constitutions and
constitutional law as could be assembled in this country at this time. As Editor of the volume, and as members of the Society's Committee on Publications,
we want to express our sincere thanks to the authors of these chapters for
their unfailing cooperation during the tedious process of editing, revising,
and coordinating their comments and materials, to the end that the discussion
as a whole might have unity and effectiveness, and might display a minimum
of the alleged weaknesses of the symposium form. They have all cooperated
"far beyond the call of duty." They have been a splendid group with which
to work!

And we are deeply indebted, also, to two others—Dr. Claude E. Hawley,
President of the Society, and Miss Laverne Burchfield, Public Administration
Service, who edited the manuscript for the printer. Dr. Hawley, as a member
of the Executive Committee, participated in the planning of this project,
before assuming the leadership of the Society. Since he became President, his
continued assistance and support have been of inestimable value at every

stage. Miss Burchfield has performed her exacting duties with such skill as to contribute in a substantial way to the quality of the finished product as it appears in the pages that follow.

W. Brooke Graves, Editor
The American University

Don L. Bowen
American Society for Public Administration

Franklin L. Burdette, Chairman
University of Maryland

Committee on Publications, Pi Sigma Alpha

August 1, 1960

contents

INTRODUCTION

myth and reality in state constitutional development

Harvey Walker

When the 13 British colonies along the eastern seaboard of the North American continent declared themselves free and independent on July 4, 1776, they faced many difficult problems. One was to secure from the British government a recognition of their independence. This recognition was accomplished only after a long, expensive, bloody war which left the new states weak and exhausted. The Treaty of Paris, signed September 3, 1783, confirmed the fruits of independence and made final the separation from England. But this legal separation did not and could not sever the many ties of blood, habits of thought, traditions, and institutions. These continued to exist, with shamefaced acknowledgment at first, as if the advocates of the policy of following tried British experience felt such a course unpatriotic, but later with frank recognition of its advantages.

A second problem arose from the necessity of common action against a formidable adversary and a common front in international affairs. Common action was secured through the First and Second Continental Congresses, whose powers were largely undefined, but grew and expanded with the necessities of the war. There was no constitution at the outset, although at the same time that the Declaration of Independence was signed, action was in progress in the Continental Congress looking toward a written instrument of government, which later (March 1, 1781) was put into effect as the Articles of Confederation.

The third problem, which will be the main preoccupation of this volume, was the devising of satisfactory institutions of government for the individual states, whose colonial governments had begun to fall apart as the armed conflict with England drew closer. Despite the fact that the Declaration of

3

Independence had been issued by the Continental Congress, as a representative of all the colonies, it was quite generally agreed that each one of them individually became free and independent, not all of them collectively. Thus it was that the first constitutions adopted by the various states between 1776 and 1781, and even those adopted between 1781 and 1787 when the Constitutional Convention met, were based on unitary rather than federal assumptions.

The eminent historian, Allan Nevins, has presented a scholarly and thorough analysis of the period of early constitutional development in the United States.[1] He recounts the contributions of such leaders as John Adams, R. H. Lee, John Rutledge, James Madison, George Mason, and John Dickinson in the framing of these documents, for which few if any precedents then existed. He speaks of their educational background, which gives some clues to their philosophical predilections on such matters as separation of powers, universal suffrage, individual liberty, and governmental stability. He emphasizes the strong tendency in each state to follow the familiar principles and practices of its colonial charter, so far as they could be made applicable to the facts of independent existence. To his great credit he does not fall into the error of facile generalization so common among Americans of asserting that American institutions of government were consciously and faithfully copied from those of the mother country. The influence of English example can be seen in some aspects of colonial governments, but the fledgling states inclined to follow colonial institutions as better adapted to American life than the more remote and constantly less influential model. As Nevins says: "Not only upon the [colonial] practice of a century and a half, but upon the political theorizing of the same period—the writings of Harrington, Milton, Hume, Locke, Blackstone, Montesquieu and others—were the new American constitutions built."[2]

The task of writing the first state constitutions was indeed formidable. There were no precedents for such a procedure. Britain even to the present day has never attempted to reduce the outlines of her governmental structure and procedures to a single document, and much of what Englishmen refer to as constitutional law rests upon unwritten custom. The institutions of Crown and hereditary nobility were repugnant to American ideals. The monarchies of continental Europe still preserved many aspects of absolutism, and the kings and emperors were not desirous of suffering the restrictions which a written constitution might bring. The French Revolution came in the year in which the American federal Constitution went into effect. The colonists, become citizens of states, had to depend upon their own resources in pre-

---

[1] Allan Nevins, *The American States during and after the Revolution, 1775-1789* (New York: Macmillan Co., 1924).

[2] *Op. cit.*, p. 119.

paring their governmental documents. And documents they were, despite British precedent.

What considerations led to the development of written constitutions in America? Many theories have been advanced. One of the most obvious is that the constitution-writers had in many cases lived under written charters as colonists and found it convenient to appeal to these documents against the arbitrary actions of royal governors. They were familiar with Magna Carta, the Habeas Corpus Act, and the Act of Settlement. They had aspired to claim the rights of freeborn Englishmen against the Crown, and they were equally anxious to guarantee their own liberties as citizens of states by formulating carefully worded bills of rights to protect them against excesses by their own governments. Also, they had imbibed deeply of the political theories of Locke and Montesquieu,[3] they believed in natural law and the social contract, and they wished to see their rights guaranteed and their theories translated into action in the governments which they established. Written constitutions seemed to be the best way to accomplish all these objectives.

The concept of the separation of governmental powers also required the use of a written constitution. While the implications of this concept were only dimly perceived by the Founding Fathers, they were convinced of its indispensability in the establishment and maintenance of a democratic republic. There were no models to consult. Montesquieu's description of the British scheme, in *The Spirit of the Laws,* was rapidly becoming obsolete even as he wrote. Parliamentary supremacy over the Crown was asserted in the Act of Settlement and has not since been seriously disputed. While the English judiciary has long enjoyed independence, it never has exercised judicial review in the American sense. And a legislative body blended with the Cabinet as the true executive offers little evidence of the type of separation of which Montesquieu wrote.

The separation of powers, which was a basic tenet of the Founding Fathers, has proved to be one of the least successful concepts of the American scheme. Americans profess devotion to it—but usually only to pay it lip service, since the rise of political parties that bind together all the parts of a government into a working whole has rendered it obsolete. Where the concept has been applied it has stultified governmental action. Fortunately, few realistic political leaders pay any attention to it today except in Fourth of July orations. It was not applied even in the first states, in whose constitutions it was so bravely enunciated. A careful examination of these documents will show that legislative supremacy was the rule. Furthermore, they established a mutually inconsistent scheme of checks and balances, by which each branch

---

[3] John Locke, *Of Civil Government, Two Treatises of Government;* Charles Louis de Secondat, Baron de Montesquieu, *The Spirit of the Laws.*

was given some functions in the areas generally confided to the others in order to mitigate the rigors of a strict separation.

One result of their work which the early state constitution framers did not expect, but which has given strength to their institutions, is the firm establishment in the American system of the principle of judicial review. In the main, this principle has worked well. That it has is due, however, to several factors entirely independent of the separation of powers. One is the competence and independence of the judiciary. Another is the general willingness of citizens to respect judges and to accept and obey their decisions. To the extent, however, that judges lack moral stature or legal knowledge, or base their decisions on political considerations, the acceptance level declines. To protect judges from improper pressures and to assure the highest quality performance possible, they should have opportunity in the judiciary for lifetime apolitical careers. Then judicial review could be raised to the level of statesmanship, completely independent of partisan considerations. There are some indications that progress is being made slowly in this direction.

Judicial review, although not specifically mentioned in any state constitution, rested upon important colonial experience.[4] The colonists were accustomed to having the decisions of their courts reviewed by the Judicial Committee of the Privy Council, sitting in London. This venerable court, which continues to the present day, heard appeals from the colonial courts in all parts of the British Empire, deciding them according to the concepts of British justice, a stern test indeed. So when the new state courts began to assert their right to disallow legislative acts which were in conflict with the state constitutions, the people accepted the decisions, even if the legislatures, jealous of their prerogatives, were not inclined to do so.

THE SIGNIFICANCE OF FEDERALISM

The framers of the first state constitutions did not have to reckon with federalism. Despite the existence of the Continental Congress, each new state was in theory, and almost in fact, completely sovereign and independent. Their cooperation in the conduct of the war was voluntary. There was little more to bind them together than common need for the strength which such cooperation would bring. Recognition of the need for interdependence for other purposes came slowly, as a result of experience in dealing with each other, with foreign countries, and with their internal problems. The proposal for formal common action on a limited number of subjects, represented by the Articles of Confederation, was not finally ratified until 1781, although it

---

[4] Charles Grove Haines, *The American Doctrine of Judicial Supremacy* (Berkeley: University of California Press, 1932), chap. III.

was prepared and agreed to by the representatives of the states in Philadelphia on July 9, 1778.

In the Articles the Confederation adopted for the first time the name "United States of America," but in the second article each state declared that it retained "its sovereignty, freedom and independence, and every power, jurisdiction and right which is not by this Confederation expressly delegated to the United States." Each state had a single vote on all questions in the Congress, the right of withdrawal of a state from the Confederation was expressly recognized, and amendments to the Articles were to be made only by the unanimous consent of the states. By the Articles the states gave up certain powers, such as conducting foreign affairs, declaring war, and making peace. The Congress was given sole power to enter into treaties and alliances, to resolve disputes between two or more states, to regulate the value of money, to fix the standards of weights and measures, to establish and operate a postal system, and to appoint the higher naval and army officers in the armed forces. Thus the states began a process of transferring powers to the central government which continues to the present day.

The powers of the national government under the Articles of Confederation soon proved inadequate and the framework of government established by this document was found to be unsuited to the needs of the time. It was followed by the Constitution, framed at Philadelphia in 1787 by delegates of 12 of the 13 states, and ratified and put into operation in 1789. Two of the original states were outside the Union when the new roof was raised, but both came in within 18 months to make the Union complete.

The Constitution was placed in operation, then, without strict regard to the amending procedure provided in the Articles of Confederation, which required unanimous agreement. The eventual accession of all of the original states presumably cured this defect.

By the new and more perfect union the powers and sovereignty of the states were diminished further by delegations of exclusive power on additional matters to the federal government, such as regulation of interstate and foreign commerce and the issuance of patents and copyrights. It was assumed by the Constitutional Convention, and echoed by the authors of *The Federalist,* that the central government established by the Constitution was one of enumerated powers. Yet, in the ratifying conventions in the several states complaints were heard that such an important matter should not be left to implication but should be expressly stated. Accordingly, when the first Congress met, a bill of rights was formulated and submitted to the states for ratification as a series of amendments to the original document. The last of these, which became the Tenth Amendment, declared in phrases reminiscent of the Articles of Confederation, "the powers not delegated to the United

States by the Constitution, nor prohibited by it to the States, are reserved to the States respectively or to the people." It was assumed, when this amendment was ratified, that it would establish forever the limited character of the powers of the national government and the indefinitely expandible character of those of the states. Subsequent developments have not borne out these expectations.

In the first place, the Supreme Court of the United States, which was created by the Constitution as the arbiter of disputes between the national and state governments, early established and still maintains a policy of broad interpretation of the powers granted to the national government. This interpretation has enabled Congress to legislate upon and to provide for the administration by national agencies of a host of matters never contemplated by the framers of the document. One has only to consider the expansion of the commerce clause to cover national regulation of interstate telegraph, telephone, railroad, bus, truck, and air traffic, as well as radio and television, to see the effect of this policy. If the Supreme Court had insisted that only such matters as could have been intended by the framers to be assigned to the national government should fall within congressional jurisdiction, all of these new inventions would have been subject to state control under the Tenth Amendment.

In the second place, the Constitution conferred upon the national government power to deal with many matters which already were regulated by state laws, such as control over weights and measures and bankruptcy proceedings. These areas have been occupied by the national government only gradually. In the meantime, state laws were continued. But as federal law and administration were provided, state laws and the agencies established to enforce them were superseded. These developments made it appear that the national government was taking over state powers when actually it was merely occupying fields long confided to its care. A recent example of this relationship, in which the Congress had declined for a time to legislate in a field of action (regulation of insurance as interstate commerce) which was confirmed as rightfully belonging under its jurisdiction, is offered by the decision of the Supreme Court in the Southeastern Underwriters case, and the subsequent congressional action leaving the field to the states.[5]

A third aspect of the problem of federal-state relations is the expansion of the general welfare clause to extend national government jurisdiction to almost any area of general public concern. The Congress was not given direct authority to legislate for the general welfare, but it was given power "to lay and collect taxes, duties, imposts and excises to pay the debts and provide for

---

[5] *United States* v. *Southeastern Underwriters Assn.*, 322 U.S. 533, 64 S. Ct. 1162, 88 L. Ed. 1440 (1944) ; 59 Stat. 33 (1945).

the common defense and general welfare of the United States." Under this clause it may accomplish, and has accomplished by indirection, what it was not authorized to do directly. It now uses its taxing power to collect vast sums which are thereupon granted to the states, under conditions which amount to regulation of the activity financed. No one can now foresee the limits to this power, which conceivably could result in the reduction of the states to mere administrative appendages of the national government. The Tenth Amendment and the concept of the states as the repositories of residual power seem far from present-day realities.

These developments do not mean, however, that the states will disappear. They cannot unless the Constitution is drastically amended (some say by unanimous consent, since this is required if the states are to be deprived of their equal representation in the Senate), or unless it is disregarded when a new Constitution is written, as the Articles of Confederation were ignored by the Philadelphia Constitutional Convention. Even a change in state boundaries requires the consent of the states involved, as well as of Congress, so a redrawing of boundary lines to establish regions or larger and more populous states must also await constitutional changes.

In short, it may be assumed that under our Constitution the federal system will continue, even though the power and authority of the national government continues to increase. History has shown that despite the transfer of many state activities to federal control, the tasks to be performed by the states have not declined, but have increased, new ones being added frequently in response to public demand. In some cases these represent a centralization of activities once locally performed. But even so, additions of new local government duties and functions have more than kept pace with losses of old ones to state administration. In short, the rendering of useful services by governments is growing at all levels.

The effects of these social, economic, and governmental developments over the period of American national history on the drafting and amendment of state constitutions are enormous. No longer may state constitution-makers proceed with their work oblivious of higher authority and confident that they may exercise sovereignty and independence. Their product not only must fulfill the desires and wishes of their citizens, but also must be harmonious with the Constitution and with federal laws and treaties as well as with the complex of federal administrative regulations and any interstate compacts into which they may have entered with the consent of Congress.

These remarks apply not only to new state constitutions but also to the older ones. The march of national progress, the adoption of amendments to the national Constitution, and the ever-growing number of interpretations of its meaning by the Supreme Court of the United States cause a process of gradual obsolescence in the fundamental law of the states. No state now using a constitution framed and adopted before 1935 could fail to derive substantial benefit from a general review to discover and remove obsolete matter. It is not enough to say, as some do, that these obsolete provisions simply are disregarded. One ideal of every democratic state should be to inform its citizens fully on the nature and content of its fundamental law. When only the lawyers know what provisions are or are not in effect, how can school children gain a true conception of the institutions under which they live and in whose operation they must soon participate?

Federalism in the United States today is far more than a voluntary cooperative venture in which the states have joined in order to secure their defense and to handle their foreign relations.[6] The national government, with its vast powers of taxing and spending to promote the general welfare and its growing concern over and participation in the welfare of the individual citizen, tends to overshadow the states with their reserved powers. Even the jealously guarded citadel of state authority, the police power, is being taken over by indirection in many areas where national action can be hung on constitutional pegs. The only real "state right" today is the right to decline to accept federal aid, but not to refuse to pay federal taxes. Even the long-asserted rights of nullification and secession are no longer available to dissident states. In true democratic fashion the "states rights" minority must, today, gracefully bow to the will of the "strong federal" majority, however distasteful this may be. There is no turning back, short of revolution.

AMERICAN CONTRIBUTIONS TO CONSTITUTIONAL THEORY

Since the framing and adoption of the first state constitutions by the revolutionary British colonies in America and the formation of their federal union under the Constitution, the United States has constituted the greatest laboratory for constitutional government which the world has ever known. The whole world has watched its successes and its failures, and country after country has been deeply influenced by its example. Unfortunately, attempts at imitation have not always produced the desired results in the new ground to which American institutions have been transplanted, a fact that indicates that such copying is not always wise. Constitutions must be developed out of the life and aspirations of the people, not borrowed from others. Their fundamental concepts, to be useful and lasting, must be in tune with the particular culture and times. This requires continuous adaptation.

---

[6] William Anderson, *The Nation and the States, Rivals or Partners?* (Minneapolis: University of Minnesota Press, 1955); Leonard D. White, *The States and the Nation* (Baton Rouge: Louisiana State University Press, 1953); Arthur W. Macmahon, ed., *Federalism Mature and Emergent* (New York: Doubleday & Co., 1955).

The development of constitutional government in the United States has led to many innovations, most of which are today considered standard practice. First is the practice of a written constitution which establishes the principal organs of government, distributes the powers of government among them, and defines the relationships that shall exist between the government and the people. Such constitutions have been adopted in nearly all national states today as well as in the component units of the federal system in those countries which have adopted the federal form.

Second is the idea that constitutions are distinct from and superior to ordinary statute law. This concept, however, is not universally accepted, as some countries permit amendments to be made by simple statutory enactment. Also, it may be noted that despite the establishment of the constitution nominally as the fundamental law, in some countries this precept is honored more in the breach than in the observance, as when a dictator assumes power and construes the constitution to suit his own purposes.

Third, and arising out of this distinction between constitutional and statutory law, is the idea that the fundamental law should be made by the people, while statute law can be made by representative legislatures. Thus, in the United States, we have come to accept the constitutional convention as the proper organ for proposing constitutional revision and even amendment. Also, we feel that adoption of the proposals emanating from constitutional conventions should be by vote of the citizens.

Fourth, and also a corollary to the fundamental law concept, is the practice developed so fully in the United States of judicial review of the product of representative assemblies to establish its conformity with the constitution or to nullify it if it is found to be inconsistent with that document. Nowhere in our country is this principle expressly sanctioned by a constitutional provision, but by common consent it is adhered to in every state as well as in the national government. In the few cases in which the public has not accepted the decisions of the national or state supreme courts as being just and equitable solutions to constitutional problems, the tendency has been to amend the constitution rather than to resort to forcible resistance.

Fifth, and related to the exercise of judicial review, which can be successfully undertaken only by an independent judiciary, is the concept of the separation of powers, under which the powers of government are distributed among three equal branches—executive, legislative, and judicial—each free from control by the others. As pointed out earlier, this concept was borrowed from the political theorists of the eighteenth century, without having the sanction and support of previous trial. While it has become a sort of trademark of American constitutions, it is one of their least successful features and is made practical only by the inconsistent but parallel doctrine of checks and balances.

Sixth, American constitutions include bills of rights designed to reserve to the citizen certain fundamental liberties. Such catalogs of individual rights were not unknown before 1776, but the idea that they should be made an indispensable part of a written constitution was new with the first fundamental state laws.

Seventh, although they did not originate in this country, it is in the American states and municipalities that the institutions of initiative and referendum have reached their widest use, extending even to popular proposal and ratification of constitutional amendments.

Eighth, it is in the United States that one finds the widest and most intensive development of the idea of the federal state, in which the functions of government are distributed in the fundamental law between a national or central government and local or state governments. This concept, too, has been widely copied, although many of the imitators have changed details to adapt it to what seemed to be local needs. As pointed out earlier, this division of authority is subject to frequent and drastic changes as well as to slow evolution, which in recent years have been largely in the direction of centralization. It is logically asserted that a desire to establish a workable federalism was the chief reason why the United States turned to written constitutions— so that the functions of the separate parts of the governmental system would not be so vague and indefinite as to open the way to continual conflict. The political function of the United States Supreme Court in maintaining this balance between the central government and the states has been an important and a distinguishing feature of our system.

MYTHS AND REALITIES OF THE STATE CONSTITUTIONAL SYSTEM

Every political and legal system develops a mythology or rationale which purports to explain and justify its existence and usefulness in a logical and convincing manner. In this, the American system differs little from others. Although Americans pride themselves on being realists in such matters, the stock explanations of how the system is constructed and how it works often represent a large element of oversimplification, or even wishful thinking. Like all social institutions, nations, states, and governments change, and explanations need frequent revision if they are to be kept up to date.

There are many examples of this mythology in the American scene. A few which relate to government and its activities will be examined in the light of contemporary knowledge. The case of the separation of powers doctrine has already been discussed. Others which affect constitution-drafting and revision include: (1) the concept of state sovereignty, (2) the constitution as fundamental law, (3) the concept of majority rule, (4) the independence of the judiciary, (5) the relation of legislative form to legislative product, (6) democracy and local self-government, (7) the democratic objectivity of the constitutional convention, (8) the desirability of universal suffrage, (9) the responsibility of political parties, and (10) the place of the expert in government. There are many others, but these should suffice. Obviously, space will permit only a brief statement of each stereotype and the evidence which impeaches it, and a hint of what is required for a realistic approach to the problem.

1. Theoretically, the idea that the states continue to be sovereign and independent as to those functions reserved to them under the Tenth Amendment is unassailable. Actually, the policy of the United States Supreme Court in encouraging the expansion of national power by broad construction of the vague grants made to the national government by the Constitution is resulting in a progressive centralization of governmental authority in Washington. Of prime importance today is the indefinitely expansible character of the taxing clause for the promotion of the general welfare. State sovereignty becomes a shadow when political reality demands acceptance of federal grants on the terms laid down by the Congress. While it is true that the states cannot be abolished without constitutional amendment agreed to by all of them, their sovereignty means little if they are reduced to skeletons of their former dignity.

2. We are accustomed to describe our constitutions as the fundamental law and to make them harder to establish or to change than ordinary statutes. But the truth is that constitutions, particularly those of the states, contain many provisions which fall far short of being fundamental in character. Such particulars have been inserted in these documents for various reasons, but most of them add up to a lack of confidence in the legislative organs of the government. Since these constitutional provisions cannot readily be changed to harmonize with the changes in society and culture, they become an incubus preventing the adoption of modern legislation and tying the living present to the dead past. We must learn to distinguish what is fundamental and lasting in value from what is temporary and include only the fundamentals in our constitutional documents, leaving other matters to be acted upon by properly constructed and competent legislatures.

3. Americans are accustomed to assert that theirs is a real democracy where public questions are decided by vote, where the majority rules and the minority cheerfully bows to and follows the decisions thus reached. It is true that a larger proportion of the total population is legally qualified to participate personally in the choice of public officers and the decision of governmental issues in the United States than in many other countries. But many

persons, nearly half, who live under the American system of government are disqualified from voting because they are under age or lack an adequate period of residence or citizenship. An even greater proportion fails to participate because of indifference or neglect. It is a rare election that brings out as many as 75 or even 50 per cent of those qualified to vote. More commonly the proportion is much smaller. A vote of 40 per cent is not particularly impressive as an expression of the public will. This situation underlines the importance of great care in further extensions of the suffrage and further education of the people to encourage them to inform themselves on public questions and to participate in elections.

4. The independence of the judiciary is a carefully fostered myth that has some substance but is exaggerated in the public mind. In the national government, where appointees to the bench serve during good behavior, there is more validity in the assumption of independence than in the states in which judges are elected, often for short terms, making the courts painfully dependent upon a public opinion that may be misguided by journalistic emphasis upon occasional errors rather than upon general competence. Judges are almost universally required to be attorneys today, and thus all are bound by the lawyer's ethical code; but in many states they must depend upon the favor of political parties for their nomination or election and they share the fate of the whole party ticket, rather than being independent of it. Party influence also enters into the choice of federal judges through the custom of senatorial courtesy in confirmation and the natural preferences of a politically chosen chief executive. Although, in general, judges consciously make an effort to be impartial and to seek justice for those who come before them, there are subconscious influences of education and station in life that tend to lead them toward conservative economic and social views which are reflected in their opinions. These considerations need to be kept in mind by those who are charged with the writing or revision of state constitutions. There is no certain remedy for shortcomings in the independence of the judiciary, but it seems clear that there is ample room for improvement.

5. Another persistent myth affecting state government, which is carefully fostered by those who benefit from its continuance, that a legislature organized into two houses that possess substantially equal powers and whose concurrence is required in the enactment of legislation best preserves individual rights. Careful studies by competent scholars show that there is little truth to the assertion that a second house provides a valuable check against the follies of the first. Few bills, indeed, are passed by one house only to be defeated by the other. Where such action occurs it is more likely to be traceable to the fact that one house or the other is gerrymandered to give representation which does not reflect fairly the opinions of the electorate. In fact,

because of bicameralism and gerrymandering our state legislatures are likely to be unrepresentative of the people they are designed to serve. This is one of the most serious problems facing state constitution-makers today. Only by making legislatures both representative and efficient can this branch of the government regain the public confidence which is so essential to the discharge of its functions. Many believe that these ends can be achieved best through the adoption of unicameralism, such as exists in Nebraska, in the provinces of Canada, and in virtually all local governments in this country.

6. Local self-government, home rule for local units, freedom from state legislative control—these have long been the rallying cries of local government officials. The ineptitude of state legislatures in dealing with local problems, the unconscionable waste of time involved in the enactment of special legislation, the tendency toward political manipulation of urban populations for state and national ends have given great impetus to these demands. Yet, under modern conditions they are almost as anachronistic as the divine right of kings. The reality is that few local governments can operate at all today without state-collected, locally shared taxes. The local units simply do not have an adequate tax base. It would be unrealistic to expect such aid without some measure of state control. What is needed is not freedom from control, but more intelligent exercise of it—better legislatures, better laws, and more expert and less political administration on the part of the states. The growth of immense urban agglomerations into metropolitan areas requires rationalization even at the expense of so-called local autonomy. And state constitution-makers will be called upon to use every ounce of ingenuity they possess to reconcile the general public interest with the local interest.

7. As pointed out earlier, the constitutional convention is a distinctively American contribution to political theory and action. Mythologically, it is the personification of the sovereign people assembled for the discharge of the solemn duty of framing their fundamental law.[7] It is supposed to be above politics and to have no peers among governmental agencies. Yet, experience has shown that the convention rarely rises above the legislature in the quality and experience of its membership and that pressure groups and political parties have significant influence upon its deliberations. The cost of convening and holding a constitutional convention has become practically prohibitive. Many states in recent years have turned from conventions to constitutional commissions that consist of experts who report to the governor and legislature and whose handiwork is submitted for popular vote, if approved by these political organs of the government. The saving in time and expense and the gain in the quality of the work done should commend this new American

---

[7] Harold M. Dorr, "The Myth of the Constitutional Convention," 56 *Michigan Alumnus Quarterly Review* 22-23 (December 6, 1947).

institutional device to constitution-framers as a replacement for the constitutional convention.

8. It has long been assumed by the devotees of the democratic myth that universal suffrage is devoutly to be desired. There is little doubt that in a democracy the participation of as many intelligent citizens as possible in the choice of officials and the decision of issues strengthens the government and the society. In practice, however, with few exceptions the extensions of the suffrage in this country have not been surrounded by the safeguards needed to insure that this privilege is exercised only by those who are able to use it intelligently. Political intelligence has little direct relationship to chronological age or to citizenship. It does have a relationship to education. It has no relationship to residence, but it does have a relationship to abstract and social intelligence. The constitution-makers of the future should give careful consideration to the problem of defining those qualified to exercise the privilege of voting. The suffrage is mythologically thought of and spoken of as a right. In a well ordered state it is, rather, a privilege conferred upon those who are competent and willing to exercise it.

9. One of the most carefully documented and earnestly observed myths of our political society is that all or nearly all the evils from which it suffers may be traced to the fact that political parties are not responsible. Those who support this view point to the lack of party discipline in the United States, to the frequent inclusion on party tickets of persons nominated by direct primary of whom the party organization does not approve, and to the refusal of party members in legislative bodies to follow the party platform as evidence to support their contentions. The facts are that the major parties differ little in their platforms, that the direct primary encourages independence of the candidate from the party, and that party leadership, by and large, is not of a caliber that inspires public confidence. Parties have been largely free from control by the state. We are inclined to think and speak of them as private associations of citizens. Yet both common reason and the United States Supreme Court inform us that they are quasi-governmental entities, subject to control in the public interest. State constitution-drafters need to keep this fact in mind in preparing their documents to serve as fundamental law for the new age.

10. A frequent cliché of the professional politician and the political office holder is that "the expert should be on tap, never on top." Jacksonian democracy was based on the myth that the requirements of public posts were so simple that any reasonably intelligent citizen could discharge them to the satisfaction of the public. It may be that the simpler requirements of that less complex age made such a doctrine tolerable, but the development of science and technology, the great expansion of knowledge, and the enormous ex-

tension of public education during the last century have made it invalid today. There is no public administrative job in the present-day world that can be filled satisfactorily on a purely political basis. Mayors, county commissioners, governors, and even presidents can no longer discharge the administrative duties of their positions without professional assistance. The myth that an executive can successfully coordinate the activities of 50 or more separate agencies, each theoretically reporting directly to him, has been thoroughly exploded. The whole organization of the machinery of state administration, so far as it is dealt with in the state constitution, needs to be completely revised and reworked by the constitution-makers so that it will square with sound theory and experience in management. In fact, the less said about administrative organization and procedure in the constitution the better will be the probability that they can be kept abreast of social changes. The state laws dealing with state and local administration need a similar review and revision. It seems safe to say that the place of the expert in modern government is a central one. Unless the political executive follows expert advice, it may be that the expert should be "on top," not merely "on tap."

Summary

So ends the review of a few of the important myths of our state governmental organization and operation as they affect and are influenced by state constitutional development. Others that might have been included were passed over for lack of time and space. The scissors-and-paste-pot type of constitution-drafting so often followed in this country must be challenged if realities rather than myths are to be reflected in our constitutional documents. The framers of constitutions need to emulate the scientist who accepts no event as a fact, or no collection of similar events as obeying natural law, unless it can be observed, analyzed, classified, and subjected to experimental verification. Natural science has progressed and has grown more exact because myths have been challenged and scientific theories have been modified in the light of new discoveries. The social sciences, and particularly political science, are in sad need of similar questioning, rational doubt, and research. State constitution-making is in this sense a field ripe to the harvest.

PART I

METHODS AND PROCEDURES

chapter II

methods of constitutional change

Ernest R. Bartley

The American people believe deeply in the efficacy of written constitutions as the basis of governmental organization. They have evidenced continuing faith, based on well over a century and a half of practice, in the principle that constitutional government—whether national, state, or local—is best maintained with a fundamental written law, a document that proclaims not only that the power and authority of government are binding upon all, but more important, that governmental power and authority are limited by the purposeful action of the people. The American people have placed emphasis upon the limitation of governmental power. This emphasis has found expression in a variety of constitutional prohibitions at all levels of government, but it is particularly noticeable in the methods of state constitutional change.

The early state constitutions were brief, general documents, and the limitations on governmental power tended to be expressed generally. With few exceptions, the details of governmental organization, administration, and authority were left to the future discretion of the legislature. Since they were couched in general language, these constitutions were all fairly short, ranging in length from 5 to 16 printed pages. Such documents permitted a substantial measure of growth and change through interpretation to meet the changes in society, economics, technology, and government.

The trend to longer and longer state constitutions became pronounced with the passage of time. Old constitutions were weighted with amendments, and newly written constitutions no longer were brief like their predecessors. Limitations on governmental power and particularly on legislative authority,

NOTE: The writer acknowledges the courtesy of the Oxford University Press in permitting the use of pertinent materials found in John M. Swarthout and Ernest R. Bartley, *Principles and Problems of State and Local Government* (New York: Oxford University Press, 1958).

many of them severe, were added and expanded. In the light of the original practice, it is conceivable that an older constitution *might* be a more effective document for meeting today's complex problems than a more recent one with its mass of detail. Yet the older documents often have been amended to such a degree that the original benefits of brevity and generality have been lost.[1]

The fact that the national Constitution is brief and is written in broad, general terms has made it flexible enough so that it can be interpreted without change in the basic language to meet the demands of a rapidly expanding and changing society. State constitutions, too, must be adjustable, or adjusted in Procrustean fashion, to meet changing circumstances. If such adjustments cannot be effected, the state and its citizens must suffer—and await drastic surgery to correct the situation.

State constitutions will change, although not so rapidly as many might desire or to so great a degree and in such fashion as others might like. Yet change there will be. In a dynamic society, time and circumstances will inevitably work their imperfect will on a state's fundamental law. Constitutional change is not alone a process of constitutional revision. Constitutional change takes many forms—interpretation by a variety of methods of an existing document, formal amendment, piecemeal revision, a rearrangement or a rewrite of the basic law, or a complete constitutional revision. One fact is certain: however large or small the change or changes effected, they will be the result of many interacting social, economic, and political forces. And conversely, the blocking of constitutional changes will be the result of the interactions of other social, economic, and political forces. Constitutional change and growth, whether of minor or major character, cannot be divorced from the change and growth of society generally.

Constitutional Change by Interpretation

A constitution is never rewritten in its entirety by interpretation, but a word, a phrase, a clause, or even a section may grow or change through this process. And the cumulative effect of many individual interpretations may be "constitutional" growth. While commentators on the national Constitution uniformly agree on the importance of interpretation—by Congress, President, courts, and the people through custom and usage—as the prime medium of national constitutional growth, there has sometimes been a tendency to ignore interpretation as a medium of state constitutional change. There is an awareness that the great edifice that is national constitutional power results almost entirely from the broad construction given to the general language of the

[1] Fifteen states, for example, have amended their constitutions over 70 times each.

fundamental law, yet state constitutional change is likely to be equated with formal rather than interpretive methods.

The importance of interpretation to state constitutional change and growth should not be overlooked. State constitutions do change and grow by interpretive action of governors, legislatures, courts, and the people—but with one striking difference of degree when compared with national constitutional growth. The detailed language of most state constitutions leaves far less room for change and growth by interpretation. As a medium of state constitutional change, interpretation may be secondary to the more formal processes of amendment or revision.

The constitutional prohibitions on state borrowing, found in the fundamental laws of a number of states, provide typical examples of constitutional growth by interpretation. A provision against state borrowing prevents a state from securing directly the necessary funds to carry out vitally needed capital improvement programs. States so limited, however, have not allowed constitutional language to prevent them from "borrowing." Through subterfuge (and at an increased monetary cost in interest rates, since the credit of the state cannot be pledged) many states issue "revenue certificates" or create special agencies for the purpose of borrowing money when capital improvements cannot be financed out of current revenue. Specific state revenues, rather than the credit of the state as such, are pledged when these certificates or bonds are issued. In the strict legal sense the state has no debt. This sort of evasive action taken by state legislatures, frequently at the stimulus of state chief executives, and usually with the concurrence of state courts, is a striking illustration of constitutional change by interpretation.

In notable degree, the state judiciaries must bear responsibility for generally construing state constitutions so strictly that change and growth by interpretation become difficult or impossible. The doctrine of strict constitutional construction, fairly effectively (though certainly not uniformly) negated by Chief Justice John Marshall and many of his successors on the national level, has consistently guided the high courts of many states. The philosophy of strict construction has been to a great extent the product of the state court judges themselves, though one must never discount the fact that the high degree of specificity in state constitutional language has been a major contributing factor by making easier the judicial rationalization of a philosophy of strict construction.

Careful study shows that state constitutional change by interpretation and informal processes does occur but that state constitutions have not been broadly susceptible to growth by political, judicial, and popular interpretation. The many limitations placed upon the instruments of state government, together with the common practice of outlining governmental powers in detail, discourages substantial constitutional growth and change through interpretive means.

CONSTITUTIONAL CHANGE BY AMENDMENT

The emphasis in any discussion of state constitutional change and growth must be, then, upon the more formal means—amendment or revision. And of these, the process of amendment, difficult or easy, is more frequently utilized to effect necessary change. Indeed, there can be noted a lamentable, though completely human, tendency to attempt piecemeal patching of a state's fundamental law by amendment rather than to undertake the more onerous, though often obviously necessary, path of full-scale revision.

Some states resort infrequently to the amending process, others often. Tennessee, for example, was not able, even in the face of stark necessity, to amend its 1870 Constitution until 1953. Alaska and Hawaii, of course, have yet to amend their constitutions. By contrast, the Louisiana Constitution of 1921 has been amended 326 times and the California Constitution of 1879 over 370 times.[2]

In every state but one, two steps must be accomplished before an amendment can be added to a constitution: (1) the amendment must be initiated, and (2) the amendment must be ratified. Each step is subject to considerable variation from state to state. (See Table 1)

The Process of Initiating Amendments

There are three methods by which the states initiate amendments to state constitutions: (1) through legislative action, (2) through state convention, and (3), in a baker's dozen of states only, through formal initiative petitions. Most states allow the use of either of the first two methods; a few permit any of the three.

Initiation by the Legislature. All states except New Hampshire provide at least technically for some method of legislative initiation. While 16 states allow a majority of the members elected to initiate an amendment, most states require an unusual majority of both houses, customarily two-thirds or three-fifths of the members elected. About a dozen states require that an amendment, to be initiated, must be passed by unusual majorities at two successive sessions of the legislature. There are numerous other variants. A few states place restrictions on the number of amendments that the legislature may

---

[2] Alabama, Florida, New Hampshire, New York, Oregon, South Carolina, and Texas each have amended their constitutions over 90 times. The present (1938) Constitution of New York is regarded as a "rearrangement" of the Constitution of 1894. A rearrangement is not considered a new constitution, or a revision of an old one, for no substantive changes of importance are made.

submit to the voters at any one time, or place a time limit during which a defeated amendment may not be resubmitted to the people.

It is generally accepted that when the situation appears to call for extensive or technical amendments or when the political climate seems to demand it, the legislature may establish a special commission that often, though not invariably, is called a constitutional revision commission. The make-up and activities of such commissions are discussed later, for these groups are rather more likely to be created for over-all revisionary purposes than for the preparation of specific amendments. Yet they are occasionally created to bring *recommendations* to the legislature so that that body may then decide whether formally to initiate a specific amendment or amendments.

Initiation by State Convention. Though it is customary to think of a state constitutional convention primarily as an instrument for drafting an entirely new constitution or overhauling an old one, the convention is also used for the purpose of initiating amendments to an existing document. Indeed, in New Hampshire this is the only method available for initiating amendments; and by this technique the New Hampshire Constitution of 1784 has been amended over 90 times.

The procedure for calling a convention usually involves action by the legislature, followed by an affirmative vote of the people. The customary legislative margin required is either a majority or a two-thirds vote. So far as popular ratification of the convention call is concerned, in 15 states a majority of the persons voting at the election must vote "aye," whereas in 18 states only a simple majority of those voting on the question must be favorable. In only a very few states, including Alaska, can a convention be called solely upon the action of the legislature. In 9 states the constitution makes no provision at all for calling conventions,[3] though most constitutional lawyers contend that in these states conventions can always be called as an inherent right of the people acting through elected representatives. Conventions have been held in some of them, and the courts have found the procedure valid. Eleven states now provide that the question of calling a convention must be submitted to the people at stated intervals—every 7, 10, 15, or 20 years—regardless of legislative attitude on the matter, though the requirement has been ignored in a number of cases.

The association of the convention method with full-scale reworking of a constitution has tended to obscure its use for amending purposes, yet its utility in securing amendments cannot be ignored.

Initiation by Initiative Petition. In 13 states, amendments to the state constitution may be initiated directly by the people through the use of the initia-

---

[3] Arkansas, Connecticut, Indiana, Mississippi, New Jersey, North Dakota, Pennsylvania, Texas, and Vermont.

TABLE 1

METHODS OF AMENDING STATE CONSTITUTIONS

(Other than Constitutional Initiative)

Proposal by Legislature	Popular Ratification	States
2/3 members elected.....	Majority vote on amendment....	California, Colorado, Georgia, Idaho, Kansas, Louisiana, Michigan, Montana, Texas, Utah, Washington, West Virginia
....	Majority of votes cast..........	Illinois,[a] Wyoming
....	Majority vote on amendment and approval of next Assembly ...	South Carolina
2/3 each house..........	Majority vote on amendment....	Maine, Alaska
(b)	Majority of votes cast..........	Mississippi
3/5 members elected.....	Majority vote on amendment....	Alabama, Florida, Kentucky, Maryland, Nebraska, New Jersey,[c] Ohio
3/5 each house..........	Majority of votes cast..........	North Carolina
Majority members elected.	Majority vote on amendment....	Missouri, New Mexico, North Dakota, Oregon, South Dakota
....	Majority of votes cast..........	Oklahoma
Majority each house......	Majority vote on amendment....	Arizona, Arkansas, Minnesota
Majority members elected; two successive sessions..	Majority vote on amendment....	Indiana, Iowa, Massachusetts, Nevada, New Jersey,[c] New York, Pennsylvania, Virginia, Wisconsin
....	3/5 votes on amendment.......	Rhode Island
Other...		Connecticut,[d] Delaware,[e] New Hampshire,[f] Tennessee,[g] Vermont,[h] Hawaii[i]

[a] Ratification may be by a majority of voters at election of members of General Assembly or 2/3 vote on amendment.

[b] 2/3 vote on each of 3 successive days.

[c] Either method of initiation may be used.

[d] Majority lower house; 2/3 each house, next session. Ratification by majority of voters in town meeting.

[e] 2/3 members elected, two successive sessions. No popular ratification.

[f] Amendments proposed by convention.

[g] Majority members elected; 2/3 members elected, next session. Ratification by majority of votes cast for Governor.

[h] 2/3 vote Senate, majority House; majority members elected next session. Ratification by majority voting on amendment.

[i] 2/3 vote into each house, after either or both houses give Governor 10 days written notice of final form of proposed amendment or (with or without notice to Governor) majority vote of each house at two successive sessions. Ratification (general election) majority of votes cast, such majority being at least 35% of total votes cast; ratification (special election) majority of votes cast, such majority being 35% of registered voters. Special requirements are set to change representation of senatorial districts.

TABLE 2

AMENDMENT OF STATE CONSTITUTIONS BY INITIATIVE PETITION

State	Signatures Required[a]	Ratification
Arizona	15% vote for Governor	Majority vote on amendment
Arkansas	10% vote for Governor[b]	Majority vote on amendment
California	8% vote for Governor	Majority vote on amendment
Colorado	8% vote for Secretary of State	Majority vote on amendment
Idaho	([c])	Majority of votes cast
Massachusetts	3% vote for Governor	Majority vote on amendment[d]
Michigan	10% vote for Governor	Majority vote on amendment
Missouri	8% vote for Supreme Court Justice[e]	Majority vote on amendment
Nebraska	10% vote for Governor[f]	Majority vote on amendment
North Dakota	20,000 signatures	Majority vote on amendment
Ohio	10% vote for Governor[g]	Majority vote on amendment
Oklahoma	15% of highest vote cast	Majority of votes cast
Oregon	10% vote for Supreme Court Justice	Majority vote on amendment

[a] On basis of last preceding general or biennial election.
[b] Including 5 per cent of vote in each of 15 counties.
[c] Constitutional provision has never been implemented by Legislature.
[d] Must be at least 30 per cent of total vote cast.
[e] In at least 2/3 of congressional districts. Legislature may reduce percentage; currently set at 5 per cent.
[f] Including 5 per cent in each of 2/5 of counties.
[g] Including 5 per cent in each of 1/2 of counties.

tive petition. A specified number of signatures on the petition is required—usually those of 8 or 10 per cent of the voters casting ballots for the governor or some other officer at the last general election. After signature verification by a designated state officer the proposed amendment goes on the ballot for ratification or rejection by the people. In 4 states, signatures must be distributed among the various counties or congressional districts; in theory this requirement prevents steam-roller tactics by large urban areas.

The "constitutional initiative" has been of greatest importance in California, where its use has been extremely frequent, and in a few other states like Oregon, where it has been employed often but in some moderation. In some other states, little attention has been paid to it; in Idaho, for example, the provision for constitutional initiative has not even been implemented.

The Process of Ratifying Amendments

With the single exception of Delaware, where the legislature can amend the Constitution by its own action, ratification of amendments is by the people no matter how the amendment may have been initiated. The majority of votes required varies considerably. In over three-fourths of the states, when the legislature has initiated the proposal, all that is necessary is a majority vote on the amendment itself. In the other states various degrees of difficulty in the form of special majorities are encountered. Some states utilize different majorities depending upon the method of initiation.

The Amending Process

The mass of technical detail on state amending processes is substantial. Certainly it constitutes evidence of a desire to prevent undue haste in changing fundamental law. Yet the apparent mechanical ease or difficulty of amendment has not always facilitated or prevented extensive use of the amending process. Of two states with outwardly similar provisions for amendment, one will use the process seldom and the other frequently.

The contrast tells us a great deal about American state constitutional change. Its essence is not in legalisms and forms, important as they often are. Rather, the process of change is the product of the demands of the people acting through the institutions of society—the ballot box, the pressure groups, the courts, political parties, the myriad instruments of a complex organism.

CONSTITUTIONAL CHANGE BY CONSTITUTIONAL REVISION

That the demands of the people may be imperfectly translated by the various means is recognized. Minor constitutional defects, and often some major ones, can be cured by amendment. But if the necessary changes in a state's constitution are too long delayed or cannot be accomplished by amendment or interpretation, resort must then be had to a thorough revision or overhauling of the fundamental law.

To bring such a movement to fruition requires a great deal of time and effort; in state after state proved and demonstrated need for constitutional revision has not been sufficient, standing alone, to bring it about. Many years of small irritations, and a number of dramatic large ones, inevitably are required. Pressures for revision must build to the point where those preventing change have no alternative but grudgingly to give way.

The Problem: Needs and Obstacles

There are always substantial and powerful forces that will oppose any extensive constitutional revision. There are always groups that stand to lose—or think they stand to lose—in power, prestige, economic position, or legal status if a constitution is substantially rewritten. Rewriting will bring up for reassessment and redetermination the constitutional provisions under which they hold power.

The rural interests that dominate the overwhelming majority of state legislatures form one such element. Constitutional provisions guarantee rural dominance in many ways—by providing that not more than two or three counties shall form a senatorial district or that a single county may not be split into two senatorial districts, by giving each county a senator regardless of population, by giving each county at least one member of the lower house, and by other methods. But whatever the method, the direct benefits to the less populated rural counties of such inequitable representation are substantial. By statute, tax monies collected in large populous areas build roads and schools, contribute to operating expenses, and generally aid the financing of improvements and services in less populous areas.

The conservative elements of the urban population, moreover, not wishing to run the risk of seeing local governments controlled by the "radical" elements, combine with the rural legislators to consolidate and insure conservative rule. Thus, any suggested constitutional change that would alter the basis of legislative representation is met by a phalanx of interests solidly in opposition.

Certain business interests find it advantageous to have a weak governor and diffused executive responsibility in order that they may continue practices that would almost certainly be abolished under a strong, responsible executive. A state merit system, central purchasing, judicial reform, the executive budget with adequate controls, elimination of elective cabinets—name any progressive constitutional reform and, with the naming, opposition groups let loose their blasts.

Associations of county officials—sheriffs, judges, tax collectors, assessors— are very powerful politically in many states; these groups will fight vigorously any constitutional revision that would eliminate the archaic system of electing hordes of county officials. Educational pressure groups that have managed to get their views (and particularly a guarantee of tax sources!) incorporated into a constitution have a stake in the status quo. In states where homestead exemption provisions exist, homeowners are extremely sensitive to any possibility that their exemptions may be lowered, even though schools, police, welfare, and other community and state needs may suffer. These groups and countless others are almost invariably opposed to basic change, or at least basic change that will affect their favored positions. They oppose revision, at least as applied to their situations, as a matter of course.

There are, moreover, substantial constitutional and legal barriers to revision. The difficulties that hedge constitutional amendment in many states carry over to revision as well. In some states, the constitution itself specifies the make-up of future constitutional conventions, thus insuring that future conventions will be "stacked" in favor of points of view representing the status quo. In Florida, for example, a convention if called must be chosen on the same basis as the existing House of Representatives. The inequity of such an arrangement and the certainty of perpetuating it even with a constitutional convention are obvious.

But there are favorable factors, too, in the modern United States, factors that give hope to movements for constitutional revision. More than ever before, large numbers of civic and study groups are today willing and eager to devote the necessary time and effort to the problem. In most states there are professional students that have made extensive and critical studies dealing with the organization and powers of state government. Of even greater importance, the build-up of social, economic, and political counterpressures has often become so great that there is no very satisfactory alternative to rewriting the fundamental law.

There is increasing realization among ever-larger groups of people that many of the practices and procedures followed by virtually all states are now badly outmoded and that newer and tested methods in state finance, personnel practices, education, highway development, and so forth, would give increased efficiency and effect substantial savings on the taxpayer's dollar—or at least insure more effective use of that dollar. There is growing awareness, too, of the increasingly inequitable arrangements which are perpetuated by many state constitutions, the insured dominance of rural elements in the majority of legislatures, for example.

Thus there are numerous factors favorable to the cause of revision, but talking about the subject is not enough. Carefully planned programs for stimulating citizen action and support are vital. These programs must be based upon realistic appraisals of the groups certain or likely to oppose revision. Merely demonstrating the need is not going to get the job done; active, organized support is necessary.

The forces standing against revision have as a major ally the conservatism and apathy of the average citizen who is willing to suffer what he knows rather than risk the unknown quantity that constitutional revision may produce. The history of constitutional revision wherever successfully accomplished has been one of constant and unremitting efforts for citizen education over a period of years. Citizen demand, and only citizen demand, eventually overcomes the interests standing in opposition to change. Great economic, social, and political pressure is required to overcome entrenched interests and citizen inertia.

The odds against revision are usually great, but they are not necessarily overwhelming. By one method or another Georgia (1945), Missouri (1945), and New Jersey (1948) have managed to get revised and somewhat more satisfactory constitutions. The New Jersey Constitution, in particular, contains a number of features that may well become models. Extensive efforts in Oklahoma, by contrast, were soundly beaten some few years ago.

The Initiation of Constitutional Revision

Legislatures and Constitutional Commissions. The steps involved in constitutional revision are not greatly dissimilar from the process of growth and change through constitutional amendment, so far as the legal requirements are concerned. As a matter of fact, it is possible in some states, as in Georgia in 1945, to initiate a new constitution as a single amendment or series of amendments which, upon ratification by the voters, becomes a new constitution. It is important to remember, however, that no general discussion of constitutional revision can go much beyond outlining procedures and indicating generally the importance of understanding the cold political fact that some powerful groups will lose power by revision. The probabilities of success in any specific state, on the other hand, depend upon many factors peculiar to that state.

In 4 states—Florida, Delaware, Missouri, and Kentucky—the process of over-all revision by amendment is not possible, for these state constitutions contain provisions restricting amendments to no more than the revision of one article. Full-scale revision, requiring the shifting of material from one article to another in a new and interlocking fashion, is practically out of the question. The people, in voting on the finished product might accept some and reject others of the amendments, with resulting chaos.[4]

More common in initiating constitutional revision has been the use of a constitutional revision commission. This instrument is created or authorized by the state legislature. Being legally the creature of the legislature, the commission's powers may (and usually are) limited to specific subjects. Ordinarily, a constitutional revision commission is a governmentally financed study and recommendatory group. Commission membership is customarily appointive, with some members chosen by the governor, some by the chief justice of the state supreme court, some by the two houses of the legislature, and, occasionally, some by citizens' or professional organizations like the state bar association. Commission recommendations must receive legislative approval, in the form of amendments or a new constitution, before such recommendations are submitted to the voters. This requirement of legislative approval often has resulted in the substantial destruction of a commission's work.

There is much to be said for the use of a constitutional revision commission

---

[4] An interesting variant of the process of constitutional change by amendment was attempted in Florida in 1957-58. The Legislature utilized a device known as the "daisy chain," an approach that interlocked the single amendment so that if one failed, all would fail. The voters were not allowed to pass on this attempt, however, for the Florida Supreme Court found the action invalid and knocked the attempt at revision off the 1958 ballot.

when it is so composed as to be representative of the various major interests of the state; when it is dominated by one of those interests, little can be expected of it. It is much less expensive than the convention method. Properly composed, persons of high caliber can often be induced to accept responsibility for its single-purpose operation. The members may be less involved in state politics than legislators.

On the other hand, if the legislature summarily refuses to accept the recommendations of a dedicated, competent commission, the cause of constitutional revision will be set back for years to come.[5] There are those, too, who argue that the commission method, with its appointive personnel, is less democratic than the convention method. This argument is advanced particularly in those instances where the commission has completely revised a constitution.

Constitutional Conventions. The most generally used instrument of constitutional revision and the only one common to all of the 50 states is the constitutional convention. The constitutional convention can truly be said to be the first and basic legislative body in the sense that it establishes a framework for the determination of public policy. From the first conventions held in Delaware (1776), Massachusetts (1779), and New Hampshire (1778), to those of New Jersey (1948), Hawaii (1950), and Alaska (1955-56), the nation has seen well over 200 state constitutional conventions. Sixteen states, including Alaska and Hawaii, have held only one convention; at the other end of the scale are Louisiana (10), Georgia (12), Vermont (11), and New Hampshire (14). Since the New Hampshire legislature cannot initiate amendments, the convention has had to serve that purpose.[6]

The convention method, based upon the people's election of delegates for the specific purpose of constitutional revision, carries with it a sanction and a prestige not found in other methods. Historically and legally, the convention is the direct "voice of the people" in matters affecting general constitutional overhaul. For these reasons, even in those states where the constitution does not specifically provide for conventions, the rule has been that the right to hold conventions is inherent in the people. Such an interpretation squares with democratic theory and the emphasis placed on written constitutions.

The customary initial action to convene a convention, even in those states where the constitution does not provide for a convention, is in the hands of the legislature. In a very few states, like Georgia, Maine, and Alaska, the legislature may act on its own initiative and provide for calling a convention; no approval of the electorate is necessary. In the great majority of the states,

---

[5] Constitutional revision by commission is discussed in Chapter VI.

[6] The use of conventions as instruments of constitutional change is discussed in subsequent chapters.

however, including the most recent addition to the federal Union, the action of the legislature serves to place the question of calling a convention upon the ballot for approval or rejection by the people.

Upon receiving the approval of the electorate by the constitutionally required margin,[7] the legislature then has the duty of passing the necessary implementing legislation providing for selection and apportionment of delegates, appropriations to meet expenses, time and place of convening, and other administrative details. Since the convention is the "voice of the people," delegates are then elected, and the convention starts its work at the time designated. The final product of a convention generally, but not invariably, is submitted to the people for ratification. The total process may thus be long, especially if the legislature chooses to "drag its heels" at one or more stages.

Mention has already been made of the fact that about one-sixth of the states have consitutional provisions requiring the periodic submission to the voters of the question of whether or not a convention shall be held. The fact that the legislatures in such states have often ignored the requirement (there is no legal way to force them to act, of course) has caused recent constitution-makers to make such provisions an administrative rather than a legislative responsibility. The Alaska Constitution, for example, requires the secretary of state to submit the question to the voters each 10 years; Hawaii places a similar responsibility on the lieutenant governor. In this way the issue cannot be legislatively side-stepped.

Since the "starter mechanism" for holding a convention is, in most instances, the state legislature, the question not infrequently arises as to the power of the legislature, in the convention call, to limit the actions of the convention, or to prevent the convention from proposing changes on particular subjects. Some legislatures have been reluctant to call conventions, for fear the convention might exceed the limitations set out in the call and thus upset some particular set of power relationships that the legislature wished to preserve. Thus, a rural dominated legislature, not certain of the extent to which it can go legally or politically in limiting a constitutional convention on the reapportionment issue, may choose not to call a convention at all rather than run any risk of losing power.

From the point of view of practical politics, a so-called "limited constitutional convention" once in session is bound to be hard to control by means of a section of a legislative act passed weeks or months before. The average American is pretty well imbued with concepts about controlling his own destiny; both convention delegates and citizens are apt to assume some degree of right in the convention to ignore legislative instructions. And the more

---

[7] The popular vote necessary to approve the convention call differs considerably from state to state.

knowledgeable citizen will recall that the delegates who traveled to Phila-delphia in 1787 came with instructions, some very specific, to rewrite the old Articles of Confederation; this same convention tossed out the Articles, amendable only with the unanimous consent of the 13 states, and drafted a new document to be effective upon ratification by only 9 states.

Further, if the results of the convention's work are ratified by the people (and sometimes even if the work is not submitted to the people for ratifica-tion), the courts will normally be loath to upset such a determination. The question of whether the convention was limited by the legislature will nor-mally become moot,[8] or will resolve itself into a political issue to be decided at the polls.

Yet the issue of the limited convention is not one that can be handled simply by stating the practical aspects. The question has been a vexing one in a number of jurisdictions. Legislators who did not wish to see a convention called have marshaled legal arguments, and those who favored have coun-tered with other points of view. Legal scholars have disputed among them-selves the authority of a legislature to limit the power of a convention.

An early and frequently cited commentary argues that the convention is bound by the terms of the legislative act, providing the limitations are in harmony with the convention system.[9] A later student, also much cited in argument and judicial decisions, takes the view that the issue turns on who passes the convention act: if the legislature passes it, the restrictions are not binding; if the people pass it, they are. And of course it is clear that the legis-lature cannot limit a convention in derogation of the state constitution.[10] Still a third noted writer on the topic states that the convention is neither superior nor subordinate to the legislature; the convention is independent within its proper sphere.[11]

The apparent trend, if one adds only the totals of the relatively few judicial pronouncements on the subject, is rather in the direction of the convention holding power to exceed legislatively imposed limitations. The practical effect

---

[8] See, e.g., statement of Chief Justice Agnew in *Woods' Appeal,* 75 Pa. 59 (1874): "The change made by the people in their political institutions, by the adoption of the proposed [Pennsylvania] Constitution since this decree, forbids an inquiry into the merits of this case. The question is no longer judicial. . . ."

[9] John A. Jameson, *The Constitutional Convention* (New York: Charles Scribner's Sons, 1867), pp. 352, 378 ff., 573.

[10] Roger S. Hoar, *Constitutional Conventions* (Boston: Little, Brown & Co., 1917), p. 121. Some state constitutions make the convention, within its sphere, independent of legislative authorization and control. See *Carton* v. *Secretary of State,* 151 Mich. 337, 115 N.W. 429 (1908).

[11] Walter F. Dodd, *Revision and Amendment of State Constitutions* (Baltimore: Johns Hopkins Press, 1910), pp. 80, 92. The principal judicial pronouncements in support of this viewpoint are found in *Frantz* v. *Autry,* 18 Okla. 561, 588-603, 91 P. 193 (1907).

is to cause legislatures to pause even longer than they might otherwise in calling needed conventions.[12] Yet, allowing legislatures to set the limits of convention authority would lead to perpetuation of the very abuses and inefficiencies causing agitation for a convention as well as striking at a principle of democratic government many persons believe to be fundamental.

Ratification of Constitutional Revision

The instrument prepared by the constitutional convention or by the legislature (whether or not acting through a constitutional commission) is normally submitted to the voters for approval or rejection. The right of the people to have a voice in the formulation of their basic law would appear to be so fundamental as to be beyond argument. Sound constitution-making should certainly allow such a vote.

Yet there have been notable exceptions. About 50 constitutions were promulgated without a vote of the people in the first 80 or 90 years of national existence. The bulk of these promulgations were in the Revolutionary period and in the days of secession and reconstruction. The Louisiana Constitution of 1898 was declared effective by the convention, though in this instance authorization of the procedure had been accomplished by a prior popular vote. The South Carolina convention in 1895, though uninstructed, acted on its own initiative.

The Virginia (1902) and Kentucky (1891) conventions were specifically instructed by the respective legislatures to submit their efforts to popular vote. The Kentucky convention submitted the Constitution to the people and, after adoption, the convention reassembled, proceeded to amend the document in substantial measure, and promulgated it without further vote of the people.[13] In Virginia, the convention promulgated a fundamental law in defiance of legislative instructions. Various state officials, including the Governor, swore allegiance to it. The judicial branch held the document binding.[14]

The political reasons behind efforts to promulate new constitutions with-

---

[12] The proposed new constitution for Florida, struck from the ballot by Florida Supreme Court order in 1958, contained a novel provision. The section would have required any future constitutional convention to submit its work back to the Legislature *before* submission to the people, and would have allowed the Legislature to make changes in the convention's instrument by an unusual majority. The writer, and others, were vigorously opposed to this section (and to many others!), for it gave the Legislature a whip hand in the pre- and post-determination of topics to be considered by the convention.

[13] *Miller* v. *Johnson*, 92 Ky. 589, 18 S.W. 522, 15 L. R. A. 524 (1892). The political branches of Kentucky government recognized the new document. For an interesting set of cases on the point see 15 L. R. A. 524.

[14] *Taylor* v. *Commonwealth*, 101 Va. 829, 44 S. E. 754 (1903).

out vote of the people differ considerably from state to state. But one may note that the constitutions of the twentieth century have almost without exception been submitted to the people. The theory of democratic government demands such a procedure.

Full-Scale Revision versus Specific Amendment

Because of the considerable legal, political, social, and economic difficulties involved in accomplishing full-scale constitutional revision, some authorities argue that the best approach is to work out amendments for one or two articles at a time. Over a period of years, full-scale revision can thus be accomplished in effect without the tremendous effort needed for a one-time full-scale operation. Combinations of forces that might unite, temporarily, to defeat complete revision, might be splintered by use of the amendment-by-amendment, divide-and-conquer, approach. It it were possible for such a long-term effort to be properly coordinated and citizen interest in it sustained, the argument in its favor might be overwhelming. Certainly a specific, single amendment is to be preferred when there is a special problem demanding immediate attention, for the amendment-by-amendment approach shows tangible results much more quickly.

The hard fact of the matter is, however, that whether one provision or a whole document is involved, the drafting of constitutional materials is an onerous and difficult job, and their construction in a form acceptable to the people is a task that frequently approaches the impossible. Single amendments are often rejected. In the use of the amendment-by-amendment approach, there is a great risk that key parts of the over-all program may be lost by popular refusal, or that lack of coordination over the years will make necessary later change of large portions earlier amended. Full-scale revision, of course, results in a coalescence of the forces of all who have fault to find, major or minor, with the completed effort. Yet single-shot constitutions were approved in 1945 in Missouri and in 1948 in New Jersey. The question of full-scale revision as against the amendment-by-amendment method would seem to be a matter of judgment, its answer dependent upon the demands of an individual situation. If true constitutional revision is the objective, no general statement can be made that one or the other of the approaches is superior.

SUMMARY

State constitutions change and grow as society changes and grows. The nature and amount of change will reflect the pressures that are being exerted in society. The democratic credo of popular control of government is nowhere put to a more severe test than in the direction taken in constitutional change.

At no point in the governmental process is the need for informed citizen participation greater—and possibly at no point in the governmental process is informed citizen participation apt to be at a lower ebb.

The restricted and specific nature of most state constitutions increases the importance of formal methods of constitutional change and growth. The continued and meaningful position of the states in the American federal system demands that state and local governments be able to meet adequately the myriad problems raised by an increasingly complex civilization. Constitutional change to insure the ability of state governments to meet these present and future challenges is not only desirable—it is imperative if the notable trend to national centralization of control over problems once deemed local is to be halted.

chapter III

recent constitutional conventions in the older states

John P. Keith

The constitutional convention is as indigenous to the United States as baseball, and it appears at times to have been almost as popular a national pastime. Massachusetts generally is credited with calling the first constitutional convention, in 1779. Since then the states have convened more than 180 constitutional assemblages.[1] There is no question that, over the years, for thorough-going constitutional revision the constitutional convention has been "old stand-by."

From 1900 to 1923, a period in which 3 new states were admitted to the Union and emerging concepts of public administration were influencing others, 19 constitutional conventions were held. A 15-year hiatus ensued in which only New Hampshire resorted to a convention (1930), and this one was held only because it is the sole method of introducing amendments to that state's Constitution. In this period there seemed to be justification for a developing feeling among constitutional scholars that perhaps the constitutional convention was outmoded.

State interest in conventions was reasserted in the two decades 1938-58, with 12 conventions held in 7 states: Missouri, New Hampshire, New Jersey, New York, Rhode Island, Tennessee, and Virginia. As further evidence of the viability of the constitutional convention, it should be recalled that during the same period responsible officials or groups in nearly half the states gave attention to the convention question, although in 6 of these states the voters rejected at the polls convention proposals.[2]

---

[1] Albert L. Sturm, *Methods of State Constitutional Reform* (Ann Arbor: Institute of Public Administration, University of Michigan, 1954), p. 150 and Table X (Michigan Governmental Studies No. 28).

[2] John E. Bebout, "Recent Constitution Writing," 35 *Texas Law Review* 1071-89 (Oct., 1957).

THE NEW LOOK IN CONVENTIONS

The experience of the 7 states holding constitutional conventions in the period 1938-58 provided not nearly such clear-cut evidence in support of the convention as a means of constitutional revision, or of the interest of the states in modernizing their fundamental law, as at first appears. In the past, constitutional conventions had been looked upon as *the* method of constitutional reform by which the task of revision could be completed at a single stroke. Yet of the 12 conventions under consideration, only that of Missouri acted in that unlimited manner. The others were limited by the call that established them, or themselves chose to limit their proposals, to amending the constitution then in force. And only in the case of New Jersey did a limited convention submit a new document to the people, albeit incorporating without alteration the "untouchable" provision of its old Constitution.

The New Jersey Constitutional Convention of 1947 was forbidden to alter the apportionment of legislative seats—an apportionment designed for earlier times that had failed to keep abreast of the state's urban growth. Nevertheless, in other respects the New Jersey revision was more comprehensive, thoroughgoing, and basic than was that of Missouri and, until Alaska and Hawaii entered the Union, provided New Jersey with the most modern state constitution.

But even admirers of New Jersey's accomplishment (and most students of state government can be so classed) must have misgivings at the serious shortcoming that the convention limitation imposed. With a government that is modern in every respect except in legislative representation, this primarily urban state is hobbled when it comes to acting on serious policy questions that are of crucial importance to its urban areas. In this situation the question may well be asked: Is not the value of a much-admired court system and a revamped administrative structure in part negated when decisions affecting urban growth, such as sources of future water supply, do not adequately reflect the needs and wishes of a majority of the population?

Despite the large success of the New Jersey convention, the limited convention generally takes on the coloration of a supplementary amending process. In several states, perhaps fortunately, it is at least questionable whether a limited convention is possible by virtue of directives in their constitutions appearing to call for unlimited conventions—for example, Alabama, Michigan, and New York.[3]

Limited Conventions Submit Amendments

Rhode Island. Rhode Island was stymied for half a century in attempts to

---

[3] Art. XVIII, sec. 286; Art. XVII, sec. 4; Art. XIX, sec. 2, respectively.

revise its fundamental law by the convention process. The state Supreme Court in an advisory opinion in 1883 had declared that the Constitution could be amended only in the mode which it itself described, and the Constitution called only for legislative submission of amendments and not for a convention. Rhode Island's limited convention of 1944 was made feasible, at least in a political if not in a legal sense, by the court's reversal in 1935 of its earlier advisory position.[4] The 1944 convention considered and rushed through a proposed amendment enabling the legislature to exempt members of the armed forces from voter registration requirements. The amending process was considered too protracted to accomplish the purpose, calling as it does for approval by two separately elected legislatures prior to submission to the people for ratification.

The amendment went unchallenged in the courts, possibly because it would have been politically unwise to contest soldier voting while American forces were engaged the world over. In any event, Rhode Island appears to have acquired a taste for the limited convention, for the General Assembly and the Governor issued a call for another limited convention in 1951.

The 1951 assemblage submitted eight proposals to the people, of which six were adopted: home rule for cities and towns, permanent registration, permission for tax-exempt veterans to vote in town meetings considering financial questions, state borrowing in anticipation of tax collections, repeal of the state poll tax, and condemnation of land for parking facilities.[5] Defeated were proposals for judicial tenure and for a pay increase for legislators. The defeated proposals, like several of those adopted, appear hardly momentous enough to require constitutional sanction. (Furthermore, a similar legislators' pay increase amendment had been defeated at the polls only the previous November.) At the time of the election the attention of people interested in constitutional change was centered on the outcome of the home rule issue. Certainly the addition of a provision for home rule to Rhode Island's Constitution was a salutary advance in state-local relations. And it might be argued that some of the other measures adopted were equally important. Nevertheless, it should be borne in mind that the whole process of adopting these six amendments, from the passage of the act authorizing the Governor to call a special election on the question of holding a limited convention to the special election in which the people voted on them, took just a little over two months. The convention itself lasted only two and one-half days. The ease with which Rhode Island circumvented the normal amending

---

[4] *In re Opinion to the Governor,* 178 Atl. 433 (1935) reversing *In re the Constitutional Convention,* 14 R.I. 649 (1883).

[5] "Rhode Island Has 'Quickie' Constitution Convention," 40 *National Municipal Review* 360-62 (July, 1951).

procedure by the use of the limited convention presaged further use of the device.

In 1955 Rhode Island held its third limited convention, this one of 10 hours duration. It took up three matters, two of which would seem to be within the competence of an unfettered legislature: a salary and mileage allowance increase for state legislators and judicial tenure, both of which previously had been defeated at the polls. The third question was the granting of power to cities and towns to redevelop slums and substandard areas, including the power to condemn private property for the purpose of redevelopment.[6] The questions were submitted to popular vote less than a month after the convention adjourned; the first two issues again went down to defeat, but the third was approved.

After the election the *Providence Journal* editorialized that "Gimmicks Won't Do," referring to the defeated legislative pay and judicial tenure amendments.[7] The editorial might well have questioned the advisability of piecemeal amendment of fundamental law by the limited convention, for now that Rhode Island has found a method by which its long unaltered Constitution can be amended it is using it with a will.

In December, 1957, a special session of the legislature authorized an election on the question of a limited convention. The vote in the special election, held in January, 1958, was favorable; the convention was convened and quickly adopted two propositions; and these proposals were approved by the electorate on February 27. One amendment empowers the legislature to prescribe the time, place, manner, and extent of voting by absentee and shut-in voters. Legislation permitting absentee and shut-in balloting prior to election day ". . . had previously been declared unconstitutional by the State Supreme Court after the 1956 election, when Governor Roberts would have been defeated if the absentee ballots had been ruled valid."[8] The second amendment repeals an outmoded requirement of a house-to-house canvass of voters every two years.

It is probably safe to predict that the Rhode Island legislature will continue to use its newly-found convention "gimmick." Furthermore, it would seem that a relatively easy method has been uncovered of transferring to popular vote the burden of hard legislative decisions. The disturbing fact in the situation is that the limited convention, by facilitating the freezing of non-constitutional matters into organic law, may well prove to be another way to

---

[6] "Rhode Island Convention Proposes Three Amendments," 44 *National Municipal Review* 367-68 (July, 1955).

[7] "Rhode Island Voters Defeat Two of Three Amendments," 44 *National Municipal Review* 421-22 (Sept., 1955).

[8] "Absentee Voters Aided in Rhode Island," 47 *National Municipal Review* 172-73 (Apr., 1958).

manacle the legislature. When a power-impoverished legislature feels compelled to ask for constitutional authority for a proposed action, each such application approved by the people begets by implication a constantly diminishing sphere of legislative authority.

Virginia. In 1945 the Old Dominion followed Rhode Island's lead by calling a limited convention in order to evade the Constitution's time-consuming amending procedure. Like Rhode Island, the assemblage proceeded to alter the constitutional provisions concerning registration and poll-tax payment for members of the armed services. The anti-poll-tax forces seized upon the occasion to press for a more fundamental consideration of the constitutional suffrage provisions and a test case was brought before the Supreme Court of Appeals. The majority opinion of the court (the Chief Justice dissenting) stated that if a majority of the voters express themselves in favor of a substantively limited convention, then the convention will be legally restricted as defined in the act.[9]

Virginia held another "quickie" limited convention in 1956, again prompted by the desire for haste in revamping fundamental law. The United States Supreme Court announced its school desegregation decision in May, 1954, and handed down its "with all deliberate speed" decree a year later. Virginia's Governor called a special session of the General Assembly in November, 1955; that body passed an act calling for a referendum on the question of a convention in January; and the voters approved the limited-convention proposal. Delegates were elected the following month and the convention met March 5, 1956; two days later it acted to amend the Constitution so that the General Assembly is permitted to appropriate funds for private schools. The amendment took effect that same day. Once again the regular amending process was short-circuited.

Tennessee. A few years back a newsman opined that "Tennessee Looks for a Sisyphus,"[10] implying that only a giant could succeed in rolling an amendment over the requirements set forth in Tennessee's 1870 Constitution. And the 83 years in which the Constitution did remain unaltered supported that implication. An amendment required not only approval by two successive legislatures, but also ratification by a majority of those voting for state legislative representatives in the last preceding election—a difficult qualification to determine, let alone surmount.

The Constitution did provide, however, that the General Assembly by a

---

[9] *Staples* v. *Gilmer*, 183 Va. 613, 33 S.E. (2d) 49 (1945). And see the highly critical comment on this case by R. K. Gooch, "The Recent Limited Constitutional Convention in Virginia," 31 *Virginia Law Review* 708 (June, 1945).

[10] Charles McD. Puckette, *The New York Times Magazine,* Feb. 27, 1949, p. 16.

simple majority vote could submit the question of holding a constitutional convention to the people and that ratification required only a simple majority of the ballots cast. Even so, nine times the question was put to the voters, and nine times it was rejected.

The use of a limited convention was first proposed in 1926, but the proposal was defeated at the polls. In 1949, a limited convention was again proposed, directed to consider nine sections of the Constitution. Sponsors of the provision, in order to test the validity of the limited-convention amending process, challenged the right of the secretary of state to place the question on the ballot. The state Supreme Court upheld the limited convention, but the proposal again was rejected at the polls.[11]

Nevertheless, Tennessee's long-sought answer proved to be the limited constitutional convention. Reform forces, by restricting their objectives to six of the less controversial matters and by stepping up their campaign of public information, succeeded in persuading the 1951 legislature again to submit the question of holding a limited convention. In August, 1952, the proposal carried by almost a two-to-one vote. Delegates were elected in November, 1952, and deliberated in convention for six weeks during the spring and summer of 1953. Several familiar topics were among the matters considered: increasing compensation of legislators, abolishing the poll tax, and inaugurating home rule. The other subjects upon which amendments were drawn were extending the Governor's term of office to four years (and conversely weakening his position by forbidding a Governor to succeed himself) ; strengthening the veto power of the Governor; and revamping the Constitution's amending process—certainly significant constitutional matters. All received the necessary popular majority for ratification in November, 1953, thus concluding a two-year amendatory process.

An important conclusion can be drawn from Tennessee's experience: either omit statutory material from the basic law or make the amending process simple—the former being much the preferred course. Tennessee's convention clarified but may not have eased its amending process. A majority of those voting for Governor (instead of for state representatives) was substituted as evidence of popular ratification, but the two-successive-legislature hurdle was retained. At the same time, legislative salaries and per diem and travel allowances were refixed in the Constitution. This time, however, an escape clause was provided: two successive legislatures may now increase legislators' pay rate, the higher scale taking effect after the second legislature adjourns.

---

[11] H. L. Trewhitt, "Tennessee Amends Her Constitution," 27 *State Government* 119-22, 128 (June, 1954).

Interestingly, the limited convention specifically was given constitutional recognition, and only legislative and popular majorities are required for its employment. As though recognizing the fact that the limited convention might supersede the refurbished, but still difficult, amending procedure, the convention itself provided that future conventions may be held not more often than every six years. Looking forward to the sixth summer since the convention of 1953, a referendum election was held in November, 1958. The vote being favorable, a constitutional convention will be held in Tennessee beginning July 21, 1960. The convention will be limited ". . . substantially to reduction of the minimum voting age to eighteen and to fixing the terms for county trustees and sheriffs."[12]

Tennessee must be recorded as another example of the limited convention serving as a supplemental, more expeditious, and possibly more studied amending procedure than that provided by legislative proposal and popular ratification of amendments. Nevertheless, this new auxiliary amending form does not allow for thorough review of the constitution and a melding of the new with the best of the old. As has been well said, "The process of a piece-meal amendment tends generally to addition, or at best to substitution, not to subtraction [in already prolix constitutions]."[13] Observing what appeared to be a dangerous trend among the states, the constitutional convention in the territory of Alaska specifically excluded use of the limited convention.[14]

Limited Convention in New Jersey Submits New Document

Undoubtedly, the most important limited convention to date is that of New Jersey in 1947. This convention contributed to the legitimacy of the limited convention and excited interest in its use. It illustrated perhaps better than any other convention, limited or unlimited, the need for research and citizen participation in the convention process; it was preceded by a constitutional commission and a legislature-convention affording contrast with these other methods of constitutional revision; and it produced one of the most admired state constitutions.

Leadup. Agitation for constitutional revision in New Jersey began gaining momentum in 1940, but in 1941 the New Jersey Legislature denied Governor Charles Edison's request for a convention and a war of nerves began. It was suggested in reputable quarters that a constitutional convention could be called without assistance from the Legislature, even though such a develop-

---

[12] "Limited Constitution Convention in Tennessee," 48 *National Civic Review* 135 (Mar., 1959).

[13] John E. Bebout, "Recent Developments in the Use of the Constitutional Convention in the States," (paper delivered at the 1955 Annual Meeting of the American Political Science Association), p. 14 (mimeographed).

[14] Art. XIII, sec. 4, Constitution of the state of Alaska.

ment would be tantamount to a peaceful revolution.[15] There was enough validity to the argument, however, to lend it credence.[16]

As a compromise the Legislature established a Commission on Revision of the New Jersey Constitution, feeling that it could better control a commission than a convention, especially with respect to the delicate subject of reapportionment. The commission presented a revised constitutional text to the Legislature in 1942, and this text served as a basis for discussion when the people of New Jersey in November, 1943, authorized the bicameral Legislature to act as a convention.

The legislature-convention did an adequate job and drafted a vastly superior instrument to the century old constitution which then existed. Political considerations in no way connected with the method of revision defeated the draft when it was presented to the people in November, 1944.[17]

Interestingly, this legislature-convention was the first limited convention; the call ratified by New Jersey voters forbade it to change the bill of rights or the existing legislative apportionment. Furthermore, the 1944 convention served to establish a pattern for limiting the convention of 1947.[18]

Convention of 1947. The call for this assembly, as ratified by the people, also included a restriction prohibiting the reapportionment of legislative seats. This was a stratagem to placate rural south and west Jersey that was agreed to in order to obtain the opportunity for revision. Unfortunately, it excluded from review an essential and especially important matter. Some have contended that retaining a

. . . Senate which enables representatives of 15% of the people to veto any legislative act is a more serious threat to effective democracy than all of the other weaknesses of the old constitution put together.

John Bebout has said in discussing the recent development of the limited convention concept:

I approach this subject with mixed feelings because it happens that I had some part in establishing the first clear precedent for a limited constitutional conven-

[15] John E. Bebout and Julius Kass, "How Can New Jersey Get a New Constitution?," 6 *University of Newark Law Review* 34-49 (Mar., 1941). See Bebout, "Recent Developments in the Use of the Constitutional Convention in the States," *op. cit.*, pp. 8-9, for a summary of the argument and for an indication of the sympathetic view of Arthur T. Vanderbilt on the question.

[16] John P. Keith, *Methods of Constitutional Revision* (Austin: Bureau of Municipal Research, The University of Texas, 1949), p. 23.

[17] *Ibid.*, pp. 10-11. The Georgia legislature of 1945, as Bebout has pointed out, "came close to essaying the role of the constitutional convention" when it submitted to popular vote "in somewhat altered form the revision prepared by the Constitutional Commission of 1943-44. . . ." See "Recent Constitution Writing," *op. cit.*, p. 1071.

[18] Bebout, "Recent Constitution Writing," p. 1074.

tion. I still believe that the ultimate achievement of a vastly improved constitution for my own state of New Jersey was worth the price but I confess to lingering qualms of conscience.

Regarding the limited conventions in Rhode Island, Virginia, Tennessee, and New Jersey he has stated: "I personally have no doubt that each of these limited conventions has achieved useful results. . . ." However, he has also declared:

. . . I regard as the most difficult problem in constitutional government . . . how to keep representation in the legislature abreast of population growth and movement.

One cannot help but conclude with Bebout that

. . . the availability of the limited constitutional convention may be a means of achieving progress but it may also prove effective in keeping some states from making the kind of progress they most need.[19]

CONVENTIONS AS PART OF THE AMENDING PROCESS

New Hampshire may amend or revise its eighteenth century Constitution only through the convention process. The New Hampshire Constitution mandates town selectmen to take the sense of the qualified voters at town meetings throughout the state every seven years to determine the need for holding a convention to amend or revise the Constitution.[20] Of recent years, the electors appear to be returning to the practice of the early years of statehood by voting affirmatively on holding a convention.[21] The Constitution provides that delegates be "chosen in the same manner, and proportioned, as the representatives to the general court."

In the past 20 years New Hampshire has had several conventions, but the actions they have taken have not been especially important or successful. Failures to secure ratification of their proposals occur in part, at least, because of the large majority required for ratification by the Constitution—two-thirds of the qualified electors present and voting in town meetings.

Following the convention of 1938, only one amendment was accepted by the electorate. It served to dedicate motor fuel and vehicle taxes to highway purposes. Ten years later, in November, 1948, the qualified electors approved one of six proposals submitted by the convention of that year: an amendment authorizing an extension of legislative adjournments from two to five days.

---

[19] Bebout, "Recent Developments in the Use of the Constitutional Convention in the States," pp. 4, 6, 7.

[20] Part II, Arts. 99, 100.

[21] Sturm, *op. cit.*, Table X, p. 114.

The 1956 convention, of 449 delegates, submitted six proposed amendments for ratification in two batches. The first three were ratified in 1956. They included

. . . measures that permitted absentee voting in primaries, increasing the minimum amount involved in civil suits before a jury trial can be demanded, and allowing the Governor to retain gubernatorial powers when absent from the state on official business.[22]

The other three amendments were submitted and adopted at the November, 1958, general election. These amendments revamp obsolete constitutional language; for example, one removed a limitation restricting the right to vote to males even though women had voted in New Hampshire for years.

In New Hampshire the constitutional convention is a required step in the amendatory process. There is no constitutional barrier, however, to a convention acting as an instrument for complete revision of the organic law. As one observer has said:

Although the New Hampshire constitution is one of the shorter and in many respects more generally approved state constitutions, many in the state hoped that the 1956 convention would avail itself of the opportunity to do a thoroughgoing job of revision rather than content itself with amendments.[23]

The use to which the convention has been put in New Hampshire may well be another indicator of the trend ahead in constitutional conventions as the limited convention becomes increasingly popular.

UNRESTRICTED CONVENTIONS

Two unlimited, or unrestricted, conventions have been held in older states in comparatively recent years: New York in 1938 and Missouri in 1944. Both states have in their constitutions a mandatory provision that the question of constitutional revision shall be submitted to the voters every 20 years.

Both states received assistance from the National Muncipal League in the campaigns directed toward securing a favorable vote on the question of holding the conventions. In New York the League organized a Special Committee on the New York State Constitution, representative of a majority of the colleges, many other schools, and a large number of citizen organizations, to conduct an information campaign. This effort has been credited with helping to bring about the favorable vote in 1937. In 1957, however, the convention question was rejected by the New York electorate.

---

[22] W. Brooke Graves, "State Constitutions and Constitutional Revision, 1955-1957," *The Book of the States, 1958-1959* (Chicago: The Council of State Governments, 1958), p. 7.

[23] *Ibid.*, p. 6.

The National Conference on Government of the National Municipal League, held in St. Louis in 1940, gave much attention to modernizing state constitutions. Subsequently, a well planned and organized citizen effort succeeded in obtaining a favorable vote on the convention question and on the document submitted for ratification.

Creation of a favorable popular climate for constitutional revision is a difficult but most important task. The methods by which citizens of Missouri and other states developed public support have been described elsewhere.[24]

CONVENTION PROCEDURE[25]

Delegates usually are chosen at the preconvention referendum on the question of constitutional revision, although some states prefer separate elections. The constitutions of New York and Missouri provide for the method of selection of delegates. In New York, a total of 168 delegates were elected at the general election subsequent to ratification of the convention question: 3 from each of the 51 senatorial districts and 15 at large. The delegates were nominated by the political parties as provided in the Constitution. In Missouri, 83 delegates served: 2 from each of the 34 senatorial districts and 15 at large. The Constitution of Missouri gave the major political parties equal representation; the odd man was chosen by agreement. This provision proved to be of considerable importance to the success of the convention by reducing party manuevering to a minimum.

In New Jersey, 81 delegates were elected to the 1947 convention. Each of the 21 counties, which in New Jersey are coterminous with senatorial districts, was represented by at least 1 delegate and the other 60 delegates were apportioned to counties on a population basis. It has been said that

The recent Missouri and New Jersey conventions both demonstrate the ability of a convention to raise politics to the level of statesmanship . . . both conventions had some leading members who would not have been in an ordinary legislative session, and both bodies had other members who were obviously challenged by the special nature of their assignment to rise considerably above the level of their normal day to day political behavior.[26]

The organization and rules of a convention are similar to those of the lower house of the particular state legislature, although often they are modified to provide increased opportunity for discussion and deliberation.

---

[24] See Charlton F. Chute, "How to Get a New Constitution," 36 *National Municipal Review* 124-30 (Mar., 1947), and John P. Keith, *Public Relations Program for a Citizen Committee* (Austin: Bureau of Municipal Research, The University of Texas, 1950), *passim.*

[25] Adapted from Keith, *Methods of Constitutional Revision*, pp. 29-33.

[26] Bebout, "Recent Developments in the Use of the Constitutional Convention in the States," p. 16.

Constitutional conventions are expensive. New York appropriated $1,300,-000 for the convention of 1938, which lasted approximately four months. Missouri paid $697,145 for its year-long convention. New Jersey restricted its convention to 90 days, and the work was completed within the stipulated period at a cost of $350,000.

EVALUATION OF RECENT CONVENTIONS

A brief evaluation of the limited convention is in order; thereafter follows a short critique of the accomplishments of the major recent constitutional conventions in the older states.

Stipulated Conventions

The adoption of home rule by Rhode Island and Tennessee, of permanent registration by Rhode Island, and of a four-year gubernatorial term and a strengthened veto power by Tennessee should be lauded as progressive steps. Some amendments submitted by the several limited conventions, however, amount to no more than constitutional tinkering. Others fall somewhere between.

In a true sense, only New Jersey held a limited convention, that is a convention that was authorized to inquire into the entire constitution except for one provision. The other conventions popularly referred to as "limited" were, in fact, "stipulated"—for only one or a few enumerated constitutional matters were within the conventions' purview.

It is pointless to inveigh against the limited constitutional convention. What was a theoretical concept only short years ago is today's reality. Still, the pronounced trend toward stipulation of subject matter for conventions is of concern. Forces in opposition to genuine constitutional revision will undoubtedly seize upon this feature as a means of forestalling legitimate reform efforts. They will act to head off constitutional alteration by substituting form for substance—or, to state it bluntly, by agreeing to conventions without power. Henceforth, the strategy of any effort for constitutional revision will have to take this new obstacle into account.

Major Conventions

Despite the fact that the New Jersey convention was limited in one highly important respect, it nevertheless produced the most classic state document of its time. The Missouri convention also submitted a thoroughly revised fundamental law for adoption. New York, unlike the others, asked the people to vote on a series of coordinated amendments, most of which were approved.

By looking at the constitution as a whole, the New Jersey convention was able to resist the pressures of special interest groups and to produce a more readily understandable, uncluttered, and cohesive document than its predecessor. Missouri's planning for a modern constitution likewise resulted in the submission of a briefer and clearer draft than the old constitution it supplanted. On the other hand,

. . . the net effect of the New York Convention of 1938 was in the opposite direction. That can be attributed to the fact that all the planning for that convention was in terms of specific additions or changes. Simplification was not set up by any responsible official or citizen agency as a prime objective, and there was no planning or preparation for it.[27]

Accomplishments

Only a few of the accomplishments of the major conventions will be highlighted; a thorough review of substantive and procedural achievements would be long and tedious.

Noteworthy was the action taken with respect to the executive department in New Jersey and Missouri. In New Jersey the Governor's term was increased to four years and he is allowed to succeed himself once. He is given full responsibility for the executive branch via the appointive power and exercises considerable influence over legislation by virtue of a strong veto power. Missouri did not eliminate competing constitutional officers, but it gave the Governor extensive powers with which to reorganize the state administration and it strengthened his fiscal control powers.

New Jersey and Missouri also made great strides in court reorganization. New Jersey replaced a complex and antiquated court system with an integrated judiciary and gave supervisory power for the administration of the court system to the Chief Justice. New Jersey judges are appointed by the Governor with the advice and consent of the Senate. In Missouri, judges are selected under the so-called "Missouri Plan" which calls for initial appointment by the Governor from a list proposed by a commission composed of bench, bar, and public members. Thereafter, an appointee runs for election on the basis of his record on a nonpartisan ballot to determine whether he shall be retained in office.[28] Both constitutions vest in the Supreme Court substantial judicial rule-making power.

Missouri met the difficult issue of legislative reapportionment head on. The duty of refixing boundaries of electoral districts was removed from the legislature and placed with the secretary of state for the lower house and with a commission appointed by the Governor for the Senate. New Jersey

[27] Bebout, "Recent Constitution Writing," p. 1088.

[28] Adopted by an initiated amendment in 1940 and readopted by the convention of 1943-44.

established annual legislative sessions and all three states made some changes designed to improve consideration of legislation.

Missouri, the originator of constitutional home rule, and New York modestly extended their home rule coverage. New Jersey, while not adopting home rule, enjoined the courts to construe liberally municipal powers and authorized the Legislature, if petitioned by a county or municipality, to adopt local laws for the petitioning unit upon a two-thirds vote.

New York's convention, acting in a Depression-influenced climate, moved to tighten fiscal restrictions on state and local government; Missouri in the period of the Second World War, on the other hand, liberalized local tax and debt limits. New Jersey did not impose either tax or debt limits; it did require, however, that local tax assessments be based on the same standard of value.

The constitutional protections affording basic rights and privileges were continued in force with little alteration, although in all three states provisions were added giving labor the right to organize and to bargain collectively. All three states, likewise, recognize the state's police power as extending to housing and the reclamation of blighted areas.[29]

Lessons

The constitutional convention continues to be the most efficacious method of conducting thoroughgoing constitutional reform. Preparatory research for and public participation in recent conventions have undoubtedly enhanced their effectiveness. The conventions themselves served as examples of "democracy in theory and practice" and added to popular understanding of basic American constitutional theory. Fears of radical departures from previous practice proved to be groundless; the conventions submitted modernized, somewhat stronger versions of their previous fundamental laws. State constitutional revision by the convention method continues to be but a part of the continuing evolution of American government, an evolution essential to a dynamic society.

---

[29] For fuller reviews of convention accomplishments see Bebout, "Recent Constitution Writing," and "Papers Delivered at the Panel on State Constitutional Developments, Forty-Fourth Annual Meeting, American Political Science Association, Chicago, 1948" (mimeographed).

chapter IV

constitutional conventions in Hawaii, Puerto Rico, and Alaska

Henry Wells

Between 1950 and 1956, Hawaii, Puerto Rico, and Alaska, in that order, drafted constitutions. Students of government have acclaimed all three documents as admirable examples of what a contemporary American constitution should contain. In view of the fact that they have acquired the reputation of being model state constitutions, it is important to understand the unusual and highly favorable conditions under which they were written.

The framers of these documents in no case were amending or rewriting an existing constitution. They were engaged in one of the most challenging of all political enterprises: the drafting of a basic law for a new body politic. As inhabitants of American territories, they were undertaking to create the constitutional framework of a political order yet to be established—statehood in the case of Alaska and Hawaii, and commonwealth status (the moral equivalent, if not the legal counterpart, of statehood) in the case of Puerto Rico. Their incentive to do the job right was the greater because they believed they had it in their power to hasten or delay the arrival of that new body politic. If their work was well received, they could hope for early achievement of the more dignified and responsible political status to which they aspired. If it was sharply criticized or rejected, they could expect their hopes to be still longer deferred. For in each case they knew that the constitution they were drafting had to meet not only the approval of their fellow citizens of the territory but also that of Congress, in whose hands lay the final determination of their political status.

These circumstances account both for the traditional, even conservative, main outlines of the new constitutions and for their innovations of detail, many of which represent significant improvements on the corresponding provisions of state constitutions. Conscious of the need for congressional approval, the delegates to all three constituent assemblies avoided radical departures from the familiar American system of government—an attitude reinforced by their own experience with territorial government, which Congress had long since established along traditional lines in its organic acts for the territories. But conscious also of their unique opportunity to lay the foundations for a stable and effective government of their own, they did not hesitate to reject features of state constitutions and of their own organic acts which experience had shown to be unworkable or unwise. In their search for the best possible provisions, the delegates consulted expert opinion on a wide variety of constitutional questions and always took account of their own local needs and circumstances. The result, in all three cases, was a constitution admirably suited to modern conditions. If additional proof were needed, these documents further demonstrated the capacity of the people of all three territories for full self-government.

How the Conventions Came into Being

The legislatures of Hawaii and Alaska had the same end in view when they authorized the calling of a constitutional convention. They looked upon the drafting and local ratification of a constitution as a device for achieving statehood. Nothing had come of the orthodox approach which Hawaii and Alaska had been pursuing for years: patiently urging Congress to pass an enabling act which would authorize the calling of a constitutional convention and define the process and requirements for admission. But 15 states had been taken into the Union without prior authorization by Congress, and 7 of these had drafted constitutions and elected state officers and legislators prior to admission. Their example seemed worth following.

Legislative action in calling the conventions had been preceded by many months of agitation for such measures on the part of public officials, party leaders, citizens' groups, and statehood commissions in both territories. As early as 1948 a State Constitution Committee, appointed by the chairman of the Hawaii Statehood Commission, had begun to draft a tentative state constitution for Hawaii, and a group of students at the University of Hawaii were engaged in a parallel enterprise.[1] Upon the adoption of Act 334, approved May 20, 1949, these and other voluntary efforts were suspended and the machinery for electing delegates to a constitutional convention was set in motion. Primary and general elections were held on February 11 and March 21, 1950, and the convention got under way on April 4.

It was not until 1954 that similar pressures began to build up in Alaska. In January of that year the keynote speaker of a convention of the Democratic party in the territory urged the calling of a constitutional convention and

---

[1] Norman Meller, "A New Constitution for Hawaii," 21 *State Government* 129-32 (1948).

the election of provisional senators and a representative to Congress. In February, an Anchorage citizens' group which called itself "Operation Statehood" set up a committee to promote the drafting of a constitution. By midsummer the movement had spread to other cities, with Fairbanks the headquarters of an Alaskawide organization. Later in the year the League of Alaskan Cities proposed the immediate calling of a constitutional convention.[2] Governor Ernest Gruening, other territorial officials, and the Alaska Statehood Committee, an agency supported by territorial appropriations, also urged the drafting of a state constitution. In March, 1955, the territorial Legislature enacted the appropriate legislation. On September 13, delegates were elected, and on November 8, 1955, the Constitutional Convention began its work.

The Puerto Rico convention had a different history. Private citizens' groups had nothing to do with the calling of it—unless a political party led by elected officeholders may be said to be such a group. The drafting of a constitution by and for the Puerto Rican people had been suggested at least as early as 1922, but the movement that led to the constituent assembly of 1951-52 had its origins during the campaign preceding the insular general election of 1948. One of the planks in the Popular Democratic party platform of that year called for congressional action to permit Puerto Rico to draft a constitution that would supersede the insular-government provisions of the organic act. The party's overwhelming victory in the November election was taken by its leader, Governor Luis Muñoz Marín, as a mandate to make a locally drafted constitution a reality. Accordingly, he and his advisers prepared an enabling act which the resident commissioner for Puerto Rico introduced in the next Congress. After a few minor modifications, the measure was adopted as Public Law 600 of the 81st Congress (approved July 3, 1950).

Enacted "in the nature of a compact" between Congress and the Puerto Rican people, P.L. 600 stated that its provisions would take effect only after the act itself had been ratified by the Puerto Rican electorate. When so approved the act authorized the Puerto Rico legislature to call a constitutional convention. It also provided that upon approval of the constitution by the Puerto Rican people and by Congress, specified internal-government provisions of the organic act would be superseded.[3]

---

[2] Victor Fischer, "Statehood for Alaska Urged by Its Cities," 44 *National Municipal Review* 92 (1955).

[3] P.L. 600 declared that the remaining provisions of the organic act would go into effect under a new title: the Puerto Rican Federal Relations Act. As the name indicates, these provisions deal mainly with Puerto Rico's relationships with the United States—including such matters as United States citizenship, reciprocal free trade, exemption from federal taxation, and the applicability of federal laws in Puerto Rico.

The first step in the constituent process, therefore, was the holding of an islandwide referendum to determine whether the electorate wished to approve or reject P.L. 600. The referendum was held on June 4, 1951—i.e., after nearly a year of public discussion of the act and its implications. Its approval was a foregone conclusion, for the Popular Democratic party was strongly in favor of it, as were the Socialists and about half of the leaders and members of the Statehood (Republican) party. Only the Independence party vigorously urged rejection of the act. The opposition of the *independentistas* and a number of statehood partisans was sufficient to stir up a lively pre-referendum debate, which in turn aroused public interest in the constitutional issues involved and undoubtedly contributed to popular understanding of them. Over 65 per cent of the registered voters participated in the referendum, and of these 76.5 per cent voted to approve P.L. 600. Soon thereafter the Legislative Assembly adopted an enabling act which provided for the election of delegates, outlined the preliminary organization and defined the powers of the convention, and made arrangements for holding a referendum in which the new constitution would be submitted to the electorate for their approval or rejection. The election occurred on August 27, 1951, and the convention held its inaugural session on September 17.

THE NATURE OF THE CONSTITUTIONAL CONVENTIONS

Composition

The number of delegates and the method of their election were prescribed in each case by the territorial enabling act which called the convention and made financial and other arrangements for it. The Hawaii statute provided for 63 delegates, the Puerto Rico for 95,[4] and the Alaska for 55. It was no accident that the Alaska Constitutional Convention contained exactly the same number of delegates as the one that had met in Philadelphia during the summer of 1787.

Despite the variations in size, all three conventions consisted of a broad cross section of their communities. This fortunate circumstance was in large part a consequence of provisions of the enabling acts concerning the election of delegates, which differed substantially from the provisions of the several organic acts concerning the election of members to the territorial legislatures. The changes were uniformly in the direction of securing more broadly representative bodies. To this end each enabling act provided for delegates chosen from newly drawn electoral districts. In Puerto Rico and to a lesser extent in Alaska, the new electoral arrangements became the model on which the con-

---

[4] Only 92 were elected, however. The Independence party refused to nominate candidates and hence did not claim even the 3 delegates-at-large which it could have seated without electoral contest.

ventions fashioned their constitutional provisions concerning the election of legislators.

In each convention all geographical areas were well represented—including outlying islands in the case of Hawaii and remote settlements in the case of Alaska. Although lawyers were, as usual, the most numerous occupational group (16 in the Hawaii convention, 32 in the Puerto Rico, and 13 in the Alaska—respectively 25, 35, and 24 per cent of the total), a wide diversity of professions, trades, and businesses was represented. Organized labor fared best in the Puerto Rico convention, where 9 delegates were labor leaders. There were only 2 in the Hawaii convention and none in the Alaska.[5] In all three conventions a considerable proportion of the delegates had had previous governmental experience—as members of the legislatures and as holders of other territorial and local offices.

The party affiliations of Hawaiian and Alaskan delegates followed roughly the distribution of party strength in the two territories. Republicans slightly outnumbered Democrats in the Hawaii convention (29 to 21), but there were 13 independents. Democrats outnumbered Republicans about two to one in the Alaska convention. In Puerto Rico, the Popular Democratic party was somewhat overrepresented: 70 delegates were *populares,* 15 were Statehood, and 7 were Socialist delegates. In all three conventions a pervasive spirit of cooperation and of common dedication to the task at hand seldom permitted party feeling to exert a divisive influence. It should be noted, however, that party identity and discipline remained strong throughout the Puerto Rico convention. The leaders of the Popular Democratic delegation, which held 76 per cent of the seats, were in a position to ride roughshod over minority-party opposition, but they exhibited commendable self-restraint. Socialist and Statehood delegates had full opportunity to express their views and were able on occasion to extract concessions and amendments from the majority-party policymakers.

Organization

Since all three conventions adopted the pattern of organization that is traditional with American assemblies, public and private, they differed from one another only in structural details. The key elements of each convention were the presiding officer, the secretary, and the standing committees.

Officers. The Hawaii convention elected a president, four vice presidents, and a secretary from its own members, and several minor officials who were

---

[5] One of the Hawaiian labor leaders, an ILWU official, was expelled by the convention for refusing to testify before the House Un-American Activities Committee, which was holding hearings in the islands at the time. Although there were no AFL or CIO representatives in the Alaska convention, at least two of the delegates were leaders of fishermen's associations.

not delegates. The Puerto Rico and Alaska conventions each elected a president and two vice presidents from among the delegates, but chose nondelegates for the other offices.

The president of the Hawaii convention was Samuel Wilder King, an able and respected public figure who had served as Hawaii's delegate to Congress. Dr. Antonio Fernós Isern, Puerto Rico's resident commissioner in Washington since 1946 and the person mainly responsible for getting P.L. 600 through Congress, presided over the Puerto Rico convention with a combination of tact and firmness that reflected his skill as a parliamentarian. Described elsewhere in this volume[6] is the tremendous contribution which William A. Egan made to the success of the Alaska convention as president of that body. Mr. Egan had been president of the territorial Senate.

The main job of the three secretaries (Hebden Porteus, Hawaii; José Berríos Berdecia, Puerto Rico; Thomas B. Stewart, Alaska) was to direct the permanent staff or secretariat in such a way as to keep the convention machinery running efficiently. They were able to rely to some extent upon experienced personnel from the staffs of the legislative chambers for many of the routine but always high-pressure tasks connected with recording testimony and debates; maintaining official files and records; distributing documents to delegates, the press, and the general public; paying delegates and staff; and performing countless other essential housekeeping functions.

Committees. The standing committees of each convention may be divided into two categories: those concerned with procedural and administrative matters (e.g., rules, agenda, administration, style and drafting) and those responsible for preparing draft articles. Although the number of committees in the first category was about the same in all three conventions (4 in the Puerto Rico and Alaska, 5 in the Hawaii), the number in the second category differed considerably. The Puerto Rico convention used only 6, whereas the Alaska convention established 10 and the Hawaii convention 15 "substantive" committees.[7]

---

[6] See Chapter V.

[7] The substantive committees of the *Puerto Rico convention* were: Preamble, Ordinances and Amendments to the Constitution; Bill of Rights; Legislative Branch; Executive Branch; Judicial Branch; and Transitory and General Provisions. *Alaska convention:* Ordinances and Transitional Measures; Preamble and Bill of Rights; Suffrage, Elections and Apportionment; Legislative Branch; Executive Branch; Judiciary Branch; Resources; Finance and Taxation; Local Government; and Direct Legislation, Amendment and Revision. *Hawaii convention:* Bill of Rights; Legislative Powers and Functions; Executive Powers; Judiciary; Taxation and Finance; Local Government; Education; Health and Public Welfare; Industry and Labor; Agriculture, Conservation and Land; Hawaiian Homes Commission Act; Suffrage and Elections; Revision, Amendments, Initiative, Referendum and Recall; Ordinances and Continuity of Law; and Miscellaneous Matters.

One explanation for the greater number of substantive committees in the Hawaii and Alaska conventions than in the Puerto Rico convention is that the former had to resolve a number of controversial issues with which the latter did not have to contend. Although the three conventions had similar institutional characteristics, they were the instruments for reconciling very different political forces and issues in quite distinct social and physical environments. In Alaska, for example, legislative apportionment (the claims of the populous centers versus those of the hinterland for representation) and control of natural resources, especially the question of whether to prohibit the use of fish traps in the salmon industry, were issues that had long agitated public opinion and seemed to require consideration by separate committees. In Hawaii such matters as the disposition of lands set aside for persons of Hawaiian descent and the long-standing controversy over public education, especially the method of selecting members for the state board of education, also called for special treatment. No comparably divisive issues confronted the Puerto Rico convention.

Other explanations for the variation in the number of committees deserve mention. There is reason to believe that the necessity of accommodating certain political leaders with chairmanships helps account for the unusually large number of Hawaii committees. Conversely, the Popular Democratic policy of allocating chairmanships to only the ablest and most trusted lieutenants of the party leader, Governor Muñoz Marín, helps explain the small number of Puerto Rico commitees.

The size of convention committees naturally depended upon the number of committees and of delegates available to man them. Six of the Puerto Rico convention's 10 committees contained 11 members, 3 contained 15, and 1 (the Bill of Rights Committee) had 17 members. Of the 92 delegates, 58 had only one committee assignment, 32 belonged to two committees, and 2 delegates (members of the 7-man Socialist delegation) served on three committees each. All of the delegates who served on more than one committee were drawn from the top leadership of the parties represented in the convention. Nine of the 14 Alaska standing committees had 7 members each, and the rest contained 9 members each. Each delegate (excluding the president of the convention) was a member of two committees. The 20 Hawaii committees contained from 7 to 15 members each.

In all three conventions the president made the committee assignments and named the committee chairmen. In the Alaska convention he acted on the advice of an *ad hoc* "committee on committees," whose recommendations took account of party strengths and regional and economic interests. The president of the Puerto Rico convention informally consulted the leaders of the three party delegations before making his assignments and gave the two minority parties proportional representation on every committee. The president of the Hawaii convention attempted to give delegates at least some of the committee assignments they requested. Because of overlapping memberships, it was sometimes difficult in all three conventions to schedule committee meetings in such a way as to avoid conflicts.

Consultant Services. All of the conventions made use of technical and research assistance, but to varying degrees and under different circumstances. The Hawaii and Puerto Rico conventions established no advisory and research facilities of their own but freely availed themselves of university-based professional help tendered them as a public service. The Alaska convention, on the other hand, had the benefit of a research and consultant program which had been authorized and financed by territorial legislation and was thus an integral part of the over-all organization of the convention.

The Hawaii convention received most of its professional assistance from the Legislative Reference Bureau of the University of Hawaii. Before the convention began, the bureau prepared a series of reports on the provisions of the 48 state constitutions. These comparative studies, compiled under the title *Manual of State Constitutional Provisions,* were widely used by the Hawaiian delegates—and later by consultants as well as delegates to the Puerto Rico and Alaska conventions. Once the sessions had begun, the bureau rendered the convention the kind of assistance it was accustomed to providing to the legislature. Its professional staff did research for delegates and committees; digested, analyzed, and even drafted proposals for sections and articles; drafted committee reports; and on occasion served as consultants to committees. The expenses which the bureau incurred in rendering these services were underwritten in part by the Hawaii Statehood Commission.

The Puerto Rico counterpart of Hawaii's Legislative Reference Bureau was an *ad hoc* group of investigators organized by the director of the School of Public Administration at the University of Puerto Rico and financed jointly by the University and the Carnegie Corporation. Some six months before the constituent assembly convened, the research team began its task of preparing reports on matters to be dealt with by the convention. Submitted in mimeograph form[8] as the substantive committees got down to work, the reports covered such topics as the bill of rights, the legislative branch, the judicial branch, the amendment process, and the constitutional implications of P.L. 600. These studies summarized and evaluated the salient features of American and European systems of government, presented alternatives, and in a few instances made specific recommendations. Throughout the duration

---

[8] The reports were later published as a 600-page book: Escuela de Administracion Publica, *La Nueva Constitución de Puerto Rico* (Río Piedras: Ediciones de la Universidad de Puerto Rico, 1954).

of the convention individual members of the research group were called upon to provide research assistance to committees, to give expert testimony at public hearings, to assist in translating the constitution into English, and to aid in preparing *Notes and Comments on the Constitution of the Commonwealth of Puerto Rico,* a document submitted to the members of Congress when the constitution itself was before them for approval or rejection.

The Alaska convention had well-integrated research and consultant services because the territorial Legislature had put $50,000 at the disposal of the Alaska Statehood Committee for the purpose of making preliminary arrangements for the convention, including the establishment of library facilities and preconvention research. In addition, $25,000 was budgeted for consultant services out of the $300,000 which the enabling act appropriated for general convention expenses. The Statehood Committee engaged the Public Administration Service of Chicago to prepare a series of reports on the main subjects that would presumably have to be considered by the convention. Published in three mimeographed volumes before the sessions began, the PAS *Constitutional Studies* were frequently referred to by the delegates in their committee work and in floor debates. A PAS representative was also present throughout the convention to assist in coordinating the work of consultants and to serve as consultant to the Committee on the Executive Branch. During the months prior to the opening session, the executive officer of the Alaska Statehood Committee (who later was elected secretary of the convention) had lined up a panel of experts to advise the convention at various stages of its work. As these consultants were needed, PAS arranged for their travel, expenses, and compensation. Two Alaskan and seven "stateside" consultants (other than PAS personnel) were on the payroll at one time or another, their period of service ranging from two to five weeks.[9]

The committees of all three conventions also received assistance from executive agencies of the respective territorial governments (and from county agencies in the case of Hawaii), from the business and professional communities, and from local university faculties.

---

[9] The professional staff of the Legislative Reference Bureau which aided the Hawaii convention consisted of Norman Meller (director), Robert G. Dodge, Robert M. Kamins, Hideto Kono, and John B. McClurkin. The Puerto Rican research group consisted of Pedro Muñoz Amato, director; Carl J. Friedrich and A. Ceçil Snyder, consultants; and Francisco Ayala, Jan P. Charmatz, Gordon K. Lewis, Raúl Serrano Geyls, and Henry Wells, research associates. Consultants to the Alaska convention included John D. Corcoran and Emil J. Sady, PAS representatives; Ernest R. Bartley, John E. Bebout, Weldon Cooper, Shelden D. Elliott, Dayton D. McKean, Vincent Ostrom, and James Kimbrough Owen. The author is deeply indebted to Messrs. Meller, Kamins, Snyder, Serrano Geyls, and Sady, as well as to Victor Fischer and Thomas B. Stewart (respectively a delegate and secretary of the Alaska convention), for reading an early draft of this chapter and making invaluable suggestions for its improvement.

Procedure

The Founding Fathers drafted the Constitution of the United States in 16½ weeks. The Alaska and Hawaii conventions finished their work in slightly less time, 13 and 15 weeks respectively, whereas the Puerto Rico convention took a bit longer—20 weeks.[10] The relative brevity of the Alaska convention is to be explained mainly by the fact that its enabling act limited its duration to 90 days—75 convention days, including week-ends and holidays, and a 15-day recess for the purpose of holding public hearings. The other two conventions had no such deadlines to meet.[11]

It should be noted, moreover, that the Alaska convention was peculiarly fortunate in its physical arrangements, which were more conducive to uninterrupted labor than were those of the other two conventions. The Alaskan delegates did their work and took their meals in the new student union building on the University of Alaska campus—5 wintry miles from such distractions as Fairbanks had to offer, and some 500 miles from the williwaws of Juneau politics. The Hawaiians and Puerto Ricans, by contrast, held their conventions in their respective capital cities—the one in the Armory, across the street from historic Iolani Palace in Honolulu, the other in the capitol in San Juan. Unlike the Alaskan delegates, whose isolated convention site precluded such activities, many of the Hawaiian and Puerto Rican delegates were able to practice their professions and conduct their businesses between sessions and committee meetings.

An explanation for the relatively long duration of the Puerto Rico convention may be found in its procedure for considering draft articles, which differed on several counts from the one followed by the other conventions. The Puerto Rico procedure was to consider and amend a committee proposal section by section in committee of the whole, after which the convention would adopt the article as reported by the committee of the whole and refer it to the style and drafting committee. On second reading the convention repeated the process in plenary session, again considering the article section by section as reported by the style and drafting committee. It devoted four weeks to each of the two stages, the second of which was by no means a duplication of the first but rather a period of searching review and constructive amend-

---

[10] The dates in question are the following: Philadelphia convention—May 25 to September 17, 1787; Hawaii convention—April 4 to July 22, 1950; Puerto Rico convention—September 17, 1951 to February 6, 1952; Alaska convention—November 6, 1955 to February 6, 1956.

[11] The Puerto Rico enabling act specifically stated that "the duration of the Constituent Assembly shall be prolonged until it decides to dissolve itself or until the Constitution which it has drafted and approved goes into effect." (Act 1, sec. 32, *Laws of Puerto Rico, 1951,* approved July 3, 1951.) The act originally called for a referendum on the constitution to be held on January 21, 1952 (sec. 33), but this provision was later amended.

ment of provisions tentatively agreed upon. The Alaska and Hawaii conventions were more expeditious. The former dealt with committees' draft articles only in plenary session. The latter discussed and amended them in committee of the whole but only rarely would amend a provision in later plenary sessions.

In most other respects the three conventions followed a similar pattern of work. Initially, each went through a stage of organizing itself—adopting rules, electing officers, setting up committees—which lasted about a week. Then followed a period of intensive committee work, during which only routine business came before the brief plenary sessions. The substantive committees familiarized themselves with their respective areas of responsibility, began to review proposals and petitions, held public hearings, and eventually worked up draft articles and accompanying reports.

Public hearings constituted an important phase of the work of the substantive committees, each of which held at least one. They served the dual purpose of enabling the committees to ascertain the views of interested parties and of helping to inform the general public of the issues before the convention. Attendance and participation varied with the accessibility of the convention site and with the degree of public interest in the articles under consideration. The three hearings held by the Bill of Rights Committee of the Puerto Rico convention, for example, were well attended and elicited vigorous expression of views, especially on the proposed clause concerning separation of church and state. There was good press coverage of committee sessions in all three conventions. In Hawaii some proceedings were broadcast over the radio, and in Alaska certain hearings were both broadcast and televised.[12]

As the committees finished their tasks, the conventions began to meet daily in committee of the whole and/or in plenary session to consider their proposals. In the Puerto Rico convention the scheduling of this stage of its work, and indeed of all convention business, was the responsibility of the Agenda Committee. The rules of neither of the other two conventions provided for such a steering committee. In Hawaii, the calendar for each session was drawn up by the secretary under the supervision of the president and after consultation with the committee chairmen. In Alaska, the job of keeping the convention to a tight work schedule fell to an informal group composed of the committee chairmen, whose meetings were called and presided over by the president of the convention.

---

[12] After the Alaska committees had reported their draft articles to the convention, additional public hearings were held at various points throughout the territory. The timing of these hearings has been criticized by some observers, mainly because the 15-day recess during which they were held coincided with the Christmas holidays, when a number of citizens who would otherwise have testified may have been too busy to attend.

As soon as the convention had accepted an article or amended it to its liking, the nearly finished product was referred to a style and drafting committee for polishing. In the Puerto Rico convention this process occurred twice: after consideration of the article in committee of the whole and after the action taken on second reading. The style and drafting committees of all three conventions had the responsibility not only for improving the language of individual articles but also for fitting sections and articles together into a consistent and coherent whole. In carrying out these functions the committees inevitably uncovered defects of substance as well as form, although theoretically they were to concern themselves only with form, and did not hesitate to refer matters back to the substantive committees or to recommend to the plenary body last-minute changes of substantive importance.[13]

Participants in each of the conventions have since observed that at the outset many of the delegates were unsure of themselves and even rather suspicious of one another, but that they grew in self-confidence and mutual esteem as they became familiar with parliamentary procedure, began to understand the constitutional issues that confronted them, and got to know one another. In Hawaii and Alaska, the conventions evolved into cohesive bodies of dedicated men and women who came to think of themselves as partners in lofty and historic enterprises that demanded their best efforts and closest cooperation. This was less true of the Puerto Rico convention, where party lines remained visible to the very end. And yet even there, as in the other conventions, the extraordinary pressure of the final sessions, which involved long hours of unremitting collective effort, gave rise to an intense *esprit de corps* and produced in most delegates an unforgettable sense of pride and accomplishment.

EVALUATION OF THE CONVENTIONS' WORK

The crucial test of any constitutional convention is the document that it comes up with. If the constitution is clearly written, bare of the policy-making details that are better left to ordinary legislation, and consonant with current

[13] During its last 10 days the Puerto Rico convention devoted three long sessions to substantive matters which the chairman of the Committee on Drafting, Style and Enrollment presented for its reconsideration. Among them was the radical proposal to eliminate a section already approved on second reading which would have provided for a lieutenant governor and to substitute for it a section naming the secretary of state as successor in the event of a vacancy in the office of Governor. In this, as in all other matters brought up for reconsideration, the convention accepted the chairman's substitute proposals—though not without strenuous minority-party opposition in a few instances. See *Diario de Sesiones: Procedimientos y Debates de la Convención Constituyente de Puerto Rico*, vol. I, pp. 825-74. See also the chairman's able rebuttal of minority-party charges that the style committee was a "super-convention" (*Ibid.*, pp. 874-75).

views on the best possible arrangement of governmental functions and institutions, then the convention may be said to have done its work effectively.

By this standard the constituent assemblies of Hawaii, Puerto Rico, and Alaska all deserve high marks. Their constitutions are well drafted, even readable! As state constitutions go, these three are brief: approximately 8,800 words in the Puerto Rico Constitution, 12,000 in the Hawaii, and 12,300 in the Alaska. The reason for this brevity is that all three stick close to fundamentals—with a few exceptions, such as the debt-limit provisions of the Hawaii Constitution (Art. VI, sec. 3), and the restrictions on abolition or consolidation of municipalities in the Puerto Rico Constitution (Art. VI, sec. 1), which may give future generations cause to regret the framers' zeal. In general, all three documents reflect the changes that have occurred in informed opinion on constitutional questions since the framing of the Arizona and New Mexico constitutions of 1912—the last previous state constitutions to have been drafted *ab initio*.

Two generations ago, for example, it was still fashionable to require that executive department heads and judges be elected by the people. The territorial conventions of the 1950's sought to avoid diffusion of executive authority and responsibility, to which overuse of the elective principle had given rise in many states, by authorizing the governor to appoint his key subordinates.[14] Under the Puerto Rico Constitution the governor is the only elected official in the executive branch; under the Hawaii and Alaska constitutions, only the governor and his successor in the event of a vacancy in the office (the lieutenant governor and the secretary of state, respectively) are elected. Following the example of the New Jersey Constitution of 1947, the Hawaii and Alaska constitutions also attempt to strengthen the governor's position by limiting the number of executive departments to a maximum of 20.

Having been accustomed to appointive judgeships under their respective organic acts, the framers of the three constitutions saw no adequate reason to turn to the elective method of selecting judges. The Hawaii and Puerto Rico constitutions provide for the appointment of judges by the governor, with the advice and consent of the senate, whereas the Alaskan Constitution embodies an adaptation of the so-called Missouri plan: appointment by the governor from a panel of names drawn up by a judicial council, each judge being subject to approval or rejection by the voters at the first general election

---

[14] In all three cases the governor appoints with the advice and consent of the Senate. Under the Puerto Rico and Alaska constitutions, his department heads (except for the Alaska secretary of state) hold office at his pleasure; but under the Hawaii Constitution, their removal by the governor also requires the advice and consent of the Senate—a provision carried over from the Hawaii organic act.

held more than three years after his appointment and periodically thereafter.

During the 40-year interval since the framing of the Arizona and New Mexico constitutions, a number of other concepts had received wide acceptance among those interested in state constitutional reform. Although some of them had been put into effect by revisions of the Missouri, New Jersey, and other state constitutions, it remained for the three territorial conventions to embrace virtually all of them. Since the relevant provisions have been thoroughly canvassed elsewhere,[15] and are also discussed at various points in this volume, only two examples of such reforms need be mentioned here.

The first has to do with the legislative branch. The general reluctance of state legislatures to authorize their own reapportionment, even when constitutionally required to do so, led the territorial conventions to opt for a widely recommended procedure: the assignment of responsibility for decennial reapportionment to a nonlegislative agency. Prescribing the formula to be followed in each case, the Hawaii Constitution gives the job to the governor, the Alaska to the governor as advised by a five-man reapportionment board, and the Puerto Rico to a board consisting of the chief justice of the Supreme Court and two other members, both appointed by the governor from different political parties. The Hawaii Constitution contains certain traditional but much-criticized limitations on legislative sessions, whereas the other two documents adhere to more modern principles. Although the Hawaii Legislature is to meet annually in regular session, it can deal with general legislation only in odd-numbered years and for only 60 days; in even-numbered years it meets for only 30 days and is restricted to consideration of the budget, "urgency measures," and a few other matters; but both types of session ("general" and "budget") can be extended 30 days by the governor. By contrast, the Puerto Rico and Alaska legislatures meet annually in regular session, unencumbered by any constitutional restrictions on the business or length of sessions.

The other area of significant innovation is judicial reorganization. All three judiciary articles embody principles generally agreed upon by advocates of reform in the administration of justice in the states. Particularly noteworthy are the provisions of the Puerto Rico Constitution, which go beyond even those of the much-praised New Jersey Constitution in establishing a unified court system and in laying the groundwork for an efficient program of court administration. The Puerto Rico judiciary article is unique in setting up "a

[15] See John E. Bebout, "Recent Constitution Writing," 35 *Texas Law Review* 1071-89 (October, 1957); W. Brooke Graves, "A New Bill of Rights?" 46 *National Municipal Review* 238-44 (1957).

unified judicial system for purposes of jurisdiction, operation and administration" (Art. V, sec. 2). Although the Alaska Constitution also unifies the courts for purposes of operation and administration (Art. IV, sec. 1) and the Hawaii Constitution does so in effect without stating the principle, neither document adopts unification for purposes of jurisdiction. The framers of the Puerto Rico Constitution took this step in order to eliminate the vexing jurisdictional conflicts which had often arisen in Puerto Rico and most state court systems and frequently resulted in cases being decided on technicalities rather than on their merits. All three constitutions attempt to achieve prompt disposition of cases through operational and administrative unification. Each one makes the chief justice administrative head of all the courts, with power to appoint an administrative director and to assign judges from one court to another so as to equalize case loads and expedite the clearing of dockets. The Puerto Rico and Alaska constitutions empower the Supreme Court to adopt rules of administration for the courts, and all three constitutions require the Supreme Court to make uniform rules of practice and procedure in civil and criminal cases—the rules being subject to change by the legislatures of Puerto Rico and Alaska. The Puerto Rico Constitution is unique in requiring the Supreme Court also to adopt uniform rules of evidence.

Although by any academic standard a constitutional convention may have done its work well, its labors do not count for much if the voters reject the finished product. In all three territories the framers had the satisfaction of seeing their efforts vindicated at the polls. After wide distribution of the documents and vigorous prereferendum debates on their proposals, Hawaiians voted three to one to approve their new Constitution, Puerto Ricans approved theirs by a four-to-one margin, and Alaskans theirs by a vote of over two to one.

The Puerto Rico Constitution, having been changed in three minor respects to meet the terms of congressional approval, took effect on July 25, 1952. The Alaska Constitution became effective on January 3, 1959, and the Hawaii Constitution on August 21, 1959—the dates on which the admission of the respective territories to statehood was officially proclaimed. In all three cases the transition to a new body politic has been orderly and efficient, and the governments established under the new constitutions have proved to be effective and responsible.

chapter V

staging a state constitutional convention

John E. Bebout and Emil J. Sady

More than 200 constitutional conventions have been held in American states and territories since the 13 colonies declared their independence. These conventions, which have in many instances been the occasions for political drama of a high order, have played a significant role in shaping the form, structure, and content of the governments of the 50 states and have had much to do with the making and development of our federal Republic.

In view of the amount of historical and other research to which American institutions in general have been subjected, it comes as a shock to have to recognize, as the consultants to the Alaska Constitutional Convention of 1955-1956 were forced to do, how little systematic attention had been given to the state and territorial constitutional conventions. Among the likely reasons for this neglect may be noted: (1) the sheer number of conventions resulting from the number of territories and states that have had occasion to hold them; (2) the brief life of a convention, giving it the appearance of a "one-shot" operation; (3) the sketchy nature or relative inaccessibility of the records and other source materials available on a majority of the conventions that have been held; and (4) the stubborn fact that from the beginning of our history national institutions and political events have tended to preoccupy scholars and "practical" men of affairs.

Whatever the reason, the neglect of the constitutional history of the states in general and of the role of state constitutional conventions in particular is unfortunate both from practical and from philosophical points of view. It has deprived students of institutions, ideas, and behavior of a

NOTE: Adapted from a paper prepared for the annual meeting of the Southern Political Science Association, Gatlinburg, Tennessee, November 8, 1956.

rich source of important materials. There is room here for much reward-
ing work not only by generalists but by specialists in such varied fields as
law, administration, politics, public finance, comparative government, and
political theory.

The present primary concern, however, is not over the loss to pure
scholarship but rather over the lack of guidance that the neglect of scholarship in this area has meant and continues to mean to the evolution of
our constitutional system. It is believed that a number of recent events,
including the Columbia University Centennial Conference on Federalism,
the report of the Commission on Intergovernmental Relations, the
American Assemblies on State Government, and recent or current re-
searches in state government and politics, all indicate an awareness that
American federalism has moved into a new phase. The growing importance
of interlevel collaboration as against interlevel separation and competition has been widely accepted and is buttressed by decisions of the United
States Supreme Court. This acceptance is making it possible for students
and statesmen to see state and local institutions in a new light and to
reckon their future in terms of their functional importance rather than in
terms of static theories or outworn shibboleths of decentralization. The
new federalism is viable, not rigid—and is responsive increasingly to
practical tests of capability and performance.

Moreover, there is growing recognition that in the future what is or
may be written in our state constitutions will, because of its effect on state
competence, have significant influence on the shifting division of labor,
responsibility, and prestige between national and state governments. Under the circumstances, it is possible to think now in terms of giving purposeful management and research guidance to future efforts at revision of
state constitutions that might have been inconceivable or futile to attempt
·in an earlier epoch.

Prosaically, a constitutional convention is an *ad hoc* representative body
charged with the duty of preparing and proposing, as the case may be, a
new constitution for a territory seeking statehood or commonwealth
status or a revision of or amendments to an existing constitution. This
bare statement, however, does not begin to suggest the potential significance of a constitutional convention in an American territory or state.[1] A
constitutional convention may have an invigorating effect on the political
life of the state that cannot be immediately connected with specific alterations in the constitution. Properly planned and managed, properly

---

[1] This chapter is not concerned with such narrowly limited constitutional conventions
as the 1945 Virginia convention called simply to propose a quick amendment to permit
absentee voting by servicemen.

"staged" in short, a convention is a means by which the people of a state can subject their basic political institutions to a probing reexamination and reappraisal. Any society needs to review occasionally its fundamental institutions and practices. Such review is particularly important in a society such as ours where words in constitutions and charters that are beyond the reach of ordinary legislative processes tend to have a controlling effect on the scope and direction of public policy.

Lest it be thought that too large an independent creative role is being claimed for constitutional conventions, one may stress the essentially continuous character of the acts of creation and of change in our constitutional system. Constitutional conventions in the states have proved to be instruments, not of revolution, but of normal constitutional evolution. They need, therefore, to be studied, planned, and managed, not as unique episodes, but rather as vital periodic events in the life of the states.

These thoughts regarding constitutional conventions in general help to explain why the first constitutional convention of Alaska has special value for persons interested in understanding and strengthening our constitutional way of life. Alaska was preparing its first state constitution. Consequently, the Alaska convention took both a more fundamental and a more comprehensive view of its task than would the typical convention in an already admitted state. For this and other reasons, this chapter will contain frequent reference to the experience which the authors shared with the Alaska Convention.

THE BEGINNING OF A CONSTITUTIONAL CONVENTION

The staging of any state constitutional convention begins long before the first meeting of the delegates or even before their election. Just where to find this beginning in the case of a particular convention, it is not easy to say. In Alaska it might be traced to the launching of the active movement for statehood, but it took definite form in late 1954 as discussion focused on the desirability of having the territorial Legislature pass an act (which it did on March 19, 1955) providing for the election of delegates and the convening of the convention.

In the case of the New Jersey convention of 1947, the time might be fixed at the moment of the recommendation that a convention be called, i.e., in Governor Driscoll's inaugural address in January, 1947. A more realistic and meaningful time would be the gubernatorial campaign of 1940 in which Charles Edison and his unsuccessful Republican opponent both talked about the need for a new constitution. This set off a long train of events which led eventually to the inauguration of the new Constitution in 1948. These events included, among many others, acts of leadership by Governors Edison, Edge, and Driscoll and by Arthur T. Vanderbilt and other political figures; intensive organization and applied civic education carried on by the League of Women Voters and various other civic and interest groups, singly, and in concert through the New Jersey Committee for Constitutional Revision and the New Jersey Constitution Foundation; a report of an official commission on revision of the New Jersey Constitution submitted in 1943, followed by extensive hearings by a joint legislative committee thereon; and rejection by the voters in 1944 of a proposed new constitution that was submitted by the state Legislature acting as a constitutional convention under authority granted by the electorate the previous year.

The staging of the limited Tennessee Constitutional Convention held in 1953 began at least as far back as the appointment by Governor Jim McCord in 1945 of a commission to study the need for revision. Important aspects of the intervening build-up included research and educational activities by the League of Women Voters and other civic organizations and by university faculty, and rejection by the voters of a proposal to call a somewhat less limited convention in 1949.

This sketchy recital makes clear the variety and the importance of citizen and official activities which in these days normally precede the holding of a successful constitutional convention. These activities constitute an integral part of the total process of staging such a convention.

In a real sense, then, a constitutional convention is a great deal more than a single body of men and women. The elected delegates are only *some* of the central figures in a process that may involve substantially all of the active citizenry and institutions of a state. One of the best measures of the importance of a particular convention in the life of a state is the extent of the involvement of the state's leadership and citizenry before, during, and after the formal meeting of the delegates.[2]

These larger aspects of the convention process are worthy of much more detailed study than they have been given. One may venture to predict that such studies would reveal some determinants of "success" and "failure" in constitutional conventions. Moreover, they would reveal much about the actual working of our system of government, about the motivation and action of civic and pressure groups, about political leadership, and about other matters of enduring interest to political scientists and thoughtful citizens.

_____

[2] For example, see a paper by John E. Bebout, "Recent Developments in the Use of the Constitutional Convention in the States," presented at the annual meeting of the American Political Science Association, Boulder, Colorado, September 8, 1955. Copies may be obtained from the National Municipal League.

Constitutional Roadblocks

There are many things that must be done prior to the first meeting of a successful convention. Subject to variations in order and priority resulting from differences in legal and other circumstances, they include the campaign to induce the people and the legislature to call a convention, the preparation and enactment of enabling or facilitating legislation, the election of delegates, the preparation of background materials and other aids for the use of delegates, and the planning of numerous details regarding the location, physical requirements, and the organization, procedure, and management of the convention.

Precisely how some of these matters are determined will depend upon established constitutional and legal provisions. To the extent that constitutional provisions do not determine such matters, they must generally be written into an enabling act passed by the legislature. What is included in the enabling legislation and how it is drafted may have a decisive effect upon the convention.

Representative Character. The most important preconvention decision has to do with the basis of representation. The nearer the convention is to being fairly representative of the people of the whole state, the more likely it is to realize the potentialities which are inherent in the constitutional convention system. The success of the Alaska convention, as indicated by the quality of its product and the acceptance of its work by the people, was undoubtedly due in the first instance to the fact that the enabling act made it the most representative body ever assembled in Alaska.

Unfortunately, circumstances would make it difficult to achieve as representative a body in many established states. In some, the existing constitution prescribes a basis of representation and election which ties the convention to an outmoded pattern of representation in the state legislature. On the other hand, in states like New Jersey which have no constitutional provision for future conventions, the representative pattern is left to the legislature which is almost certain to create it substantially in its own image, however distorted a reflection that may be of the existing population picture. So the New Jersey convention of 1947 was composed in precisely the same manner as the joint meeting of the two houses of the state Legislature. Some observers of the New Jersey convention are convinced that the resulting overrepresentation of the smaller counties had a decisive influence on certain crucial issues, particularly on the rejection of a proposal for an automatic vote on the question of calling future constitutional conventions.

The New Jersey Senate, fearing that a convention might alter or abolish it, had insisted that the act providing for a referendum on the calling of a convention contain a proviso that the convention must not change the basis of representation in the Legislature. This action highlights one of the crucial unsolved problems of American government. Put in the form of a question, the problem is: How can the people of a state maintain their freedom of action with respect to future changes in their constitution against the opposition of a legislature which in the course of time becomes more and more unrepresentative? The delegates to the Alaska convention recognized this problem very clearly. Hence, they tried to make the calling and election of future constitutional conventions as independent as possible of the state Legislature and provided further that "no call for a constitutional convention should limit the plenary power of the convention to propose any amendment or revision of the constitution which it might see fit." Thus, certain decisions of the first Alaska convention will play a crucial and—it may be expected—a beneficial role in the staging of the next convention.

Procedural Requirements. The legal provisions affecting the representative character of a convention are not the only ones that have a profound effect upon the problem of staging a convention. Others include such "road-blocks to conventions" as the requirement of extraordinary legislative or popular majorities for the calling of a convention.[3]

In many states the most effective roadblocks to a convention are found not in procedural but in substantive provisions of their constitutions. In Illinois, Ohio, and Pennsylvania, for example, one of the strongest sources of opposition to a convention has been the fear of certain interests that it might propose elimination of the existing prohibition against a state income tax. Every state constitution contains substantive provisions that tend to be dear to powerful groups. When one or a combination of these interests is strengthened by constitutional obstacles to the calling of a convention, the citizens and political leaders who are concerned about state government as a whole have a very difficult problem in developing a strategy for staging a constitutional convention. This situation accounts in part for the current tendency in states where it is constitutionally possible to do so to look to limited constitutional conventions like those held in New Jersey and Tennessee.

The choice between a limited and an unlimited convention poses some extremely difficult value judgments. Is it better, in a given situation, to try for reasonably sure but perhaps relatively minor improvements via a

---

[3] See Wilbert L. Hindman, "Road-Blocks to Conventions," 37 *National Municipal Review* 129-32, 144 (March, 1948).

limited convention or to play for larger stakes against heavy odds via an unlimited convention?

Even where a limited convention is ruled out by design or by law, it is necessary for those seeking revision to choose issues and campaign tactics carefully in order to develop the widest possible support with the least risk of arousing antagonisms that might defeat the whole project. Decisions must be made not only on which issues to emphasize but also on such matters as the selection of the organizational sponsorship, the leadership, and the launching platform for the campaign. Thus, the League of Women Voters proved to be an acceptable organization for convening the business, labor, and other groups that organized the New Jersey Committee for a Constitutional Convention in 1941, whereas an initial call from certain other organizations would undoubtedly have been less effective. Thus also, the sponsors of the movement for a constitutional convention in Missouri, mindful of the urban-rural conflict in the state, carefully sought out leadership from rural areas and small towns[4]

Preparatory Work

It has already been observed that a constitutional convention affords an opportunity for a salutary reexamination of basic institutions and practices. Without such a reexamination, no convention can have an adequate understanding of what if any, changes in the fundamental law it ought to propose to the people. Preconvention preparation, therefore, should include much basic research and publication designed to identify and clarify the significant issues, problems, and alternative courses of action across the whole spectrum of subjects dealt with in the constitution. A review of the preparatory work done for a number of conventions serves to suggest the following lines:

1. All important problems should be studied in depth and in some cases by more than one person or organization.
2. Comparative data should be evaluated in terms of results. Much time and print are wasted in mere compilations of comparative data on how particular matters are handled in different states, a procedure which may lead unsophisticated citizens and convention delegates to assume that majority practice is necessarily best practice.
3. The results of research should be made readable for the persons who must make use of them. Otherwise, the delegates may overlook important material.
4. The pros and cons of alternative positions should be objectively presented. However, the existence of a substantial consensus among informed persons

---

[4] See Charlton F. Chute, "How to Get a New Constitution," 36 *National Municipal Review* 124-30 (March, 1947).

should not be obscured by a foolish attempt to make it appear that there is an equal amount of merit on both sides of every question.

5. The right and the duty of the convention to make up its own mind on questions both of policy and of form and style should be respected. Consequently, in general, the preparatory material should avoid including draft articles implying a single answer to any given problem. Preparatory material may, however, properly include draft provisions in order to test the possibility of translating proposals into constitutional language.

A great deal of excellent preparatory work has been done for a number of constitutional conventions, including that done for Alaska by the Public Administration Service, which benefited from careful study of the strong and weak features of earlier jobs. The failure to meet the enumerated specifications as fully as is desirable may be due in some cases to inadequate appreciation of what a convention can and should mean to a state. It also may reflect the common failure to start early enough and to provide adequate money and staff for the needed work.

As indicated earlier, research and education should be directed to the general public as well as to the convention delegates. If a convention is worth having, the preparation for it is worth all the effort that qualified public and private research and educational organizations and interested individual scholars can devote to it. Excellent work has been done in different states by university bureaus of public administration; by state and local bureaus of governmental, legal, or economic research; by individual scholars or voluntary committees of scholars; and by legislative councils and various other permanent state agencies. There is room for all such agencies, but experience would seem to indicate that there should be, in almost every case, at least one temporary official committee for preparatory research and one general citizens committee devoted primarily to the education of the public. One reason for a temporary state commission is that almost every permanent agency will be limited to some extent, if not in its objectivity then at least in its scope and resources for a special task of this sort. Alaska was peculiarly fortunate in having the well-established Statehood Committee, which was essentially independent of the territorial government although supported by public funds, to sponsor the preparatory research.

Ordinarily, official preparatory research has been beamed directly to the constitutional convention. However, there have been numerous special constitutional commissions like the New Jersey commission of 1941-42 and the Minnesota commission of 1947-48 which have been given the responsibility for reviewing the constitution and recommending desirable changes. The report of such a commission becomes public property and is bound to have an important effect both on public thinking and on that of the delegates to any future constitutional convention. In some cases such an official recommending commission is an important, if not an indispensable, part of the preparation for a convention.

The state of New York in 1956 took an unprecedented step in establishing a commission, appointed jointly by the Governor and the presiding officers of the two houses of the Legislature, to begin preparing for a convention which would have been held in 1959 if the people in November, 1957, had voted "yes" on the call for the convention which appears automatically on New York ballots every 20 years. This action was a recognition of the fact that a constitution as long and detailed as that of New York cannot be revised properly unless a massive job of preparatory research has been undertaken.

After the people somewhat unexpectedly turned down the call for a convention, the commission was replaced by a special joint legislative committee with substantially the same composition and staff. This committee was authorized to continue study of the Constitution and to make specific recommendations for constitutional change to the Legislature. The mandate of the committee, as in the case of its predecessor commission, included a special directive to study the possibility of "simplifying" the Constitution.[5] At the beginning of the legislative session in 1959 the committee, in turn, was reconstituted as the Temporary State Commission on the Revision and Simplification of the Constitution with substantially the same mandate.[6]

The consultants to the Alaska convention were often frustrated by the lack of reference tools and basic research on important issues with which the convention was confronted. No amount of preparatory work for a specific convention can meet entirely the need for up-to-date comparative and analytical material on constitutional issues or for guidance based on pertinent experience throughout the country on various problems connected with the conduct of a convention and the technical aspects of the task. While still in Alaska, the authors began to discuss these needs with the late Kimbrough Owen who was consultant to the Committee on Style and Drafting. As the needs were itemized, it became apparent that

---

[5] The first published staff report issued by the committee is *The Problem of Simplification of the Constitution.* Legislative Document No. 57, Albany, 1958. This was prepared by an Inter-Law School Committee under the chairmanship of Professor Walter Gellhorn of the Columbia University Law School.

[6] In its first report, *First Steps Toward a Modern Constitution,* Legislative Document (1959) No. 58, issued December 31, 1959, this commission recommended a substantial revision and simplification of a number of articles and sections of the Constitution. Several of its proposed amendments were given first passage by the Legislature in 1960.

concerted efforts of several organizations and many scholars would be required fully to meet them. The state constitutional study programs now being carried on by the National Municipal League and the Legislative Drafting Research Fund of Columbia University, with financing by the Ford Foundation, were developed partly as a result of this exploratory discussion in Fairbanks.

THE SETTING OF THE CONVENTION

Planning the physical arrangements for the convention, its organization, and the conduct of its proceedings will be significantly affected by the legal, political, and preparatory background already discussed. Of crucial importance in this connection is the leadership which emerges from this background both inside and outside the convention. The stage for the election of the convention delegates should be set so as to insure that there will be within it persons with a statewide point of view, capable of commanding the respect of the public outside and the affection and cooperation of the men and women inside the convention—people, moreover, who will have effective continuing communication with leaders of similar stamp who are outside the convention.

This ideal state of affairs was approximately achieved in Alaska, notably so with respect to the effectiveness of the leadership inside the convention. It was also substantially achieved in New Jersey. Noteworthy aspects of leadership in the New Jersey convention were: (1) the presence in the convention of a number of the outstanding leaders of the long-time civic campaign for revision, and (2) the close and effective liaison between Governor Driscoll and the leadership of the convention, particularly in bringing about certain compromises of a political nature which smoothed the way to agreement and to the overwhelming popular acceptance of the Constitution.

The Convention Site

The decision on the place of holding a convention has a good deal to do with what happens when it meets. The decision to locate the New Jersey convention in the gymnasium on the campus of Rutgers University in New Brunswick was dictated by the desire to get it and its members out of the atmosphere of the State House and its pervasive aroma of legislative maneuvering, midnight lobbying, and official protectiveness. While the distance between New Brunswick and Trenton is short in miles, the political distance between the Rutgers University gymnasium and the State House is considerably greater.

It was in all probability a stroke of genius on the part of those who planned the Alaska convention to follow the New Jersey example and locate it at the University of Alaska, which was remote in miles as well as in political atmosphere from the territorial capital in Juneau. In Fairbanks the delegates were able to develop a sense of community in the service of Alaska as a whole that would have been more difficult to achieve in the distracting environment of Juneau or even of Anchorage. It is also a matter of some importance that both the New Jersey and the Alaska conventions were on university campuses which boasted no barrooms or cocktail lounges.

Once the delegates arrived at the university campus in the morning they were likely to stay there until the end of the last session of the day—often late into the evening. It should not be supposed that smoke-filled rooms in the city of Fairbanks where the delegates stayed played no role in the work of the Alaska convention. They were important and on the whole beneficial, but factors of time and distance kept them from diverting members from their duties in the scheduled sessions of the convention and its committees.

Of course, no state could find a retreat quite so protected as mid-Alaska in midwinter, but the New Jersey and Alaska precedents are commended to the planners of future conventions in other states.

The Convention Timetable

The timetable of the convention can greatly affect its ultimate effectiveness, though more study needs to be given to comparative experience with this factor. Both the New Jersey and the Alaska conventions operated on strict timetables set by their enabling acts. Each was of about three months' duration and in each case the day of adjournment was kept constantly and purposely in the minds of the delegates—a policy that appeared to have the salutary effect of giving everybody a sense of urgency. In general, there was evident a strong feeling of obligation to avoid filibustering or diversionary tactics that might endanger success. It is true that in the case of the Alaska convention at least some matters might have been reconsidered and some drafts further refined if the time schedule had not been quite so tight. Yet more time might well have been wasted without producing any noteworthy improvement in the document.

In drawing up an enabling act it might be well to consider setting a tentative date of adjournment subject to postponement only by action of an extraordinary majority of the convention. This action would set a goal which probably would be kept but would still enable a convention which found itself unexpectedly bogged down over some important or difficult issue to extend its time and thus perhaps save itself from disaster or futility. The experience of the Missouri Constitutional Convention, which was not limited as were the New Jersey and Alaska bodies and which met almost continuously for exactly one year, is instructive on this point. It may have been necessary for the members of that body to continue to meet together over a considerable period in order to establish the rapport and the sense of corporate responsibility to the whole state which ultimately developed and produced an excellent result. Conceivably, the convention might have risen to the occasion earlier if the law had required it —but it would be dangerous, without much further study, to assume that it would have.

Another matter of timing has to do with the arrangements for giving the public an opportunity to review tentative decisions of the convention and to develop a sense of participation in the ultimate stage in the process of constitution-writing. In New Jersey, which is a small state, the convention committees published tentative reports which were then subjected to extensive public hearings at which individuals and organizations were invited freely to express themselves in the convention hall in New Brunswick. The record of these hearings became an integral part of the convention record and bulks larger than the formal debates in the convention itself. They played an important role both in shaping the final decisions on many issues and in preparing the public for the campaign for adoption of the new Constitution.[7] The Alaska convention, operating in an entirely different physical setting, sought to achieve a somewhat similar result by providing for public hearings at various centers throughout Alaska during a 15-day recess about halfway through the convention, after the committees had completed tentative drafts of their articles.

INTERNAL ORGANIZATION OF THE CONVENTION

The internal organization of the convention is vitally important. The convention is a distinctive instrumentality of the people, presumed to possess all powers required to accomplish its purpose. (Several questions that arose in Alaska on the powers of the convention revealed the need for an up-to-date study on this general subject.) The convention must organize itself, establish its procedures, and assume responsibility for the services of the convention staff. Key points in convention organization

---

[7] On the importance of the public hearings held by the committees of the Missouri convention, see Dean William L. Bradshaw's observation that they "were excellent conferences or seminars on all phases of state and local government." "The Convention Goes to Work," in *Modernizing State Constitutions* (New York: National Municipal League, 1948), p. 20.

are: (1) selecting the president; (2) organizing the committees; (3) managing the secretariat; and (4) selecting and using consultants.

Leadership of the Convention

A constitutional convention is a wonderful laboratory for the exercise of the combined arts of politics and administration. The president of the convention has a crucial role which may be a major determinant of its success. Without doubt, the personality, the native political wisdom, the complete integrity, and the inherent likeableness of President William A. Egan was an essential factor in the success of the Alaska convention.[8] President Egan demonstrated a remarkable sense of timing which made him appear completely patient when patience was a virtue and extremely urgent when urgency was a necessity. He knew how to apply the rules of procedure to produce the widest consensus and how to use good sense or human sympathy to smooth out a difficulty. He helped inexperienced delegates over rough spots and gradually welded a group of extreme individualists into a thoroughly effective working body. There were personal conflicts and stormy debates, but they were not allowed to divide the convention or to impair its functioning.

This tribute to President Egan's leadership has been paid primarily to illustrate the kind of leadership that should be sought for in every convention. There is good reason for surmising that a study of the record would show that President Clothier of Rutgers University as the chairman of the New Jersey convention and Mr. Robert Blake, a conservative Democrat who in effect sat between the Republicans and the rank-and-file of Democrats, in the Missouri convention made equally important contributions to the success of these bodies.

The Convention Secretariat

The convention needs a working secretary who is not a delegate to assume responsibility for such tasks as the following under the direction of the president or the committee on administration:

1. Maintaining the official records of the convention.
2. Selecting and supervising the staff and arranging for the pay, travel, working space, and other requirements of the delegates.
3. Numbering and duplicating convention documents.
4. Arranging for tape and stenotype records of convention sessions.
5. Providing professional library services and maintaining an historical record of the convention.

---

[8] Mr. Egan was later elected as one of the provisional United States senators for Alaska and became the first Governor of the state of Alaska.

6. Arranging public hearings, preparing news releases, and otherwise facilitating the convention's public relations as directed by convention officers.
7. Printing and distributing the final document and explanatory materials.

The secretariat functions of the convention may be performed by the personnel of some existing body, such as a legislative council or preparatory commission, or they may be organized separately by the convention. In either case, the secretariat should be under the complete control of the convention. It is more likely to be free of cumbersome influences if it is established separately, but it will need access to some governmental office to facilitate fiscal and other housekeeping services. It will need access, also, to competent legal advice.

Careful programing of convention work is essential to effective convention administration. The convention's administrative needs change as the work progresses. For example, the Alaska convention passed through four distinct phases: (1) the organizational phase; (2) a period of intensive committee work; (3) a period during which some committees were completing their work while the convention began to consider committee proposals; and (4) the final phase during which the convention was in almost continuous plenary session. Each phase had distinctive administrative requirements. The transition from one phase to another makes special demands on the officers and staff, not only in work load but also in adaptation. It seems reasonable to assume that other constitutional conventions which remain in continuous session will pass through similar phases. This factor should be considered in convention planning.

Committee Organization and Procedure

As in any large representative assembly, the burden of the work of a constitutional convention must be borne by the committees. A comprehensive study could and should be made of this subject. All that can be done here is to pass on a few insights, hunches, caveats, and suggestions. In the first place, the number of committees should be strictly limited. This rule is dictated by several considerations. One is the interlocking nature of the subject matter areas with which a convention deals. If these areas are broken down into too many separate units there are too many artificial jurisdictional lines between committees, with the consequent multiplication of opportunities for conflict, inconsistencies, and errors of omission and duplication in committee work and in the finished product of the convention. Another vital consideration is the fact that the length of the constitution and the extent of extraneous material included in it may be affected by the number of committees. It is almost axiomatic that there will be one section of the constitution for every substantive committee that is created. Finally, holding down the number of committees limits the number of assignments for each delegate and facilitates scheduling of convention work to avoid conflicts in committee meetings. A delegate will more fully participate in the preparation of a constitution if he is on one or at most two substantive committees having broad coverage.

The selection of committee members calls for a good deal of wisdom and finesse. In Alaska the task of designating committee chairmen as well as of assigning delegates to committees was given by rule to the president —an arrangement which produced cohesiveness in convention organization.

The natural tendency to load committees with people whose personal enthusiasms lead them to covet the assignments, or whose business or professional interests or experience presumably make them somewhat expert in the particular subject matter field, should be strictly curbed. Too many lawyers on the judiciary committee or too many businessmen and bankers on the finance committee may adversely affect the content or the public acceptance of the provisions they write. Specialists tend to forget that their business is to draft constitutional provisions for the people of the whole state, not just for themselves. At the same time, members who feel less well informed than the specialists on a committee may defer too easily, though not always gladly, to "superior" knowledge. In general, the only safe rule is to make each committee, so far as possible, a cross section of the convention as a whole without ignoring the value of having persons on certain committees with sufficient technical knowledge to be able to talk with consultants or with professionally equipped lobbyists and critics in their own language.

The question of whether committee meetings should be private or should be held in a fish bowl is almost certain to arise in connection with the adoption of rules of procedure, despite the fact that in practice the issue is likely to lack substance. There can be no dispute that committees should invite a certain amount of public participation, which means that they must let the public in from time to time on the results of their deliberations. Yet much committee work must be done under circumstances which protect the delegates against the introduction of irrelevancies from uninformed observers. Moreover, delegates should feel free to express themselves, without fear of being ridiculed or misunderstood, while they are trying experimentally to arrive at an understanding of themselves and their colleagues. The chances are pretty good, of course, that if the meetings were open to the public most of them would be held in substantial if not complete privacy. On the other hand, if all official committee meetings are actually attended by the public, it is certain that much of the most important committee work will be done in unofficial conferences at odd times and places. One way of avoiding unnecessary debate on the matter is to provide in the draft rules for both "public meetings" and "executive sessions" of committees.

One of the problems of convention management is to allocate time properly between committee work and meetings of the whole convention either in formal session or in committee of the whole. In our experience, this allocation is something which the president and some kind of steering committee, which may well be made up basically if not exclusively of committee chairmen, as in Alaska, will need to work out as the convention progresses. The same is true of the handling of committee reports at the various stages or "readings" at which they are considered by the convention as a whole. The convention's work must be programed to ensure adequate consideration of draft articles at each stage and to avoid jamming up toward the end of the convention.

Up to this point, attention has been centered on subject matter committees, with only incidental attention to the need for some kind of steering committee. There is, of course, a need for other committees, including at least one to assist the chairman and the secretary with respect to the purely business and formal aspects of convention management and another, of the utmost importance, usually known as the committee on style and drafting.

Selection and Use of Consultants

Conventions will find it useful, if not essential, to have specialists in various fields available for consultation. The selection of consultants and the definition of their role at conventions merit study. As a start for an agenda for such a study a number of views held by the authors are here listed:

1. Consultants should be selected as much for their flexibility, ability to get along with people, and willingness to submerge themselves and their prejudices in the service of the convention as for their technical knowledge. Some of the consultants should be chosen because of their qualifications as constitutional generalists rather than their knowledge of particular specialties.
2. There should be a clear understanding regarding the lines of responsibility and channels of communication between convention officers, committees, and delegates on the one hand and consultants on the other.
3. Consultants should be free to speak in committee meetings or with individual delegates, but should avoid taking sides publicly on controversial issues and

should never appear before the convention as a whole or at public hearings except on request or specific authorization of the convention.

4. Delegates should not use the names of consultants as weapons in debate. Consultants should be quoted, if at all, on the convention floor, only to indicate technical backing of items in the committee reports.

5. Consultants should recognize at all times that it is the convention, not they, writing the constitution and should so behave that there never can arise any criticism on this score.

6. Consultants have an obligation, however, to maintain complete integrity and should not refrain from calling attention through recognized channels to information or errors which may be germane to the work of the convention. A consultant has an obligation to see that the technical reasons for his disagreement with a committee or convention action are made known to and considered first by the responsible committee and then by the president or steering body of the convention. He should, however, scrupulously avoid lobbying for any point.

7. While a consultant may be engaged to advise on a particular segment of the constitution, he has an obligation to recognize the relationship between his work and that of others serving the convention. In his work he should advance the sense of common responsibility for the whole constitution which is necessary to a properly functioning convention.

8. It would also be desirable to have more of the consultants than was possible in the case of Alaska serving from beginning to end of the convention. On the other hand, there is certainly need in every convention for the occasional or part-time consultant, and it is also desirable for a committee not to get all its technical assistance from or through a single person.

9. At least one or two specialists in style and drafting should be included among the consultants. The Alaska Constitution reflects in part the superior skill of the late Kimbrough Owen who served as consultant to the hard-working and able Committee on Style and Drafting.

CONCLUDING STEPS IN THE CONVENTION'S WORK

Problems of Draftsmanship

The problem of refining and harmonizing the language of all proposals and keying them in an orderly and consistent manner into a single document or, in the case of amendments, into the existing document is one of the most difficult and important assignments that can be given to any members of a constitutional convention. The task of future committees on style and drafting will be immeasurably lightened when a competent manual on the subject is prepared for the use of constitutional draftsmen.[9] Until that time, every such committee and its consultants will continue to be pioneers plodding not an untrodden but still an essentially trackless field. The absence of such a manual makes it particularly important that the committee on style and drafting should start to meet at the beginning of the convention with a view

---

[9] The Legislative Drafting Research Fund of Columbia University Law School is now engaged in preparing material to meet this need.

to agreeing on some usages with respect to words, phrases, punctuation, capitalization, and organization that can guide the subject matter committees in their initial reports and lighten the load in the closing days of the convention. A good job of preparatory work in this field for a particular convention would include a special glossary explaining established usages of words and phrases in the constitution of the state.

If proper preparation has been made before and in the early weeks of a convention, the final task of the committee on style and drafting should not be too time consuming, but in scheduling the work of the convention it would ordinarily be desirable to set aside about a week between final action on substantive matters and the date set for the submission of the final report of the committee on style and drafting. During this period other members could well be occupied in disposing of various business matters, in reviewing the constitution for any oversights, and in planning for the program of public education on the proposals of the convention which, it is believed, following New Jersey and Alaska precedents, are necessary and proper functions of any constitutional convention.

One of the problems that concerned the Committee on Style and Drafting of the Alaska convention was distinguishing between style and substance. Obviously, this distinction cannot always be confidently drawn. When in doubt, the committee sometimes dealt with the question alone and sometimes worked the problem out with the one or two subject matter committees concerned. This experience leads to speculation on the desirability of formalizing the job of auditing the semifinal draft of the whole constitution for substance. Of necessity, convention delegates tend to concentrate on particular segments of the constitution, either those handled by their subject matter committees or others in which they happen to have a personal interest. Few have the time or the background to make an adequate assessment of the document as a whole and of the various ways in which decisions with respect to the substance of one article may affect another article.

Sensing this need, the consultants at the Alaska convention during its final days obtained the permission of the president to make a confidential report to the committee chairmen on substantive issues which they felt merited a final reconsideration before the document was approved for submission to the people. Limitations of time and competence necessarily limited the consultants' review, but on the whole their report was well received and proved helpful.

The final document will reflect many things: the knowledge and ability of the delegates; their leadership and ability to work together; the relationship between delegates and the general citizenry; the efficiency of the secretariat; and the contribution of technical advisers. An efficient secretariat and helpful advisers will not ensure a good constitution, but delegates will be under a grave handicap if their administrative and technical backstopping are poor.

Convention Sponsorship of Its Work

The view has already been expressed that a constitutional convention should be expected not only to write and formally submit a proposed constitution or constitutional amendments but also to assist in the education of the public on the meaning and importance of its proposals until they have been adopted or rejected at the polls. This is an essential part of the continuing process of constitution-making or revision, of which the convention is simply the central feature or agency. It has always been recognized that the convention should publish its proposals and perhaps accompany them with a formal address to the people.

Beyond that, it is suggested that every convention should be authorized to distribute to all voters a popular summary—an explanation of the constitution —and to sponsor talks and other presentations, especially by the delegates for the enlightenment of the general public. The convention record should be made available to the public for whatever help it may provide in the campaign for the adoption of the constitution and, of course, should be published for posterity. It goes without saying that planning for these activities should begin long before and continue through the convention. They are simply the culminating phase of the task of a constitutional convention.

IN CONCLUSION

It seems appropriate to end this over-long and distressingly sermonlike discourse with a few words on what might be described as the higher law of constitutional conventions. If some readers suspect that the authors have been a bit "touched" by their experience in Alaska and perhaps elsewhere, let them believe it, for it is true. To be close to a constitutional convention that approaches the greatness of which such a body is capable is to have something akin to a religious experience. There can be no doubt that in such a body members may attain heights of statesmanship seldom equaled in their political or private lives.

chapter VI

revision by constitutional commission

Bennett M. Rich

The constitutional commission continues to thrive, although as a device for achieving constitutional change the commission has had a rather meager record of accomplishment. Notwithstanding this record, or perhaps without reference to it, several new commissions have been established recently. Within the decade of the 1950's, approximately one-quarter of the states created constitutional commissions or made use of some similar device.[1]

CLASSIFICATION OF COMMISSIONS

Constitutional commissions may be classified in four categories. Three of these—the statutory commission, the executive commission, and the legislative commission—are concerned almost exclusively with constitutional matters. The fourth category, denominated for want of a more imaginative term as the special advisory body, embraces a variety of official groups concerned directly or indirectly with constitutional amendment and revision.

Statutory commissions are of two types: the classic, or true commission, and the preparatory commission. The classic commission, the largest single category, may be defined as one created by law—a joint product of the legislative and executive branches—for the purpose of recommending constitutional change to the legislature. All of the nineteenth century

---

[1] The growing literature on constitutional commissions is limited for the most part to commentaries on individual state commissions. However, see the excellent study by Albert L. Sturm, "Constitutional Commissions and Other Official Groups," in his *Methods of State Constitutional Reform* (Ann Arbor: Institute of Public Administration, University of Michigan, 1954), pp. 121-47. See also Bennett M. Rich, "Revision by Commission," 40 *National Municipal Review* 200-6 (Apr., 1951).

commissions and many in the twentieth century have been of this kind. There have been at least six in this category during the 1950's—Florida, Kentucky, New York, North Carolina, Pennsylvania, and Vermont.

The Florida Constitution Advisory Commission was by far the largest. The enabling act, adopted in 1955, required the Governor to share his appointing authority with a number of agencies. Indeed, he selected only 8 of the 37 members. Eighteen members were legislators: the President of the Senate, the Speaker, and the 8 members of each house constituting the Florida Legislative Council. The Chief Justice of the Florida Supreme Court appointed 5 members and the Board of Governors of the Florida Bar appointed 5. The attorney general was a member also.

The Constitution Review Commission of Kentucky was given statutory status in 1950. Created a year earlier by executive order, the commission was continued by law as an independent agency of state government. The law provided also for a 4-year term of office. Of the 7 members, all appointed by the Governor, 1 was to be selected from each appellate court district.

New York's Temporary State Commission on the Revision and Simplification of the Constitution was established early in 1959. It continues studies initiated by the 1956 statutory preparatory commission and the 1958 legislative commission, both described below.

The North Carolina Constitutional Commission, established in 1957, is classified in the table below as a classic or true commission. North Carolina has the distinction of being the only state in which the approval of the Governor is not required as the final step in the legislative process. However, Governor Luther H. Hodges played a significant role by recommending, in a message to the General Assembly, that a commission be established. The legislature complied and authorized the Governor to appoint a 15-member body.

Pennsylvania's Commission on Constitutional Revision, created in 1957, also consisted of 15 members. The Governor, the Speaker, and the President pro tempore of the Senate each made 5 appointments. The enabling act authorized the commission either to recommend amendments, or, if it determined that a general revision was required, to act somewhat in the capacity of a preparatory commission for a convention.

For a half century Vermont has followed the practice of setting up a constitutional commission at the end of each decade to consider suggested amendments. The Constitution provides that amendments may be proposed at 10-year intervals only. In 1959, a commission of 8 members was established.

Not all of the constitutional commissions created by law are required to report to the legislature. The mandate, instead, may be to prepare materials for a constitutional convention. The one example in the 1950's was the New York Temporary State Commission on the Constitutional Convention. Created in 1956, the commission was given a broad mandate to conduct studies and to compile information not only for the use of the delegates, but also for the use of the people both before and during the convention. Appointments to the 15-member body were shared equally by the Governor, the temporary President of the Senate, and the Speaker of the Assembly.

The second category of constitutional commissions consists of those created by action of the executive alone. In 1957, Governor George Docking appointed a 21-member Kansas Commission on Constitution Revision, instructing the group to establish their own objectives and procedures. More recently, in August, 1958, Florida's Governor LeRoy Collins appointed a Special Constitution Advisory Committee of 5 members.

Commissions responsible to the legislature alone constitute a third category. New York's Special Legislative Committee on the Revision and Simplification of the Constitution, created in 1958, was of this kind. Oregon had a Governor's and Legislative Constitutional Committee in 1953 and West Virginia set up a 48-member legislative Commission on Constitutional Revision in 1957.[2]

The fourth category—the special advisory body—is a catchall which fits no easy pattern. It may be argued that this category should be eliminated since, in the final analysis, any official advisory body fits one of the three major classifications. However, the principal categories of commissions include only those officially created bodies with constitutional matters as their principal concern. The special advisory body, on the other hand, may have constitutional revision as one of many concerns.

One type of special advisory body is the existing state agency which

---

[2] Admittedly, the problem of classification of the interim legislative committee is difficult and somewhat arbitrary. At what point, for example, does an interim committee merit the classification of a legislative constitutional commission? Professor Dodd, writing in 1910, made a sharp distinction between a commission and a joint legislative committee established to draft amendments. Joint committees established by Louisiana in 1894 and by Georgia in 1901 for the specific purpose of preparing amendments were dismissed by Dodd as "merely legislative committees and not commissions acting independently of the legislative bodies. . . ." Walter F. Dodd, *The Revision and Amendment of State Constitutions* (Baltimore: Johns Hopkins Press, 1910), p. 263n. Professor Dodd's recognition of the semi-independence of the commission may be an appropriate bench mark for purposes of classification. If any considerable portion of the membership of a legislative committee is from outside the legislature, then it would seem appropriate to designate the body a legislative commission.

either by direction or on its own initiative considers constitutional revision. For example, in 1946 the Louisiana State Law Institute, an official law revision body, was directed by statute to prepare the draft of a new constitution.[3] Texas offers a more recent illustration of a similar approach; in 1957, the Legislature requested the Legislative Council to make a constitutional study. By the same resolution, an 18-member Citizen Advisory Committee was authorized.

The "Little Hoover Commissions" may also fit into the category of the special advisory body. Many of them made recommendations on constitutional matters. For example, a completely revised constitution was included in the draft of the Connecticut Commission on State Government Organization in 1950.[4] Kentucky's Committee on Functions and Resources of State Government recommended a number of constitutional changes in its survey of the state's needs.[5]

The table below includes known commissions of the three principal categories. No effort has been made to compile a full listing of the host of agencies making up the fourth category, although a few examples are included.

The classification of commissions according to the manner of their creation is, admittedly, somewhat artificial. Two broad categories based on purpose might serve equally well—those recommending change to the legislature, and those preparing materials for a convention. However, one clue to the chances of success of a commission—and by success is meant a substantial acceptance of its recommendations both by the legislature and by the people—may be found in the manner of a commission's creation.

Commissions established by law have at least the nominal support of both the legislative and the executive branches. They may, indeed, have the enthusiastic support of one or both. Commissions created by one branch may or may not have support from the other branch. Those created by the chief executive alone may be expected to have particularly rough sledding. The Kansas commission of 1957, for example, was appointed by the Governor, a Democrat, after the Republican Legislature had refused to act. Similarly, the recently appointed executive commission in Florida was established only after the courts had thrown out the Legislature's "daisy chain" plans—of which more later.

---

[3] Kimbrough Owen, "Constitutional Revision in Louisiana: The Preliminary Stage," 20 *State Government* 304-6 (Dec., 1947).

[4] Commission on State Government Organization, *The Report* (State of Connecticut, 1950).

[5] Committee on Functions and Resources of State Government, *Final Report, Findings and Recommendations* (Frankfort: Dec., 1951).

TABLE 3
CONSTITUTIONAL COMMISSIONS BY STATE AND TYPE, WITH YEAR OF ESTABLISHMENT AND OTHER INFORMATION

State	Year	Page Citation to Statutes	No. of Members
I—Statutory Commissions			
A. To Recommend Revision			
California	1929	741	15
Florida	1955	1246	37
Georgia	1943	1680	23
Kentucky	1950	777	7
Maine	1875	3	10
Michigan	1875	563	18
Minnesota	1947	1111	21
New Jersey	1852	546	3
	1854	544	3
	1873	844	14
	1881	187	9
	1894	556	20
	1905	185	5
	1941	1084	7
New York	1872	2178	32
	1890	402	38
	1959	ch. 4	15
North Carolina	1913	449	20
	1931	796	9
	1957	1689	15
Pennsylvania	1919	388	25
	1957	927	15
Rhode Island	1897	121	15
	1912	475	9
South Carolina	1948	2226	16[a]
Tennessee	1945	703	7
Vermont	1908	571	5
	1919	310	8
	1929	222	8
	1939	417	8
	1949	428	8
	1959	J. Res. R-29	8
Virginia	1926	797	7
West Virginia	1929	503	11
B. Preparatory to Convention			
New York	1914	758	5
	1956	1765	15
Massachusetts	1917	23	3

TABLE 3 (Continued)

State	Year	Page Citation to Statutes	No. of Members
II—Commissions Created by the Chief Executive Alone			
A. To Recommend Revision			
Florida	1958		5
Kentucky	1949		7[b]
Kansas	1957		21
Michigan	1942		32
Washington	1934		9
B. Preparatory to Convention			
New York	1938		42
III—Commissions Created by the Legislature Alone			
A. To Recommend Revision			
California	1947	Assembly Concurrent Resolution No. 89	20
Oregon	1953	Senate Joint Resolution No. 28	17[c]
New York	1958	Concurrent Resolution	15[c]
West Virginia	1957	Senate Concurrent Resolution No. 5	48[c]

IV—Special Advisory Bodies (illustrative only)

A. Existing Agency Directed to Prepare Revision

State	Date	Agency
Louisiana	1946	Louisiana State Law Institute
Oklahoma	1947	Legislative Council
Texas	1957	Legislative Council

B. Broad-Purpose Commission

Connecticut	1949	Commission on State Government
Kentucky	1952	Committee on Functions and Resources of State Government

[a] The act provided for 21 members; however, the 5 members from the court system were not appointed.

[b] Also, 41 persons on subcommittees named by commission.

[c] Governor shared in appointment of members.

Of the three legislative commissions created during the last decade, all provided for executive appointment of a portion of the membership. This would seem to indicate that there is no significant difference between the statutory commission and the legislative or executive commission so far as the relationships with the chief executive are concerned. The sponsors may simply have chosen the concurrent resolution as an easy parliamentary device.

The recent New York experience attests to the invalidity of such an assumption. A bill reconstituting the Temporary State Commission on the Constitutional Convention, more popularly known as the Rockefeller Commission, was vetoed by Governor Harriman on the ground that (1) 15 members were too many, (2) two-thirds of the members were appointed by the legislative leaders, and (3) the members of a permanent body should be appointed by the chief executive.[6] Since the Republican majorities in the Senate and the Assembly were insufficient to override the veto, the Legislature's only means of continuing the commission was by concurrent resolution.

A Special Legislative Committee on the Revision and Simplification of the Constitution was thereupon created. The 15-member body was to consist of 5 persons appointed by the temporary President of the Senate, 5 by the Speaker of the Assembly, and 5 by the Governor. The membership was to be limited to 10 in the event the Governor failed to abide by the legislative request. Rather than appear to be against continued study of the Constitution—an untenable position equivalent to being in favor of sin—Governor Harriman appointed 5 persons to the commission. In this instance, then, the creation of the commission by resolution rather than by statute did not come about merely because of the ease of the parliamentary procedure. The manner of creation of the commission, in short, was directly linked to the political maneuvering incident to a gubernatorial election.

COMPOSITION, PROCEDURES, AND FINANCING

The list of members of a constitutional commission usually reads like a who's who of the state. Persons prominent in business, education, and government are selected. The jury to determine the guilt or innocence of the existing constitution is unquestionably of the blue-ribbon variety.

In any governmental commission, a major problem is to secure members who are interested and who can devote a sufficient amount of time so that their judgments are informed. The constitutional commission is no exception. The subject matter of a constitution is highly complex. In every state there are a number of so-called "hot potatoes" which require on the part of the commission member not only an extensive background of information but an astute political sense. The big-name commission

---

[6] *New York Times,* Feb. 11, 1958, p. 25.

member may have neither the time nor the disposition to "bone up" on the issues and to seek patiently for appropriate solutions. Emphasis on a big-name commission may, in fact, be completely misplaced.

As one might expect, no two constitutional commissions operate in quite the same manner. However, there seem to be no significant differences based upon classification; that is, the executive commission operates in much the same manner as the legislative or statutory commission. Committees are often established in order to divide the work and at the same time to obtain a degree of specialization. No accepted pattern has emerged, however, as to the best means of committee operation. In Pennsylvania, the 15 committee members were assigned to seven substantive areas: legislative, executive, judiciary and human rights, state finance, education and social welfare, suffrage and elections-amendment and revision, and local government. The Kansas commission followed a similar plan; of 9 committees, 7 dealt with substantive and 2 with procedural matters, a general steering committee and a committee on publicity and public consultation.

The plan of attack of Oregon's Governors and Legislative Constitutional Committee was in sharp contrast to the substantive-area approach. Four subcommittees were created to analyze on a section-by-section basis Oregon's 25,000 word Constitution. An executive secretary acted as a liaison among the subcommittees in the consideration of interconnected sections. Of 232 sections in the Constitution, the committee determined that all but 66 were in need of change. A constitutional convention was recommended as the only means of obtaining an integrated constitution.[7]

Public hearings are now standard practice although, again, there is a considerable variation in the manner of holding them. The Pennsylvania commission held hearings in Pittsburgh, Harrisburg, and Philadelphia. Of 18 presentations at Pittsburgh, 10 were by individuals and 8 by local organizations. At the Harrisburg hearing, representatives of 11 statewide associations testified—associations such as the Pennsylvania State Grange, the Pennsylvania League of Women Voters, and the Pennsylvania Association of Boroughs. The chairman of the Florida commission reported that "protracted public hearings were held over the state."[8] In contrast, the West Virginia commission planned but two hearings, one in January, 1958, to obtain the views of the state's legislators and one in May, 1958, to which the public was invited. The North Carolina commission con-

---

[7] *Report of the Governor's and Legislative Constitutional Committee* (January 10, 1955), pp. 11-12, 25.

[8] Florida Constitution Advisory Commission, *Recommended Constitution for Florida* (n. d., n. p.).

ferred with state officials and with representatives of state organizations, but held no public hearings.[9]

Legislative provision of funds for technical assistance is spotty. The Florida commission received an appropriation of $100,000; the Pennsylvania commission received $50,000. The Legislature of Kansas appropriated $5,000 to its Legislative Council whose Special Committee on the Constitution worked with the commission; preliminary research studies were financed by a grant from the Ford Foundation. New York's Special Legislative Committee had an initial allocation of $150,000. In contrast, $500 was appropriated for the Vermont commission.

ROLE OF THE LEGISLATURE

Commission members face a dilemma immediately upon their organization. Should they try piecemeal amendment or should they go for all-out revision?[10] Will their contribution have the greatest ultimate effect as the result of a bold and imaginative approach? Or should they limit their recommendations to what they believe the legislature will accept?

To follow the first course offers the commission an opportunity to raise the public's sights and to dramatize needs. To follow the second offers some assurance that the commission's recommendations will be looked upon with favor by the legislature.

The legislature can make or break a constitutional commission. It may exercise an absolute veto, since whatever the commission recommends must receive the approval of both houses. Indeed, extraordinary majorities are sometimes required, and favorable action in more than one legislative session may be necessary before a proposal of the commission reaches the stage of a public referendum.

The commission is hampered not alone by the fact that its recommendations must be screened by the legislature. There is the further handicap that recommendations finally accepted by the legislature must be presented as proposals for amendment in the form prescribed by the constitution. In many states, this additional burden spells doom for revision efforts.

The strategic position of the legislature is illustrated strikingly by the recent Florida experience. Legislative efforts to control the end result

---

[9] John L. Sanders, "The Proposed Constitution of North Carolina: An Analysis," 25 *Popular Government* 2 (Feb., 1959).

[10] The constitutional amending clause may furnish the answer to this question. In Florida, for example, the Supreme Court has held that general revision may be accomplished only through the process of the constitutional convention.

were always evident. The first means of control was through direct representation on the commission, and legislative members were but one short of an absolute majority. A second means of legislative control also stemmed from the enabling act. The commission's jurisdiction was limited. Several constitutional issues were removed from consideration, such as the prohibition on the issuance of state bonds and the prohibition on the levying of an income tax. Nor was the system of distributing to the counties taxes on the pari-mutuel pools to be disturbed.

Notwithstanding the large number of legislators on the commission, the rather limited proposals for revision contained in the report were entirely unacceptable to a joint legislative committee.[11] Significant changes in the recommendations were made in several areas, including a different formula for representation, the elimination of limited home rule provisions, and the elimination of a provision for the use of the initiative in amending the Constitution.

One of the most extraordinary recommendations of the Legislature concerned the holding of a constitutional convention. At present, the concurrence of two-thirds of each house is required before the question of holding a convention may be submitted to the voters. Not satisfied with this restrictive provision, the Legislature added the requirement that the proposed constitution be returned to the Legislature for review and possible amendment. When returned, the constitution could be "submitted to the electorate only after it had been approved by three-fifths of the members of each house." The only means of avoiding this procedure was for the Legislature to agree by a three-fourths vote of the membership of each house that convention proposals would go directly to the electorate.[12]

The recommendations of the Legislature were grouped into 14 proposed amendments. Owing to the "interlocking details" of the various proposals, the Legislature declared by resolution that all had to be approved. If one failed, all 14 failed. The legality of the so-called "daisy chain" package was contested, and the Supreme Court declared the proposal in violation of the existing amendment clause.[13] Thus ended, momentarily, the revision effort. The Florida experience is one of the best—

---

[11] See *Revised Florida Constitution Proposed by the Legislature and Explanation of Changes* (Tallahassee: R. A. Gray, Secretary of State, n. d.).

[12] See Manning J. Dauer, *The Proposed New Florida Constitution: An Analysis* (Gainesville: Public Administration Service, University of Florida, 1958), pp. 17-18 (Civic Information Series, No. 30).

[12] *Rivera-Cruz* v. *Gray*, 104 So.2d 501 and *Pope* v. *Gray*, 104 So.2d 841.

or worst—illustrations of the manner in which a legislature, through its power of review, may emasculate the work of a commission.[14]

EVALUATION

An assessment of the results of the commissions established in the 1950's is premature. As of mid-1960 a status report only is appropriate. Of the six classic or true commissions established by law to recommend constitutional change, four had completed their work. The fifth—New York—began operation as a statutory body in January, 1959, and the sixth—Vermont—was scheduled to report in time for the 1961 legislative session. The Constitution Review Commission in Kentucky recommended the constitutional limit of two amendments in 1952 and another two in 1954-1955.[15] In each instance the legislature submitted one of the proposed amendments to popular referendum. Both were rejected. Subsequently, the functions of the commission were transferred to the state's Legislative Research Commission.

The alteration by the Florida Legislature of the recommendations of the Constitution Advisory Commission has already been described. The commission was replaced by a Special Constitution Advisory Committee to the Governor. This new body has recently submitted a report for the consideration of the Legislature.[16]

Extensive reports were submitted in early 1959 by the commissions in North Carolina and Pennsylvania. The North Carolina group, with 58 recommendations for substantive change, submitted a fully revised constitution.[17] In contrast, by a vote of 9 to 6, the Pennsylvania commission favored the submission of amendments. These were divided into three categories. Joint resolutions were prepared covering 35 recommended changes in the first two categories, those "critically needed" and those "desirable" but not "vital."[18]

The operations of the lone statutory commission preparatory to a convention, that of New York, were abruptly terminated when the people of

---

[14] For an analysis of the revision effort, see William C. Havard, "Notes on a Theory of State Constitutional Change: The Florida Experience," 21 *Journal of Politics* 80-104 (Feb., 1959).

[15] Kentucky. *Report of the Constitution Review Commission,* 1952 and *Constitution Review Commission Biennial Report,* 1954-1955.

[16] Florida. *The 1959 Recommended Constitution.* Mimeographed.

[17] North Carolina. *Report of the North Carolina Constitutional Commission* (Raleigh: 1959).

[18] Pennsylvania. *Report of the Commission on Constitutional Revision* (Harrisburg: March, 1959).

the state voted against calling a convention. The legislative commission which replaced the preparatory body has, in turn, been succeeded by a new statutory agency. Its first recommendations, which included completely new articles on local government, suffrage, and defense, were released December 31, 1959.[19]

The Kansas Commission on Constitution Revision submitted a progress report early in 1959.[20] It recommended four separate amendments relating to home rule, taxation, the powers of the executive, and the composition of the Legislature, including a board of apportionment. The Legislature has agreed to submit one of the four—home rule for cities—to the electorate in the 1960 general election.

From the remaining commissions operating in the present decade, little of a positive nature has developed. In Oregon, nothing came of the legislative commission's recommendations for a constitutional convention.[21] Lacking funds, the Texas Legislative Council has delayed the start of any thoroughgoing study.[22]

On balance, over a period of several decades the record of the constitutional commission has been undistinguished.[23] Substantial changes, it is true, have been achieved in a few states, and one or more amendments have been adopted in a number of states following the use of the commission device.

What accounts, then, for the continued popularity of the commission as opposed to the relative eclipse, once again, of the constitutional convention? The reasons vary from state to state. One motivating factor may

---

[19] The reports issued by the New York commissions are: Temporary State Commission on the Constitutional Convention, *First Interim Report*. Legis. Doc. No. 8 ([New York] Feb., 1957). *Second Interim Report*. Legis. Doc. No. 57 (New York: Sept., 1957). The Temporary Commission on the Revision and Simplification of the Constitution, *First Steps Toward a Modern Constitution*. Legis. Doc. No. 58 (New York: Dec., 1959).

[20] Kansas. *Progress Report of the Kansas Commission on Constitution Revision* (Topeka: 1959).

[21] Oregon. *Report of the Governor's and Legislative Constitutional Committee* (1955).

[22] However, see *Interim Report to the 56th Legislature and the People of Texas from the Citizens Advisory Committee on Revision of the Constitution of Texas* (March 1, 1959).

[23] No study has been published of the influence of constitutional commissions upon subsequent constitutional and statutory changes. Such a study would be complicated by the time lag which often occurs between the proposal of a commission and the acceptance of the proposal in the form of a law or a constitutional amendment. For a recent illustration, see Lloyd M. Short, "Minnesota Adopts Three Constitutional Amendments," 46 *National Municipal Review*, 28-29 (Jan., 1957).

be the ease in setting up a commission as distinguished from the formal and formidable convention process. Practical considerations also play a part; constitutional barriers to a convention may lead to the commission approach as an alternative.[24]

Commissions may be established for no ascertainable reason other than that they are a normal means of seeking solutions to difficult problems. The national government and the state governments create scores of special commissions. What more natural course for a governor or a citizen group to pursue than to advocate the creation of a special body to consider constitutional change?

For the members of a state legislature, also, the creation of a commission has certain built-in advantages. The commission offers a forum for the more ambitious, and it can be used as a delaying tactic for those primarily interested in the over-all strategy of maintaining the status quo. The fact that the commission is in existence gives the appearance of doing something. Momentarily, the legislator has a respite from the hot breath of the ardent reformer.

To a legislator bent on holding the line, the establishment of a constitutional commission provides the perfect answer. Nothing the commission does can have any legal effect without legislative approval. Recommendations do not go on the ballot automatically. Every proposal must go back to the legislature for approval, modification, or rejection.

To all concerned, then, the commission device seems a happy answer. And sometimes efforts of a commission are crowned with success. Frequently, however, the results are disappointing to those seeking constitutional change.

By its very nature the constitutional commission is at a disadvantage in promoting public acceptance of its recommendations. The commission meets sporadically, and it is extremely difficult to sustain interest in its operations. When the commission's studies are concluded, its membership may be reluctant to campaign for public support until the legislature has acted. Then, too, legislative amendments may take away the zeal of the commission for a promotional campaign.

---

[24] Fear of failure to obtain the required legislative majority for a convention resulted in Georgia's Constitutional Commission in 1943. Headed by the Governor, the commission proposed a number of substantial changes which, after some modification by the General Assembly, were submitted as a package and approved by the people. In this instance, one observer has declared, "the commission and legislature together may be said to have been accepted as substantially the equivalent of a constitutional convention." John E. Bebout, "Recent Constitution Writing," 35 Texas Law Review, 1076 (Oct., 1957).

The constitutional commission has a place. It can assist in educating the public concerning important constitutional issues. It can propose amendments of a technical nature. Occasionally, it can effect substantial revision. However, the commission lacks the strong legal position and the dynamic character and the drama of a convention. Notwithstanding the contributions of a number of excellent commissions, the commission device is no substitute for a convention. No amount of wishing can make it so.

chapter VII

use of the amending procedure since world war II

W. Brooke Graves

For a long time, the American people have been passing upon dozens, scores, even hundreds of state constitutional amendments each year, but up to this time no one has known very much about them. Actually, how many are there? With what subjects do they deal? What are the voting habits of the electorate in passing upon them? Are all or most of the proposals submitted approved, or is it general practice to vote them down on the theory that somebody might be trying to get away with something?

Does a sufficient percentage of the proposals submitted deal with basic problems of government to make this method of constitutional change a really useful device for revising and modernizing state constitutions? In other words, can piecemeal amendment be made to work, so that a constitution may be kept up to date without periodically going through the ordeal of general revision by a constitutional convention?

GENERAL OBSERVATIONS

Background of the Study

These are important questions to which the answers ought to be known. On this account, and because so much has been said about the excessive number and the poor quality of state constitutional amendments, the author undertook to find out what the facts are.[1] The effort to assemble this informa-

---

[1] The Division of Governments, U. S. Bureau of the Census has from time to time provided information regarding the number of proposals voted upon in the several states, but little has been done by way of analyzing their contents. See *State Proposals Voted Upon* and *City Proposals Voted Upon* (Washington, D. C.: Government Printing Office, annually, except 1938-1946).

tion began several years ago with a sampling of the proposals submitted to the electorate in the biennium 1953-1955.[2] The analysis of the information regarding this sample proved to be so interesting that the few who saw the report unanimously agreed that the scope of the study should be enlarged and extended to include all proposals submitted in all the states over a longer period of time.

Such a study became possible in 1957 in connection with the National Municipal League's project on state constitutions and constitutional revision, financed by the Ford Foundation. The period selected for analysis was the 11 years following World War II, extending from 1946 to 1956, inclusive. Table 4, a summary table, shows the number of propositions submitted, the number of subject matter changes involved, and the number of each adopted and defeated, state by state, during this period.

The report here presented is still regarded as preliminary. Although complete information on the proposals submitted to the voters in all states during this period was finally obtained, the data still seem inadequate, both in quantity and coverage, especially when a sizable number of important proposals affecting such topics as local government, home rule, metropolitan areas, and taxation are known to be pending. It has been decided, therefore, to extend the present study by bringing up to 15 the total number of years included.

What Is a Constitutional Amendment?

First of all, one may raise the question: What is a constitutional amendment? The question is by no means so foolish as it sounds, nor is the answer so obvious. As a practical working basis, one generally is compelled to take the position that a constitutional amendment is whatever language on whatever subject, formulated and submitted to the voters for their approval or rejection in accordance with some procedure authorized in the constitution for accomplishing constitutional change.

Under such a necessary rule of thumb, many things are included which properly should not be classified as constitutional material, whereas other things which might be so classified are excluded. For Minnesota, for example, there is included a revision and rewrite of a 1916 amendment setting forth in detail a description of all the routes in the state highway system; this proposal was originally adopted "to keep the highways out of politics." For 5 Southern states (see Table 5), one is obliged to include dozens and

---

[2] The sample consisted of approximately 200 proposals from 25 states, concerned with 33 major topics. This was, it is now known, about half of the normal biennial grist.

TABLE 4
NUMBER OF CONSTITUTIONAL AMENDMENTS SUBMITTED, ADOPTED, AND
DEFEATED, AND NUMBER OF SUBJECT MATTER CHANGES INVOLVED,
BY STATE, 1946-1956, INCLUSIVE

State	Number of Propositions			Number of Subject Matter Changes Involved		
	Sub-mitted	Adopted	De-feated	Sub-mitted	Adopted	De-feated
1. Alabama	133	64	69	213	105	108
2. Arizona	25	13	12	31	21	10
3. Arkansas	23	10	13	29	14	15
4. California	109	72	37	137	95	42
5. Colorado	27	10	17	34	17	17
6. Connecticut	10	9	1	10	9	1
7. Delaware						
8. Florida	51	31	20	61	39	22
9. Georgia	205	193	12	292	275	17
10. Idaho	8	8	0	9	9	0
11. Illinois	10	6	4	10	6	4
12. Indiana	3	3	0	3	3	0
13. Iowa	2	2	0	2	2	0
14. Kansas	8	6	2	8	6	2
15. Kentucky	9	6	3	10	7	3
16. Louisiana	216	166	50	264	199	65
17. Maine	22	19	3	25	22	3
18. Maryland	31	31	0	33	33	0
19. Massachusetts	5	5	0	5	5	0
20. Michigan	28	23	5	30	25	5
21. Minnesota	19	9	10	22	12	10
22. Mississippi	11	7	4	11	7	4
23. Missouri	13	7	6	22	11	11
24. Montana	10	7	3	13	9	4
25. Nebraska	23	13	10	24	13	11
26. Nevada	12	12	0	14	14	0
27. New Hampshire	9	4	5	9	4	5
28. New Jersey	14	8	6	25	15	10
29. New Mexico	43	26	17	50	29	21
30. New York	50	45	5	71	64	7
31. North Carolina	23	18	5	30	26	4
32. North Dakota	22	10	12	29	10	19
33. Ohio	23	19	4	34	29	5
34. Oklahoma	32	17	15	51	28	23
35. Oregon	31	21	10	44	29	15
36. Pennsylvania	13	7	6	18	11	7
37. Rhode Island	47	41	6	71	65	6

TABLE 4 (Continued)

State	Number of Propositions			Number of Subject Matter Changes Involved		
	Submitted	Adopted	Defeated	Submitted	Adopted	Defeated
38. South Carolina	106	106	0[a]	166	166	0[a]
39. South Dakota	18	10	8	27	14	13
40. Tennessee	9	9	0	12	12	0
41. Texas	50	38	12	59	47	12
42. Utah	13	12	1	14	13	1
43. Vermont	3	3	0	5	5	0
44. Virginia	10	8	2	10	8	2
45. Washington	14	12	2	20	17	3
46. West Virginia	10	7	3	16	11	5
47. Wisconsin	17	11	6	25	16	9
48. Wyoming	14	8	6	18	12	6
Total	1,584	1,172	412	2,116	1,589	527

[a] While no proposition was defeated at the polls, the action of the electorate is not final. After popular approval, amendments have to be ratified by the General Assembly before becoming a part of the Constitution; there were about 30 propositions which, during the period covered by this study, failed to receive such ratification.

scores of items of local legislation, none of which have any proper place in a constitution. Many other illustrations might be cited.

In the realm of excluded materials, one may note the propositions submitted to the voters in some states in the form of "public questions." The results of such voting are conclusive and binding, thereby distinguishing these referendums from the so-called advisory referendums. Some of these propositions involve debt increases in significant amounts for specific purposes; in many states, such questions have to be handled as constitutional amendments. The public questions procedure, while it involves submitting a specific policy question to the people, at least functions without incorporating each bond issue approved into the basic law of the state.

AMENDMENTS RELATING TO CONSTITUTIONAL CHANGE

Amendments affecting the process of constitutional change were not, as one might have expected, a field of major activity in the period under review; 36 proposals of this general character were submitted in 19 states. Connecticut and Maine codified existing constitutions. New Jersey adopted a com-

TABLE 5

NUMBER OF GENERAL AND LOCAL CONSTITUTIONAL AMENDMENTS
ADOPTED AND DEFEATED, SELECTED STATES AND YEARS

State	Year	Propositions		General		Local	
		Adopted	De-feated	Adopted	De-feated	Adopted	De-feated
Alabama	1946	9	0	6	0	3	0
	1948	9	7	1	3	8	4
	1950	6	0	1	0	5	0
	1952	4	1	2	1	2	0
	1954	6	0	3	0	3	0
	1956	4	10	4	2	1	7
Total		38	18	17	6	22	11
Florida	1946	1	5	9	2	1	3
	1948	8	3	3	3	5	0
	1950	5	0	5	0	0	0
	1952	2	9	1	3	1	6
	1954	6	1	4	1	2	0
	1956	7	1	5	1	6	0
Total		29	19	27	10	15	9
Georgia	1946	0	0	0	0	0	0
	1948	17	0	0	0	17	0
	1950	35	2	2	2	31	0
	1952	45	1	8	2	36	0
	1954	43	4	7	0	32	0
	1956	54	4	8	0	42	4
Total		194	11	25	4	158	4
Louisiana	1946	25	5	15	7	10	0
	1948	32	9	21	8	11	1
	1950	16	8	6	4	8	6
	1952	34	0	23	0	11	0
	1954	23	8	12	4	11	4
	1956	36	19	21	16	13	7
Total		166	49	98	39	64	18
South Carolina	1946	11	11	0	17	17	0
	1948	26	26	0	47	47	0
	1950	39	39	0	66	66	0
	1952	14	14	0	16	16	0
	1954	10	10	0	12	12	0
	1956	6	6	0	8	8	0
Total		106	106	0[a]	166	166	0[a]

[a] While no proposition was defeated at the polls, the action of the electorate is not final. After popular approval, amendments have to be ratified by the General Assembly before becoming a part of the Constitution; there were about 30 propositions which, during the period covered by this study, failed to receive such ratification.

pletely revised Constitution, and Illinois, Minnesota, and Tennessee adopted amendments designed to improve the amending procedure by making it more workable or more democratic in operation.[3]

Maine in 1950 adopted a proposal designed to make possible the rearranging (or codification) of the Constitution, by putting it in a readable and usable form and making it one continuous document without the necessity for cross references to amendments. Similarly, Connecticut in 1953 adopted a codification of its Constitution for the first time since 1819, incorporating into it some 47 amendments without other revision. New Jersey in 1947, by approving a public question, formally adopted its new Constitution, thereby bringing to a successful conclusion a full decade of effort to revise the state's century-old document.

CONSTITUTIONAL PROTECTIONS

Some 39 proposals in the area of bills of rights were submitted in 19 states; they related to several different aspects of the field and included various phases both of substantive rights and of the rights of property.

Substantive Rights

Proposals in the field of substantive rights dealt with the basic freedoms, freedom from discrimination, the rights of women, and the rights of accused persons. In the first category, Maryland in 1948 and North Carolina in 1946 adopted amendments relating to freedom of conscience, Massachusetts in 1948 to freedom of speech. Proposals relating to the relatively new field of freedom from discrimination were submitted in 5 states and adopted in 2. North Carolina adopted a very general, preamble-like statement regarding human rights, but Ohio in 1953—following the lead of New Jersey in 1947—voted to eliminate the word "white" and thereby make the provision for military duty apply to all male citizens.

The two rejected proposals were submitted in California in 1946 and in New Mexico in 1948. The former, submitted in the form of a proposition

---

[3] Illinois in 1946 defeated once again its famous Gateway Amendment, but adopted it upon its sixth submission in 1950. This amendment was intended to break the roadblock which had for more than half a century operated to prevent change in the Illinois Constitution. Only 9 amendments had been adopted since 1870, only 3 since 1890. Minnesota defeated two such proposals in 1948, defeated them again in 1952, but approved both in almost identical form in 1954.

Tennessee in 1953 adopted an amendment easing the requirements for ratification of amendments by substituting a majority of votes cast for a vote equal to or exceeding that of all votes cast for members of the General Assembly—a requirement that had, for a period of more than 80 years, operated to prevent use of the amending procedure, thereby conferring upon Tennessee the dubious distinction of being the only state with an unamended constitution.

or public question, declared it to be state policy that all persons have the right to equal opportunity to secure employment; ". . . hence it shall be unlawful to hire, discharge, or discriminate in conditions of employment because of race, religion, color, national origin, or ancestry." Provision was made for the establishment of a commission to enforce this policy. The second, in New Mexico, provided that ". . . no person shall be denied employment because of membership or non-membership in, or other relationship to a labor union, nor be compelled against his will to pay dues in such an organization as a prerequisite to employment or as a condition of employment." This, of course, was the now familiar right-to-work formula.

Four states extended to women the right and the duty of serving on juries,[4] and 3 states adopted and 1 defeated proposals affecting the rights of accused persons. Of this second group, the North Carolina provision adopted in 1946 is most significant: "In all criminal prosecutions, every person charged with crime has the right to be informed of the accusation and to confront the accusers and witnesses with other testimony, and to have counsel for defense, and not be compelled to give self-incriminating evidence, or to pay costs, jail fees, or necessary witness fees of the defense, unless found guilty."

Michigan in 1952 adopted a provision relating to search and seizure, and California rejected one on the composition of the grand jury and the eligibility of the chairman for service. North Carolina in 1950 affirmed the right of any person, when represented by counsel, to waive indictment in all except capital cases, under such circumstances as the General Assembly may prescribe. Texas in 1956 authorized legislative relief for persons who have been fined and imprisoned for offenses of which they were not guilty.

Two states adopted constitutional provisions relating to subversion—Michigan in 1950 defining the term and establishing offenses and penalties; California in 1952 providing that "public employment shall not be held by, and no tax exemption shall be extended to, any person or organization advocating overthrow of Federal or State Government by force or unlawful means and advocating support of a foreign government against the United States in the event of hostilities." Legislation to enforce this provision was authorized.

Rights of Property

The 3 Pacific Coast states adopted amendments relating to land ownership by noncitizens. Five states adopted 7 amendments having to do with eminent

---

[4] They were: North Carolina (1946), Oklahoma (1952), Texas (1954), and West Virginia (1956). Texas had previously rejected this proposal in 1949. North Carolina in 1956 extended the legal rights of married women with respect to ownership of property, and Ohio in 1953 removed constitutional restrictions on the eligibility of women to hold certain public offices.

domain,[5] and 5 states adopted 8 amendments dealing with different aspects of the problems of racing, betting, and wagering.[6]

In California in 1952 and 1954 amendments were adopted repealing restrictions, adopted in 1879, prohibiting property ownership by Chinese and eliminating restrictions on the rights of resident foreigners, eligible for United States citizenship, to hold property other than real estate. It thereby gave Chinese the same rights as were enjoyed by resident foreigners of white or African descent. Oregon in 1946, however, took a step in the opposite direction by adopting an amendment prohibiting any Chinese who was not a resident of the state at the time of the adoption of the Constitution from ever holding any real estate or mining claim or working any mining claim within the state.

Washington adopted 2 amendments in 1950 and 1954 dealing with another aspect of the problem of land ownership. The first, a reciprocity provision, had the effect of permitting ownership of land by Canadians who are citizens of provinces wherein citizens of Washington may own land; the second redefined the term "alien," permitting the Legislature to determine the policy of the state respecting the ownership of land by corporations having alien stockholders.

Two proposals submitted in Texas dealt with the problem of rural fire protection, the first in 1949 being approved, the second in 1951 being rejected.

POPULAR CONTROL OF GOVERNMENT

Proposals having to do with popular control of government fall into three groups: initiative and referendum, suffrage and elections, and ballots and elections administration. None of these groups is large, there being 10 propositions relating to the first, 61 to the second, and 7 to the third. Only 1 in the first group was defeated, 19 in the second, 3 in the third.

---

[5] Alabama and Rhode Island authorized local units to acquire land for public housing, slum clearance, and redevelopment projects; Louisiana for highway purposes, harbors and terminals and terminal facilities, and for public works of a permanent nature. North Dakota and Wisconsin adopted provisions largely of a procedural nature, and provisions of this character were also included in the Louisiana highway amendment.

[6] The voters of Arkan as rejected an amendment declaring that horse and dog racing were unlawful and approved another authorizing horse racing and pari-mutuel betting thereon in Hot Springs and Gaylord County and the regulation thereof by the General Assembly. In California in 1946 a proposition or public question which would have authorized dog racing and pari-mutuel betting in certain counties was rejected. Another similar proposal was defeated in 1950. In 1948, Colorado voters authorized the General Assembly to pass a pari-mutuel law; in 1952, Oregon voters defeated such a proposal. In 1954, Michigan rejected a proposal to authorize bingo, and Colorado rejected a proposal to outlaw slot machines except in those local units, where by local option, they had been authorized.

Initiative and Referendum

California and Oregon were the only states submitting proposals on the constitutional initiative.[7] Proposals relating to initiated measures involved four problems: control of legislative change of measures previously adopted, financing, petition requirements, and procedure.[8] Petition requirements were voted upon in 3 states—Maine, Massachusetts, and Washington—all providing for additional signatures on petitions.[9]

Suffrage and Elections

Proposals in this area may be grouped under qualifications for voting, absentee voting, ballots and voting machines, and elections administration. General provisions relating to qualifications for voting were considered in 5 states—Alabama, Minnesota, Mississippi, North Carolina, and South Carolina. Of 8 propositions submitted, 7 were adopted. A rewrite job, intended to clarify voting qualifications but not to change the meaning, was rejected in Minnesota. By 2 amendments, Mississippi sought more fully to prescribe the qualifications of electors; it included a requirement for constitutional interpretation designed to restrict Negro voting. A North Carolina proposal providing that "every person born in the United States and every person who has been naturalized, twenty-one years of age, and possessing the qualifications set forth in this article, shall be entitled to vote at any election . . ., except as herein otherwise provided," was amended a few years later to emphasize age (21 years), residence (1 year in the state, 6 months in the district), and literacy (ability to read and write the English language). The

---

[7] California extends to this area the application of the familiar one-subject rule, prohibiting the submission of proposals including more than one subject and providing that such measures hereafter submitted shall not become effective. Oregon increased from 8 to 10 per cent the number of voters' signatures required to put an amendment on the ballot, based on the number of legal votes for justice of the Supreme Court in the last regular election.

[8] On legislative change, California now authorizes the Legislature to propose amendments to or the repeal of initiated laws, provided that such changes shall be submitted to the people for their approval or rejection. In Washington, it is provided that no act approved by the people shall be amended or repealed within two years following such approval, except by a two-thirds vote of all members of the Legislature or by direct vote of the people. Maine voters rejected a proposal to make temporarily inoperative any measure adopted by the people which fails to provide a revenue adequate to support the service or function for which it provides.

[9] For a referendum petition Maine requires not less than 10 per cent of the total vote for Governor in the last gubernatorial election. Washington stipulates 8 per cent of the last vote for Governor for an initiated measure, 4 per cent for a referendum petition. Procedurally, Maine and Massachusetts changed the dates for filing on initiated measures. In the former, 45 days is provided instead of 30, after the date of the convening of the Legislature, in order to give ample opportunity for the Legislature to take the action proposed.

South Carolina proposal dealt with the qualifications of voters in municipal elections.

Idaho and Missouri adopted amendments giving Indians the right to vote. California voters rejected and Connecticut voters approved proposals looking toward removal of the voting disqualification of persons who, having been convicted of an infamous crime, had completed paying the penalties imposed for such conviction. Three proposals to lower the voting age were submitted; Kentucky voters approved and Oklahoma and South Dakota voters rejected the extension of the suffrage to persons 18 years of age who were otherwise qualified. Several states passed upon questions involving the poll tax as a qualification for voting. In Alabama, the exception from the poll tax was extended to veterans of the Korean and other conflicts, and the cumulative character of the tax—except for a period of two years—was abandoned. Rhode Island, South Carolina, and Tennessee abolished the poll tax as a prerequisite for voting, but proposals to accomplish this purpose were rejected in Arkansas, Texas, and Virginia.

The residence requirement was considered in 4 states;[10] questions on registration, of which only 1 was rejected, were considered in 7 states;[11] general propositions on absent voting also were considered in 6 states.[12]

---

[10] California voters adopted a proposal designed to preserve the eligibility of electors who move from one county to another within 90 days prior to an election, by permitting them to vote in the county of their former residence. Louisiana voters reduced the state residence requirement from two years to one, without affecting other residence requirements effective in the parish, precinct, or municipality. Mississippi voters first rejected, later approved, a statement that persons, in order to become qualified electors, "shall have good moral character and that the wife of a minister, legally residing with him, shall be qualified to vote after a residence of six months in the election district, or incorporated city or town, if otherwise qualified"!!! North Carolina, as noted, established a one-year residence requirement.

[11] Alabama adopted qualifications for registration of voters. Arkansas granted the General Assembly power to enact laws providing for registration of voters and to require that the right to vote in any election should be dependent upon such registration. Louisiana voters adopted one and rejected another proposition dealing with registration administration; they also rejected one to empower the Legislature to provide absentee registration to persons, even including those not of voting age, who are entering or serving in the Armed Forces. Maine, Nevada, New York, and Texas exempted military personnel in service from the requirements of the registration law, along with spouse, parent, or child accompanying them. Rhode Island voters adopted two amendments to provide for permanent registration.

[12] In Maryland, absent voting was authorized under certain conditions, as it was in New Hampshire, but in this case for primary elections only. New Mexico first rejected in 1951, then approved, an authorization to the Legislature to provide for absent voting, but it took three propositions submitted in 1953 and 1955 to accomplish this result. New York adopted two proposals to enable persons unable to appear personally at the polling place on election day, because of illness or disability, to vote absentee. Pennsylvania extended this privilege to incapacitated war veterans, Rhode Island to shut-ins.

Ballots and Elections Administration

With relation to ballots and elections administration, Colorado voters adopted a provision for a secret ballot and Ohio voters one for an office column ballot and requiring that each candidate must be voted for separately. Louisiana authorized the use of voting machines in two parishes, and Rhode Island authorized a $500,000 bond issue to purchase 300 machines. Two unsuccessful attempts were made in Georgia to write into the Constitution the county unit system for all officers elected on a statewide basis. Michigan adopted two proposals on elections administration and one to establish a bipartisan state board of canvassers. Rhode Island defeated an attempt to repeal the direct primary.

THE EXECUTIVE

In the period under review, 163 propositions relating to the executive were submitted to the voters in 43 states; of these, 114 were approved and 49 rejected, as shown in Table 6. In other words, the ratio of adoptions to re-

TABLE 6

NUMBER OF CONSTITUTIONAL AMENDMENTS RELATING TO THE EXECUTIVE SUBMITTED AND ADOPTED AND NUMBER OF STATES SUBMITTING, BY TYPE, 1946-1956, INCLUSIVE

Type	Proposals Submitted	Proposals Adopted	Number of States
The Governor			
Governor's office	28	25	18
Executive powers	5	4	5
Legislative powers	6	6	5
Executive clemency	3	3	3
Administrative organization			
Departmental structure	2	2	2
In re specific services	20	11	9
Public officers			
General provisions	11	9	9
Qualifications	13	6	11
Method of selection	13	11	13
Tenure	25	12	17
Compensation	31	19	17
Filling vacancies	6	6	5
Total	163	114	...

jections was better than two to one. These proposals related to the governor's office, administrative organization, and public officers.

Governor's Office

The proposals relating to the governor's office may be grouped under such convenient headings as qualifications and election, tenure, compensation, disability, and succession. In general, it may be said that the proposals themselves and the disposition of the voters to approve them indicate a trend toward longer terms and higher salaries. The amendments also represented an effort to clear up uncertainties regarding disability and succession—uncertainties which may, on occasion, become both annoying and embarrassing. All of these changes are in accord with recommendations which students of state government have long been urging.

Maine and New York adopted important changes relating to qualifications of candidates for governor and elections for that office. Maine eased the citizenship requirement by changing from natural born to 15 years. New York took steps to prevent in future a situation in which the Governor and lieutenant governor would be of different political parties by providing that each voter should cast a single vote for these offices. It also provided that there should be no election of a comptroller or an attorney general except at the time of electing a Governor, vacancies in such offices to be filled by the Legislature. New York many years before had provided for the election of major state officers in an "off-year" election.

Three states—Colorado, Ohio, and Tennessee—increased from two to four years the term of the governor and other elected state officials. Arkansas tried twice to make this increase, in 1950 and 1954, but failed both times. Ohio and Tennessee imposed a limit on reeligibility—Ohio "for a period not longer than two successive terms," and Tennessee "without the possibility of immediate succession." California voters rejected a proposal to limit eligibility to two successive terms, and Idaho and Maryland authorized successive four-year terms. Massachusetts and Virginia (the latter already had a four-year term) changed the date of the inauguration. Four states approved substantial increases in the governor's salary, New York establishing a new maximum of $50,000.[13]

---

[13] California in 1946 fixed the minimum of $10,000 and forbade increases after the 1947 session during a term of office. In Maryland, an increase from $4,500 to $15,000 was provided for in 1954. In 1953, New York voters authorized the Legislature to fix the salary at not more than $50,000—which amount was thereafter provided by statute—thereby doubling the constitutional salary previously existing. At the same time, the salary of the lieutenant governor was also doubled, the new figure being $20,000. Texas voters authorized the Legislature to fix the salaries of the Governor and other officers.

Three states—California, Kentucky, and New Hampshire—struggled with the troublesome question of disability. California in 1946 provided that the secretary of state, attorney general, treasurer, and controller, in the order named, should assume the powers and duties of the Governor in the event of his disability. Kentucky in 1953 and New Hampshire in 1956 conferred upon the governor the power and authority to transact official business while absent from the state. Succession in case of vacancy was presented to the voters in 9 states. An order of succession was established in 5: Arizona, California, Michigan, Oregon, and Texas. Massachusetts, New Mexico, and New York, taking cognizance of then recent difficulties experienced in other jurisdictions, made provision for succession in case of the death of the governor-elect, and Connecticut took action regarding the qualification of the lieutenant governor as Governor under these circumstances.

In view of the generous size of the sample, and even of the number of proposals relating to the executive, the powers of the governor received little consideration. Only 5 propositions were submitted relating to the executive powers—2 on appointing powers, and 3 on military powers. Minnesota voters authorized their Governor, when filling a vacancy in an elective office, ". . . to appoint until the end of the term for which the person who vacated the office was elected, or the first day of January following the next general election, whichever is sooner . . .," rather than until the next annual election, as formerly provided. Utah voters conferred upon their Governor power to fill vacancies in certain offices. Alabama and Vermont voters adopted amendments organizing or reorganizing their National Guard units; Ohio voters removed from their Constitution provisions for the election of officers of the militia.

Only two aspects of governors' legislative powers came up for consideration by the voters—special sessions and veto power. Louisiana adopted a provision requiring the Governor to give the Legislature written notice at least five days in advance of calling a special session. New Mexico provided that, while special sessions may be called by the Governor, only business specified in the call shall be transacted during such sessions.

Four states—Florida, Georgia, New Mexico, and Tennessee—gave evidence of concern about or interest in the veto power of the governor by increasing the time available to him for consideration of bills left on his desk after the legislature had adjourned. Tennessee also broadened the veto power by authorizing the item veto for appropriation bills.

Three states—Maine, Nevada, and South Carolina—were concerned with executive clemency. Maine extended the powers of Governor and Executive Council to offenses in juvenile delinquency. Nevada authorized the Governor, justices of the Supreme Court, and the attorney general, under certain conditions, to remit fines and forfeitures; it also authorized the Legislature to enact laws conferring upon the district courts power to suspend execution of sentence. South Carolina, on the other hand, sought to limit the pardoning power, restricting it to reprieves and commutations of the death sentence, and establishing and vesting all other clemency in a Probation, Parole and Pardon Board.

Administrative Organization

Since details of administrative organization do not rightfully belong in a constitution, it is gratifying to find that relatively few proposals of this character found a place on the ballot. Montana adopted an amendment establishing a Department of Labor by separating the Bureau of Labor from the Department of Agriculture and, in another amendment, set up a Board of Pardons. Colorado reorganized its state Department of Education in 1948, and again in 1952. Ohio created a state Board of Education, and Oregon changed the method of selecting the state superintendent of public instruction. Louisiana and Oklahoma each adopted a proposal relating to the reorganization of the fish, game, and wildlife agencies; Louisiana voters rejected two other proposals relating thereto.

Similarly, with regard to highways, Louisiana adopted one and rejected two proposals having to do with organizational matters. New Mexico and Oklahoma both rejected proposals for a state highway commission. The former would have given full powers over all highway matters to the commission and would have created five highway districts. Louisiana first rejected and then adopted a proposal to establish a Liquefied Petroleum Gas Commission. West Virginia removed its state superintendent of public instruction from the state Public Works Board. Louisiana adopted one and rejected two proposals having to do with public welfare organization.

State Administrative Services

In the limited space available, it is difficult to do more with the proposals dealing with state administrative services than to indicate their enormous number and their highly diversified character. Of some 574 proposals submitted, dealing with 14 different major state services or functions, 450 were approved and 124 rejected (Table 7). Although, as has been noted, few of these matters have any proper place in a constitution, the tendency to deal with them at least in part in constitutional provisions is well-nigh universal. Of the 14 subjects, education was considered in 35 states, highways in 24, veterans in 23, public welfare in 17, and corporations and public health and hospital matters in 10 states each. At the other end of the scale, only cor-

TABLE 7

NUMBER OF CONSTITUTIONAL AMENDMENTS RELATING TO STATE
ADMINISTRATIVE SERVICES SUBMITTED AND ADOPTED AND NUMBER OF
STATES SUBMITTING, BY SERVICE, 1946-1956, INCLUSIVE

Service	Proposals Submitted	Proposals Adopted	Number of States
Corporations (incl. banking)	12	9	10
Corrections	5	3	3
Education	266	246	35
Highways	41	29	24
Housing	16	15	7
Industrial development	47	23	8
Labor	6	5	5
Liquor control	14	6	9
Natural resources (incl. agriculture) ...	14	8	7
Public health and hospitals	34	26	10
Public lands	13	8	9
Public utilities	7	3	6
Public welfare	36	24	17
Veterans	66	58	23
Total	577	463	...

rections and labor among the 14 subjects were considered in amendment proposals in 5 or fewer states.

In only 7 states were no proposals submitted relating to any of the 14 subjects.[14] Various reasons seem to explain some of this nonaction. New Jersey had a new, thoroughly revised Constitution near the beginning of the period under review, and some of the other states have withstood the temptation to embody major portions of the administrative code in their constitutions.

THE LEGISLATURE

Proposals for change in the provisions relating to the legislature occupied an important place in constitutional change in the 11 years following World War II, 138 proposals being submitted in 39 states. Aside from half a dozen proposals of a miscellaneous nature, the following aspects of the legislative process were presented for decision by the voters: apportionment, compensation, tenure, method of filling vacancies, sessions, local legislation, powers, and procedure. California voters rejected in 1956 a proposal to

---

[14] They were: Connecticut, Delaware, Indiana, Iowa, New Hampshire, New Jersey, and Washington.

change the name of the lower house from The Assembly to the House of Representatives.

Legislative Organization

Nine states considered general or partial reapportionment of the senate and 5 adopted these proposals, but only 3 considered and 2 approved reapportionment of the lower house. Reapportionment of both houses was on the ballot in 10 states; it was approved in Illinois and New Mexico, and also in South Dakota two years after an initial defeat. Some type of automatic apportionment was voted on five times: approved in Illinois and Texas, defeated in Colorado, and in Oregon first defeated and later adopted.[15] These data tend to confirm the view that it is easier to accomplish change in senatorial than in house apportionment, and much easier to accomplish either alone than the two together.

Nationwide, the question of increasing legislative compensation received— as it should—a considerable amount of attention. As has long been the case, the voters seemed reluctant to deal with the question on a realistic basis, in keeping with generally recognized needs. Of 40 proposals submitted in 23 states, only 20 were adopted, and the increases provided in some were ridiculously inadequate. Salary increases were voted in a number of states; increases in per diem and travel allowances in some; and in a few, increases in both were provided.[16]

---

[15] The Illinois reapportionment, accomplished by the widely publicized Blue Ballot in 1954, was the first since 1901. It was provided that, in future, if the General Assembly fails to apportion, a special commission shall be established to make the required apportionment. Texas created a Legislative Redistricting Board because of the failure of past legislatures to redistrict after each decennial census. Two reapportionment proposals were defeated in Colorado in 1954 and 1956, the former carrying an automatic procedure to insure future reapportionments when due.

Oregon had an active decade in the field of apportionment. In 1946, the voters rejected a proposal to increase the number of senators from 30 to 31, and in 1950, a reapportionment plan which would have allotted to each county at least one representative. This action was followed in 1952 by an initiated proposal making a current reapportionment and requiring reapportionment every 10 years, the secretary of state to act if the Legislative Assembly failed and, again, giving the Supreme Court power to compel compliance. As a result of this action, an amendment was adopted in 1954 authorizing the legislature to divide counties having more than one senator or representative into subdistricts for the election of members.

[16] Salary increases were voted in Alabama, Florida, New York, and Rhode Island. California provided $500 per month; Connecticut, $500 per session; Oklahoma, $100 per month; Oregon, $600 per year; Texas, $25 per day not to exceed 120 days; Utah, $500 per legislative term. California authorized members to draw per diem expenses not in excess of allowances to members of boards and commissions. Maine, Missouri, North Carolina, and South Carolina provided travel allowances for members. Kansas, Michigan, New Mexico, Oklahoma, Tennessee, and Utah provided for increases both in compensation and for expenses and allowances.

The voters of 5 states passed on questions of legislative tenure, 2 endorsing and 3 rejecting longer terms.[17] Of 6 states that voted on questions involving the method of filling vacancies, only Wyoming rejected the proposal—a proposal that would have repealed existing provisions. Each of the others prescribed a method or procedure to be followed; in South Dakota, for instance, the Governor was authorized to appoint to fill vacancies occurring in either house.

Questions involving legislative sessions were reviewed by the voters in 22 states, three types of questions being involved. They were (1) proposals fixing regular and special sessions in 6 states;[18] (2) questions regarding special sessions in 4 states;[19] and (3) the question most widely considered— biennial vs. annual sessions—the trend being in the direction of the latter.[20] Virtually all of the states adopting annual sessions provided that the session in the even-numbered year should be devoted—some of them exclusively devoted—to budgetary and fiscal matters. The trend toward more frequent meetings of the legislature is encouraging, but the effort to establish a barrier between fiscal and policy questions is a little ridiculous, since it is impossible to consider either without reference to the other.

Powers and Procedures

Nine states submitted 12 proposals relating to various aspects of legislative powers, of which 4 were defeated. The California electorate rejected a proposal to permit members to hold office and serve as members of boards and commissions created to apportion state funds to state and local agencies. The voters of California, along with those of New Mexico, North Dakota, and Ohio adopted, while those of Montana rejected, proposals applying to one or both houses, authorizing them to provide for the selection, term, and compensation of their officers and employees.

---

[17] In California, a proposal was defeated that would have established four-year terms for both houses, one-half of the membership of each house to be elected every two years. Nebraska and Texas also rejected four-year terms, but such tenure was approved in Ohio and Oregon.

[18] Alabama, California, Connecticut, Florida, Missouri, and New Mexico.

[19] Alabama rejected and Arizona adopted a provision permitting the legislature to convene itself in special session. Louisiana, as noted above, required the Governor to give advance notice in writing of his intention to call a special session, and New Mexico authorized the Governor to call a special session, but limited the business that might be transacted to subjects mentioned in the call.

[20] Of 12 states voting on this question, in one form or another, 7 voted for annual sessions, 5 for biennial sessions, as follows: for annual sessions: Arizona, California, Georgia, Kansas, Louisiana, Maryland, and Michigan; for biennial sessions: Connecticut, Mississippi, New Mexico, North Carolina, and West Virginia. Louisiana's decision in 1954 was reaffirmed in 1956.

In an effort to control "political appropriations," Louisiana voters adopted a requirement of a three-fourths vote to appropriate funds during special sessions called prior to a gubernatorial primary and near the end of a term. Four years later, in 1956, the voters of this state established a requirement of a two-thirds vote to levy new taxes or to increase existing taxes.

New Hampshire voters authorized the General Court to adjourn for periods not to exceed five days. Texas voters authorized their Legislature to grant aid and compensation to persons fined and imprisoned for offenses of which they were not guilty. Washington voters granted their Legislature power to fix the salaries of elected state officials, but limited its power to amend within two years measures approved by direct vote of the people.

A dozen proposals governing procedural matters were passed upon by the voters of 8 states. Only 2 were defeated. Oregon and South Dakota both struggled with the time-honored problem of the three readings, both confirming ancient practice, the latter by rejecting a two-reading proposal. Oregon also established an emergency committee to serve from session to session, with power to allocate funds, and liberalized requirements with regard to title. Vermont added to its oath of office a provision for assurance that the new officer is not a dual officeholder.[21]

Although local legislation constitutes a serious problem in a few states, it did not show up as a major issue in the period 1946-56. Most of the local amendments dealt with taxation and finance, schools, or public works. There were only 6 general proposals in this field, 3 of them in Georgia where 2 dealt with problems of specific counties and the third had to do with the advertising of local legislation in the press. Proposals submitted in Kansas, Tennessee, and Virginia were of a more substantial character.

In Kansas, in 1954, the Legislature was authorized to designate "urban areas" and to enact special legislation with regard thereto; otherwise, general laws with uniform application throughout the state should be adopted. A Tennessee proposal, growing out of the limited Constitutional Convention of 1953, established home rule for cities and counties as to local legislation, requiring approval of a state act by a two-thirds vote of the local legislative body. Virginia, which is not supposed to have local legislation, adopted in

---

[21] Alabama voters defeated and those in Georgia approved a validation. In Florida, a proposal was adopted relating to adjournment and the signature and vetoing of bills. In Georgia, the legislature was authorized to consider at any later session during the life of a given General Assembly business pending at adjournment of any regular session. Louisiana adopted a detail regarding the titling of acts and statutory revision and codification. Maryland provided for reconsideration of bills vetoed by the Governor and for their passage over his veto by a three-fifths vote. Maryland also established a cut-off date for the introduction of bills: 10 days before adjournment in even-numbered years, 20 days before adjournment in odd-numbered years.

1948 a purely organizational proposition, abolishing the Joint Committee on Special, Private and Local Legislation in the General Assembly.

THE JUDICIARY

In view of the serious need for revision and modernization of state court systems, it is significant that they were given extensive attention in some 160 proposals for change in the constitutions of 32 states. The number of such proposals presented in the 11-year period tended to impugn the oft-repeated assertion that "nothing is ever done about the courts." Many of these proposals, to be sure, were of a routine character, creating new courts, authorizing more judges, or extending the jurisdiction of established courts. Some, however, marked real improvements in organization or advances on questions of policy.

The proposals submitted may be grouped, for brief consideration here, under the following headings: judicial personnel, including qualifications and selection, compensation, filling vacancies, tenure, and retirement; organization of the courts, including general provisions, the minor judiciary, problems of individual courts, and jurisdiction; and judicial procedure, including, in addition to general provisions, the jury system, both grand and petit.

Judicial Personnel

Questions relating to the qualifications of judges were considered in 2 states, California voters rejecting 2 proposals and Michigan voters approving 1 in this area. In 5 proposals in 4 states, questions having to do with the selection of judges were considered.[22] The compensation of judges received considerable attention, 15 proposals relating to this subject being submitted in 9 states.[23]

If the generally overburdened courts are to keep abreast of their dockets,

---

[22] Connecticut in 1948 changed its method of selection, providing for the appointment of minor court judges on nomination by the Governor instead of election by the General Assembly. Louisiana now requires the Governor to call special elections for the filling of new district judgeships created by the Legislature. It is further provided that such judges must be members in good standing of the state bar association. Both Michigan and New Mexico took steps to improve electoral procedures, as applicable to the judiciary, by establishing a nonpartisan method of election. Michigan, in addition, cancelled noncontested judicial primaries.

[23] Of these, 6 were rejected. Arkansas, Kansas, and New Mexico (after twice defeating the proposal), authorized the legislatures to fix judicial salaries. Michigan, Ohio, Utah, and Wyoming authorized increases in certain judicial salaries, but Georgia twice defeated such proposals. Both New Mexico and Ohio voters rejected a provision prohibiting increases or decreases during the term for which the judge was elected or appointed.

provision must be made for filling even temporary vacancies. Voters in several states were confronted with proposals in this general area. New York voters in 1955 rejected 2 proposals for the appointment of temporary judges to serve during the illness or temporary disability of incumbents. Alabama and California voters each adopted two amendments regulating the filling of judicial vacancies. Maryland adopted 1 such proposal. Louisiana, New York, and Pennsylvania each adopted provisions authorizing the assignment of judges, as a means of filling temporary vacancies, and Georgia adopted 2 such provisions.

Questions relating to judicial tenure and retirement received considerable attention. Connecticut increased the tenure of probate judges from two years to four. Florida and Georgia adopted amendments dealing with tenure of certain local court judges, and Wisconsin a general tenure provision. Rhode Island voters twice rejected proposals for life tenure of judges (the second time in the form of service up to 70 years of age), and Nevada specified that judges should not be eligible to any other office, except a judicial office during the term for which they were elected or appointed.

Provisions relating to judicial retirement were adopted in 8 states, in 1 following an earlier rejection. Georgia, Louisiana, and North Carolina made their retired judges eligible to preside over their respective courts, and authorized the legislature to provide for such service. Florida and Washington voters provided for retirement for higher court judges at age 75, with a proviso that the legislature might prescribe a lesser age or other causes for retirement. New York and Wisconsin were the other states adopting retirement provisions.

Organization of Courts

Some 19 proposals relating to judicial organization were presented to the voters in 10 states; of these, only 6 failed of adoption. Twelve provided for the establishment of additional lower courts, and only half a dozen can be said to have been of any real importance. California voters rejected a proposal for a new court of tax appeals, but adopted another establishing a uniform system of municipal and justice courts throughout the state, providing for municipal courts in the larger cities and that there should be only one kind of court in a district. New York made its Court of Claims a constitutional court. Maryland reorganized its circuit courts, and Minnesota, by consolidation, improved its over-all judicial structure. North Carolina authorized the General Assembly to divide the state into judicial districts, with one court in each. The same number of proposals, none of them important, were submitted on the minor judiciary. Only 2 of these were defeated. Four Alabama proposals relating to court officers—clerks and registrars—were all defeated.

Many of the proposals took the form of creating individual courts or types of courts. There were more than 30 of these in about a dozen states, dealing with everything from the supreme court to the probate courts.[24]

Seven amendments in 5 states were adopted dealing specifically with questions of jurisdiction. In Georgia, higher appellate courts were authorized to review by writ of error all final judgments of juvenile courts. Louisiana enlarged the jurisdiction of the First City Court of New Orleans and the criminal jurisdiction of the City Court of Shreveport. New York similarly increased the monetary jurisdiction of the City Court of New York and of the county courts outside of New York City; Washington increased the monetary jurisdiction of its superior courts. New Mexico adopted a general provision regarding the jurisdiction of its probate courts.

Judicial Procedure

Only a few proposals were considered on procedural matters. Alabama dealt with court costs in a single county. California deleted a time limit on appeals to the Supreme Court. Louisiana dealt with criminal appeals in one parish court, New York with appeals to its highest appellate court—the Court of Appeals. Ohio provided for the revision of the procedures of its courts of record. Texas authorized judges to deny bail to professional criminals, with 60 days as the maximum time for holding an individual in jail without bond. Louisiana rejected a proposal to liberalize bail in felony cases. Utah adopted an amendment relating to prosecution by information and indictment and to grand juries.

Seven states adopted and 1 rejected propositions relating to juries and grand juries. California rejected a grand jury proposal. Florida provided for jury trials of civil cases in certain municipalities in a single county. New Hampshire sought to preserve the right of trial by jury in civil cases in which the value in controversy exceeds $500. Maryland asserted that the jury should be the judges of law as well as of fact, North Carolina that "no person shall be convicted of any crime but by the unanimous verdict of a jury in open court," but authorized the legislature to provide other means of trial for petty misdemeanors, with the right of appeal. Texas now permits

---

[24] Mississippi enlarged its Supreme Court and Florida tried unsuccessfully to do so, as well as to establish a system of appointment by the Governor for Supreme Court justices. Louisiana and Texas voters considered the organization and jurisdiction of district courts. Maryland, as noted, reorganized its circuit courts. Florida added 4 amendments relating to the office of county judge in individual counties, and 4 states adopted amendments relating to their probate courts. California, Louisiana, and Virginia provided for the establishment of municipal courts, and specialized courts likewise received attention. Florida, Louisiana, and Wyoming adopted provisions establishing juvenile courts, and Louisiana adopted 2 amendments relating to family courts. Georgia and Louisiana provided for the establishment of traffic courts in certain cities.

waiver of jury trial, in cases other than those involving a criminal offense, for insanity reasons. Oklahoma and West Virginia each provided that service on grand and petit juries should not be limited to male persons.

TABLE 8

NUMBER OF CONSTITUTIONAL AMENDMENTS RELATING TO TAXATION AND FINANCE SUBMITTED AND ADOPTED AND NUMBER OF STATES SUBMITTING, BY TYPE, 1946-1956, INCLUSIVE

Type	Proposals Submitted	Proposals Adopted	Number of States
Taxation			
Property taxes	18	7	14
Miscellaneous taxes	17	11	10
Taxes for school support	39	23	7
Taxes for community development	16	12	11
Highway and road taxes	10	6	9
Taxes for hospital support	7	6	1
Taxes for miscellaneous purposes	9	6	4
Tax administration	32	19	16
Tax exemptions	64	59	16
Tax limitations	14	9	8
Special assessments	12	10	4
Earmarking of revenues	34	20	18
Fiscal administration	22	14	13
Public works	25	20	13
Debt			
General	18	12	15
Loans for particular purposes	6	4	5
Debt limitations	48	44	11
Public school financing	43	42	11
Financing higher education	11	9	5
Financing hospital construction	6	5	3
Financing slum clearance and housing	8	8	2
Public works financing	23	20	8
Financing highways and bridges	15	13	13
Financing public buildings	12	10	8
Financing payments to veterans	29	25	16
Total	538	414	

TAXATION AND FINANCE

As might be expected, proposals on taxation and finance accounted for a considerable percentage of the total number of propositions submitted. One reason for the tremendous number is that, in some jurisdictions, many measures of purely local application have to be submitted to a statewide vote. In general, the proposals may be classified in four main groups, as indicated in Table 8.

Taxation

Tax proposals were much too numerous and varied to be considered here in any detail. Comment will be limited to property taxes, other tax sources, and such problems as exemptions, limitations, earmarking of receipts, and tax administration. For lack of space, no comment will be made on special levies (mostly on general property), receipts from which were earmarked for such specific purposes as school support, community development, highways, hospitals, and other purposes.

Some of the more significant proposals relating to the property tax may be noted. Arkansas and Nebraska rejected and Texas approved proposals to abolish the state ad valorem tax. In 1949 and 1950, California voters repealed obsolete material relating to the property tax, added new material, and revised its tax provisions; it rejected a prohibition on state and local units to impose personal property taxes on tangibles or intangibles. Louisiana voted to require a two-thirds vote in the Legislature to levy new taxes or to increase existing taxes. North Dakota voters twice rejected (in 1950 and 1954) a proposal for a graduated property tax. Alabama authorized various municipalities to levy additional ad valorem taxes.

With the exception of 6 propositions on severance taxes, the proposals relating to other tax sources were widely diversified in character. Voters in Colorado rejected a 5 per cent levy on all petroleum and petroleum products, voters in Nebraska rejected a severance tax on minerals, and Pennsylvania voters rejected a tax on private forest preserves. Louisiana voters approved three amendments authorizing severance taxes and, in the first two instances, earmarking revenues therefrom. Proposals of other forms of taxation approved included: California—tax position of the State Compensation Insurance Fund; Georgia—local business taxes; Michigan—sales tax; Nebraska —grain, sales, and income taxes. Proposals rejected included: Alabama—rate of the corporate income tax; New Hampshire—graduated inheritance tax and tax on public utilities.

Proposals relating to tax exemption were legion—some 64 of them in one-third of the states, of which all but 5 were approved. Exemptions show a distressing tendency to multiply in number and to expand in scope, taking an ever larger bite out of the revenues of the governmental jurisdiction that authorizes them. A few of the proposals dealt with application of the exemption principle to particular tax forms; most of them, however, were concerned with questions of application to organized groups or as a benefit to some idea or institution thought to be entitled to special consideration, such as the family (homestead and household furnishings exemptions), promotion and development, educational, religious, and charitable purposes, or for veterans.

Tax limitations came up for consideration 14 times in 8 states; fortunately, 5 of these proposals were rejected. Some of them, it may be noted, were designed to ease rather than to aggravate existing restrictions. Voters in 4 states passed on a dozen special assessment propositions relating mostly to individual counties, and approved all but 2 of them.

Of 34 proposals in 18 states on the earmarking of revenues, 20 were approved. Some of these were concerned with the receipts from individual taxes, others with support of particular governmental services and functions. State income tax revenues were earmarked in Alabama; severance tax revenues in Louisiana, New Mexico (two proposals), and South Dakota; timber tax revenues in Louisiana; and sales tax revenues in Michigan. Most important were motor vehicle or highway user taxes, earmarked in 13 states.[25] In addition, earmarking for roads occurred in Louisiana; for veterans compensation, in Minnesota and Oklahoma; for industrial safety, in Nevada; for general state expenses, in New Mexico; for state institutions, in North Dakota; and for schools in 6 states.[26] In view of the adverse effects of such practices on sound budgeting and financial control, this record is highly unfortunate.

Thirty-two questions relating to tax administration were presented to the voters of 16 states, and slightly more than half of them were approved. They dealt chiefly with general organization,[27] assessment and collection, and with such specific problems as centralized administration, city-county cooperation, delinquent taxes, and tax refunds. Those relating to assessment and collection were by far the most numerous; significant among these was the defeat in Arkansas of a proposition to require full-value assessment, of 2 proposals in California on assessment procedure, of centralized administration in two Florida counties, and for the appointment of assessors and boards of equalization and assessment in Nebraska counties. Among those approved

[25] They were: Alabama (two proposals), California, Florida, Louisiana (five proposals), Massachusetts, Michigan (three proposals), Missouri (two proposals), Montana, Ohio, Oklahoma, Tennessee, Texas, and Wyoming.

[26] They were: Alabama, Minnesota, Oklahoma (four proposals), South Dakota, Texas and Wyoming.

[27] Such proposals were adopted in Florida, Georgia, Nebraska, Texas, and Utah.

were the Georgia proposal of city-county cooperation for tax collection in Atlanta and Fulton County and provisions for the reduction or extinguishment of certain delinquent taxes in Louisiana, Montana, and Oklahoma.

Fiscal Administration

As shown in Table 8, 22 proposals on fiscal administration were presented in 13 states; of these, 14 were adopted and 8 rejected by the voters. While at least one could be found relating to each major aspect of fiscal administration, there were 4 on budgeting and 10 on trust funds and fund management. With regard to budgeting, California and Maryland adopted annual legislative sessions and provided that the new session in the even-numbered years should be devoted to fiscal matters. Florida placed its budget director in the Constitution, and Maryland, in a second amendment, provided for the submission of the budget. The 10 changes relating to trust funds and fund management were designed either to protect such funds or to make their assets available for loan, under certain conditions, in aid of purposes thought to be worthy or otherwise desirable, such as loans to veterans.

Public Works

Of 25 propositions in 13 states relating to public works, all but 5 were adopted. Some were proposals on state financing and some on local. In the former category, Alabama voters in 1946 approved a general authorization to the state to acquire, construct, develop, and operate harbors, seaports, and public airports and landing fields. In the same year, Michigan voters limited state control over certain internal improvements, and in 1954 Illinois authorized the sale of a canal and directed that the funds therefrom be appropriated for the operation of other canals and waterways owned by the state. Six states voted on proposals for the financing of public buildings; these proposals were approved in 4 states and rejected in 2.[28] Proposals relating to the financing of local public works—16 in number—ranged all the way from a municipal auditorium to water and sewerage works. Of 4 for the financing of special water districts, 2 in Rhode Island were approved and 2 in Louisiana were rejected.

Debt

Although it does not make much sense for a state—and still less for a local unit—to be obliged to amend the state constitution in order to make the loans necessary for the continued performance of governmental services and functions, such a procedure, as the table clearly indicates, is widely

---

[28] Approved in California, Ohio, Oklahoma, and Texas; rejected in Maine and New Jersey.

followed. A few of these amendments were of a general character, but most had to do with the financing of such individual services and functions as education (secondary and higher), hospitals, slum clearance and housing, public works, and payments to veterans. These last proposals will not be discussed here; they either liberalized existing debt limitations or authorized incurring debt in specific amounts for specified purposes.

As is shown in Table 8, 18 proposals of a general nature were presented to the voters of 15 states, who approved exactly two-thirds of them. Provisions were included on debt administration, power to incur debt, and procedure in liquidation. For instance, Alabama voters denied to one county the right to repeal a sales tax levy until the interest and principal of certain bonds or warrants had been paid and adopted a proposal regulating the issuance of bonds by certain public corporations. California extended from 50 to 75 years the maximum permissible term of statutory debt and established procedures for submission to the voters of proposals for incurring new debt in the local units of the state.

Debt limitation was one of the most prolific sources of proposals for constitutional change, accounting for no fewer than 48 propositions in 11 states. All but 4 were approved, thereby providing conclusive proof that, during the postwar years, the voters displayed an extraordinary willingness to approve new loans or changes in the rules which would make such loans possible.

PUBLIC OFFICERS AND EMPLOYEES

Public Officers

Proposals having to do with public officers included general provisions, qualifications (including reeligibility), method of selection, tenure, compensation, and method of filling vacancies (see Table 6 above). A good many of these proposals were applicable to local officers only, or to local and state officers. Most interesting, perhaps, of the general provisions was one in California, in 1950, prohibiting the submission to electors of any constitutional amendment or law naming any individual to hold office and declaring that any such measure shall hereafter not go into effect. This was an obvious effort to prevent a repetition of an unfortunate incident of a few years before. New York extended the coverage of its dual office-holding provision.

The proposals on qualifications for certain offices for the most part had to do with county officers. Seven states either removed or relaxed restrictions on reeligibility of such officers.[29] Thirteen states proposed and 11 adopted miscellaneous provisions affecting the method of selection of public officers,

---

[29] They were: Illinois, Kansas, Nebraska, Pennsylvania, South Dakota, Washington, and Wisconsin.

and 3 modified the wording of the prescribed oath of office. Two adopted provisions for the bonding of state and local officers: Louisiana provided for bonding in the amount of $5,000 for the secretary-treasurer of each community center and playground district in a specified parish, and Maryland required all state's attorneys to put up corporate surety bonds.

Questions involving tenure both of state and of local officers received extensive consideration (25 proposals in 17 states) had approximately a 50-50 break on acceptance. Arizona, Arkansas, Colorado, and New Mexico rejected proposals to give state officers four-year terms; but two years later Colorado approved this proposition, and Connecticut, Illinois, and Ohio also adopted this provision during the period under review. Four-year terms for county officers were defeated in Alabama, Arizona, and New Mexico and adopted in Colorado, Indiana, and Texas. Proposals of five-year terms for sheriff were adopted in Maryland and rejected in South Dakota and Wisconsin. The method of filling vacancies demanded the attention of voters in 5 states, with 6 proposals approved. Most of them provided for recess appointments in specified vacancies or types of vacancies.

Compensation of state or local officers accounted for 31 proposals in 17 states, with 19 proposals adopted. Alabama submitted a dozen proposals (of which 5 were adopted), 11 of which authorized the Legislature to fix, alter, and regulate the fees, allowances, and other compensation of officers in individual counties. Florida and Georgia, like Alabama, struggled with the fee system for local officers. Although there was a clear tendency to permit the amount of compensation to be established by legislative action, a few jurisdictions still persisted in setting salaries in specified amounts by constitutional provision.[30]

Personnel Administration

Civil service and personnel administration did not receive extensive consideration by the voters in the period under review; 49 proposals were submitted in 17 states, and 38 were adopted. Most aspects of personnel administration were touched upon at least once. For convenience, they may be classified in three groups: state, general; county and municipal; and compensation and retirement.

Significant in the group of state proposals were 5 to provide a constitutional basis for the merit system. Such propositions were approved in Alabama, Florida, and Louisiana; they were rejected in Arizona and Colorado.

Louisiana voters rejected a proposal for handling appeals on personnel

---

[30] Among these may be noted Arkansas, Kentucky, Maryland (sheriffs at $7,500, and a $2,000 increase for the secretary of state). Six states enlarged legislative authority to set salaries: Georgia, North Dakota, Ohio, Oregon, Texas, and Washington.

actions detrimental to the interests of the employee. Maryland voters approved a loyalty and security provision. Colorado voters approved a proposal for greater security of tenure. Exemptions from civil service coverage were passed upon in California, Colorado, and New York. California approved exemptions for part-time and for certain professional employees; Colorado approved them for certain top-level administrative positions; and New York tightened up its provisions on veterans preference.

Four states—Colorado, Georgia, Louisiana, and Texas—passed on proposals for local civil service systems; in Colorado and Texas these proposals were rejected. Of 6 proposals in 4 states designed to increase compensation for local employees, all were approved. Questions involving retirement benefits in some form accounted for half of the proposals in the personnel field. All were aimed at greater security of pension funds, greater benefits, or wider coverage—in some instances for the state as a whole, in others for specified local units.

Local Government

Problems of local government came in for a tremendous amount of attention in the constitutional amendments submitted to the voters during the period under review, 286 such proposals being submitted in 25 states. This statement, however, does not present a true picture because a few more than half of these proposals were presented in 3 states—Alabama, Georgia, and Louisiana—and 90, or almost one-third of the total, were presented in Georgia alone. Outside the South, the problem of local legislation was relatively unimportant. The subject matter coverage was extensive, including proposals of two major types: general government and administrative services and functions.

When it is generally agreed among students of the subject that administrative services and functions—even those relating to state services—have no proper place in a constitution, it is somewhat distressing to find that approximately two-thirds of the proposals submitted in the field of local government had to do with such activities, including education; fire protection; law enforcement; health and hospital facilities; highways, bridges, and tunnels; port development and facilities; public works; recreation; and some miscellaneous functions. Because of limitations of space and the fact that these matters do not belong in the constitution, the discussion here will be confined to the proposals relating to general government.

General Government

Approximately one-third of the proposals submitted fell in the category of general government, including such matters as charters and charter-drafting, home rule, metropolitan areas, city-county consolidation, community development, personnel, and the fiscal powers of cities and counties.

Twenty-one proposals relating to charters and charter-drafting were submitted in 6 states, 17 of them in 3 states—California, Louisiana, and Maryland. All but 6 were approved by the voters. California voters in 1948 refused to liberalize the provisions regarding the submission of new borough charters, but in 1956 approved such a change for the submission of county charters. They approved a plan to permit any chartered city or city and county the alternative of establishing the borough form of government either for the entire territory or for a part thereof. Three Louisiana amendments created charter commissions in specific local units.

Fiscal provisions relating to specific units were adopted in Louisiana, Maryland, and New York. Vermont authorized cooperative relations between towns in the maintenance of "a competent number of schools." Wisconsin voters rejected a proposal broadening municipal powers of eminent domain.

Metropolitan Areas

Two states—Georgia and South Carolina—adopted and Louisiana defeated proposals relating to metropolitan areas. Two proposals in Georgia dealt with industrial areas, one authorizing creation of such areas adjacent to the city of Savannah in Chatham County, another requiring the city of Atlanta to assume and pay a proportionate part of the Fulton County school district bonds upon extension of the corporate limits. Louisiana voters rejected a proposal that would have permitted East Baton Rouge Parish to zone outside incorporated municipalities. South Carolina voters authorized the city of Chester to extend water and sewer services to property owners outside the city limits and to levy assessments and issue bonds for support of such services. These changes are probably more significant as indicators of a trend than they are individually.

Seven proposals in as many states involving city-county consolidation were presented to the voters, and all but 1 was approved.[31] Problems of community development—in most cases in individual cities or communities—

---

[31] This, in Alabama, would have authorized the Legislature to provide for the merger or consolidation of the various municipalities in Jefferson County and the county, or any part of them, under one municipal governing body. Florida and Georgia voters adopted amendments consolidating city and county offices. In New Mexico, in areas where the population of the city and county exceeds 50,000, the people may frame their own charter for a consolidated government, and amend the same, in the manner provided by the Legislature in general law. Such charter shall designate the necessary officers. In 1951, city-county consolidation in Philadelphia, pending since 1923, was finally achieved. The amendment abolished all county offices and provided for the performance of county functions by the city of Philadelphia. In Tennessee, one of the changes proposed by the limited constitutional convention of 1953, ratified by

were given review. Some 28 proposals in 5 states, 20 of them in Georgia, dealt with this problem.[32] Five proposals dealt with planning and zoning, 2 in Georgia, 3 in Louisiana; all were adopted.

Many of the proposals created or authorized the creation of authorities. Georgia adopted 5 such proposals, including the Savannah District Authority, the Waycross and Ware County Development Authority, the Vidalia Development Authority, and possibly the Savannah Airport Commission. Maryland voters enlarged the powers of the Baltimore Redevelopment Commission.

Georgia adopted 11 amendments authorizing as many counties to levy a tax earmarked for a fund to be used in assisting, promoting, and encouraging the location of industry within their boundaries.

Local Administration

Twenty-eight questions on personnel matters dealt, for the most part, with methods of selection and the compensation of local officers. Many proposals in both categories were defeated. Georgia voters authorized extension of the merit system in Fulton County and ratified its extension by the General Assembly. Arizona now permits its cities to employ nonresidents as city managers. Alabama, Maryland, and South Dakota adopted, and Wisconsin rejected, changes in the tenure of sheriffs. Three states dealt with other county officers—Oregon with the powers and duties of the coroner and the surveyor, Pennsylvania with the term of the treasurer, Utah with the powers, duties, and tenure of county attorneys.

Several states adopted more general provisions relating to county offices. Idaho provided for the elimination of the office of county superintendent of public instruction as an elective county office and prescribed the county officers to be elected. A defeated Oklahoma proposal named the county officers, created their offices, and provided for a four-year term for the incumbents. South Dakota voters twice defeated and Washington voters approved proposals to permit all county officers to hold office for any number of consecutive two-year terms to which they might be elected. It is always

the people, authorized city-county consolidation. Finally, Washington voters authorized the formation, under a charter, of combined city and county municipal corporations in areas having a population of 300,000 or more.

[32] Georgia adopted a new article on slum clearance and urban redevelopment. California, Georgia, and Pennsylvania adopted provisions relating to finance, the first authorizing the financing of such projects from taxes on property within the project area, the second authorizing municipalities having such projects to enter into contract to exempt from local and municipal taxes the increase in value attributable to such projects, the third authorizing the General Assembly to exempt by general laws redevelopment authorities from taxes on land acquired for urban redevelopment for a period not to exceed 25 years.

difficult to muster popular support for questions involving increases or possible increases in compensation of public officials. In Alabama, 12 amendments were submitted, each authorizing the Legislature to fix, alter, and regulate the fees, allowances, and other compensation of officers in 12 different counties. Only 4 of them were approved. Georgia voters approved an amendment defining the persons eligible to participate in the pension system established in Fulton County.

Numerous proposals involved the fiscal powers both of counties and of cities, including taxes and debt, and limitations on both. Alabama and Louisiana authorized various municipalities to levy additional ad valorem taxes for general revenue purposes; Louisiana also approved such taxes for support of employee pension systems. Tax limitations were imposed in New York, debt limitations in Georgia. Revenue anticipation certificates were authorized in Georgia, revenue bonds in Georgia and Louisiana. Fiscal changes affecting the counties were generally similar. One Alabama county was authorized to levy a privilege license tax on gasoline and other motor fuels, and one Georgia county to impose an occupation license tax. Revenue certificates were authorized in one Georgia county, refunding bonds in another. Four amendments relating to the assessment and collection of taxes in 4 Florida counties were adopted, whereas 2 proposals having a similar effect in 10 other counties were defeated.

INTERGOVERNMENTAL RELATIONS

Intergovernmental relations, important though they have always been, continued to receive scant attention at the hands of those making or amending state constitutions. Only 43 proposals in this area, submitted in about two-thirds of the states, were passed upon. Of these, 27 were approved and 16 rejected, as shown in Table 9.

TABLE 9

NUMBER OF CONSTITUTIONAL AMENDMENTS RELATING TO INTER-
GOVERNMENTAL RELATIONS SUBMITTED AND ADOPTED AND
NUMBER OF STATES SUBMITTING, BY TYPE, 1946-1956, INCLUSIVE

Type of Relationship	Proposals Submitted	Proposals Adopted	Number of States
Federal-state	15	7	12
Interstate	6	6	5
State-local	22	14	13
Total	43	27	

Federal-State Relations

Most of the proposals in the field of federal-state relations dealt with fiscal matters, but there were a few exceptions. Aroused over alleged federal encroachments, Arkansas voters required their General Assembly ". . . to oppose in every constitutional manner, including interposition and nullification, all deliberate, palpable and dangerous invasions or encroachments upon rights and powers belonging to the States and people, or by any nation or group of nations acting under apparent authority of the United States government." California and Vermont adopted provisions on dual office-holding in the federal service and their respective state services. Ohio undertook to correct provisions in its Constitution which conflicted with those of the United States Constitution. North Dakota considered the question of jurisdiction over United States and Indian lands. Questions relating to taxation accounted for the rest of the proposals.

Louisiana sought to make its gasoline tax applicable to gasoline sold to United States agencies, except when sold in large quantities to be used by the Armed Forces. It also authorized a grant of land for a Naval Research Training Center. Four states—Nevada, Utah, Virginia, and Washington—adopted authorizations for a state tax on federal property within their borders if and when such taxation should be authorized by the Congress, and Wisconsin repealed the prohibition on taxation of federal lands. Wyoming removed the exemption of federal property when used for non-governmental purposes.

Interstate Relations

While interstate relationships have increased steadily in number and in importance, this trend was not perceptible in the constitutional amendments submitted to the voters. There were only 6 proposals of this character. Two, in Arizona and California, dealt with boundary questions. Louisiana ratified the Southern Regional Education Compact and extended tax exemption to out-of-state donations to tax-exempt institutions. Maryland approved the interstate desertion and nonsupport compact. South Carolina voted to change its provisions regarding divorce.

State-Local Relations

Many of the proposals involving state-local relationships were financial; others involved questions of home rule. Voters in Alabama and Oregon rejected tax limitation proposals applicable to local units. Debt limitation proposals proved to be somewhat more acceptable, being approved in Louisiana, Montana, and Pennsylvania, rejected in Alabama. Michigan adopted a proposal to share sales tax revenues with certain municipalities.

Alabama and Nebraska turned down proposals on state aid for schools. New York voters approved a large bond issue to make funds available for loans to local units for slum clearance and low-rent housing projects.

Ten proposals involving home rule were passed upon in 7 states, all but 1 of them being approved. California, Colorado, Rhode Island, and Tennessee voters approved home rule proposals relating to cities and towns, Louisiana and Washington to cities, California to counties. Contrariwise, California voters also extended state control over local units in the field of education by authorizing a county board of education, by county charter, to be elected rather than appointed. Florida voters defeated home rule for its counties, but approved it for Dade County.

Georgia voters approved a curb on local legislation by the state, providing in 1952 for the submission of amendments that affect only a county or counties to voters in the units concerned, not to the voters of the state as a whole; it also authorized the General Assembly to provide for self-government for municipalities. Louisiana voters improved the status of the city of New Orleans by authorizing a home rule charter, with restrictions regarding its amendment and replacement, and by transferring responsibility for the fixing of water service rates from the Legislature to the local Sewerage and Water Control Board. In Nevada, it was provided that tenure in office or dismissal of any officer in any municipality governed by a home rule charter should be governed by the charter, rather than by any existing provision of the state Constitution or laws.

CONCLUSION

What general conclusions appear to be justified from the survey work on constitutional amendments that has been completed thus far? Does this survey of a decade of experience with and practice in the use of the amending procedures of the state constitutions provide a sound basis for viewing them as a possible substitute for general revision?

Perhaps the first observation that might be made is that voters tend rather generally to approve the propositions submitted to them. This is not to say or to imply that they approve all proposals indiscriminately, for there is considerable evidence that they do not. But they do approve a much larger number than they reject, as is clearly evident from the figures in Table 4.

A second observation about these proposals is that they tend to center, as they should, around current major problems of state government. While various inconsequential proposals are voted upon, most of the amendments deal with one or another of a group of topics of major concern in the states today, i.e., the governor, the legislature, the courts, suffrage and elections, taxation and finance, public officers and employees, local government, intergovernmental relations, and such administrative services as education, highways, and veterans. The exact nature of the proposals in these various fields has been summarized in the foregoing discussion.

A few of the proposals dealt with more than one subject, and so had to be counted under more than one subject heading, thereby swelling somewhat the number of actual constitutional changes involved. A few of them, in a group of 5 Southern states, were local in character, and should never have been submitted to the electorate—certainly not on a statewide basis. On these, see Table 5. Otherwise, the great majority of the proposals dealt with matters of general concern throughout the state.

A fourth point which is illustrated over and over again, in state after state, is that often proposals submitted once and rejected by the voters are later submitted again and frequently adopted in the same or similar form. While a second rejection may be regarded as conclusive, there are instances in which a proposition has been submitted three or more times. In such cases, one may assume that the state leaders regarded the proposal as sufficiently important to justify the expenditure of time and effort involved both in a resubmission and in the campaign of public education necessary to inform the voters and change the minds of an appreciable number of those who formerly had been opposed to the proposition.

There is little or no basis for viewing the amending procedures as a possible substitute for general revision. While it is true that many desirable changes were brought about in the constitutions of many states, these altogether represent only a very minor if not an insignificant percentage of the changes that were urgently needed if the documents of which they were to become a part were to be thoroughly revised and modernized. Not only does the piecemeal amending procedure result in sporadic coverage of significant matters; it also provides a mechanism by which an unbelievable quantity of constitutional underbrush finds its way into instruments already burdened with considerable amounts of such material.

PART II

THE CONTENT OF STATE CONSTITUTIONS

chapter VIII

what should a state constitution contain?

David Fellman

For a variety of historical reasons, and not because of abstract cogitation, the American people have always regarded the written constitution as the essential basis of legitimate government. The colonial experience with the common law and written charters, to which appeal was constantly made in recurring disputes with the home government; the concept that the state rested on contract, which dominated political thinking in the eighteenth century; and the appeal to a higher law as justification for revolution established for us the proposition that government is not the state, but only its agent, deriving its just powers from the consent of the governed as set forth in a written constitution emanating from the people. Thus, Chief Justice John Marshall spoke in an authentic American genre when he wrote in one of his most celebrated opinions:

> That the people have an original right to establish, for their future government, such principles as, in their opinion, shall most conduce to their own happiness, is the basis on which the whole American fabric has been erected.[1]

THE AMERICAN IDEA OF A CONSTITUTION

Pursuant to a resolution adopted by the Continental Congress on May 15, 1776, the people of the various states began to write constitutions, and they have been at it ever since. The original state constitutions summarized the political ideas which then prevailed.[2] It is an interesting paradox that these documents of the Revolution were essentially conservative in tone; they did

---

[1] *Marbury* v. *Madison*, 1 Cranch 137, 176 (1803).

[2] On these constitutions see: Allan Nevins, *The American States during and after the Revolution, 1775-1789* (New York: Macmillan Co., 1924); Walter F. Dodd, *The Revision and Amendment of State Constitutions* (Baltimore: Johns Hopkins Press, 1910), chap. 1; William C. Morey, "The First State Constitutions," 4 *The Annals* 201-32 (Sept. 1893); William C. Webster, "Comparative Study of the State Constitutions of the American Revolution," 9 *The Annals* 380-420 (May, 1897).

not break much new ground, but sought largely to conserve the prevailing values of their age.[3] They were very brief documents, running from about 5 to 16 pages of ordinary print, and they stated very concisely certain basic principles regarding popular sovereignty, the separation of powers and checks and balances, individual liberty and the supremacy of law, and the superiority among governmental institutions of the legislative body as the authentic voice of the people.

In the ensuing years, however, as new states entered the Union and old constitutions were occasionally revised, these documents necessarily changed in response to the evolving patterns of American life. It has well been remarked that a study of our state constitutions "affords a perfect mirror of American democracy,"[4] since they have always articulated the varied and changing interests and conditions of the American people. They reflect the steady growth of executive power, the erosion of popular confidence in the legislature through the multiplication of constitutional limitations, the extension of popular participation in government as a consequence of the flowering of a democratic spirit, the rise of corporations to a dominant position in the economy, the Civil War and Reconstruction, the steady growth of commerce and industry, and the development of vast new urban communities.

It cannot be gainsaid that the American people have had a very considerable experience in tinkering with their state constitutions. Louisiana has had 10 constitutions in its history, Georgia 8, South Carolina 7, and Alabama 6. Four states have had 5 constitutions each, and 8 states have had 4 each. While 18 states have had only 1 constitution each, all of them have been amended many times. There have been 134 state constitutions in all, and it has been estimated that the present documents have been amended over 3,000 times. Of existing constitutions, only 7 were drafted before 1850,[5] 7 were drawn up between 1851 and 1865, and all the others date since the end of the Civil War, with the largest bulge in the curve appearing in the period 1876-1900. All but 10 states have constitutions which antedate 1900. There have been a few general constitutional revisions in recent years, in New York in 1938, Missouri[6] and Georgia in 1945, New Jersey in 1947, and Tennessee in

---

[3] See Clinton Rossiter, *Seedtime of the Republic* (New York: Harcourt, Brace & Co., 1953), chaps. 12-14; Benjamin F. Wright, *Consensus and Continuity, 1776-1787* (Boston: Boston University Press, 1958).

[4] James Q. Dealey, *Growth of American State Constitutions* (Boston: Ginn & Co., 1915), p. 117.

[5] Massachusetts, 1780; New Hampshire, 1784; Vermont, 1793; Connecticut, 1818; Maine, 1820; Rhode Island, 1843; Wisconsin, 1848.

[6] See William L. Bradshaw, "Missouri's Proposed New Constitution," 39 *American Political Science Review* 61-67 (Feb., 1945); William F. Swindler, "Missouri's Constitutions: History, Theory and Practice," 23 *Missouri Law Review* 32-61 (Jan., 1958).

1953. The adoption of constitutions since 1950 by Puerto Rico, Hawaii, and Alaska has stimulated a great deal of fresh interest in the whole problem of drafting such documents.[7]

Though no two state constitutions are alike in all details, all of them conform roughly to a common pattern. First there is a preamble, repeating in rather stock phrases certain first principles regarding the nature and purposes of government. Then there is a bill of rights, spelling out in familiar language the basic rights of conscience and of property and the rights of persons accused of crime. The next three articles usually deal with the legislative, executive, and judicial branches of the state government, in that order, describing their structure, powers, and limitations. At the end is an article dealing with the methods of constitutional amendment or revision and a schedule for the transition to the new dispensation. In addition, most state constitutions have articles of varying length and detail on a wide variety of additional subjects, notably education, local government, the suffrage, public finance, corporations, and other business organizations. While the state constitution generally is not regarded as a grant of powers to the legislature, since the legislature has all powers not denied to it by either the federal or its state constitution,[8] the contemporary documents reflect the modern interest in new social services by authorizing or even directing legislative activity in regard to welfare and health activities, care of the aged, social security, unemployment, workmen's compensation, and the like.

However detailed state constitutions may be, as in the case of the federal Constitution custom plays a large role in the actual functioning of state government. No document can say everything, though some states have overloaded their constitutions with details. Some of the most significant aspects of state government are not provided for in constitutional language. Many of the most important activities of the political parties fall within the scope of custom. The party caucus in the legislature, which may very well dominate the formal proceedings, is a product of custom, as is the representation of minority parties on legislative committees. The elaborate body of practices that defines the relationships between the governor and the legislature is largely unwritten.

CONTEMPORARY CRITICISMS OF STATE CONSTITUTIONS

If students of contemporary state government agree upon anything, it is

[7] See John E. Bebout, "Recent Constitution Writing," 35 *Texas Law Review* 1071-89 (Oct., 1957) ; S. Gale Lowrie, "Hawaii Drafts a Constitution," 20 *University of Cincinnati Law Review* 215-38 (Mar., 1951). See also J. Alton Burdine, "Basic Materials for the Study of State Constitutions and State Constitutional Development," 48 *American Political Science Review* 1140-52 (Dec., 1954).

[8] Walter F. Dodd, "The Function of a State Constitution," 30 *Political Science Quarterly* 201-21 (June, 1915).

that modern state constitutions are seriously defective and need considerable revision.[9] While very little has been written in a systematic way about the proper contents of a state constitution,[10] the consensus of informed opinion holds that most state constitutions need a great deal of attention both to style and to content. Thus a committee of distinguished legal scholars recently reported, after surveying the New York Constitution from the point of view merely of simplification, that it was "literally amazed by the extent to which . . . [it] contains hollow phrases, defective provisions, and creakingly antiquated policies."[11] After close study of 54 of the 199 sections of this Constitution, it concluded that 23 of them should be stricken from the document altogether as superfluous or no longer useful, and that at least 18 should be rewritten and shortened substantially "in order to achieve clarity, flexibility, and understandability."[12]

Speaking of the Louisiana Constitution, which is one of the worst and certainly the most long-winded of all, an able legal scholar has written:

A layman who starts out to study the Louisiana Constitution . . . is confronted with a Herculean task. . . . The document will trip, entangle, infuriate and then exhaust him. The difficulties presented to the inquiring citizen include the vast detail, the dispersion of subject matter, confusing terminology, incon-

---

[9] See Robert H. Pealy, ed., *The Voter and the Michigan Constitution in 1958* (Ann Arbor: Bureau of Government, Institute of Public Administration, University of Michigan, 1958); William H. Cape, *Constitutional Revision in South Dakota* (Vermillion: Governmental Research Bureau, University of South Dakota, Report No. 39, Aug., 1957); Robert B. Dishman, *A New Constitution for New Hampshire?* (Durham: Public Administration Service, University of New Hampshire, Governmental Series No. 6, Apr., 1956); Albert L. Sturm, *The Need for Constitutional Revision in West Virginia* (Morgantown: Bureau for Government Research, West Virginia University, 1950); William N. Ethridge, Jr., *Modernizing Mississippi's Constitution* (University: Bureau of Public Administration, University of Mississippi, 1950); Dillard S. Gardner, "The Continuous Revision of Our State Constitution," 36 *North Carolina Law Review* 297-313 (Apr., 1958); Clarence N. Callender, "The Constitution of Pennsylvania—Should It Be Revised?" 29 *Pennsylvania Bar Association Quarterly* 205-15 (Mar., 1958).

[10] See W. Brooke Graves, "What Should a Constitution Contain?" Governor's Committee on Preparatory Research for the New Jersey Constitutional Convention (May, 1947); H. V. Thornton, "What a Constitution Should Contain," *Oklahoma Constitutional Studies* (Oklahoma City: Constitutional Survey Commission, 1950), pp. 1-8; William Bennett Munro, "An Ideal State Constitution," 181 *The Annals* 1-10 (Sept., 1935); National Municipal League, *Model State Constitution,* 5th ed. (New York: 1948).

[11] Inter-Law School Committee, *Report on the Problem of Simplification of the Constitution* to the New York Special Legislative Committee on the Revision and Simplification of the Constitution, Staff Report No. 1 (Apr., 1958), p. 330.

[12] Commenting on this report, the *New York Times,* June 2, 1958, remarked editorially that the state Constitution was characterized by "haphazard arrangement, slipshod and confusing phraseology, relics of long-gone fears, verbosity, frustrated efforts to fit law to new circumstances, a testimonial to the force of inertia."

sistencies, errors, references to other legal documents, informal amending procedures, duplication of material, contradictions and omissions.[13]

Such criticisms are standard. A California constitutional commission found in 1930 that the state document was "an instrument bad in form, inconsistent in many particulars, loaded with unnecessary detail, encumbered with provisions of no permanent value, and replete with matter which might more properly be contained in the statute law of the State."[14] A recent painstaking survey of the Florida Constitution called attention to such faults as excessive detail, obsolete matter, dispersion of materials, inconsistencies and contradictions, the incorporation by reference of materials outside the document, and errors.[15] In 1955, a constitutional committee in Oregon recommended changes for the improvement of syntax, the deletion of statutory, obsolete, and unnecessary matter, the rearrangement and clarification of mislocated and poorly-worded provisions, the resolution of ambiguities, and the alteration or removal of the statements of objectionable policies. Of the 232 sections of this Constitution, the committee would leave untouched only 66.[16]

The final report (1955) of the Commission on Intergovernmental Relations drew attention to the crucial importance of the problem under discussion. It said:

Early in its study, the Commission was confronted with the fact that many State constitutions restrict the scope, effectiveness, and adaptability of State and local action. These self-imposed constitutional limitations make it difficult for many States to perform all of the services their citizens require, and consequently have frequently been the underlying cause of State and municipal pleas for Federal assistance.

And it added:

It is significant that the Constitution prepared by the Founding Fathers, with its broad grants of authority and avoidance of legislative detail, has withstood the test of time far better than the constitutions later adopted by the States.

The commission concluded that there is "a very real and pressing need for the States to improve their constitutions."[17]

---

[13] Kimbrough Owen, "The Need for Constitutional Revision in Louisiana," 8 *Louisiana Law Review* 1-104 (Nov., 1947).

[14] *Report of the California Constitutional Commission,* December 29, 1930 (Sacramento: 1931), p. 9.

[15] Manning J. Dauer and William C. Havard, "The Florida Constitution of 1885— A Critique," 8 *University of Florida Law Review* 1-92 (Spring, 1955).

[16] Oregon. *Report of the Governor's and Legislative Constitutional Committee* (Jan. 10, 1955), p. 7.

[17] Commission on Intergovernmental Relations, *A Report to the President for Transmittal to the Congress* (Washington: Government Printing Office, 1955), pp. 37-38.

THE PROBLEM OF DETAIL

The most obvious, and in many ways the crucial, fault of state constitutions is that they are too detailed. They simply attempt to say far too much on too many subjects. This was not always so. The Virginia Constitution of 1776 had about 1,500 words; the New Jersey Constitution of 1776 about 2,500 words; the New York Constitution of 1777 some 3,000 words; and the longest of them, that of Massachusetts (1780), had about 12,000 words, which, incidentally, is the size of the Model State Constitution. Today, 37 state constitutions are longer than the original Massachusetts document.[18] Of the 8 state constitutions which have under 10,000 words each, 7 were drafted before the Civil War.[19] The dubious honor of being the wordiest of all is held by the Louisiana Constitution, which in 1960 included 201,423 words, and which, since its adoption in 1921, has been swelled with 356 amendments. The second longest document is California's, which has been amended 321 times since 1879 and runs to about 75,000 words. Other very long state constitutions are those of Alabama (1901) with 57,000 words and 140 amendments; Texas (1876) with 43,000 words and 133 amendments; Washington (1889) with 36,422 words and 32 amendments; and Oklahoma (1907) with 35,940 words and 39 amendments. The newly-revised Missouri Constitution (1945) has about 30,000 words, and the New Jersey Constitution of 1947 has some 12,500. The Constitution of Alaska (1956) has 12,000 words; that of Hawaii (1950) 11,412; and that of Puerto Rico (1952) 8,560. Clearly, the current accent in constitution-writing is on brevity.[20]

Almost any constitution will supply examples of details that hardly rise to the dignity of a place in such a document. The Oklahoma Constitution devotes 20 pages to the division of the state into counties and the definition of their boundaries (Art. XVII), has over 300 words on the piddling subject of free transportation by railroads (Art. IX, sec. 13), and even stipulates that home economics must be taught in all public schools (Art. XIII, sec. 7). At the same level of importance is a provision in the South Dakota Constitution which authorizes a twine and cordage plant at the state penitentiary (Art. XI, sec. 1) and a clause in the Constitution of South Carolina which defines what shall constitute a "durable hard surface" street in the city of Greenville (Art. X, sec. 14). Many state constitutions spell out in precise sums the

---

[18] For a table showing the size of all state constitutions see Council of State Governments, *The Book of the States, 1958-1959*, Vol. XII (Chicago: 1958), p. 11.

[19] Rhode Island (1843), 6,650 words; Connecticut (1818), 6,741 words; Indiana (1851), 7,816 words; Iowa (1857), 7,997 words; Vermont (1793), 8,000 words; Kansas (1859), 8,052 words; Maine (1820), 9,000 words; Tennessee (1870), 9,460 words.

[20] Alfred De Grazia, "State Constitutions—Are They Growing Longer?" 27 *State Government* 82-83 (Apr., 1954).

salaries of public officers and prescribe the election of a large variety of public officers (e.g., the Constitution of Texas provides for the popular election of the inspector of hides and animals and the public weighers, Art. XVI, secs. 64, 65). Small wonder that someone recently suggested to the Kentucky Constitution Review Commission that a clause be added stipulating that "no whiskey be sold in the State under four years old and made from 100 percent corn or Rye, No neutral spirits added."[21] Why not?

Local government is one of many subjects which state constitutions are apt to treat with excessive detail. For example, about one-sixth of the long California Constitution is concerned with details of city and county government (Art. XI), and the Louisiana Constitution devotes 28 pages to the government of New Orleans (Art. XIV, secs. 20-31.1).

Another subject upon which state constitutions lavish words is public finance. The South Carolina Constitution sets up certain local debt limitations and then devotes almost 14 pages to spelling out exceptions (Art. VIII, sec. 7) ; it also has 12 pages of exceptions to the revenue provisions (Art. X, sec 5). The Louisiana Constitution has several thousand words on the one-cent-per-gallon tax on nonmotor fuels, even going so far as to define the term as meaning "all volatile gas-generating liquids having a flash point below 110 degrees F. . . ." (Art. VI-A). Ten per cent of the California Constitution deals with revenue and taxation (Arts. XIII, XVI).[22] The Texas Constitution spells out the upper limit of taxation by rural fire-prevention districts (Art. III, sec. 48-d).

Many state constitutions have elaborate sections on the highway system, the Louisiana Constitution devoting 25 pages to the subject (Art. VI, secs. 20-23). Education, elections, corporations, and court procedure also are given a great deal of space. Some constitutions, like that of Delaware (Art. V, secs. 7-8), incorporate what is in substance a corrupt practices statute.[23] The New York Constitution includes all sorts of minor matters—a section on veterans' preference in regard to civil service appointments (Art. V, sec. 6), an elaborate section on the elimination of railroad grade crossings (Art. VII, sec. 14), a clause permitting pari-mutuel betting (Art. I, sec. 9), long sections on the debt limits of municipalities (Art. VIII), and elaborate provisions on the bribery of public officers (Art. XIII, secs. 2-5). Most of these matters belong in the statute books.

Why have the state constitutions become such wordy documents? All ob-

---

[21] Kentucky: Constitution Review Commission, *Report* (1950), p. 6.

[22] A good example of detailed limitations on indebtedness will be found in the Oregon Constitution, Art. XI, sec. 7 and Art. XI-a, d, e, f.

[23] See Paul Dolan, "The Constitution of Delaware," 59 *Dickinson Law Review* 75-85 (Oct., 1954).

servers agree that the principal reason has been the growth of popular distrust of the legislature; and some provisions are really commands to the
legislature to make sure that it does certain things. For example, the Oklahoma Constitution directs the Legislature to revise the statutes periodically
(Art. V, sec. 43) and to legislate against monopolies (Art. V, sec. 44), and
the Illinois Constitution directs the General Assembly to enact safety laws
for miners (Art. IV, sec. 29). Many state constitutional provisions reflect the
growing complexity of the social and economic order in regard to such matters as corporations, public utilities, and social legislation. Some constitutional
provisions, such as those dealing with social security and labor, were designed to overcome the anticipated opposition of conservative courts. Court
decisions have often been overruled by constitutional amendments. The
triumph of Jacksonian democracy explains the elaboration of provisions
dealing with the suffrage and the election of more and more public officers.
The need for new governmental machinery to handle emerging problems has
led to the expansion of constitutions to create new administrative agencies.
The rapid growth of government business in recent decades has resulted in
new constitutional sections dealing with such topics as the civil service, public
works, and the letting of contracts.

Very often an item is inserted into a state constitution because, as in the
case of homestead exemptions, the makers of the document feel that it is
particularly important and should be put beyond the possibility of legislative
tinkering. Furthermore, members of constitutional conventions often get
into the odd habit of assuming that in some special way they are endowed
with more wisdom and righteousness than members of future legislatures are
likely to have. Thus, a member of the Illinois Convention of 1870 declared:

> It is assumed that when we depart from this hall all the virtue and all the
> wisdom of the state will have departed with us. We have assumed that we alone
> are honest and wise enough to determine for the people the ordinary, and in
> many instances even the most trivial, questions affecting the public welfare; as
> if the mass of people of the state of Illinois were not as competent hereafter to
> select others that are honest and capable as they were to select us.[24]

In addition, many constitutional provisions represent either the hopes or
fears of special interest groups who want their particular views nailed down.

Finally, it remains to be noted that a democratic people will necessarily
find the quickest and surest means of having their way. In some states it is
as easy to amend the constitution as it is to adopt a statute by the initiative
and referendum. Writing a new constitution, or amending it, has often been

---

[24] Quoted by Walter F. Dodd, *State Government,* 2d ed. (New York: Century Co.,
1928), p. 96.

found to be a quicker and simpler method of securing reforms than legislative action. The American people, Lord Bryce observed in his celebrated book on our governmental system, have "a conscious relish for power," and "there is an unmistakable wish in the minds of the people to act directly rather than through their representatives in legislation."[25]

Of course, the more detailed a constitution is, the more often it has to be amended. Thus, it is the fate of a long constitution that in the very nature of things it has to grow longer. There is simply more to amend. It follows that wordy constitutions must be changed frequently, so that they get wordier still. It is an inexorable vicious circle.

If there is any proposition which meets with approval among informed students of American public law, it is that most state constitutions are too long, and that constitutional verbosity entails many undesirable consequences. It deprives the legislature of adequate control over its normal functions. Governor Driscoll, in his opening address to the New Jersey Constitutional Convention of 1947, said:

> When legislation is permitted to infiltrate a constitution, it shackles the hands of the men and women elected by the people to exercise public authority. The longer a constitution, the more quickly it fails to meet the requirements of a society that is never static.[26]

That constitutional verbosity leads to inflexibility is illustrated in a recent decision of the Supreme Court of Oklahoma holding that the state Corporation Commission had no jurisdiction over air transport.[27] The state Constitution (Art. IX, sec. 18) gives the commission jurisdiction to regulate "all transportation and transmission companies," but, unfortunately, it goes on to define the term by listing railroads, steamboat lines, express companies, and the like. Of course, when the enumeration was written air transport was unknown. From a strictly legalistic point of view, the holding that an enumeration excludes all things not in the list was not a bad decision, but from a policy point of view it makes no sense at all.

The wordy state constitution is a constant invitation to litigation and therefore burdens the courts. For the more the constitution says, the more bases there are on which to contest in court the legality of legislative and executive actions. In fact, courts frequently make rulings they wish they could avoid, for after all it is a cardinal principle of American law that a constitutional provision controls all other acts of government. For example, the Texas Constitution (Art. V, sec. 12) stipulates that all indictments must

---

[25] James Bryce, *The American Commonwealth*, rev. ed. (New York: Macmillan Co., 1913), Vol. I, p. 444.

[26] *Record of the New Jersey Constitutional Convention of 1947*, Vol. I, p. 7.

[27] *Application of Central Airlines*, 199 Okl. 300, 185 P.2d 919 (1947).

conclude with the words "against the peace and dignity of the State." On one occasion a man was convicted on an indictment that said, erroneously, "against the peace and dignity of the *statute.*" The Texas Court of Appeals felt obliged, however reluctantly, to set aside the conviction, saying:

> However much we may feel disposed to consider a matter prescribed by the Constitution ill-advised or useless—however much we may be inclined to doubt the propriety of inserting into the organic, fundamental law of the State requisites of forms with regard to procedure and practice in the courts—the answer is, the people themselves, the source of all power and authority in a republican government, have spoken it; and with regard to their *ipse dixit,* when contained in the Constitution, which is but the expression of their sovereign will, the courts can only bow in humble obedience, and say *"ita est scripta."*[28]

Excessive constitutional detail is bad for many reasons. It solidifies the entrenchment of vested interests. It makes temporary matters permanent. It deprives state legislatures and local governments of desirable flexibility and diminishes their sense of responsibility. It encourages the search for methods of evading constitutional provisions and thus tends to debase our sense of constitutional morality. It makes frequent recourse to the amending processes inevitable. It hinders action in time of special stress or emergency. It stands in the way of healthy progress. It blurs the distinction between constitutional and statute law, to the detriment of both. It creates badly written instruments full of obsolete, repetitious, misleading provisions. Above all, it confuses the public, and in fact makes it certain that few will ever bother to read the state constitution. This is extremely unfortunate, since one of the main purposes of a constitution is to educate the public in first principles. How can the people be expected to respect a constitution they never read, and which may in fact be altogether unreadable? Long ago Chief Justice John Marshall made this crystal clear:

> A constitution, to contain an accurate detail of all the subdivisions of which its great powers will admit, and of all the means by which they may be carried into execution, would partake of the prolixity of a legal code, and could scarcely be embraced by the human mind. It would probably never be understood by the public. Its nature, therefore, requires, that only its great outlines should be marked, its important objects designated, and the minor ingredients which compose those objects be deduced from the nature of the objects themselves.[29]

OTHER FAILINGS OF STATE CONSTITUTIONS

Contemporary state constitutions are ripe for drastic revision for many other reasons: among them, to purge them of obsolete or unnecessary words,

---

[28] *Cox* v. *State,* 8 Tex. App. 254, 306 (1880).
[29] *McCulloch* v. *Maryland,* 4 Wheat. 316, 407 (1819).

phrases, and clauses, to correct errors and eliminate duplications, to rearrange dispersed sections, to get rid of inconsistencies and contradictions, and to restate confusing or even unintelligible terminology.

Almost any constitution will supply examples of obsolete and unnecessary clauses. Even some words are obsolete. There is not much point today in calling the legislature a "General Court," as does the New Hampshire Constitution (Part II, Art. 2), or in referring to citizens as "subjects" (Part II, Arts. 14-16). Nor is there much excuse in our day for such words as "doth" and "hath" and "dwelleth." No utility is served by incorporating specific figures for salaries in the constitution (e.g., Florida Constitution, Art. IV, sec. 29), where the legislature is allowed to change them and in fact has done so. Constitutional provisions forbidding outlawry (e.g., Texas Constitution, Art. I, sec. 20), or dueling (e.g., Pennsylvania Constitution, Art. XII, sec. 3), or hereditary privileges (e.g., West Virginia Constitution, Art. III, sec. 19), or titles of nobility (e.g., Oregon Constitution, Art. I, sec. 29), or the quartering of troops in private homes (e.g., Nebraska Constitution, Art. I, sec. 18), or feudal land tenures (e.g., New York Constitution, Art. 1, sec. 10) are completely obsolete today.

Many constitutional provisions are obsolete because of the passage of time. Thus the South Dakota Constitution, which went into effect in 1889, still directs the Legislature to submit the question of woman suffrage to the voters at its first session (Art. VII, sec. 2). Provisions in the Florida Constitution (Art. IX, secs. 12, 14) granting tax exemptions to certain interests for a period of years have been obsolete since the tolling of the period. The provisions of the Pennsylvania Constitution of 1873 on state sinking and reserve funds are archaic (Art. IX, secs. 11-13). The clause in the New Hampshire Constitution (Part I, Art. 6) which authorizes the towns to support "public protestant teachers of piety, religion, and morality" is obsolete. So also is the West Virginia provision relating to the disabilities of citizens who participated in the Civil War (Art. VIII, sec. 20).

Many state constitutional clauses are obsolete because the problems to which they were addressed are no longer with us. For example, the section of the New York Constitution (Art. III, sec. 17) which spells out certain restraints on the construction of street railways is obsolete because no one in his right mind would even dream of building a street railway today. Similarly, the New York provision (Art. I, sec. 13) relating to land transactions involving Indians is obsolete. Iowa's limitation of leases to a period of 20 years (Art. I, sec. 24) grew out of the antirent disturbances on the Van Rensselaer manor in New York in the 1840's, and is now archaic.[30] The

---

[30] See Note, 39 *Iowa Law Review* 486-94 (Spring, 1954); Henry Christman, *Tin Horns and Calico* (New York: Henry Holt & Co., 1945).

West Virginia provision that railroad officials are not eligible for membership in the Legislature (Art. VI, sec. 13) is but the echo of a dead controversy.

A staff report of the California Joint Interim Committee on Constitutional Revision, 1947-1948, listed 81 provisions of the state Constitution which it regarded as obsolete. Among them were a solemn assertion of the right to fish (Art. I, sec. 25), a prohibition of slavery (Art. I, sec. 18), a meaningless clause on aliens (Art. I, sec. 17), a clause dealing with emergency relief administration in the 1930 depression (Art. XVI, sec. 10), and sections dealing with dueling (Art. XX, sec. 2), the Chinese (Art. XIX), taxation (Art. XIII, secs. 15½, 16½), the election of judges (Art. VI, secs. 3, 4a, 15, 17, 25), the powers of San Francisco in connection with the 1915 World Fair (Art. XI, sec. 8a), the assessment of property damaged by the earthquake of 1933 (Art. XIII, sec. 8a), the salaries of executive officers (Art. V, sec. 19), and the liquor question (Art. I, sec. 26a).

Still other provisions of state constitutions are dispensable because they are invalid on federal grounds. A number of state documents still limit the suffrage to male citizens (e.g., Kentucky Constitution, sec. 145); such limitation, of course, is contrary to the supreme law of the land. Several constitutions forbid the enactment of legislation prohibiting emigration from the state (e.g., Kentucky Constitution, sec. 24), but any such statute would be unconstitutional on federal grounds. By the same token it is wholly unnecessary for a state constitution to forbid slavery (e.g., Utah Constitution, Art. I, sec. 21). Nor is it necessary for a state to proclaim that it is an inseparable part of the federal Union (e.g., Wyoming Constitution, Art. I, sec. 37), since it has no choice in the matter. The provision in the Oregon Constitution (Art. I, sec. 31) authorizing the legislature to regulate the immigration into the state of persons not qualified to become citizens and guaranteeing equal rights only to "white foreigners" is invalid under federal law. The New Hampshire provision (Part II, Art. 51) which authorizes the Governor to engage in war is illegal, and the declaration that the state has all powers not *expressly* delegated to the United States (Part I, Art. 7) is contrary to declared federal law.[31]

All sorts of constitutional clauses are now unnecessary or undesirable for a variety of reasons. It may have been all right for West Virginia, in 1872, to give the Governor only five days in which to make up his mind to sign or veto legislation (Art. VII, sec. 14), but modern conditions require more time.[32] Provisions requiring automatic reapportionment by the legislature (e.g., Pennsylvania Constitution, Art. II, sec. 18) simply do not work. The

---

[31] *McCulloch* v. *Maryland,* 4 Wheat. 316 (1819).
[32] The Model State Constitution gives the governor 15 days (Art. III, sec. 315).

relating of representation in the New Hampshire Senate to direct taxes paid (Part II, Art. 26) is not consonant with modern thinking. And a large majority of state constitutions are out-of-date on the subject of representation in the legislature.[33]

It is wholly unnecessary for a state constitution to declare (e.g., Texas Constitution, Art. III, sec. 42) that the legislature may pass laws to carry the document into effect. It is also unnecessary for the document to declare that statutes in violation of the constitution shall be declared void by the judiciary (e.g., Georgia Constitution, Art. I, sec. 4, par. 2). It is hardly necessary for the constitution to authorize the legislature to pass vagrancy laws, or to establish rural fire prevention districts, or to enact laws prescribing the qualifications of medical practitioners (Texas Constitution, Art. III, secs. 46, 48-d, Art. XVI, sec. 31).

Constitutions often contain meaningless clauses which ought to be rephrased or deleted. No one has ever been able to figure out, for example, what the California Constitution means when it declares (Art. V, sec. 6) that the Governor "shall transact all executive business with the officers of government. . . .", or when it says (Art. XVII, sec. 2): "The holding of large tracts of land, uncultivated and unimproved, by individuals or corporations, is against the public interest, and should be discouraged by all means not inconsistent with the rights of private property." And what does the Pennsylvania clause (Art. II, sec. 13) really say which asserts that "the sessions of each House and of committees of the whole shall be open, unless when the business is such as ought to be kept secret"?

The tidying up of constitutions would also correct errors in grammar and spelling and misnumbering. Quite a few Florida sections have been misnumbered (Art. V, sec. 49, Art. VIII, secs. 12-15, 20-21), and there are two sections 14a in the Louisiana Constitution. Something of a prize should be awarded to those who wrote section 71 of Article VII of the Louisiana Constitution. This article devotes 97 sections to the subject of the judicial system. Section 71 deals with coroners, and declares, "provided, this *article* shall not apply to any parish in which there is no regularly licensed physician, who will accept the office." Taken literally, this means that such a parish would be removed from the state's judicial system, and presumably live in something of a state of nature.

There are also contradictions to resolve. Thus the South Carolina Constitution declares that the General Assembly "shall make no law respecting an establishment of religion or prohibiting the free exercise thereof" (Art. I, sec. 4), but it also says that "no person who denies the existence of a

---

[33] See, e.g., W. Duane Lockard, "Constitutional Revision in Connecticut," 27 *Connecticut Bar Journal* 163-69 (June, 1953).

Supreme Being shall hold any office under this Constitution" (Art. XVII, sec. 4). The West Virginia Legislature is directed to enact "proper laws" for the registration of all voters (Art. IV, sec. 12), but in the next breath is forbidden to establish a board of registration of voters (Art. VI, sec. 43). One section of the Florida Constitution decrees that there shall be no more than 15 judicial circuits (Art. V, sec. 45), and a later section creates another one (Art. V, sec. 51).

Another piece of unfinished business is the rearrangement of badly organized constitutional provisions. One might well begin with the provision in the New York Constitution (Art. I, sec. 9) which permits pari-mutuel betting and which is located in the bill of rights. In the very same section is a provision that no divorce shall be granted except by judicial proceedings. Surely, here are two fish in the wrong pond! The same document also has provisions relating to the removal of judges in four different sections (Art. VI, secs. 9, 9a, 10, 17) and excess condemnation provisions in two (Art. I, sec. 7, Art. XVIII, sec. 8). Materials in the Louisiana Constitution dealing with the executive branch are scattered in 17 different articles, taxation in 6, and local government in 7. One section of the South Dakota Constitution fixes the per diem pay of legislators (Art. III, sec. 6), but 33 pages and 18 articles later the legislators are authorized to fix their own salaries (Art. XXI, sec. 2).

Still another bad habit of constitution-makers is the incorporation by reference of all sorts of nonconstitutional documents. Thus a 1945 amendment to the Georgia Constitution incorporates a statute enacted by the legislature in 1902 (Art. I, sec. 6, par. 1). The section of the Florida Constitution which deals with the distribution of the gasoline tax to the counties incorporates a 1931 statute (Art. IX, sec. 16), and another section of this document even incorporates by reference certain resolutions of a county commission (Art. VIII, sec. 11). The Louisiana Constitution, which is so rich in examples of what is wrong with state constitutions, includes by reference sections of seven previous constitutions, many state and federal laws, municipal ordinances, and even several resolutions or contracts of governmental boards. A competent scholar has computed that it gives some degree of constitutional status to 179 documents.[34] One section (Art. XIV, sec. 23.1) dealing with sewerage, water, and drainage in New Orleans incorporates by reference an 1899 statute which has been amended 10 times!

THE UPDATING OF STATE CONSTITUTIONS

State constitutions need frequent attention to make sure they are in tune

---

[34] Owen, *op. cit.*, p. 9.

with the times.[35] Many traditional clauses in bills of rights are ripe for re-examination, and some deadwood, such as clauses dealing with the right to bear arms, the quartering of troops, and the granting of titles of nobility, can be pruned away.[36] While most of the traditional guaranties are still accept-able, recently-revised documents spell out such rights as the right of labor to organize and bargain collectively, the right of the worker to just compensa-tion and to a reasonable working day, the right to social security, and the right of employed minors and women to special protection.[37] While provi-sions against discrimination are by no means novel, the newer constitutions are especially meticulous and, indeed, often quite eloquent on the subject.[38] There are new clauses dealing with such current problems as wiretapping[39] and fairness in legislative investigations.[40] The Model State Constitution includes a clause which is designed to strengthen the whole conception of a bill of rights by specifying that any citizen may go to court to restrain the violation of any constitutional provision (sec. 113).

A great many clauses dealing with the legislature need rethinking, as the interesting suggestions of the Model State Constitution on this subject would indicate. For it directs attention to the very structure of the legislature, with the recommendation of a unicameral in place of the traditional bicameral body, with authority to sit as long as it wishes whenever it wishes, and with many suggestions regarding such matters as automatic reapportionment, improvement of committee procedures, and aids to legislation.[41] One of

---

[35] Here and there are gaps to be filled. An illustration of a rather obvious omission occurs in the New Hampshire Constitution which, with an elaborate bill of rights of 38 sections, has no guaranty of free speech.

[36] See William A. Schnader, "Dead Wood in the Pennsylvania Constitution," 25 *Temple Law Quarterly* 399-409 (Apr., 1952).

[37] See W. Brooke Graves, "A New Bill of Rights," 46 *National Municipal Review* 238-44 (May, 1957). The North Dakota bill of rights, Art. I, sec. 23, asserts the right of workers to obtain employment, and several state constitutions say in some fashion that low-income people have a right to low-cost housing. Massachusetts Constitution, Amendment 43; New York Constitution, Art. XVIII, sec. 1; South Dakota Constitution, Art. XIII, sec. 17.

[38] See especially New York Constitution, Art. I, sec. 11; New Jersey Constitution, Art. I, sec. 5; Alaska Constitution, Art. I, sec. 3; Puerto Rico Constitution, Art. II, sec. 1; Hawaii Constitution, Art. I, secs. 4, 7, 12, and Art. IX, sec. 1.

[39] See New York Constitution, Art. I, sec. 12; Puerto Rico Constitution, Art. II, sec. 10.

[40] See Alaska Constitution, Art. I, sec. 7; Puerto Rico Constitution, Art. II, sec. 8.

[41] The new constitutions of Hawaii (Art. III, sec. 11), Alaska (Art. II, sec. 8) and Puerto Rico (Art. III, sec. 10) provide for regular sessions annually. See Belle Zeller, ed., *American State Legislatures* (New York: Thomas Y. Crowell Co., 1954); A. E. Buck, *Modernizing Our State Legislatures* (Philadelphia: American Academy of Politi-cal and Social Science, 1936); Council of State Governments, *Our State Legislatures,* rev. ed. (Chicago: 1948).

the most widely discussed features of modern state government is the failure of legislatures to carry out constitutional provisions requiring the periodical reapportionment of the legislative seats. From the point of view of population a very large majority of state legislatures are unrepresentative. Since American courts refuse to order legislatures to do their constitutional duty by writ, one solution is to provide for some sort of automatic reapportionment by a non-legislative body, as has been done in a few recent instances.[42]

Constitutional articles relating to the state executive are also subject to widespread debate. In the words of the final report of the Commission on Intergovernmental Relations:

> Today few States have an adequate executive branch headed by a governor who can be held generally accountable for executing and administering the laws of the State. . . . Typically, though not universally, the governor is the nominal chief of a sprawling State administration consisting of scores of separate departments, commissions, and agencies. . . . Few governors have been supplied with modern staff agencies and tools of management adequate to the administrative responsibility presumed to be vested in them.[43]

What is required for the state executive branch is concentration of authority and responsibility, functional integration, the removal of boards and commissions from purely administrative work, the coordination of staff services, and provision for an independent audit.[44] While the office of governor has become much more powerful than it was in the early days of the Republic,[45] its power still is kept dispersed and disintegrated and does not measure up to the requirements of modern administration. The main objective of the sections of the Model State Constitution dealing with this subject is to create an adequate governorship by making the executive branch

---

[42] The Texas Constitution was amended in 1948 to provide for automatic reapportionment by a five-member ex officio Legislative Redistricting Board if the Legislature fails to do its duty. (Art. III, sec. 28) The Missouri Constitution of 1945 shifted responsibility to the secretary of state for the reapportionment of the lower house, and to an appointed commission for the upper house. (Art. III, secs. 2, 7) The Alaska Constitution authorizes the Governor to reapportion every 10 years, with the assistance of an advisory board. (Art. VI, sec. 3) The Constitution of Hawaii goes further by providing that if the Governor does not apportion every 10 years, then any registered voter may sue for a writ of mandamus in the Supreme Court of the state. (Art. III, sec. 4) Automatic reapportionment is also provided for in the Puerto Rico Constitution by a board consisting of the Chief Justice and two members appointed by the Governor. (Art. III, sec. 4)

[43] Report, op. cit., pp. 42-43.

[44] See Arthur E. Buck, The Reorganization of State Government in the United States (New York: Columbia University Press, 1938), pp. 14-15; Council of State Governments, Reorganizing State Government (Chicago: 1950).

[45] See Leslie Lipson, The American Governor: From Figurehead to Leader (Chicago: University of Chicago Press, 1939); Coleman B. Ransone, The Office of Governor in the United States (University: University of Alabama Press, 1956).

a reality. An important step in this direction is short ballot reform.[46] Other needs of the office of governor are now being debated: longer terms of office, control of department heads, the item veto, power over administrative reorganization, and more effective budgetary controls.

It is equally necessary to create a judicial department, since all that most states have today is a congeries of various types of courts having various sorts of jurisdictions. Roscoe Pound has made it abundantly clear that in each state the whole judicial power should be vested in one single great court, divided into departments or divisions and containing a great deal of internal flexibility.[47] Such is the central point of the article of the Model State Constitution on the judiciary, for it would make all courts of the state parts of a unified "general court of justice," consisting of a single supreme court department and other departments. The chief justice would be elected by the voters for an 8-year term, and he in turn would appoint all other judges for 12-year terms from lists of three presented to him by the judicial council. After an appointive judge has served four years, he would have to submit his record to the voters. In addition, the Supreme Court would have the rule-making power. Thus the purposes of this article are to unify the court system, give it internal flexibility, and give the judges political independence. Both the Missouri and New Jersey constitutions have taken important strides in this direction, as have the new constitutions of Alaska, Hawaii, and Puerto Rico.[48] Most state constitutions, however, still have a long road to travel before they begin to approximate the desired goal of judicial integration.

Most other major sections of state constitutions need rethinking. Certainly this is true for provisions that deal with local government. It is time to reconsider all the restrictions imposed upon the legislature in connection

---

[46] Under the terms of the New Jersey Constitution of 1947, the Governor is the only executive official elected from the state as a whole, and the same is true for Puerto Rico. In Hawaii only the Governor and the lieutenant-governor are elected by the whole body of voters, and in Alaska only the Governor and the secretary of state.

[47] *Organization of Courts* (Boston: Little, Brown & Co., 1940). See also Arthur T. Vanderbilt, *Minimum Standards of Judicial Administration* (New York: National Conference of Judicial Councils, 1949).

[48] Since 1940 the Governor of Missouri has been appointing judges from lists supplied by a commission, and later the judges run for election upon their records. This feature was retained in the constitutional revision of 1945, and in addition the Supreme Court was given general rule-making powers and the authority to transfer judges temporarily. The New Jersey revision created a genuinely integrated court system, with the judges subject to appointment by the Governor, subject to confirmation by the state Senate. The new constitutions of Alaska, Hawaii, and Puerto Rico all create unified judicial systems, give the highest court rule-making power, and provide for appointive rather than elective judges; the latter two empower the Chief Justice to appoint an administrative director for all courts.

with local government that often make desirable flexibility impossible.[49] The emphasis in the newer state constitutions is upon local home rule.[50] It is also imperative that adequate provision be made for urgent problems growing out of urban growth, such as annexation and consolidation of local units, intergovernmental cooperation, city-county consolidation, debt limitations, local budgeting, slum clearance, and urban renewal. Equally pressing in a great many states is the question of reviewing the sections dealing with state finance. Here, too, the current tendency is to reduce restrictions upon the legislative power and to simplify and liberalize provisions on this subject.[51]

Finally, attention should be directed toward the amending procedures set forth in state constitutions. If a state constitution is to serve its proper purposes, the door must be open to change by reasonable procedures.[52] Where the amending process is too difficult, such as the requirement of an extraordinary popular vote,[53] the document tends to get out of date; on the other hand, if the amending process is too easy, then the constitution tends to get out of hand. Ideally, the amending process should be more difficult than the ordinary legislative process, but not impossibly difficult. Furthermore, every generation has a right, and indeed an obligation, to review its constitution, and a few documents make periodic review, or at least its possibility,

---

[49] See Charles C. Binney, *Restrictions upon Local and Special Legislation in State Constitutions* (Philadelphia: Kay & Bro., 1894) ; Thomas F. Green, Jr., "A Malapportian Provision of State Constitutions," 24 *Washington University Law Quarterly* 359-81 (Apr., 1939).

[50] See Missouri Constitution, Arts. VI, VII; New Jersey Constitution, Art. IV, sec. 7, para. 10; New York Constitution, Art. IX; Georgia Constitution, Art. XV, sec. 1; Hawaii Constitution, Art. VII, secs. 1-2; Alaska Constitution, Art. X; Model State Constitution, Art. VIII.

[51] In the new constitutions of Alaska, Art. IX, sec. 14, Hawaii, Art. VI, sec. 8, and Puerto Rico, Art. III, sec. 22, there are no detailed limits on state and local taxation and borrowing, and all provide for an independent postaudit by an auditor appointed by the legislature. The Missouri revision, Art. IV, secs. 13, 15, 22-28, Art. VI, secs. 23-29, greatly liberalized the sections dealing with debt limits and tax rates, reorganized the state's fiscal agencies, and created a genuinely independent postaudit by an elective state auditor.

[52] On this general subject see: Dealey, *op. cit., supra,* note 4; Dodd, *op. cit., supra,* note 2; Christian L. Larsen and Conrad Cowan, *South Carolina Constitution Amendment Procedures* (Columbia: Bureau of Public Administration, University of South Carolina, 1948), pp. 19-58; Thomas R. White, "Amendment and Revision of State Constitutions," 100 *University of Pennsylvania Law Review* 1132-52 (June, 1952); Albert L. Sturm, *Methods of State Constitutional Reform* (Ann Arbor: University of Michigan Press, 1954).

[53] See K. C. Sears and C. V. Laughlin, "A Study in Constitutional Rigidity," 10 *University of Chicago Law Review* 142-76 (Jan. 1943) ; 11 *ibid.* 374-442 (June, 1944).

automatic.[54] Such provisions are altogether consistent with sound democratic theory, for in the last analysis the constitution belongs to the people and should express their will. Finally, there has been a highly desirable tendency in recent years to provide for adequate preliminary spadework through the use of commissions or other special bodies charged with the function of doing research and writing informed reports on the problems that are likely to arise. Extensive research preceded constitutional revision in New York in 1938,[55] and more recently in Missouri, New Jersey, Alaska, Hawaii, and Puerto Rico. Of course, independent scholars have also made significant contributions in this field.[56]

THE QUALITIES OF A GOOD CONSTITUTION

What, then, are the proper attributes of a good constitution? It is difficult to generalize, since a constitution must be both stable and flexible. Serving as the legal underpinning for the commonwealth, it must supply the stability which orderly government requires; yet it will fail of its purposes if the door is closed too tightly against change and adaptation. Indeed, in many ways the central problem is to find a proper balance between stability and change. John Dickinson once wrote:

> The largest number of controversies and causes of dissatisfaction that arise under a written constitution are connected with the question of progress. . . . The function of a written constitution is to provide . . . a principle and framework of order within which change can proceed without endangering stability.[57]

Furthermore, there has never been an ideal state constitution, and no constitution could possibly be ideal for all states. A document which is suitable for the needs of a maritime state might not do very well for an arid, inland state. Also, every viable constitution must necessarily reflect the power struc-

---

[54] In New Hampshire the question of calling a constitutional convention must be submitted to the voters at least once every 7 years, Art. 100; in Iowa, every 10 years, Art. X, sec. 3; in Michigan, every 16 years, Art. XVII, sec. 4; and every 20 years in New York, Art. XIX, sec. 2, Ohio, Art. XVI, sec. 3, Missouri, Art. XII, sec. 3a, Maryland, Art. XIV, sec. 2, and Oklahoma, Art. XXIV, sec. 2. In November, 1957, the voters of New York rejected the call for a constitutional convention to meet in 1959 by a vote of 1,275,000 to 1,175,000. The new constitutions of Alaska, Art. XIII, sec. 2, and Hawaii, Art. XV, sec. 2, provide for submission of this issue to the voters every 10 years, and the Model State Constitution, Art. XIII, sec. 1301, would submit the question every 15 years.

[55] See Vernon A. O'Rourke and Douglas W. Campbell, *Constitution-Making in a Democracy* (Baltimore: Johns Hopkins Press, 1943).

[56] See, e.g., the symposium on "Constitutional Revision in Texas," 35 *Texas Law Review* 901-1089 (Oct., 1957).

[57] John Dickinson, "The Constitution and Progress," 181 *The Annals* 11-12 (Sept., 1935).

ture of the particular society it is designed to serve; it cannot and will not function in a vacuum. Nor will a good constitution retain its quality for very long, in our sort of dynamic society, unless it can be changed to keep up with the times. Even the Model State Constitution, which the National Municipal League first published in 1921, has been revised periodically, with a fifth edition appearing in 1948, and a sixth under study today.

Certainly, the first requisite of a good constitution is brevity. It is a very great mistake for the authors of a constitution to attempt to say too much. A constitution is no place for legal codes or the appeasement of temporary interests. It should do no more than set down fundamental and enduring first principles. It must describe the basic framework of government, assign the institutions their powers, spell out the fundamental rights of man, and make provision for peaceful change. But it should do all of these things in general rather than in overly detailed language, and should attempt no more. And there is reason to believe that prevailing conditions are such that the goal of a concise constitution is now feasible, since courts today rarely stand in the way of social legislation, there has been an observable decline in the legislative appetite for special legislation, the Fourteenth Amendment of the federal Constitution sets limits to many types of state misbehavior, and modern means of mass communication are tremendously important checks upon improper legislation. An effective free press is probably a more efficacious check than formal constitutional limitations. Furthermore, there is a growing public awareness that holding legislators politically accountable for what they do protects the public interest more surely than constitutional caveats which hamstring any sort of action.

A second quality of a good constitution is readability, for one of its central purposes is to educate the public in first principles. If it is to fulfill this objective it must be something the average citizen will undertake to read. It should therefore be written in good, modern English; obsolete terminology should be avoided; ambiguous phraseology should be clarified; and repetitious or contradictory language should be corrected. The articles, sections, and clauses should be arranged in a logical and orderly way. In short, the constitution should be intelligible to ordinary people, if it is to command confidence and, indeed, general reverence. It is not merely or primarily a lawyer's document to be manipulated in litigation. It is above everything else a people's charter, a statement of their essential conceptions about government.

It follows that the authors of a constitution should use familiar language. Americans are old hands in this business, and have developed over the years—indeed the centuries—certain words and phrases to express basic ideas. These should be retained, because the familiar is apt to be readily appreciated and understood. For example, almost all state constitutions have a provision which forbids "cruel and unusual punishments." The phrase comes from the English Bill of Rights of 1689. It was suggested in the recent New Jersey convention that the words "excessive and unreasonable punishments" be substituted, but the convention wisely rejected this proposal. Since the old phrase and the new said the same thing, it was correctly decided to use the familiar one. Surely nothing would have been gained by the change, and in the process an ancient phrase which has served us well would have been needlessly abandoned.

A sound constitutional revision, even if undertaken on a comprehensive scale, will never change the basic pattern to which the American people are thoroughly habituated and which they obviously want to preserve. The Missouri Constitution of 1945 illustrates this point, since it is by no means a new document, many sections dating from the original Constitution of 1820. Though the new Constitution is shorter than its predecessor, that of 1875, by some 11,000 words, all of the traditional provisions were included. But some antiquated sections were eliminated, a great deal of detail was dropped, language was clarified and simplified, and many provisions were rearranged. New provisions were added to deal with modern problems relating to agriculture, education, forestry, health, hospitals, libraries, museums, parks, recreation, and welfare.

This, then, is another aspect of a good constitution, that it makes provision for emerging problems and reflects the best in current thinking. A constitutional convention today will have to concern itself with problems of urban growth and metropolitan government, reapportionment, aids to legislation, the short ballot, court reorganization, the extension of the merit system, revenue sources, debt limitations, the organization of local government, terms of office, highways, and the expansion of welfare services, including housing, reclamation of blighted areas, mental care, conservation, and the like. Changes in all these areas are now in the air.

Above all, as the Model State Constitution emphasizes, reality must be given to the concept of the "department." Every state constitution goes through the motions of asserting that power is divided among three departments, but in most states executive and judicial departments are largely fictions. Where the governor shares power and influence with 10 other popularly-elected officials and a large number of quasi-independent boards and commissions, one can hardly talk about an executive department as a reality. Nor is a mere congeries of courts a department in any realistic sense.

And wholly apart from the new problems, there are plenty of old problems that need rethinking. Bills of rights should be clarified and modernized. Legislatures should be made smaller and more representative, and given more effective organization. Relations between the governor and the legislature can certainly be improved through institutional changes. The last word has not yet been said on the subject of the executive budget. The governor's term of office is still a lively issue in many states. The best method of selecting judges is another. Existing initiative and referendum procedures and amending provisions are ripe for reevaluation. Intergovernmental cooperation can and should be encouraged.[58] Even the minimum age for voting is now being discussed; after all, the age limit of 21 years was not decreed in heaven.[59]

Finally, it is desirable that the writers of constitutions should stick as close as possible to reality and avoid making claims or staking out generalizations which, though theoretically desirable, are impossible of fulfillment. Otherwise, people are likely to find a constitution something of a snare and a delusion. For example, it is customary for most state constitutions to state flatly an absolute principle of separation of powers between the legislative, executive, and judicial branches. But a complete separation of powers is not possible and is, in actuality, to be found nowhere. What purpose, then, is served by making unrealistic claims? In this connection, what the New Hampshire Constitution (Part I, Art. 37) has to say makes a good deal of sense:

In the Government of this State, the three essential powers thereof, to wit, the Legislative, Executive, and Judicial, ought to be kept as separate from, and independent of, each other, as the nature of a free government will admit, or as is consistent with that chain of connection that binds the whole fabric of the Constitution in one indissoluble bond of unity and amity.

This is a wholly reasonable proposition. As far as possible, a state constitution should be a reasonable document.

---

[58] See Model State Constitution, Art. XI, secs. 1100-03.

[59] Two states have lowered the age limit to 18: Georgia Constitution, Art. II, sec. 2, and Kentucky Constitution, sec. 145; the Model State Constitution, Art. II, sec. 200, does the same. The age limit is fixed at 20 in the Constitution of Hawaii, Art. II, sec. 1, and at 19 in the Alaska Constitution, Art. V, sec. 1.

chapter IX

the bill of rights

Robert S. Rankin

The bills of rights found in American state constitutions are testaments of the high regard in which both constitution-makers and citizens hold the rights of individuals. They also indicate a realization that these rights must be made secure from interference by others and from the arbitrary exercise of governmental authority.[1] Unlike the federal Constitution where the bill of rights is found as amendments, bills of rights in state constitutions constitute the first article—a position that attests to the importance and basic character of the subject matter. Through the years there has been no diminution in this importance. The constitutions of Alaska and Hawaii, with carefully prepared bills of rights, offer eloquent proof of this statement. The emphasis that today is being placed upon civil rights and their preservation[2] is due, to some extent, to a fear that the growing power of the state, the bureaucratic character of modern government, and the complexity of current social and economic life will conspire to deprive the individual of his rights and privileges and make him an automaton. Bills of rights help allay these fears. There is good reason, then, to consider them both as fundamental law and as "insurance policies."

Each state constitution today contains a bill of rights, and in recent state constitutional conventions little or no thought has been given to excluding

---

[1] The author desires here to express his indebtedness to the National Municipal League for permission to reproduce here much of an unpublished article upon the same subject prepared under the auspices of the League.

[2] Evidence of the great current interest in civil rights in general is shown by the fact that during the month of March, 1959, there were introduced in the Senate of the United States 13 bills concerning civil liberties and 24 in the House of Representatives. This information was secured from a letter to the author from Senator Thomas C. Hennings, Jr., Chairman of the Subcommittee on Constitutional Rights of the Judiciary Committee, April 1, 1959.

such a bill. Although made over a period of nearly two centuries, they are all similar although no two are exactly alike—in part because of the basic nature of the subject matter but also because of the tendency of state constitution-makers to copy sections of the federal bill of rights and of other state constitutions. Excellence is not measured by length, and some of the early bills of rights which are relatively short are equal to if not better than some of the lengthy bills of more recent origin. The essentiality of a bill of rights rests on the principle that

A bill of rights is, in a very real sense, an expression of political faith and ideals—it sets the bounds of political authority and reserves to the individual certain freedoms believed essential to human happiness. It guarantees protection for those areas of individual difference necessary for the operation of popular government and political democracy.[3]

The provisions found in state bills of rights may be placed in three general groups. First, most bills of rights have introductory statements of the political theory that is the basis for the rights that are to follow and for the form of government that is described and outlined in other articles. Typical of this type of statement is the one found in the Constitution of the state of North Carolina that

. . . all political power is vested in, and derived from, the people; all government of right originates from the people, it is founded upon their will only, and is instituted solely for the good of the whole. (Art. I, sec. 2)

Concerning the rights of man, the Constitution of Hawaii declares,

All persons are free by nature and are equal in their inherent and inalienable rights. Among these rights are the enjoyment of life, liberty and the pursuit of happiness, and the acquiring and possessing of property. These rights cannot endure unless the people recognize their corresponding obligations and responsibilities. (Art. I, sec. 2)

The rule of law, the separation of powers, and other broad principles of democratic government are also found in these introductory statements.

In recent years some doubts have been expressed that statements like the above serve any good purpose. Austin F. MacDonald, for example, believes that they only consume space and should be deleted. He contends that

Some guarantees are phrased in such general terms that they have little or no significance; some are positively detrimental to the social development of present-day commonwealths; while still others deal with a wide variety of mat-

---

[3] *Civil Rights and Liberties, a staff paper prepared by Public Administration Service for the Delegates to the Alaska Constitutional Convention* (Chicago: November, 1955), p. 4 (mimeographed).

ters that cannot by any stretch of the imagination be classified as fundamental rights.[4]

A contrary view is taken by most constitution-makers and by many writers.

Recognizing the importance of the affirmations of basic governmental philosophy and the guarantees of personal and political rights which the Declaration embraces, the Constitutional Commission dealt cautiously with its provisions.[5]

So stated the North Carolina Constitutional Commission with respect to the declaration of rights found in that state's Constitution. And in the words of W. Brooke Graves, "since they do no great harm, perhaps the energy expended in the effort to remove them might better be applied to more vital matters."[6] Certainly, it is not inappropriate to restate the basic principles upon which the government of a state is founded.

Following the introductory statements come provisions designed to protect personal and property rights. These guarantees may be placed in two groups: the first includes rights that are substantive in nature, as freedom of religion, speech, press, assembly, and petition; the second is made up of procedural guarantees. The first list of freedoms is so generally accepted today that it is hard to realize, for instance, that "complete freedom of religion did not exist in any of the thirteen colonies, nor did the first constitutions of the original states in any instance presume to guarantee full freedom of religion."[7] Procedural guarantees have for their purpose the securing of equality before the law and a fair trial. Provisions prohibiting excessive bail and cruel and unusual punishment and requiring trial by jury and an indictment by a grand jury are examples. The broad guarantee of "due process of law" may be classified both as a substantive and as a procedural right. Property rights also are protected by the bills of rights in state constitutions. The interest of constitution-makers in the protection of property is illustrated by statements providing that private property cannot be taken for public use without just compensation and maintaining the security of homes, papers, and effects from unwarranted searches and seizures.

Each bill of rights also contains provisions that defy classification and must be lumped together in a miscellaneous group. Some are essential to the preservation of liberty; others are not. Some are placed in a constitution to

---

[4] Austin F. MacDonald, *American State Government and Administration*, 6th ed. (New York: Thomas Y. Crowell Co., 1960), p. 83.

[5] John L. Sanders, "The Proposed Constitution of North Carolina: An Analysis," 25 *Popular Government* 6 (Feb., 1959).

[6] W. Brooke Graves, *What Should a Constitution Contain?* (Trenton: State of New Jersey, 1947), p. 4. A monograph written for the Governor's Committee in Preparatory Research for the New Jersey Constitutional Convention of 1947.

[7] See Jewel C. Phillips, *State and Local Government in America* (New York: American Book Co., 1954), pp. 40-41.

put the subject beyond the control of the state legislature. "Annapolis will be the meeting place of the legislature," "lobbying is not permitted," "immigration should be encouraged" are instances of the inclusion in particular bills of rights of matters not fundamental in nature that should be left to the discretion of the legislature.

The following listing gives the subject matter of the most common provisions that are found in state bills of rights:

Subject	Number of States
Natural rights	35
Political power in the people	47
Freedom of religion	49
Freedom of speech and press	50
Freedom of assembly and petition	50
Security against searches and seizures	48
Trial by jury	50
Speedy trial	39
Protection against double jeopardy	38
Suspension of the writ of habeas corpus	50
Excessive bail	48
Imprisonment for debt	33
Military authority subordinate to civil authority	39
Quartering of troops	31
Treason	32
Power of eminent domain	50
Right to bear arms	35
Saving clause "those enumerated are not all"	50

Is a Bill of Rights Necessary?

Notwithstanding the general acceptance of a bill of rights as an integral and necessary part of a state constitution, two arguments may be raised in favor of omitting such bills. The first is that all powers exercised by a state are powers delegated from the people and those not delegated remain with the people. A bill of rights, therefore, is unnecessary. Alexander Hamilton, writing in the Federalist Papers, made this point when he said,

. . . bills of rights are, in their origin, stipulations between kings and their subjects, abridgments of prerogative in favour of privilege, reservation of rights not surrendered to the prince. . . . they have no application to the constitutions professedly founded upon the power of the people, and executed by their immediate representatives and servants. Here, in strictness, the people surrendered nothing; and as they retained everything they have no need of particular reservations.[8]

The inclusion of bills of rights in state constitutions, however, does not

---

[8] *The Federalist,* No. 84. (Everyman's Library edition, pp. 438-39.)

necessarily contradict this position. Inclusion, in effect, only means that there are certain rights reserved to the people that are more important than others. These rights are better secured by having their importance attested to in black and white in the fundamental law of the state. Certainly, nothing is lost by such inclusion and much may be gained. While only 8 of the original 13 state constitutions contained bills of rights, and these differed widely in content, today all of the state constitutions and the federal Constitution contain bills of rights. The Model State Constitution devotes Article I to a bill of rights. It may, therefore, be maintained that the inclusion of bills of rights in state constitutions is an acceptable and a desirable practice.

The second argument brought against the inclusion of bills of rights in state constitutions also is based on the claim that they are unnecessary, for the reason that the bill of rights and certain other amendments of the federal Constitution are enough to make these rights secure anywhere within the United States.

When the first 10 amendments to the federal Constitution were being considered in the first Congress, James Madison proposed another amendment that failed to secure congressional approval. It proposed that "equal rights of conscience, the freedom of speech or of the press, and the right of trial by jury in criminal cases, shall not be infringed by any state."[9] The failure to accept this amendment and the decision of the Supreme Court of the United States that the first 10 amendments of the United States Constitution were not applicable to the states increases the importance of state bills of rights.[10]

Much of the need for protection against acts of the states, however, was removed by the adoption of the Fourteenth Amendment. Rights secured elsewhere in the Constitution of the United States from interference by the federal government could now be classified as privileges and immunities with which the state could not interfere.[11] Fundamental rights were also secured against state action by the due process of law clause. In its interpretation of the Fourteenth Amendment the Supreme Court has

. . . established that the terms "liberty" and "due process of law" as used in Amendment XIV render available against the States certain fundamental rights guaranteed accused persons in the Bill of Rights and the substantive rights which are protected against Congress by Amendment I.[12]

---

[9] *The Debates and Proceedings in the Congress of the United States*, Vol. 1 (Washington: Gales and Seaton, 1834), p. 452.

[10] *Barron* v. *Baltimore*, 7 Peters 243 (1833).

[11] See *Slaughter House Cases*, 16 Wall. 36 (1873) and *Twining* v. *New Jersey*, 211 U. S. 78 (1908).

[12] Edward S. Corwin, ed., *The Constitution of the United States of America* (Washington: Government Printing Office, 1953), p. 751.

Undoubtedly the Fourteenth Amendment is a bulwark of protection against arbitrary state action but it has not removed the need for bills of rights in state constitutions. As one writer has said,

For those who would halt, or at least slow down, the exercise of federal power and who would revitalize state governments, the careful drafting of a state bill of rights to include all liberties which should be guaranteed against state action (even if they may also be protected by the fourteenth amendment) offers a major challenge. If the states cannot protect their citizens' fundamental liberties, or are careless about such protection, then obviously the basic, fundamental vitality of state governments is immeasurably weakened.[13]

Why Changes Occur in State Bills of Rights

If basic rights remained the same down through the years, then the revision of bills of rights would be unnecessary. Fundamental rights, however, do not remain entirely the same in number or in content, and some are readily discoverable and others are not easily recognizable in these changing times. Also, our ideas concerning the fundamental character of a right may change. At one time the right of petition was considered fundamental; today it is viewed as a right of little importance.[14] Not only have certain other rights been deleted from more recent constitutions but new rights have been discovered that are believed to have such importance as to merit inclusion. Society has become extremely complex and its social and economic structure differs greatly from that of the eighteenth century. The individual has found the need for additional guarantees whereby to protect himself. Robert M. Hutchins states that "the principal reason why civil liberties as traditionally defined and defended do not interest the American is that they are inadequate to express the true dimensions of the problem of freedom and justice today." Today, he maintains, an individual needs protection from the possible dangers of a police state, from the arbitrary character of the bureaucratic state, and from the "remorseless tendency of an industrial system."[15]

The increase in length of bills of rights has been due to three factors:

---

[13] James P. Hart, "The Bill of Rights: Safeguard of Liberty," 35 *Texas Law Review* 919-25, 924 (1957).

[14] That the right of petition is still used and has some effect is illustrated by the following incident. People living next to an airport in an English village protested the start of a jet flight at 1:30 every morning. The noise awakened all. Nothing was done but "the plans for the flight were junked rather hastily after the people of Longford Village warned they would exercise the right of petition by telephoning all airline officials and transport ministry officials every time a jet plane woke them up at 1:30 in the morning." *Wall Street Journal*, May 1, 1959.

[15] "Can a Free Society Survive?," *The Fund for the Republic Bulletin* (May, 1958), pp. 4, 5.

first, the failure to delete obsolete sections; second, the addition of new rights; and, third, the inclusion of many guarantees that are not basic. Illustrative of a provision that might well be deleted is the statement in the North Carolina Constitution (Art. I, sec. 29) that "a frequent recurrence to fundamental principles is absolutely necessary to preserve the blessings of liberty"—a statement that has served no particular purpose. New rights added in recent years may be illustrated by provisions for the right of labor to organize. Guarantees that are not basic may be illustrated by provisions concerning immigration and emigration.

In constitutional conventions an effort usually is made to keep bills of rights short by including only broad guarantees of rights, but this objective has not always been achieved. The New Jersey Constitution of 1947 has 21 sections in its bill of rights; the Georgia Constitution of 1945 has 39 sections; and Alaska and Hawaii have 21 and 20 respectively. The Model State Constitution in its fifth edition has only 14 sections.

METHODS AND TYPES OF CHANGES

Usually, changes in state bills of rights come at times of major constitutional revision rather than by piecemeal amendment. In the period from 1933 to 1939, for example, many amendments were added to state constitutions but none concerned bills of rights.[16] In 1944, however, an amendment was added to the Florida Constitution concerning the right of collective bargaining and there are other instances of changes of this type. However, most alterations take place at the time of a general revision. Changes in bills of rights are of three general types:

1. Editorial changes resulting from the ever-present need for editorial improvement. Errors in grammar and poor choices of words occur frequently. The North Carolina bill of rights makes the rather naive statement that "all elections ought to be free." (Art. I, sec. 10) Much improvement in the effectiveness of constitutional provisions can be made by careful editorial work.

2. Alterations of sections that do not call for fundamental change but that need to be updated and made more effective.

3. The addition of new and the deletion of old rights.

A proposed constitution, prepared for the state of Florida in 1955, made changes of all three types in the bill of rights. Editorial changes were numerous; nine alterations were made in the statements of existing rights; a provision was deleted requiring "primary allegiance to the Federal Government"; and a unique provision was added concerning self-incrimination, as follows:

---

[16] Hugh R. Gallagher, "State Constitutional Amendments," 34 *American Political Science Review* 506-11 (June, 1940).

Any public officer or public employee who, upon being called before a grand jury to testify concerning the conduct of his office or the performance of his official duties, refuses to sign a waiver of immunity against subsequent criminal prosecution or to answer any relevant question concerning such matters before the grand jury, shall by virtue of such refusal be disqualified from holding any public office or public employment for a period of five years, and shall be removed from office or employment by the appropriate authority or shall forfeit it at suit to be prosecuted by the attorney general.[17]

NEW RIGHTS AND SIGNIFICANT DEVELOPMENTS

There exists at all times a demand for the inclusion of new guarantees within bills of rights, but the nature of the desired additions and the intensity of the demand vary. Current proposals for additions that have considerable support are considered below. Of these, the right to organize and bargain collectively is particularly important.

The Right to Organize and Bargain Collectively

An outgrowth of industrialization in the United States is a demand for legal recognition of the right to organize and bargain collectively. Union leaders and workers have urged that such provisions be added to the bills of rights in state constitutions. In the words of W. Brooke Graves, this "is one of the rights now in the process of establishment,"[18] and there is considerable evidence to substantiate this view. Following the example of New York in 1938, provisions recognizing the right to organize and to bargain collectively have been added to the constitutions of Missouri in 1945, of New Jersey in 1947, of Florida in 1955. The Model State Constitution states:

Citizens shall have the right to organize, except in military or semi-military organizations not under the supervision of the state, and except for purposes of resisting the duly constituted authority of this state or of the United States. Public employees shall have the right, through representatives of their own choosing, to present to and make known to the state, or any of its political subdivisions or agencies, their grievances and proposals. Persons in private employment shall have the right to bargain collectively through representatives of their own choosing. (Art. I, sec. 103)

There also is opposition to the inclusion in state constitutions of a provision on the right to organize. Here are the bases for this opposition. The right to bargain implies the right to come to an agreement. If the terms of the agreement for which one can bargain can be regulated, then bargaining itself

---

[17] Florida Constitutional Advisory Commission, *Recommended Constitution for Florida*, Art. 1, sec. 15 (Tallahassee: 1957).

[18] W. Brooke Graves, "A New Bill of Rights," 44 *National Municipal Review* 238-44 (May, 1957).

is subject to restriction. Should the right to organize and bargain collectively be included in a constitution it should indicate a general agreement that these actions are of such basic importance that they should be protected from legislative interference unless they constitute in some way a clear and present danger to a public interest of greater importance. Actually, limitations upon the right to bargain collectively have been upheld by the courts. Today, the "hot cargo" clause controversy raises the question of whether collective bargaining should be allowed if it results in what is in effect a secondary boycott. Many people think certain limitations on the right to bargain collectively are desirable; they also feel it would be difficult to demonstrate that these restrictions would result in a clear and present danger to other fundamental guarantees. The course of legislation indicates a general agreement that employees have the right to organize and to bargain with their employers; it reveals no clear-cut evidence that collective bargaining and possibly the right to organize should be removed from ordinary legislative policy determination. The constitutions of Alaska and Hawaii do not mention the right to organize and to bargain collectively in their bills of rights.

The Control of Subversion

Constitution-makers, fully aware of the deep significance of the rights that they guarantee in a constitution, also recognize the possibility that these rights may be abused. For example, communists and others may take advantage of provisions for due process of law and protection against self-incrimination. Forty-four states now have laws which penalize those who advocate the violent overthrow of the federal or state governments. Conflicts between these statutes and certain sections of state bills of rights are immediately apparent. The resolution of these conflicts is the province of the courts. Fortunately for the states, although they have vigorously denounced the decision because of certain implications, the Supreme Court of the United States in *Pennsylvania* v. *Nelson* declared the control of subversion primarily a federal responsibility. In this case the court approved the findings of a federal district court to the effect that

Sedition against the United States is not a *local* offense. It is a crime against the *Nation*. As such, it should be prosecuted and punished in the Federal courts. . . . It is not only important but vital that such prosecutions should be exclusively within the control of the Federal Government. . . .[19]

Many state officials expressed the fear that this case was an open door for the federal government to invade a field of law occupied by the states and to supersede state law with federal law. In the more recent case of *Uphaus* v.

---

[19] 350 U. S. 497, 505 (1956).

Wyman the Supreme Court held that the Nelson case was limited to the field of sedition and that federal law in the field of sedition superseded state law only when both prescribed the same conduct. Justice Clark, speaking for the court, said that the Nelson case did not take away from the states the right to protect themselves, for ". . . all the opinion proscribed was a race between federal and state prosecutors to the courthouse door."[20] States, therefore, can continue to prosecute for sedition against the state itself and can conduct investigations in this area.

Irrespective of the agency that exercises this power, control of subversion is a difficult assignment. Most citizens deplore the thoughts and deeds of communists but are also in basic agreement with the tenet of Thomas Jefferson that "to suffer the civil magistrate to intrude his powers into the field of opinion, and to restrain the profession or propagation of principles on supposition of their ill tendency, is a dangerous fallacy."[21]

Protection against Bureaucracy in Government

American political leaders of the late eighteenth century accepted the principle of the separation of powers among legislative, executive, and judicial branches of government. One important corollary of the doctrine of separation of powers in the United States is that legislative powers should not be exercised by executive officers. However, with the rapid growth in the functions of government, legislatures have increasingly delegated legislative responsibilities to executive offices. One student of government writes, with regret, that the courts have ruled in specific cases involving the delegation of powers at the federal level to the effect that at the pleasure of the bureaucracy one may not retain a radio broadcasting license; may not plant tobacco; may not raise sugar cane; must furnish demonstrators for his product to every outlet in an area regardless of circumstances; may be summarily ousted from the directorship of a bank; and may be put out of business for violation of a bureaucratic decree, after only a hearing by the prosecuting officials and decisions by them in their own premises.[22]

Bureaucracy in state government that results from too broad a delegation to officials of legislative power and that interferes unduly with individual rights should be prevented. The courts have served as a watchdog. One additional protection is to include in a bill of rights a statement more forceful than the one in the North Carolina Constitution that reads, "the legislative,

---

[20] 360 U. S. 72, 76 (1959).

[21] *Virginia Statute of Religious Liberty* (1786) in W. W. Henning, ed., *Statutes at Large of Virginia*, Vol. XII (Richmond: R. W. and G. Barton, 1823).

[22] Spencer R. Girvan, *Rule by Executive Decree under Statutory Delegations, 1789-1950*, Unpublished Ph.D. Thesis Duke University, 1957, p. 400.

executive, and supreme judicial powers of the government ought to be forever separate and distinct from each other." (Art. I, sec. 8). This provision probably offers only mild protection against bureaucratic tyranny; a stronger statement could be made to serve a real purpose.

Equal Rights

The controversy over desegregation and the decision of the Supreme Court of the United States holding that equal but separate treatment of races by states is unconstitutional have given rise to a demand that "equal treatment" statements be included in state bills of rights. This demand is made notwithstanding the protection of persons provided by the Fourteenth Amendment to the federal Constitution. Many states have adopted antidiscriminatory legislation. Writing in 1957, W. Brooke Graves reported that 15 states and 36 municipalities had established public agencies charged with the elimination of discriminatory practices.[23] This action, however, has not lessened the demand for constitutional provisions requiring equal treatment.

There has been a mixed response to this demand. The new Georgia Constitution and the proposed constitution for Florida only reiterate that "individuals are equal before the law." The constitutions of Alaska and Hawaii, however, where minority groups exist, offer eloquent examples of this type of guarantee. In the Alaska document, in addition to a provision for equal protection of the law, there is a statement that "no person is to be denied the enjoyment of any civil or political right because of race, color, creed, or national origin. The legislature shall implement this section." (Art. I, sec. 3). The Hawaii Constitution provides that no person may ". . . be denied the enjoyment of his civil rights or be discriminated against in the exercise thereof because of race, religion, sex or ancestry." (Art. I, sec. 4). The Constitution of the Commonwealth of Puerto Rico has the strongest statement on this subject:

The dignity of the human being is inviolable. All men are equal before the law. No discrimination shall be made on account of race, color, sex, birth, social origin or condition, or political or religious ideas. Both the laws and the system of public education shall embody these principles of essential human equality. (Art. II, sec. 1)

The elimination of discrimination based upon color or religion has received wide publicity; but there are other types equally important—discrimination in employment, in membership in various types of organizations, and in the giving of preferred treatment to a favored few. These matters, as well as racial discrimination, will be a concern of constitution-makers during the

---

[23] "A New Bill of Rights," op. cit., p. 241.

next few decades. It is possible that antidiscriminatory legislation will be enacted by additional states. Also, it is probable that statements against discrimination will be added to state constitutions, particularly when they are revised in convention. Other states, however, will pass over the matter and will leave protection the responsibility of the federal courts, an attitude that Graves deplores. In his view, "the problem . . . is essentially one for the states themselves. The basic responsibility is theirs."[24] With this the author agrees, although at the present time, in spite of the Supreme Court decision, there is no agreement among states on what *is* discriminatory treatment.

Procedural Rights

A basic element of all state bills of rights is the assurance to all citizens of equal treatment in the courts. In order to insure such treatment there has been included in all recent state constitutions a broad guarantee of "due process of law." The courts then have the responsibility of spelling out the exact meaning of this term in order to give fair treatment to all. It is also common practice to list in a bill of rights individual steps and requirements that are considered necessary in order to assure a fair trial to litigants and those accused of crime. Matters such as methods of indictment, jury trial, double jeopardy, self-incrimination, excessive bail, cruel and unusual punishment, and many other procedural requirements are the subject matter of these sections.

In the revision of a state constitution a statement concerning due process of law and the important procedural requirements that merit specific attention and which are vitally important to fair court procedure should be included. The Model State Constitution provides for due process of law and the equal protection of the laws, and then stipulates that an accused person

. . . shall have the right to demand a specific statement of the charges against him, and to appear and defend himself in person and by counsel; to meet the witnesses against him face to face; to have process to compel the attendance of witnesses in his behalf; and to have a speedy public trial. . . . (Art. I, sec. 106)

Double jeopardy and excessive bail are also prohibited in this Model Constitution.

The broad interpretation given by the courts to the term "due process of law" has resulted in relatively few alterations in the number and nature of procedural rights listed in any state constitution. One suggestion of particular interest concerns trial by jury. The Pennsylvania Committee on Constitutional Revision made the following statement regarding possible modification of the right to a trial by jury:

---
[24] *Ibid.,* p. 242.

As far as *criminal* trials are concerned, there can be no quarrel with this constitutional protection of the right of an accused to have his guilt or innocence determined by the unanimous vote of a jury of 12 of his "peers," and in accordance with all rules, regulations and procedures traditionally associated with the conduct of such trials. . . .

What the Commission does believe, however, is that there is no reason for such immutability in regard to jury trials in *civil* cases, and it is therefore recommending that the right to the practice in *such* cases be left to such possible legislative modifications in the future as may from time to time be deemed desirable or even essential.[25]

The Constitution of Alaska includes the following stipulations concerning the right to trial by jury (Art. I, secs. 11, 16) :

1. With respect to petty criminal offenses the Legislature may reduce the size of a jury to six if it so desires.

2. While trial by jury applies both in criminal and in civil trials, three stipulations are made with respect to civil cases:

    a. a jury trial applies only in cases where the amount in controversy is at least $250.00.

    b. a jury of not fewer than six is required in courts not of record.

    c. the Legislature may enact a law that will permit a verdict by three-fourths vote of a jury.

Space does not permit a discussion of each procedural right, but one—the right to counsel—merits consideration here. Is this a basic right and should a statement to this effect be placed in a state constitution? An accused person can rely upon three possible constitutional bases for his request for legal counsel. The first is the Fourteenth Amendment to the federal Constitution. The second is that an accused person must have legal counsel in order that he obtain due process of law under the state constitution. The third is based on a specific constitutional provision of a right to counsel.

The Sixth Amendment to the federal Constitution states that in all criminal prosecutions the accused shall have the assistance of counsel for his defense. The Supreme Court of the United States has never held that the provisions of the Sixth Amendment are included in the Fourteenth. On the contrary, the Court in *Gallegos* v. *Nebraska* held

The Federal Constitution does not command a state to furnish defendants

---

[25] *Report of Committee on Constitutional Revision* (Harrisburg: 1959), p. 18. The recently proposed constitution for the state of North Carolina also included modifications in the requirement for trial by jury. It provides for the waiving of a trial by jury in all criminal cases except when the offense charged is a felony punishable by death or life imprisonment. In other felony cases, trial by jury may be waived "only with the consent of the trial judge and counsel for the accused." In misdemeanor cases the waiver requires the approval of the trial judge only. *Proposed Constitution of North Carolina,* Art. IV, sec. 13. See 25 *Popular Government* 38 (Feb., 1959).

counsel as a matter of course. . . . Lack of counsel at state noncapital trials denies federal constitutional protection only when the absence results in a denial to accused of the essentials of justice.[26]

In many states legal counsel is considered as essential to a fair trial and, therefore, is included in the meaning of due process. Courts in various states differ, however, as to the essential character of the legal counsel requirement. Specific cases have required that the appointee must be competent and that he be given sufficient time to prepare his case.

Inclusion in state constitutions of the legal counsel requirement gains more and more favor. Quibbling by courts about the necessity of counsel in a particular case is avoided. Also, if legal aid has value it should be afforded to the poor and to the uninformed.

In conclusion, there is justification for the inclusion of particular guarantees, such as the right to counsel, in a bill of rights. Constitution-makers have not added too many stipulations. Particularly, few additions and changes have been made in the procedural requirements included—a fact that speaks well not only for the constitution-makers but also for the proper interpretation of due process by the courts.

One last point must be made regarding procedural rights. Their value must not be depreciated because certain undeserving people receive protection from them. The avoidance of giving testimony before investigatory bodies by recourse to guarantees against self-incrimination has become common, and it has resulted at times in protecting enemies of the United States. This practice notwithstanding, the recently-adopted Alaska Constitution recognizes the basic importance of protection from self-incrimination in its provision that ". . . the right of all persons to fair and just treatment in the course of legislative and executive investigations shall not be infringed." (Art. I, sec. 7)

Wiretapping and Practices of Law Enforcement Officials

One result of the hearings conducted before the Kefauver Committee on Interstate Crime was to convince the people of the United States that crime is big business and that the criminal is using the best scientific equipment to expedite his work. To cope with this situation, law-enforcement officials have also adopted new means of securing information and convictions. In the minds of many, some of these methods, particularly wiretapping, invade private rights. Many police officers, however, consider wiretapping an appropriate aid in coping with criminals.

Should a provision forbidding wiretapping and the admission of evidence gained in this manner be inserted in state constitutions? There is no clear-cut

---

[26] 342 U. S. 55, 64 (1951).

answer to this question. Most state constitutions prohibit "unwarranted search and seizures" and leave to the courts the responsibility of determining what comes within this classification. The New York Constitution of 1938 prohibits wiretapping. The Constitution of Puerto Rico has a similar section. Neither the Constitution of Alaska nor that of Hawaii mentions wiretapping.

For several reasons there has been no strong, concerted demand to include in state constitutions a provision prohibiting wiretapping. The doubt remains that wiretapping is in all cases a violation of the right of privacy.[27] Also, it is possible there is sufficient protection of the individual in the constitutional bar against unwarranted search and seizure. And the Supreme Court has said that police methods offensive to human dignity are ruled out by the due process clause of the Fourteenth Amendment.[28]

OTHER POSSIBLE RIGHTS

The states provide their citizens with many general welfare services that are well established and are recognized as proper state functions. While there are instances where these services are classified as "rights," the general conclusion is that they are not "rights" as the term is usually employed in constitutions. Refusal to classify these services as rights has been based upon possible contradiction with accepted political philosophy; upon lack of desire for the welfare state; and upon the opinion that existing bills of rights, supplemented by proper legislation, are adequate to permit giving people what they desire and should have. Demand to have these services classified as rights is based on the premise that,

They go beyond the political forms and freedoms for which our ancestors fought and which they handed on to us, because we live in a new world in which the central problems arise from new pressures of power, production, and population, which our forefathers did not face.[29]

President Franklin D. Roosevelt, an advocate of these new services, would

---

[27] One of the best statements concerning wiretapping made by a state official is that of Mr. Thomas McBride, attorney general of Pennsylvania. He expressed the personal view that "wiretapping should be banned, that there isn't sufficient good done by it to overcome the harm that is done by that feeling of loss of freedom of decent people. . . . If you could tap only a conversation between somebody you know is committing a crime, I think the feeling of men like me would be entirely different. But the line itself is tapped. . . . And I think those people should have been allowed to talk without having their conversations listened to by anybody." U. S. Congress. Senate. Committee on the Judiciary, Sub-committee on Constitutional Rights, *Wiretapping, Eavesdropping, and the Bill of Rights,* Hearings, pt. I, pp. 25-26, May 20, 1958. 85th Cong. 2d sess. on S. Res. 234 (Washington: Government Printing Office, 1958).

[28] *Rochin* v. *California,* 342 U. S. 165 (1952).

[29] National Resources Planning Board, *National Resources Development Report for 1942* (Washington: Government Printing Office, 1942), p. 4.

have added to the freedoms of speech and worship the freedom from want and the freedom from fear. He believed that the maintenance of these new freedoms is essential to the preservation of liberty within a democratic state and our way of life. To help in securing these freedoms, to protect old rights and to guarantee new ones, there was prepared during the Roosevelt administration a new declaration of rights.[30] None of the new proposals therein contained have ever been added to the federal bill of rights as such. However, the declaration is the best illustration of what is frequently referred to as "modern rights," a group of rights that constitution-makers today must consider whenever a new constitution is prepared.

The constitutions of Alaska and Hawaii are noteworthy for the omission of references to social and economic rights. One commentator, in writing about Alaska, explains this absence on these bases: (a) recent political philosophies did not affect the constitution-makers, (b) the constitutent assembly was particularly careful not to create a document that would be unacceptable to Congress, and (c) socio-economic ills are proper subjects for legislative action rather than constitutional fiats.[31]

The right to an education is the service most likely to receive general acceptance as a "right." The Constitution of North Carolina states that, "the people have a right to the privilege of education, and it is the duty of the State to guard and maintain this right." (Art. I, sec. 27) Similar provisions are found in other state constitutions. The right to medical care, to proper housing, and to work are illustrations of the subject matter of other proposed amendments. It is reasonable to believe as states provide more services for people and as the people become accustomed to receiving them, these services will become rights that the state must guarantee its citizens.

---

[30] Here is the declaration of personal rights prepared by the National Resources Planning Board in 1942:

1. The right to work, usefully and creatively through the productive years.

2. The right to fair pay, adequate to command the necessities and amenities of life in exchange for work, ideas, thrift, and other socially valuable service.

3. The right to adequate food, clothing, shelter, and medical care.

4. The right to security, with freedom from fear of old age, want, dependency, sickness, unemployment, and accident.

5. The right to live in a system of free enterprise, free from compulsory labor, irresponsible private power, arbitrary public authority and unregulated monopolies.

6. The right to come and go, to speak or to be silent, free from the spyings of secret political police.

7. The right to equality before the law, the equal access to justice in fact.

8. The right to education, for work, for citizenship, and for personal growth and happiness; and

9. The right to rest, recreation, and adventure; the opportunity to enjoy life and take part in an advancing civilization. *Ibid.*, p. 3.

[31] P. Allan Dionisopoulos, "Indiana, 1851, Alaska, 1956: A Century in State Constitutions," 34 *Indiana Law Journal* 36 (Fall, 1958).

In Conclusion

In conclusion, there is no debate over the inclusion of a bill of rights in a state constitution. Debate occurs only over the subject matter. In the words of the staff paper for the use of delegates to the Alaska Constitutional Convention, "There can be little question that the Alaska Constitution must have a bill of rights. . . . The basic question . . . is what should and should not be included. . . ."[82]

Over the years there has been no lessening in the importance of the first article of state constitutions. However, "as the historic conditions that first inspired bills of rights recede further into the dim past, the danger increases that guarantees of personal liberty will not be fully appreciated and that in a constitutional revision they will be weakened or even abandoned."[33] The present complex social and economic structure of society, with its new concepts of social and economic democracy, the possible improper use of broadening governmental powers, and the bureaucratic character of the modern state have but increased the importance of and necessity for the inclusion of guarantees of individual rights in state constitutions.

---

[82] *Civil Rights and Liberties, op. cit.*, p. 5.
[33] Hart, *op. cit.*, p. 919.

chapter X

popular control of government: suffrage and elections

O. Douglas Weeks

Provisions relating to suffrage and elections are found in all 50 state constitutions, but in none are they concentrated in a single article. Most constitutions contain one or more articles which deal exclusively with suffrage and elections, but provisions relating to the subject usually will be found also in other articles or major sub-divisions. All but 14 constitutions have one or more provisions relating to suffrage or elections in their bills or declarations of rights. Such provisions, taken together, embrace some 20 matters. Obviously, provisions relating to elective places and offices and to election arrangements always appear in the articles providing for the legislative, executive, and judiciary departments and in those devoted to local government and the process of constitutional amendment. Provisions for the legislative initiative and/or referendum are included in the legislative article in 16 states and in amendments in 6. Finally, sections affecting suffrage and elections appear in many of the "general" or "miscellaneous" articles which form a part of most state constitutions.

In this chapter the suffrage and elections provisions in bills of rights will be considered briefly. Most attention will be given to the articles devoted to suffrage and elections, because their provisions are of primary importance. Provisions located in the legislative, executive, judiciary, local government, and amendment articles which pertain specifically to elective places and offices or special elections will not be considered, because to do so would be to overlap the subject matter of other chapters in this book. Only the sections on the initiative and referendum and other general provisions relating to elections which appear in the legislative articles of some constitutions will be touched upon. Brief attention will also be directed to pertinent sections of the "miscellaneous" articles.

SUFFRAGE AND ELECTIONS IN BILLS OF RIGHTS

A simple statement guaranteeing "free elections" is to be found in the bills of rights of 21 of the 36 states which include suffrage and election provisions in these initial parts of their constitutions. In 7 the right of suffrage is protected. Religious tests are barred in 12 states,[1] property qualifications in 5. Each of the following provisions is found in the bills of rights of 2 states: barring racial tests (Alaska and Wyoming); duelists disqualified for office (Iowa and South Carolina); rotation in office (Maryland and Massachusetts); no elections or appointments for life (Mississippi and South Carolina); no political test (Tennessee and West Virginia); and the right of voters to instruct representatives (Massachusetts and New Hampshire).

Article XVIII of the Massachusetts Declaration of Rights admonishes voters to be sure of the "piety, justice, moderation, temperance, industry, and frugality" of all they elect to public office. New Hampshire inserts her basic suffrage qualifications in her bill of rights. Vermont and Virginia have provisions that voters should have a "sufficient common interest in" and "attachment to the community," whatever meaning these original bases for property qualifications may have today.

Other items, each found in 1 bill of rights only, have to do with frequent elections (New Hampshire), dual office-holding (Maryland), incompatibility of national and state office-holding (Oklahoma), residence (South Carolina), crime as a disqualification for suffrage (Texas), and guaranteeing the vote to soldiers (South Dakota).

ARTICLES ON SUFFRAGE AND ELECTIONS

Articles on suffrage and elections are numbered all the way from I to VIII in the state constitutions and bear 20-odd different titles.[2] The content of these articles varies greatly, and in length they range from 11 pages in the Alabama Constitution to a half-page in that of Tennessee. In addition to Alabama, 8 states have excessively numerous and detailed provisions.[3] The articles in half of the constitutions occupy 2 pages or less. The constitutions of Rhode Island and Tennessee distribute their suffrage and elections provisions among three articles,[4] those of Colorado, Kansas, New York, Ohio, and

---

[1] The bills of rights of Maryland and Texas require belief in God or a Supreme Being for office-holding.

[2] Twelve states label these articles "Suffrage and Elections." Others use "Suffrage," "Elections," "Franchise," "Right of Suffrage," "Elections and Officers," and so forth.

[3] California, Delaware, Louisiana, Mississippi, New York, Vermont, Virginia, and West Virginia.

[4] Rhode Island: Art. II—"Qualifications of Electors," Art. VIII, Amendment XI—"Of Elections," and Art. IX—"Of Qualifications for Office" and numerous amendments; Tennessee: Art. IV—"Elections," Art. IX—"Disqualifications," Art. X—"Oaths, Bribery of Electors, New Counties."

Pennsylvania between two.[5] The eighteenth-century constitutions of Massachusetts and New Hampshire carry provisions in their bills of rights, in scattered sections, or in numerous amendments appended at the end.

Qualifications and Disqualifications for Voting

While the content of articles on suffrage and elections is by no means standardized, sections dealing with qualifications and disqualifications for voting are invariably included. The usual qualifications relate to minimum age,[6] United States citizenship, and residence within the state and precinct.[7] Five states require the payment of a poll tax, with certain exceptions and variations;[8] 18 provide for mandatory or optional literacy tests, with varying requirements or alternatives; and 7 specifically guarantee suffrage to women. These last provisions all antedate the Nineteenth Amendment to the United States Constitution. Voter qualifications are especially detailed in the constitutions of Alabama, Georgia, Michigan, and Mississippi, the three Southern states containing requirements in addition to those mentioned above. Seven states set forth property qualifications for elections on bond issues, and Alaska provides that they may be established by law. Idaho provides that the Legislature may "prescribe qualifications, limitations, and conditions for the right of suffrage additional to those prescribed" in her Constitution. (Art. VI, sec. 4) Wisconsin has a similar provision, but subjects all such changes to a referendum. (Art. III, sec. 1) New Mexico requires an extraordinary vote of three-fourths of the electors voting and two-thirds of those voting in each county to amend her fundamental suffrage requirements. (Art. VII, sec. 3)

As has been noted, residence is universally required for voting, and many constitutions also have provisions respecting the gaining or losing of residence. Twenty-six specify that residence may not be lost as a result of absence because of federal or state employment, civil or military or both; employment in navigation; status as a student; and/or confinement in an asylum, almshouse, or prison. Twenty states provide that residence is not gained by persons in military service stationed within the state; 2 states provide that their legislatures shall determine this matter.

---

[5] Colorado: Art. VII—"Suffrage and Elections," Art. XII—"Officers"; Kansas: Art. 4—"Elections," Art. 5—"Suffrage"; New York: Art. II—"Suffrage," Art. XIII—"Public Officers"; Ohio: Art. V—"Elective Franchise," Art. XVII—"Elections"; Pennsylvania: Art. VIII—"Suffrage and Elections," Art. XII—"Public Officers."

[6] It is 21 years in all except Georgia and Kentucky (18 years), Alaska (19 years), Hawaii (20 years).

[7] Five states require 2 years in the state; 11 set 6 months; and the rest 1 year. Residence in the precinct varies from 6 months to 1 month. Two or three states permit voting in the old precinct until residence is established in the new.

[8] 8 Alabama, Arkansas, Mississippi, Texas, and Virginia. Florida makes its adoption optional.

The common disqualifications for voting apply to criminals, idiots, and the insane or mentally incapacitated. Disqualifying crimes are usually set forth in the constitutions, but 8 states provide that the legislature shall specify them in whole or in part. The South Carolina Constitution lists 19 crimes and misdemeanors conviction for which disqualifies voters; the Virginia Constitution lists 9. Convictions for dueling, bribery, election fraud, and betting on elections are added to the usual list in a few states. Idaho bars polygamists. Louisiana applies her disqualifications to registration rather than to voting. New Mexico forbids disqualification on the basis of religion, race, color, or literacy, and Utah forbids disqualification of persons without property.

Registration

Registration of voters is made mandatory by 15 state constitutions, usually for the entire state, although in most cases the form of registration and detailed provisions for it are left to legislative determination. Alaska, Delaware, and New York authorize permanent registration; Rhode Island requires it and specifies certain arrangements for it. Alabama, Louisiana, and Virginia include detailed provisions for registration procedure. South Carolina requires registration every 10 years. In 13 constitutions the legislatures are given optional authority to provide for registration for populous areas, rural areas, or the entire state. Texas limits this authority for cities of 10,000 or over, and Washington for municipalities of over 500. In other states in which the constitutions are silent on registration, the legislatures have assumed the power to provide for it under a general constitutional mandate to regulate elections and to insure their purity.

Control of Elections

At least half of the state constitutions specifically authorize the legislatures to provide for general elections and to protect them against fraud. Sometimes bribery and various types of fraud and other corrupt practices are specified. Many suffrage and elections articles have sections on the frequency and time of elections. Some deal with various matters involving election administration. Sections specifying the qualifications or disqualifications for elective office are found in several states; Colorado, New York, Pennsylvania, and Tennessee have separate articles dealing with these matters. (Arts. XII, XIII, XII, and IX, respectively) Provisions for contested election procedures are found in the suffrage and elections articles of 7 states.

Primary Elections

The suffrage and elections articles in the constitutions of only 8 states provide for primary elections,[9] these sections all having been adopted during the early years of the present century when the movement for the direct primary was at its height.

The primary provisions of 6 of these states are fairly brief. Alabama provides that "the Legislature shall make provision by law for the regulation of primary elections . . . and for punishing frauds at the same, but shall not make primary laws compulsory." (Art. VIII, sec. 190) The Arizona section reads: "The Legislature shall enact a direct primary election law, which provides for the nomination of candidates for all elective State, county, and city offices, including candidates for United States Senator and for Representatives in Congress." (Art. VII, sec. 10) Mississippi specifies that "the Legislature shall enact laws to secure fairness in party primary elections, conventions, or other methods of naming party candidates." (Art. XII, sec. 247) Louisiana has a similar provision and further requires that the primary voter must be registered and have "such other and additional qualifications as may be prescribed by the party of which candidates for public office are to be nominated" and that apportionment of delegates in all political conventions must be on the basis of population. (Art. VIII, sec. 4) The Virginia Constitution refers to primaries only incidentally by requiring registration for primary participation and by exempting members of the armed forces from poll-tax payment and registration in primaries and general elections. (Art. II, sec. 35, Art. XVII, secs. 1-3) Oklahoma requires the Legislature to provide for a mandatory primary system applicable to all parties and to all elective state, district, county, and municipal offices, provided that nomination by petition may be substituted for nonpartisan elective offices. (Art. III, sec. 5)

The California and Ohio provisions for primary elections are more detailed. California gives the Legislature power to enact laws regulating the election of delegates to party conventions and providing for direct nomination of candidates to public office. It may also make primaries mandatory and "determine the tests and conditions upon which electors, political parties, or organizations of electors may participate in any primary election." (Art. II, secs. 2½ and 2¾) The Ohio provision is even more extended and specific:

All nominations for elective state, district, county and municipal offices shall be made at direct primary elections or by petition as provided by law, and provision shall be made by law for a preferential vote for United States senator; but direct primaries shall not be held for the nomination of township officers or for the officers of municipalities of less than two thousand population, unless petitioned for by a majority of the electors of such town or municipality. All delegates from this state to the national conventions of political parties shall be

---

[9] Alabama, Arizona, California, Louisiana, Mississippi, Ohio, Oklahoma, and Virginia; South Carolina deleted all provisions relating to primaries in 1944.

chosen by direct vote of the electors. Each candidate for such delegate shall state his first and second choices for the presidency, which preferences shall be printed upon the primary ballot below the name of such candidate, but the name of no candidate for the presidency shall be so used without his written authority. (Art. V, sec. 7)

Voting

The suffrage and elections articles of nearly all state constitutions require voting by ballot in all or most elections, but in most cases the form of the ballot is not specified. Many such ballot requirements antedate the adoption of the official ballot. Only 14 states specify a secret ballot. New Jersey leaves both matters to the Legislature. Ohio requires the use of the office block ballot in general elections. (Art. V, sec. 2a) South Dakota and Texas authorize the numbering of ballots. (Art. VII, sec. 3 and Art. VI, sec. 4, respectively) Only the Louisiana Constitution contains elaborate provisions in regard to the ballot. (Art. VIII, secs. 7, 15) Absent voting is provided for in 19 constitutions. Voting machines are authorized in 12. In addition to the frequent general mandates to the legislatures to preserve the purity of elections, 21 state constitutions forbid specified corrupt practices, some allowing the legislatures to add to the constitutional list of offenses. About the same number of states insert in their suffrage and elections articles provisions regarding the qualifications of office-holders, listing in some cases conviction for certain corrupt practices as disqualifications. Thirty-two states protect voters from arrest while going to and from the polls and while at the polls, usually except for treason, felony, or breach of the peace. Some states exempt voters from military service on election day except during times of war and public danger. Finally, 6 states require plurality elections.

OTHER PROVISIONS

Recall Elections

Between 1908 and 1926, 11 states amended their constitutions to provide for the recall of public officers by means of petition followed by a special election; Alaska was added to the list in 1959.[10] Four of these states—Oregon, Nevada, Kansas, and Idaho—place the provision for the recall in the article on suffrage and elections. Louisiana inserts it under the article titled "Impeachment and Removal" (Art. IX, sec. 9) and Wisconsin in the article on "Miscellaneous Provisions" (Art. XIII, sec. 12); Alaska provides for it in a separate article titled "Initiative, Referendum, and Recall" (Art. XI) and the remainder in amendments at the end of their constitutions. All states but

---

[10] A thirteenth state having the recall, Michigan, has no provision for it in the Constitution.

Kansas restrict the recall to elective offices, from which Alaska, Louisiana, Michigan, and Washington except judges. Most of the provisions set forth procedures in detail, only Alaska and Idaho leaving them to legislative enactment.

This is not the place to discuss the merits and demerits of the recall as an election device. Suffice it to say that it has been very rarely used for state offices and therefore may be regarded as a somewhat superfluous though harmless appendage to a state constitution.[11]

Legislative Initiative and Referendum

Only the legislative initiative and referendum are considered here,[12] the constitutional initiative and/or referendum having been dealt with above in Chapter II under methods of constitutional change. Applied to ordinary lawmaking, both devices were provided for in the constitutions of 19 states between 1898 and 1918 and in that of Alaska in 1959. New Mexico in 1911 and Maryland in 1915 adopted the legislative referendum without the initiative. Idaho is the only state in which the legislature never acted to implement the constitutional provision. In 16 constitutions the initiative and/or referendum provisions appear as a part of the legislative article; in the Alaska Constitution they are in a separate article which also provides for the recall; in the remaining 5 states they are provided for in amendments attached at the end. The provisions are brief in 5 of the constitutions; in the others they are more or less detailed, running to six pages in the Arkansas and California constitutions.

No attempt will be made here to summarize the many variations and details of procedure in provisions for the initiative and referendum. Arguments for and against these devices are numerous and need not be repeated. It should be said, however, that interest in them, outside the states where they are frequently used, and except for Alaska, seems to have spent itself with the decline of the "progressive" enthusiasms of 40 or 50 years ago. The Model State Constitution, however, includes a two-page article on the initiative and referendum. (Art. IV)

Provisions in Legislative and "Miscellaneous" Articles

Some general provisions relating to elections are inserted in a few of the legislative articles of state constitutions. They involve such matters as qualifi-

---

[11] The most recent brief treatments of the recall may be found in Howard R. Penniman. *Sait's American Parties and Elections*, 5th ed. (New York: Appleton-Century-Crofts 1952), pp. 502-507, and W. Brooke Graves, *American State Government*, 4th ed. (Boston: D. C. Heath & Co., 1953), pp. 150-153.

[12] On this subject see Harvey Walker, *The Legislative Process* (New York: Ronald Press Co., 1948), chap. 22.

cations and disqualifications for elective offices, bribery, canvassing election returns, and procedures for contested elections.

Certain provisions relating to suffrage and elections also are placed in the "miscellaneous" articles of a number of constitutions. Seven states here fix terms of office; 7 make provision for oaths of office; 5 lay down rules barring nondeists, duelists, and political corruptionists from public office. Almost identical provisions appear in the new constitutions of Alaska and Hawaii disqualifying for public office any person "who advocates, or who aids or belongs to any party or organization which advocates, the overthrow by force or violence" of the government of the United States or the state. (Art. XII, sec. 4 and Art. XIV, sec. 3, respectively) Four states authorize the legislature to provide for or protect elections of public officers; 4 fix the time of elections; 3 require plurality elections; 3 determine the incompatibility of offices. Two each provide for election returns, make women eligible to school or welfare offices, provide for vacancies in office, and define bribery and assess penalties for those convicted of it. Other items appearing in single constitutions have to do with qualifications for office, reinstatement of officers returning from military service, military absent voting for local office, absence on state or federal business in relation to residence, contested elections, election of United States senators, and allowing residents on Indian lands to vote at the nearest outside polling place.

CONCLUSIONS

From this brief review of the suffrage and elections provisions of the state constitutions several conclusions and suggestions may be drawn. In the first place, it would seem that, so far as possible, these provisions should be concentrated in a single article. Certainly, there is no particular reason why any should appear in bills of rights or in the "miscellaneous" articles. In states that provide for the recall and the initiative and referendum, a separate article might well be devoted to them. Only the Alaska Constitution has such an article. The Model State Constitution places the initiative and referendum in a separate article (Art. IV), although it is not illogical to insert brief provisions for them under the legislative article, as most states providing for them do. In such cases the recall might best be placed under the article on suffrage and elections, as is done in 4 constitutions. Provisions for elective places and elections under the legislative, executive, judiciary, local government, and constitutional amendment articles would seem to belong under such articles, which is the arrangement in most state constitutions. Elections, of course, would be improved if the short ballot were universally adopted with respect to executive, judicial, and local government offices. The new constitutions of Alaska and Hawaii are models in this respect. In most states, however, such provisions would involve fundamental reform.

The suffrage and elections articles of most state constitutions are sufficiently brief; the important question is whether they contain what should properly be in a constitution. The one-page article on the subject in the Model State Constitution (Art. II) may be as good a guide as any to those charged with amending or drafting a state constitution, although specifying a minimum age of 18 for voters and requiring permanent registration may be questioned in some situations. Certainly, no uniform set of provisions can be suggested that will fit all the states.[13] Perhaps all that need be said here is that only general and fundamental requirements should be set down—those fixing the basic qualifications and disqualifications for voting and providing in a brief way for residence, absent voting, registration of voters, methods of voting, election officers, and the times of elections. Beyond these provisions, detailed arrangements should be left for statutory determination.

[13] Model State Constitution, page 26. For exhaustive treatment and valuable suggestions on suffrage provisions, see: Kirk H. Porter, "Suffrage Provisions in State Constitutions, 13 *American Political Science Review* 577-92 (Nov., 1919).

chapter XI

the executive article

Louis E. Lambert

A feeble Executive implies a feeble execution of the government. A feeble execution is but another phrase for a bad execution: and a government ill executed, whatever it may be in theory, must be, in practice, a bad government.

Taking it for granted, therefore, that all men of sense will agree in the necessity of an energetic Executive, it will only remain to inquire, what are the ingredients which will constitute this energy? How far can they be combined with those other ingredients which constitute safety in the republican sense?[1]

HISTORICAL BACKGROUND

Hamilton's statement about the Presidency also brings the problems of the modern American state executive into sharp focus: the joining of authority with responsibility. The state governors at the time Hamilton wrote occupied a pitifully weak office. Madison at the Constitutional Convention had shrugged them off as "cyphers."[2]

The recently created office of state governor consciously and deliberately had been made weak because throughout much of the Colonial period the people had regarded the governor as a symbol of British tyranny. His had been a powerful office, frequently filled, as Charles and Mary Beard have noted, by men who were "frankly coarse and brutal . . . with the morals and manners of an English drill sergeant."[3] Though this description did not fit all of them, most were interested, as the Beards have said, in the increase

---

[1] Alexander Hamilton, *The Federalist*, No. 70 (New York: The Modern Library, 1941), p. 455.

[2] "Experience had proved a tendency in our governments to throw all power into the Legislative vortex. The Executives of the States are in general little more than Cyphers; the legislatures omnipotent." Charles S. Tansill, ed., *Formation of the Union of the American States* (Washington: Government Printing Office, 1927), p. 398.

[3] Charles A. and Mary R. Beard, *The Rise of American Civilization* (New York: Macmillan Co., 1930), Vol. I, p. 113.

of their private fortunes, and the post of governor offered considerable possibilities in this direction. The governor made appointments to many posts, administrative, judicial, and military, and even gave livings where the Church of England was established. But the colonial governor did not limit himself to the filling or granting of positions and the confirming of land grants; he also tried to lead the colonial assemblies, and to persuade them to authorize expenditures for projects devised in England for imperial purposes.

The Colonial legislatures, for their part, vigorously resisted the governors and succeeded in creating a picture of them as the embodiments of British tyranny. The reaction of the constitution-drafters in the period 1776-80 was to make the state executive weak. In fact, the provisions of these first state constitutions relating to the governor made him little more than a ceremonial figurehead. Only in Massachusetts and New York was he elected; in the other states the legislature appointed not only the governor but also a council to serve with and check him. Other executive officers who were independent of the governor also were appointed by the legislature. The governor's term of office ordinarily was one year, and strong statements in the constitutions on the separation of powers were mainly to prevent the governor from assuming any legislative leadership. Only in Massachusetts and South Carolina did the governor have a veto. Having virtually no power to appoint or remove, the governor had little authority to see that the laws were executed. Leslie Lipson repeats a story about a delegate returning home from the North Carolina convention. When asked how much power the constitution-makers had given the governor, he answered: "Just enough to sign the receipt for his salary."[4]

The framers at the Philadelphia Convention agreed, after vigorous debate, that a strong executive was needed—one who could exercise leadership and protect himself against attempts at legislative dominance. Though persons concerned with improving the office of governor have always considered the powers of the President, they have never succeeded, except possibly in New Jersey in 1947, in gaining comparable authority for the governor.

During the nineteenth century, however, legislatures caused alarm as they demonstrated that they were not able to use wisely the virtually unchecked authority given to them. To curb legislative profligacy and corruption, the constitutions of the Jacksonian period increased the powers of the governor by lengthening his term, usually to four years, and by granting him greater authority to appoint, pardon, and veto. Also, the office became elective, and as restrictions upon white male suffrage were lifted in the states, the governor,

---

[4] Leslie Lipson, *The American Governor from Figurehead to Leader* (Chicago: University of Chicago Press, 1939), p. 14.

as the chief officer with a statewide constituency, began to reflect and express public wishes.

Jacksonian democracy, however, also brought disadvantages where the governorship was concerned. A number of state administrative offices were created, and popular democracy decreed that they should be filled by the action of the voters. As the governor moved into a position of political leadership, he simultaneously suffered a loss in administrative control.

Following the Civil War, the farmer discontent that developed in several midwestern states found expression chiefly in legislation designed to curb the abuses of the railroads. But the discontents of the farmers in the 1870's did not leave much mark upon state government. While not always the independent, self-sufficient yeoman that Jefferson had envisaged, the farmer actually wanted relatively little from government.

During the 1880's and 1890's, however, urban dwellers, who progressively became a larger proportion of the population in the states east of the Mississippi River and north of the Ohio, demanded more services. The tempo of industrialization and urbanization increased, with the large manufacturing corporation as the dynamic force, and the laborer and the small businessman, feeling a threat to their health and welfare, turned to the state for protection and assistance. As specific groups agitated for particular services, political leaders, understandably, responded. Whether or not the governor had a part in expressing these demands, the response of the legislature was to "pass a law" to provide for the new service and to create an administrative body to execute the law.

Almost never was the governor given any control over these new agencies. After prescribing their duties and appropriating operating funds for their use, the legislatures tried to maintain control over them through legislative supervisory committees. Administrative direction generally was exercised by boards or commissions whose members were appointed by legislatures or governors or were popularly elected. Seldom was any recognition given to the concept of administrative leadership by the governor.

The first decade of the twentieth century prepared the way for change. Such muckrakers as Lincoln Steffens revealed with careful documentation that state political machines and state governments were controlled by "bosses" or "interests" or, frequently, by bosses for interests. Dissatisfaction was expressed with the way public affairs were being conducted on every level of government. Adoptions of the direct primary and the initiative, referendum, and recall as devices of direct democracy reflected this public dissatisfaction. Reformers agitated for the adoption of the commission form of city government and propaganda increased for woman suffrage, popular election of senators, and a progressive tax on incomes. Finding strength in deeply felt, widespread popular support, such governors as Robert M. LaFollette of Wisconsin, Hiram Johnson of California, Theodore Roosevelt of New York, and Woodrow Wilson of New Jersey announced bold legislative programs and led the way to their enactment. But even the strong governors experienced frustration when they tried to enforce the laws. The complaint of a former governor of Massachusetts of this period is atypical only in its eloquence:

> The Governor has absolutely no authority over a commission in this State. By condescension, by favor, he is permitted by the legislature to name the members of boards and with certain restrictions to remove them. . . . The Governor has no constitutional authority to issue an order to a single board in this State. . . . You give him no power. You tie his hands. You check him at every turn by an Executive Council. Yet the people hold him responsible for the efficient management of the State's business affairs.[5]

The belief that the governor should have authority to match, or at least roughly to approximate, his responsibility grew throughout the second decade of the present century. It is a goal still being pursued, sometimes vigorously, sometimes lackadaisically, but never quite attained.

Any revision of the executive article of state constitutions must take account of the movement for administrative reorganization that has developed since 1915, at times enlisting great public interest and support and at others becoming nearly quiescent. This movement is supported by the theory that certain "principles" of organization and administration are applicable in all states. "Efficiency" generally is accepted as the primary value to be attained, and "responsibility" and commensurate "authority" always are recognized.

Vigorous dissents to the basic assumptions of the movement, however, are almost as old as theories relating to the ends of reorganization. Professor Francis W. Coker, in his articles titled "Dogmas of Administrative Reform, as Exemplified in the Recent Reorganization of Ohio," in the *American Political Science Review* of August, 1922, was among the first to raise questions. Professors Harvey Walker and Charles S. Hyneman in the 1930's also questioned the basic assumptions. The following query of Hyneman is frequently quoted. After asserting that there are many grounds for discontent with American state government besides its inefficiency and wastefulness, he asks:

> What does the administrative reorganization program designed to achieve efficiency and economy offer to the man whose chief concern is that vision, imagination, and courage predominate in the execution, adaptation, or modification of policy?[6]

---

[5] Quoted in Lipson, *op. cit.*, p. 46.
[6] Charles S. Hyneman, "Administrative Reorganization: An Adventure into Science and Theology," 1 *Journal of Politics* 66 (Feb., 1939).

In the following decade Dwight Waldo in *The Administrative State* (1948) made a full-scale, systematic attack upon the basic assumptions on which the administrative reorganization movement was based. Herbert A. Simon in *Administrative Behavior* (1947) likewise sharply challenged orthodox theories. The cumulative effect of the works of these writers and others of kindred views has been to shake the earlier assurance and confidence of political scientists concerned with the theory or practice of administrative reorganization. The basic recommendation of the dissenters seems to be that the problems of each state should be considered individually; any recommendations relating to reorganization should come only after research in depth into group structures within and outside the administration and into intergroup rivalries.

Recognizing the rich diversity among our states—in area, geography, communication and transportation facilities; in the population elements of race, national origins, minority groups, urban-rural ratios, densities; in cultural patterns relating to education, religion, occupational groups; in history, customs, traditions, and beliefs; in politics, with the bewildering variations of one-party control, two-party struggles, and the in-between systems—the writer also recognizes the elements of uniformity that exist. All of our states have written constitutions that set up a republican form of government based upon a separation of powers. The governor, the legislators, and most (but not all) of the judges are popularly elected to specific terms of office. All of the states encounter problems in their relationships with one another and with the federal government. The demand for services continues to grow at an ever-accelerating rate, with a consequent urgency to provide additional funds. In no state have discerning observers reported an entirely satisfactory system of administrative organization. Probably the call of Professor Hyneman for "vision, imagination, and courage . . . in the execution, adaptation, or modification of policy" cannot be attained by institutional arrangements, by the granting or the withholding of certain powers. This is not to admit, however, that such institutional arrangements are not important.

Though the principles of administrative reorganization have not been proved scientifically, some claims, such as the desirability of an integrated administrative system under a governor who has authority to go with his responsibility, make considerable appeal to common sense. In the most recent full-scale study of the American governor in action, based upon interviews and studies in 25 states, Professor Ransone, though conscious of the attacks upon the orthodox theory of administrative reorganization, still supports the strong-governor theory:

> The whole tenor of this book is to emphasize the need for a strong governor who is equipped with both the powers and staff necessary to do an adequate job

in the formation of policy, in the explanation of that policy to the citizens of the state, and in the supervision of the agencies who will carry that policy to fruition.[7]

Most of the writers who prepared the research reports for the American Assembly of 1955, published as *The Forty-Eight States,* assumed that it was desirable to have a governor with adequate authority and responsibility. The present writer concurs in this view. His recommendations with supporting arguments, as space allows, will relate, first, to strengthening the governor so that he can provide legislative and administrative leadership; and, second, to ensuring that the strong governor shall be controllable by means of democratic institutions.

In revising a constitution it is never possible to make a completely fresh start. Arrangements that have been made to accommodate geographical, racial, urban-rural, and other differences tend to persist and some power positions may not be challenged even in the framing of a new constitution. One telling illustration is the complicated system of pledges placed upon delegates not to change the system of representation in the New Jersey Legislature, a price rural interests could exact before allowing a convention to be held.[8] When theories of good administrative organization come into conflict with hard political realities, the theories seldom win, and the leaders of reorganization must argue as persuasively as possible without being doctrinaire and must accept a half or quarter loaf when a full loaf cannot be obtained. It seems worth observing that even when administrative integration was a new idea that was presented with great assurance and confidence, no state ever completely adopted it in practice even though it accepted the idea in principle. Yet improvements have been made and governors now have powers that give them a much better chance than their nineteenth and early twentieth century predecessors had of performing their duties satisfactorily. Administrative organization and management have improved greatly since the 1920's, even though the improvement has been on an unsystematic, piecemeal basis. For most states a constitutional revision seems to offer the best chance of achieving a rounded orderly modernization of the executive department.

A More Effective Executive

Constitutional revision to make the executive branch of state government more effective and responsible must start with the office of governor. The first

---

[7] Coleman B. Ransone, Jr., *The Office of the Governor in the United States* (University: University of Alabama Press, 1956), p. 281.

[8] Bennett M. Rich, *The Government and Administration of New Jersey* (New York: Thomas Y. Crowell, 1957), p. 25.

Hoover Commission's statement from its first report puts the argument succinctly: .

The President, and under him his chief lieutenants, the department heads, must be held responsible and accountable to the people and the Congress for the conduct of the executive branch.

Responsibility and accountability are impossible without authority—the power to direct. The exercise of authority is impossible without a clear line of command from the top to the bottom, and a return line of responsibility and accountability from the bottom to the top.[9]

By substituting the word *governor* for *President* and the word *legislature* for *Congress,* this quotation becomes applicable to state government. It is not an accurate description, however, of the office of governor, for nowhere is such unity of command achieved. Though concentration of authority and responsibility in the chief executive is always a prime principle of reorganization, it is never completely attained—not in the Presidency of the United States or in the Governorship of New Jersey.

The case for an integrated executive office, however, is strong. First, since the governor is the political leader of his state, whose election attracts the greatest interest, he is held politically accountable for every important thing done (or not done) by public officers during his administration. The power to stimulate or to curb and control these officers should belong to the governor as a consequence of his political leadership and political accountability.

Second, "the activities of the government should be consistent; and the more independent agencies, the more possibilities for inconsistencies. An integrated, systematic, and rational program of activities for state government calls for an integrated, systematic, and rational arrangement of administrative agencies."[10] Such a program and such an arrangement of administrative agencies can be attained only through a governor who can direct and control.

If it is granted that a strong, responsible governor provides the best hope both for legislative and for administrative leadership, the constitutional means to attain that end may now be considered.

Term

The desirability of a four-year term now generally is accepted and all recent constitutional changes have been from a shorter term to the four-year term. Only 15 states still retain the two-year term and Minnesota will go to a four-

[9] Commission on the Organization of the Executive Branch of Government, *General Management of the Executive Branch* (Washington, D. C.: Government Printing Office, 1949), p. 1.

[10] York Willbern, "Administration in State Governments," in *The Forty-Eight States* (New York: The American Assembly, 1955), p. 119.

year term in 1962.[11] The trend toward a longer term since 1895 may be realized from the following statement from a book published in that year: "[The governor's] term of office, in nineteen states, [is] four years; in two states, three years; in twenty one states, two years; and in two states, Massachusetts and Rhode Island, one year."[12]

But whether the governor may succeed himself, or whether he may succeed himself more than once, remains a controversial question. The knowledge he may gain from serving several terms must be weighed against the possibility that he may amass a too heavy concentration of power. Though some notably successful New York governors have served several terms, neither Missouri nor New Jersey, the states which most recently revised their constitutions, adopted unlimited succession. While the Constitution of Alaska limits the Governor to "two full successive terms," the Constitution of Hawaii, the newest state, does not restrict the succession of the Governor. The limitation placed upon the presidential term by the Twenty-second Amendment, however, suggests that there is considerable opposition to the idea of unlimited succession, although 24 states still permit it.

Election

It seems desirable to separate state politics from national and to elect the governor and the state legislators upon state issues uninfluenced by the glamour of a presidential candidate or by grievances against a national administration. Only 11 states elect their governors to a four-year term during the presidential election, although there are 16 states that elect governors in every even-numbered year. Twenty-three states never elect governors during presidential elections,[13] a policy that seems wise, since it permits the voters to focus on state condidates and their programs and not be overwhelmed by the drama of electing a president.

Legislative Powers

Since the governor ordinarily runs on a legislative platform and generally is accepted by the public as an initiator of policy, he should have effective tools of legislative leadership. The right to address a joint session of the legislature at the beginning of the session for the purpose of presenting his program should be provided for in the state constitution. As emergencies arise, the governor also should be able to address the legislature to make policy recommendations.

---

[11] *The Book of the States 1960-1961* (Chicago: The Council of State Governments, 1960), p. 122.

[12] James Bryce, *The American Commonwealth*, 3d ed. (New York: Macmillan Co., 1895), Vol. I, p. 494.

[13] *The Book of the States 1960-1961*, p. 122.

A veto power is not just a shield with which the governor may protect himself and his branch of government; it can also be a sword. If the governor has the item veto and if his veto can be overriden only by a two-thirds vote in each house, he is in a strong bargaining position. To get their own particular bills enacted into law, legislators will have to come to terms with the governor on measures he considers to be of first importance.

The amount of legislation passed each session and its increasing complexity suggests the desirability of allowing the governor at least 15 days to determine his action on a bill. After legislative adjournment, the governor should have a longer period than most state constitutions now provide to decide whether bills passed in the last days of a session shall become law. The New Jersey provision allowing the governor 45 days does not seem unreasonable. The New Jersey conditional veto, which permits the Governor to recommend amendments to a submitted bill that can become valid by majority action of both houses, gives him almost the power of a third house. It is worth careful consideration.

The provision of the Model State Constitution to permit the governor and his chief officers to introduce and debate bills in the legislature (but without voting on them) seems not to have attracted much support. It seems unlikely that a constitution-revising body would give it serious consideration.

Along with granting the governor power to call special sessions of the legislature, a constitutional provision may also give him the authority to determine what business is to be considered and to forbid the legislature to consider any other business in the special session.

With such powers to call on, the governor should be able to provide the legislative leadership that is desirable. There can be no guarantee, of course, that the governor always will lead wisely in the general interest, but he can be checked by a bare majority of one house if his proposals are considered not sound. All of the powers listed, however, will be of little avail if the governor chooses, consciously or unconsciously, not to use them. If the governor becomes overwhelmed by the ceremonial aspects of his office, the hard decisions of legislative leadership may be abdicated. Various persons and groups then will move in to fill the vacuum and the public interest may not be well served.

Executive Powers

In addition to the usual grant of "executive power" or the power to see that the "laws be faithfully executed," the governor should be strengthened by an authorization such as that provided by the 1947 New Jersey Constitution:

. . . To this end he shall have power, by appropriate actions or proceeding in the courts brought in the name of the State, to enforce compliance with any constitutional or legislative mandate, or to restrain violation of any constitutional or legislative power or duty, by any officer, department or agency of the State; but this power shall not be construed to authorize any action or proceeding against the Legislature. (Art. V, sec. 1, para. 11)

Basic to the executive function is the power to appoint and remove department heads. Elective department heads and heads appointed by boards, perhaps for terms longer than the term of the governor, may be cajoled and influenced, they may recognize the party leadership of the governor, they may cooperate, but *authority* to require cooperation is lacking in such situations. The New Jersey Constitution gives the Governor power to appoint all department heads except the secretary of state and the attorney general, subject to the approval of the Senate, and these appointees serve at the pleasure of the Governor. His removal power, however, does not extend to the members of boards and commissions. The appointment and removal powers of the New Jersey Governor conform with the main stream of American administrative thinking, supported by United States Supreme Court decisions regarding the powers of the Presidency.

A model statement of the military authority that the governor should have is made in the 1954 amendment to the Constitution of Minnesota:

. . . He [the governor] shall be commander-in-chief of the military and naval forces, and may call out such forces to execute the laws, suppress insurrection and repel invasion. (Art. V, sec. 4.)

These recommendations for strong executive powers are those called for in orthodox reorganization theory. For persons who accept the powers of the President as they are, there is nothing particularly novel about them.

Administrative Powers

Administrative powers are separated from executive powers for purposes of exposition. Administrative powers here are thought of primarily as the day-to-day relationships between the governor and the officers serving under him, particularly the department heads.

If the authority of the governor to direct and supervise is to be effective, the number of agencies he administers must be manageable. The creation of an unwieldy number of agencies in state governments from the close of the Civil War until 1917 was one of the chief contributors to the early reorganization movement. Though no formula exists for discovering the "one best number" of departments, the maximum number mentioned in the "Little Hoover reports" was 20, the number provided in the New Jersey and the New York constitutions and also in the Alaska and Hawaii constitutions. The 9 suggested by the Oklahoma Legislative Council appears to be the smallest number recommended. Until some number is accepted as scientific, the 9 to 20 figure can be taken as reasonable. Whatever the maximum number is, it should be stated in the constitution as a means of preventing the legislature from bowing to the various pressures opposed to integration. The names of departments should not be specified in the constitution, however, since such listing will make the administrative structure rigid. Within the constitutional maximum, the governor and legislature should establish the departmental structure through formal statutory action. Since the administrative structure will need adjustment from time to time, the governor should have authority to initiate changes to shift agencies from department to department or even to consolidate departments. Any plans for change should be submitted to the legislature and unless rejected by a majority in each house within a specified length of time should become law.

To strengthen his supervisory powers, the governor should have a grant such as that provided in the 1954 Minnesota amendment:

. . . He may require the opinion, in writing, of the principal officer in each of the executive departments upon any subject relating to the duties of their respective offices. . . . (Art. V, sec. 4.)

A governor's "cabinet" is frequently mentioned in textbooks and administrative reorganization plans. So far as the writer can determine in no state has a cabinet become a permanent feature, though it has been tried a number of times and discarded. Since the recommended power over department heads would allow the governor to call all or any number of them into conference at any time, it seems neither necessary nor desirable to include a provision for a cabinet in the constitution.

A DEPARTMENT OF ADMINISTRATION

As an aid in providing administrative leadership, the governor should be served by a department of administration headed by a chief director and composed of such divisions as budget, personnel, planning, purchasing, accounting, and preauditing, each headed by a director. Since they will work in an intimate relationship with the governor, the chief director and the division directors should be appointed by the governor (without senatorial confirmation) and should serve at his pleasure. Perhaps only the office of chief director should be named in the constitution, with an unspecified number of "division directors" referred to, so that the governor or the legislature can reorganize the department to meet current needs. The chief director will be responsible to the governor, and the division directors will be responsible to the chief director.

Before discussing the work of the department of administration, it is necessary to state the assumptions that are being made about the legislature, particularly since the discussion will start with budgeting, which is the crux of executive-legislative relations. First, it is assumed that the legislative session will not begin until at least two months, and preferably three, after the election of the governor. If the session begins in January following the November election, the governor, exhausted by a hard campaign and with many patronage problems facing him, hardly has "an opportunity to take the initiative in the most encompassing set of policy decisions that a legislative session makes. . . . Budget decisions are, on a more general level, decisions on tax rates and tax policy and on the general scale of state activity."[14] Of course, the governor of a one-party state would have more time to engage in budget decisions before the legislative session convenes.

Second, it is assumed that the legislature will meet in annual sessions. If annual full-scale sessions are not acceptable, a brief budget-appropriation session in even-numbered years will allow the budget period to be kept to one year and thus permit greater precision in estimating revenues and expenditures.

Third, the legislature should devise effective methods for critically evaluating the budget estimates. Perhaps career employees of the postauditing agency (considered below) could be attached to finance committees of the legislature to help get the facts and significant background information. In California the legislative auditor "has the duty of maintaining liaison with the executive departments on fiscal matters and of providing the legislature with estimates by which to judge the soundness of the governor's budget."[15] Ransone also reports on developments of the same nature in Oklahoma and Wisconsin. The curious legislative-executive budget of Indiana provides for two senators and two representatives, ordinarily outstanding leaders in their houses and parties, to have an important role in budget preparation and execution.

Finally, it is assumed that an auditor will be selected by joint action of the two houses to be the director of a postauditing agency, an organ of the legislature. In addition to regular selective postaudits of the financial transactions of all state agencies, checking not only for accuracy of the accounts but also considering the legality of the actions of the administrative officers, the staff members would be available for special investigations. Inefficient and improper, even if not necessarily illegal, practices could be discovered and reported to an appropriate committee of the legislature. Evidence of illegal practices would be turned over to the governor to be transmitted to the attorney general for prosecution.

---

[14] Karl A. Bosworth, "Lawmaking in State Governments," in *The Forty-Eight States* (New York: The American Assembly, 1955), p. 106.

[15] Ransone, *op. cit.*, p. 284.

Budgeting plays a significant role in the leadership function of the governor. The budget function should be provided for in the constitution. The remaining staff functions—personnel, planning, accounting, and preauditing —will not be discussed, since they should be established for law rather than by constitutional provision. In addition to providing for the usual powers of the governor over an executive budget, it is recommended that the legislature not be permitted to increase the amount of an appropriation item (though it may decrease or eliminate the item) and that its power to add new items be restricted. The bills embodying the budget should be passed before any other appropriations are considered. The right of designated representatives of legislative committees to attend departmental budget hearings and to make inquiries also should be provided for in the constitution. A quarterly allotment system for budget execution also should be provided, as well as an authorization to the governor to reduce appropriated funds to departments when revenues fall below estimates. The chief model for these recommendations is the constitutional budget authority of the Governor of New York. The effectiveness of this system is attested to by Professor Lynton K. Caldwell.[16]

The most serious challenge to the executive budget as the vehicle of gubernatorial policy is the practice of earmarking funds; the most common example is limiting the use of gasoline taxes to highway purposes. Departments financed by earmarked funds are largely outside the financial control of the governor. Professor Ransone reports that in some states the governor can exercise control over no more than one-third or one-quarter of the total expenditures. To prevent this weakening of the executive budget, the Georgia Constitution, Art. VII, sec. 9, para. 4, prohibits the allocation of any particular tax or fund for any particular object.

When these budgeting powers here described are joined to his veto powers, the governor should be able to exert both legislative and administrative leadership.

KEEPING THE GOVERNOR RESPONSIBLE

The above recommendations have been made with a view to strengthening the governor by giving him the powers needed to provide leadership in state government. The question then arises: Will a governor with such powers be controllable by anything other than his own character and personal integrity? Will such a concentration of authority in one office affront our concept of limited government? The writer believes not. Numerous curbs on executive power exist.

Legislative power is the first and most immediate curb on the executive. In

---

[16] Lynton K. Caldwell, *The Government and Administration of New York* (New York: Thomas Y. Crowell, 1954), pp. 229-36.

recommending the strengthening of the office of governor it was assumed that the legislature also would be strengthened. The legislature would have an important role in budgeting, with representatives of legislative committees sitting in on budget hearings and having a significant part in budget execution. The postauditing body, to be as much an agency of the state legislature as the General Accounting Office is of the Congress, would permit the legislature to be fully informed on actions by the administrative organization directed by the governor. The staff of auditors would be available to carry on investigations of particular agencies, either under a broad grant of power or, preferably, under the direction of a legislative committee. The possible airing of faults and errors would serve to keep the governor and his administrative leaders on the alert. Misconduct and betrayal of public trust could be discovered and punished. Less dramatic, but perhaps more important, would be the fact that the legislative leadership would be informed so that the executive's budget could be debated intelligently. The original legislative power—the control of the purse strings—would be strengthened.

The courts ordinarily are not considered as agencies of control over the governor; none of the persons interviewed by Professor Ransone in his study of the office of the governor mentioned them in this connection. If, however, the governor is made responsible for the acts of his department heads, as has been recommended, he is involved in any errors or mistakes that they may make. Administrative agencies can be subjected to grand jury investigation, and if prosecutions and convictions follow, the governor certainly will have been controlled by the courts. The threat that the courts may be used to hold the administration in line has a salutary effect upon the governor and his department heads. Though the concept of the separation of powers today is not that held by John Adams at the time of the adoption of the Massachusetts Constitution, it still has vitality.

The political system also serves as a check upon the executive. A governor who has offended the standards of the community cannot be re-elected; neither can he expect to see his chosen successor win his place. This form of control may come slowly, however, personality and current issues playing the part that they do in politics. Do our state political systems provide any means of controlling a governor on a current basis? Certainly a strongly competitive two-party system, with the "outs" on the alert to discover and exploit any errors in administration, can serve as a curb on the executive and his assistants. Less than a majority of the states, however, have strongly competitive two-party systems. No mechanical contrivance for control can take the place of a competing party.

Political factions in a one-party state, and to lesser degree in the two-party state, can also be effective in persuading the executive to adopt and follow suitable policies. Public esteem can be gained by the group that discovers errors in policy or administration, and this esteem may be converted into political support. The more tightly the avenues to political advancement are closed to the "out" group or groups of the party, the greater the likelihood that errors will be discovered and exploited.

The maverick, the gadfly, the "spokesman for the people" can force the administration to justify its decisions, actions, and procedures. Such individuals, not concerned with moving up the political ladder, can attack vigorously and often effectively.

Even though a truly competitive two-party system does not exist in a number of the states, there is a well-developed pattern of interest or pressure groups in every state. As decisions are made or actions taken that affect a particular interest adversely, the reactions of the group and its spokesman are likely to be sharp and immediate. The group also may be successful in enlisting the support of other interest groups.

Finally, all dissenters, whether individuals or groups, can appeal to public opinion. Newspaper columnists, political reporters, radio and television commentators make available the facts and their interpretation of them. If there is evidence of indiscretion or wrongdoing in the executive branch, demands will be made for more facts for public scrutiny. Opposition elements, inside and outside the party, will be solicited for "views and opinions." Special interests will prepare statements for the public press and also will put forward their arguments in their own publications. Even though the vast majority of the people will be quiescent, well organized minorities can bring pressure directly upon the governor and other administrators through vigorous propaganda tactics that are likely to be heeded. With such methods available, the slow, cumbersome procedure of recall hardly seems realistic as a control device. Like impeachment, however, it can serve as a deterrent to sponsorship by a governor of policies not in the public interest.

A strong governor with an integrated administrative system, with appointive department heads responsible to him, with a strong staff to aid him in controlling the administrative machinery, even with effective tools for legislative leadership, does not have the powers of a dictator. He can be checked by the legislative and judicial branches of the government. Elements in the political system also will operate to check him if he or his immediate subordinates act in a way that appears detrimental to the public interest. Such a governor will be down front, center stage, with the spotlight on him all of the time. He will be answerable to the public for his own conduct and that of his subordinates. He will have to accept the blame for failures, but he can lead his state government not only with efficiency but perhaps even with courage, imagination, and vision.

chapter XII

the legislative article

Charles W. Shull

The legislative article of a state constitution should accomplish several objectives in a minimum number of words. First, it should bring a lawmaking power and body into existence. Second, it should determine the basis of representation for the chambers that are created. Also, it should state the major legislative powers to be exercised by the lawmaking body and, where desired or necessary, it should prescribe the way in which these powers may be utilized.

BICAMERALISM VS. UNICAMERALISM

The choice of the number of chambers to be created by the legislative article is strictly limited. American practice sanctions only the unicameral and the bicameral forms. At present, 49 American states have bicameral or two-chambered legislatures; Nebraska is the only state with a single-house legislature.

The decision as to whether the legislature will have one or two houses is basic. The weight of experience among the American states is heavily on the side of the bicameral system, despite unicameral operation at various times in Delaware, Georgia, Pennsylvania, Vermont, and Nebraska.[1] The operation of the two-house national Congress has been more successful than the operation of bicameral state legislatures, where procedural and other difficulties have been compounded in the relatively involved and complex operation of the two-chamber system. The basis of representation is also a greater problem in a bicameral legislature. The apparent simplicity of opera-

---

[1] The colonial legislatures of Delaware, Georgia, and Pennsylvania were unicameral. Delaware changed to bicameralism at the time of the Revolution, Georgia in 1789, Pennsylvania in 1790. Vermont entered the Union with a one-house legislature which it maintained until 1836. Nebraska became unicameral in 1937.

tion of the one-house assembly is demonstrated by the recent experience of Nebraska.[2]

Factors Affecting the Choice of Type

Factors which must be balanced in the choice between bicameralism and unicameralism are: (a) the weight of the tradition of bicameralism in the United States; (b) the argument of operational efficiency advanced in favor of unicameralism at the state level; (c) the determination of whether two distinct bases of representation can be found and will be used in the bicameral system; (d) the force of the argument that interest or pressure groups can, in the long run, control one body more easily than two; (e) a view recently voiced by Professor E. E. Schattschneider[3] that devices such as bicameralism operate to socialize conflict and thus to contain the wilder impacts of social forces, and have value to the extent that they accomplish this result.

The question of the number of legislative chambers must be met at the outset in any general or basic revision of a state constitution, and the choice is not an easy one. Justice Holmes' remark about the relationship of general propositions to the settlement of concrete cases applies to this decision, and it is not certain that either unicameralism or bicameralism should be employed in each and every state. The decision as to the number of chambers in a state legislature is intertwined with the question of the bases of representation.

There are states in which arduous search and penetrating analysis will fail to turn up more than one feasible, reasonably effective basis of representation. In others, the length of operation under a bicameral system may be the deciding factor for the retention of that type of legislative organization and structure.

State constitution-makers in the future should give consideration to the possibility of instituting a single-house legislature. Failure to face this problem in a realistic manner is to admit difficulty in the areas of representation and apportionment.

The Problem of Apportionment

With the determination of the number of chambers and their descriptive specification in the text of the legislative article of a state constitution there arises the over-all problem of apportionment. As has been pointed out by the

---

[2] For a convenient review and appraisal of the Nebraska experience, see Belle Zeller, ed., *American State Legislatures* (New York: Thomas Y. Crowell Co., 1954) Appendix A, pp. 240-55. This is the Report of the Committee on American Legislatures of the American Political Science Association. Also: A. C. Breckenridge, *One House for Two* (Washington, D. C.: Public Affairs Press, 1957).

[3] "Intensity, Visibility, Direction and Scope," 51 *American Political Science Review*, 933-42 (Dec., 1957).

author elsewhere, this problem of apportionment is composed of four factors.[4] These are the size of the chambers, the bases of representation, the frequency of reapportionments, and the mode or method of apportionment.

Constitutional provisions may relate to any or all of these matters. Since each is complex and inherently controversial, it will be appreciated that these provisions in the legislative article will be born of conflict and will beget controversy.

Size of Chambers

The temptation will be present to specify in the constitution the number of members in each chamber of the legislature. Perhaps there can be an attempt to relate size to significant characteristics in the life of the state and its people. Current informed opinion would insist upon two prime considerations beyond adaptations to local circumstances in arriving at a defensible choice with respect to size. First, efforts should be made to keep legislative chambers small. Second, in arriving at a formula for determining the distribution of seats to electoral areas, a range or possible variable number is greatly to be preferred. It seems inevitable that the future trend will be for the state legislator to serve larger areas and greater populations, on the average.[5]

Representative Bases

The choice of the basis of representation poses a difficult problem. The bicameral system, the doctrine of separation of powers, and the system of checks and balances all operate to complicate the decision on the possible bases of representation for a body such as an American state legislature.

The *sine qua non* for retention of bicameralism lies in the discovery and the determined use of different bases of representation for the two chambers. The more closely the chambers of a bicameral legislature approximate one another in representation, the less the need for two chambers.

The choice of the representative bases for legislative bodies exemplifies the conflict between (a) the desire to make certain that the body created can act with reasonable dispatch and decisiveness; and (b) the desire to make certain that all persons have their interests presented for consideration by the representative body. This problem inheres in all attempts to create or to reconstitute modern legislatures or to reapportion or redistribute memberships in them.

---

[4] Charles W. Shull, "Reapportionment: A Chronic Problem," 30 *National Municipal Review* 73-79 (Feb., 1941).

[5] For the numerical range of the present legislatures, see *The Book of the States, 1960-1961* (Chicago: Council of State Governments, 1960), p. 37.

There are two basic approaches to representation in legislative bodies. One is that sound action can flow from the aspirations of a part or segment of the population—an emphasis on class or corporate representation or, more recently, economic and social groups. The other is the belief that every person as an individual must be included in the representative base. Both views hold that the aggregate population is considered, but the latter places emphasis on the fact that the individuals are included as such.

This form of egalitarian representation, in the popular sense, ascribes to individuals a common character as units in the representative process. It treats them without regard to a multitude of other factors. It views each political unit as having a given number of people, who, in terms of right to representation, are all equal in claim. As a canon of faith this view has had power far beyond its apparent deserts. To it there is no feasible objection which can be raised short of denying the right of individuals to be considered as individuals and making the counterclaim that only as bits of a totality do they ever attain personal significance.

Abstract justice and the exigencies of ethics can be satisfied by the egalitarianism of population representation. Practical problems of representation and representative systems cannot. People are not and cannot be distributed at a uniform rate of density per square mile throughout electoral units or districts of equal surface area; and even if equal distribution of population could be achieved, the equal area would be meaningless except in arithmetical terms such as square miles, for again the earth has no uniformity of geographical features or climate.

In the process of implementing representation and representative bases the tendency, then, is to consider people as capable of description in terms of various categories. They are related to the area or region in which they live; if it is sufficiently populated to be called a village, or a city, or metropolitan community with a core city and surrounding satellites or suburbs, the individual is representationally defined as urban. If, on the other hand, he lives in an area of sparse population, he will be characterized in the pattern of representation as rural. Conflict then emerges in terms of rural versus urban power.

Within the pattern of present-day developments, the trend toward urbanization is so strong that the struggle for distinction and for prevailing representation in state legislatures is a matter of how the community in question and its residents are urban. The struggle is for recognition within the representative pattern in terms of kinds of urbanism. This is an area in which there will be greater stresses and strains in the years ahead.

If the mobility of the American people continues on anything like its recent scale, it will further complicate the search within the states for feasible bases of representation. Censuses are valuable social instruments on virtually all counts, except for the fact that they portray what is, in effect, a set picture and cannot be a cinematograph of the population which they enumerate and frequently describe. When systems of representation are based on the as-sumption that any given census has identified the human content and socio-economic composition of a community so adequately that it can be taken as the measure of what is to be represented legally in the legislature, a degree of artificiality has been injected into the representative system which obscures the argument that every person ought ethically to be included in the repre-sentative base. We catch a picture of the population in the United States, for instance, once every tenth year, and the picture has changed even before the census figures are in print.

A search must be made for something that can reveal the streams of mobility, that can disclose the deposits of political silt and fertile soil, that will show as accurately as possible the political effects of high degrees of cross-country migration and of internal mobility in metropolitan communities.

The dilemma of the American states in their search for possible representa-tive bases, particularly under bicameralism, is acute and perdurant. Land or area as bases of representation have not been used and are not likely to be under present circumstances. Governmental units are plentifully available in most states, but their great numerical range limits them severely as bases of representation. The plethora of political units that might be used actually works confusion—for example, counties cannot be treated even as a crude approximation of the states in the national Senate because their number ranges from 3 in Delaware to 240 in Texas.

Although any conclusive prescription for the choice of representative bases seems precluded at this point, certain practical suggestions will be proffered for consideration:

1. If the number of counties in a state is relatively small and there is an ade-quate spread among them in terms of population, a chamber can be con-structed upon the basis of the allocation of members proportionately to the population rank of counties. Florida and Georgia use this basis for their Houses of Representatives,[6] although they have too many counties for it to be equitable and effective.
2. If a state has a moderate number of counties without undue population spread, it may be possible to employ equal county representation in one cham-ber and devise the other, preferably the lower house, on the basis of major fractions or other devices, including equal proportions.
3. If a state has a system of semipermanent districts that is reasonably accept-able, the above suggestions relating to counties can be applied to them.
4. Consideration may be given to the award of memberships in a chamber on

---

[6] As of 1959. Florida is discussing a reapportionment proposal.

the basis of units of population established in the text of the constitution—as an illustration, one seat for each 50,000 inhabitants.

5. Consideration should be given to the development of systems of proportional representation, whether of the Hare, the Liste, or the D'Hondt or Baden type. In most states there would have to be some constitutional change to make this experimentation possible. In some states a direct application of either the Liste or the D'Hondt type would operate to guarantee seats for stipulated blocks of voters of each party and might be the means of easing the way to genuine reform in apportionment.

6. If it is decided to follow Arizona in its practice of allotting seats in the House of Representatives on the basis of units of votes cast for Governor, the number of legislative places can be controlled by enlarging the unit of votes rather than by placing a ceiling on the membership of the House as was done in Arizona.

7. Newer phases of the developing problem of representative bases would indicate that thought should be given to some use of apportionment of seats to the incorporated communities and representation for the remainder of the state through election of members at large from the unincorporated areas—with the suffrage limited to the registered voters in such areas.

8. If, after studying various alternatives, there is support for population alone, then serious consideration should be given to the possibility of a single-house legislature.

Time of Reapportionments

The choice of representative basis will condition the time of reapportionment. If population alone is the basis, the time of an apportionment must be linked with some census. Since the national government takes a census every tenth year, competition with the national government can be avoided only by placing a state census at some intermediate point within the so-called census decade. The taking of such a census involves the crucial factor of expense. When systems of proportional representation directly applicable to the election itself are utilized, the problem of timing an apportionment is solved. If the use of election results in terms of units of votes cast is employed in the apportionment process there will have to be a decision on which election and the vote for which position will be used as the base. These will be matters to be established in the constitution.

Mode or Method of Apportionment

How shall apportionment and redistribution of legislative seats be accomplished? The options are: (a) to place this power in the legislature to be used at its discretion; (b) to place it in the legislature, but to recognize that it may fail to act (as had happened often in some states), and then to create an agency which in case of legislative inaction will deal with apportionment administratively; (c) to vest the power in approximately the ways the semiautomatic federal process is accomplished; (d) to place in the secretary of state or other appropriate officer the certification of places to be filled by election.

The chief problem is to achieve reasonable treatment of number and size of chambers and the basis of representation in them and to relate these factors effectively to the mode of apportionment and vice versa, in order to avoid some haphazard or bastard type of apportionment.

PROVISIONS RELATING TO LEGISLATORS

No one will question the requirement that members of state legislatures should be popularly elected. A state constitution also will have to include provisions on term of office of legislators, their qualifications, any privileges they may enjoy, method of filling vacancies, and salaries and other compensation.

Terms and Vacancies

There must be a provision for the popular election of members of the legislature and for their term of office—in effect, the duration of an elected legislature. At present, terms in American state legislatures are either two or four years. They may be distributed in several ways: (a) two-year terms for the members of whatever chambers there are, as in Michigan, for example; (b) two-year terms for members of the lower house and four-year terms for members of the upper; (c) two-year terms for the lower chamber and four-year terms for the upper with staggered terms patterned so far as is possible on terms in the United States Senate. The Committee on American Legislatures of the American Political Science Association recommended in 1954 that "the legislative term should be long enough to permit a legislator to participate in two or more sessions."[7] A further recommendation was that the term of the Governor should equal the maximum term for members of either house.

Despite a somewhat trustful attitude on the part of earlier constitution-makers, vacancies in legislatures do occur. A constitution will necessarily have to recognize that members of the legislature may die, that they may move from their districts, and that they may be appointed or elected to other positions, including election to the Congress of the United States. A provision should be included in the legislative article to cover such eventualities. Appointment to vacancies by the governor is unsatisfactory. A practice of leaving such vacancies unfilled is also questionable, especially when they occur in the latter months of a term where only a biennial session is the rule. There should

---

[7] Zeller, ed., op. cit., p. 88.

be a clear-cut provision requiring the certification of a special election to fill vacancies—a counterpart of the British by-election—except perhaps for a vacancy occurring subsequent to the November date at which a successor legislature has been selected. In no instance ought the power of calling the by-election be left to the discretion of the governor. It is doubtful that there is need to recognize the claim that the successor in the vacancy should be of the same party as the departed member. By-elections will be watched with interest to note whether sentiment within the electoral districts remains the same or has changed.

Qualifications

Customarily, American legislatures and their chambers have the constitutional authority to judge of the elections, qualifications, and returns of their members and may censure or expel them for breaches of decorum. For the most part, qualifications consist of a few specific items such as age, citizenship, status as a qualified elector, residence in the state and in the district from which elected, provisions relating to the holding of other civil offices, and eligibility to hold offices created by legislatures in which individuals serve.

Frequently, the first three of these items are conjoined in the covering phrase "qualified elector in this state." There is a problem inherent in the fact that Georgia qualifies electors at 18 years of age; to stipulate only that a legislator must be a qualified elector would seem to be unwise. It would be well in such cases to include in the legislative article a specific age requirement, such as 21 years, or a provision for full legal age. Citizenship should be prescribed and residence, both within the state and within the district or area from which the member is elected, probably also should be provided in the legislative article.

The constitution should provide that each house shall certify that its members possess the required qualifications. In the words of the Report of the Committee on American Legislatures, "the seating of a legislator in the case of a contested or disputed election should be the prerogative of the house concerned, but should follow an investigation of the law and facts by either the courts or a special tribunal for that purpose."[8]

Privileges

The legislative article of a state constitution should provide for the traditional privileges and immunities of members of the legislature. They include freedom from arrest during a session and while going to and returning from

---

[8] *Ibid.*, p. 88.

the seat of the legislature. In practice, this particular privilege has been held not to apply to any indictible offense—treason, felony, or breach of the peace. Traditional and likewise vital is the guaranty of freedom from question for words and actions on the floor of the chamber of which a legislator is a member.

Salaries

In the matter of salaries and additional allowances for members, the following principles merit consideration. First, the constitution should not prescribe and fix legislative salaries. The legislative article may well include a provision that the legislature itself shall determine the salaries and additional compensation of its members. Such a provision may not be popular in some states, but the increase in length and frequency of sessions calls for a rectification of the salary scale of legislators. Each state will have to work out for itself the scope of the provisions relating to salaries, mileage, and other expense allowances, and possible retirement systems.

SESSIONS

American state constitutions provide for two principal types of legislative session—regular and the special. State constitutions expressly provide for the convening of regular sessions annually or biennially. They also provide that special sessions may be called by the governor. In many states the call defines the subjects that the legislature may consider in such special sessions, although new topics may be sent to the legislature by executive message and impeachment actions may be taken in either type of session.

At present, regular legislative sessions are either annual or biennial, with or without specific time limits fixed by the constitution of the state. Special sessions may be classified in diverse ways. They may be limited in length or they may be free from such limitation, which usually is set forth as a specific time limit in terms of days or is insured by a salary or per diem cutoff after a certain period of time. Special sessions may also be classified on the basis of the degree of control the governor exercises over the legislature during such extraordinary sessions. The governor may have virtually complete control of the activity of the legislature by reason of a constitutional requirement that the lawmaking body confine its attention in special session to those matters set forth in the call or subsequently suggested by the governor. Alternatively, in some states no subject-matter limitation may be imposed on extraordinary or special sessions.

It would appear that annual sessions might well become the rule in the American states. Legislation has become a matter of continuous concern in state government, and it is obvious that state legislative problems do not have an incidence or life limited to the first 60 or 90 days in each biennium. The suggestion of limiting one of two annual sessions within a legislative biennium to the consideration of financial, budgetary, or emergency matters has some merit and appeal, but it is doubtful whether this substantive division could be sustained over the years.

Agreement with the Committee on American Legislatures on the business to be transacted at special sessions seems warranted. In its words, "the call for special sessions should be authorized by the governor or by the petition of a majority of the legislators, and these special sessions should be permitted to transact any public business whether mentioned in the call or not."[9] Also, there would seem to be no valid reason today for any limitations on the duration of regular and special sessions of state legislatures, let alone including such limitations in state constitutions.

The practical effects of placing time limits on legislative sessions have been several fold. One has been to create an atmosphere of confusion, conflict, and collusion in legislative activity—the very things the limitations sought to avert. Another has been the demonstration of the maxim that time wasted is forever gone, and thus has contributed to the reduction of highly regarded procedures as well as bald weapons of delay and obstruction. Last, there is the distinct impression that many American state legislatures have performed well in spite of manifest and manifold time limit handicaps.

PROCEDURAL RULES

Many matters relating to procedures, and actual legislative rules, are found in the texts of many American constitutions. There is little reason for such inclusion and a saving in the length of the legislative article can be effected by omitting them. Most operate to restrict freedom of action and to erode the working time of the legislature. The state constitution should provide that the chambers of the legislatures should establish their own rules of procedure. Surely if the houses of the Congress of the United States have been trusted with such powers during their entire life, the popular assemblies of the states should be accorded like courtesy and evidence of trust.

Two illustrations may be cited. A direction that all roll calls shall be viva voce, still found in relation to some assemblies, is foolish. Not all measures merit a roll call; also, mechanical recording devices have been used to speed up the lawmaking process with good results. Again, an effective way to prevent action on many issues is the rather prevalent provision that a majority vote of all members elected is necessary to carry a measure. In many states the

---

[9] *Ibid.*, p. 103.

simple removal of this latter constitutional limitation in favor of following the congressional practice of a majority vote with a quorum present would practically work a reapportionment.

In Conclusion

Consideration should be given to the reconstitution of state legislative bodies as effective elements in the entire process of state government. Highly restricted and limited in many ways, state lawmaking assemblies have not been geared to cope with the growing complexities of modern legislation. They have exhibited tendencies at times to obstruct or to insist upon privileges and status rightly or wrongly conceived. On occasion, they seem to have assumed they were the entire government.

State legislatures need to be re-formed and re-shaped so that the legislative power is more fully vested in one body—though not necessarily one house. Control of the purse should be vested more clearly and securely in the legislatures; constitutional provisions that, in effect, make appropriations should be eliminated. The horizons of the American state legislatures can be widened by sound constitutional treatment, and such treatment will provide hope for their future. If it is not provided, the sun may be setting on representative government as exemplified by the legislatures of the American states.

chapter XIII

the judiciary article

Francis R. Aumann

The problem of formulating a satisfactory judicial article for a state constitution has long been with us. If there has been little success in getting such an article adopted it has not been due to indifference to the problem, or to failure to advance solutions for it. An extensive literature indicates that much thought has been given to the problem of reorganizing the judiciary to meet the needs of a changing society and to the constitutional changes required for such action.

THE MOVEMENT FOR REFORM

As early as 1906, Dean Roscoe Pound, in his great speech on "The Causes of Popular Dissatisfaction with the Administration of Justice," called attention to the need for rethinking this problem. Describing the existing state judiciary system as "archaic" in its "multiplicity of courts," its unwieldy "concurrent jurisdiction," and its "waste" of judicial power,[1] he advised the adoption of a plan of organization that would provide a system that would be flexible and responsible and capable of using its power with a minimum of waste. "The controlling idea underlying any plan of organization for our courts," he said at a later date, "should be unification, flexibility, conservation of judicial power and responsibility."[2] He suggested careful study of the British Judicature Act of 1873 as a model plan. The chief feature of this plan was the establishment of a single court, complete in itself, embracing all superior courts and jurisdictions, and including as a branch, a single court of final appeal.[3]

In 1909, in a report to the American Bar Association, Dean Pound rede-

---

[1] *American Bar Association, Reports,* Vol. 29, Part I (Baltimore: 1906), p. 395.
[2] Roscoe Pound, *Organization of Courts* (Boston: Little, Brown & Co., 1940), p. 275.
[3] See H. C. Hanbury, *English Courts of Law,* 2d ed. (London: Oxford University Press, 1953), p. 142. For discussion, see pp. 143-61.

fined the principles which he thought should govern the organization of a modern system.

The whole judicial power of the state should be vested in one great court, of which all tribunals should be branches, departments, or divisions. The business as well as the judicial administration of this court should be thoroughly organized so as to prevent not merely waste of judicial power, but all needless clerical work, duplication of papers and records, . . . thus obviating expense to the litigants and costs to the public.[4]

In 1913, the American Judicature Society, which was founded for the purpose of promoting "the efficient administration of justice," accepted the principles advanced by Dean Pound; and shortly afterward it put them into effect in the form of a model statewide judicature act which would establish a single court of justice embracing all of the judicial officers in the state from the highest to the lowest.[5]

In 1919, the National Municipal League called upon the American Judicature Society to prepare the judicial article for the first Model State Constitution and Dean Pound's ideas were followed in the resulting draft which (with the exception of its plan for judicial selection) was incorporated in the first edition of the Model State Constitution which appeared in 1921 and, with a few other exceptions, in its second and third editions as well. Although several changes were made in the judiciary article in the fourth edition which appeared in 1941, the basic objectives of the earlier plans were followed once again, as they were in the fifth edition which was prepared in 1948. The keynote of the judiciary article found in all five editions of the Model State Constitution is unification of the courts.

In 1938, the American Bar Association expressed its faith in this principle when it adopted a report recommending "that provision should be made in each state for a unified judicial system with power and responsibility in one of the judges to assign judges to judicial service so as to relieve congestion of dockets and utilize the available judges to the best advantage."[6] This was the first in a series of recommendations made by the association in a systematic

---

[4] Report of Special Committee to Suggest Remedies and Formulate Laws, *American Bar Association, Reports*, Vol. 34 (Baltimore: 1909), p. 589. In 1947 he was still stressing the point. "My proposition," he told the members of the New Jersey Constitutional Convention, "is that the whole judicial power of the state should be concentrated in one court. This court should be set up in three chief branches." *Convention Proceedings of the State of New Jersey Constitutional Convention of 1947*, Vol. VII, p. 1587.

[5] This act was first published in Bulletin 7-A of the Society, and when this bulletin went out of print it was republished in the *Journal* of the Society, Vol. XI, no. 4, Dec., 1927, pp. 99-117; see also *ibid.*, no. 3, Oct., 1927, pp. 69-83.

[6] Arthur T. Vanderbilt, ed. *Minimum Standards of Judicial Administration* (Newark: National Conference of Judicial Councils, 1949), pp. xxi-xxiii, 29, 513-14.

effort to establish some "minimum standards of judicial administration." These recommendations were made after a nationwide study of the courts had been completed by a distinguished committee of lawyers, judges, and law teachers under the chairmanship of Judge John J. Parker, and after the entire membership of the American Bar Association had had full opportunity to study the proposals before voting on their adoption. With the adoption of these recommendations the organized bar of the country was placed firmly on record as approving the principles of unification. Nor is that all. The Journal of the *American Judicature Society* has carried innumerable articles describing in detail the provisions of proposed judicial articles, based on the model plans, that have been drawn up by various state bar associations and pushed for adoption. Included among the plans that have been given special consideration are those of Illinois, Iowa, Kentucky, Florida, Minnesota, Maryland, Wisconsin, New Jersey, Puerto Rico, Hawaii, and Alaska.[7]

In short, the record of the past 50 years shows that:

1. Countless plans have been made to reorganize the courts and to draw up the kind of judiciary article for the state constitutions that would make such reorganization effective.

2. Most of these state plans have proposed a general court of justice which would be the single court of the state in all trials and appellate functions throughout the state's territory and also have provided for an executive head for the general court.

3. All of these plans have had the sponsorship of able students of judicial administration.

4. Such interested nationwide organizations as the American Bar Association, the American Judicature Society, and the National Municipal League have actively supported such plans, as have various state and local bar associations and judicial councils.

5. Very few voices have been raised in open opposition to such plans.[8]

---

[7] For discussion of the Illinois plan to modernize court systems, see Louis A. Kohn, "Modern Courts for Illinois," 42 *Journal of the American Judicature Society* 42-51 (Aug., 1958). For reference to plans for Florida, Minnesota, Wisconsin, and Illinois, see Sheldon D. Elliott, "Judicial Administration, 1955," 31 *New York University Law Review* 162-81 (Jan., 1956). This review is also published as a separate bulletin and as a part of the 1955 *Annual Survey of American Law* by the Institute of Judicial Administration, 40 Washington Square South, New York 25, New York. For draft of recent proposals for Illinois, Iowa, Kentucky, New Jersey, Alaska, and Puerto Rico, see *Judicial Articles: Selected Recent Proposals, with Explanatory Comments* (New York: Institute of Judicial Administration, May 15, 1958), 104 pp.

[8] Charles Groves Haines and Raymond Moley, both experienced students of judicial administration, do not accept the idea that mere organizational changes in the judicial system (based on plans for unification) will provide a complete solution for our judicial problems. For their comments on plans for court unification see Charles Groves Haines, "The General Structure of Court Organization," 167 *The Annals* 1, 2-11; (1933), and Raymond Moley, *Our Criminal Courts* (New York: G. P. Putnam's Sons 1930), pp. 88-90.

The record also shows that, despite these efforts, the basic features of the present-day state judicial system remain very much the same as they were a half-century ago, or even much earlier.

In some states, to be sure, an effort has been made to provide a better system for the distribution of judicial business by transferring cases from over-congested courts to those with too little to do. Unified municipal courts have been established for a long time in most of our great urban centers. Some degree of unification also has been brought to other courts of higher jurisdiction with good results. Most of these efforts have been piecemeal and incomplete, however, and, at the present time, New Jersey is the only state which has reorganized its judiciary in a way that would meet the minimum practical standards of judicial administration established by the American Bar Association or the requirements of the "model plans" established by the American Judicature Society and the National Municipal League.[9]

What is the reason for the striking disparities between planning for changes in judicial organization and in the results of such planning? One of the most persuasive explanations advanced is that few if any of the suggested reorganization plans could be put into effect without constitutional change, and that such changes are extremely difficult to make. The facts are that the inflexibility of the state constitutional amending process, and the unfortunate overloading of the state judiciary article with details applicable to another day and condition, go to the very root of the difficulty of securing judicial reform.

THE RELATIONSHIP OF THE STATE CONSTITUTION TO JUDICIAL CHANGE

"Nothing has prevented wide-spread reform in judicial administration," states a spokesman for the American Judicature Society, "except the difficulty of amending state constitutions."[10] Although this statement ignores some other extremely important deterrents, the inflexibility of the amending process undoubtedly presents a formidable road block to judicial reorganization. The difficulty presented by the amending process is increased when an overburdened judiciary article prescribes the organization of the courts in great detail; specifies the kinds of courts, their jurisdiction and appellate relationship; fixes the number of the judges; and indicates when and where they shall sit. It is increased still further when amendments to the judicial article, made on a piecemeal basis, add to the complexity of the court system. If we continue to use this patchwork technique of amending the judiciary article, the state court system will probably remain as it is now—a miscellaneous ag-

---

[9] Willard G. Woelper, "Administering the Courts in New Jersey," 36 *Journal of the American Judicature Society* 70 (Oct., 1952).

[10] "Model Judicial Article and Content Therein," 26 *Journal of the American Judicature Society* 51 (Aug., 1942).

gregation of courts, loosely connected, with overlapping functions and jurisdictions, and with no real method for coordinating and controlling its functions.

The federal Constitution is no easier to amend than are the constitutions of
many states. Its judiciary article insures more flexibility, however, by providing for the broad outlines of the judiciary in the fundamental law and leaving
many of the details of organization and operating methods to the Congress
or to the courts. If the makers of the state constitutions had followed this
course or had made the state constitution less difficult to amend, the record of
judicial reform in the states might have been quite different.

The experience in New Jersey graphically demonstrates the close relationship between constitutional change and any effective judicial reform. In 1947,
New Jersey, after a long and bitter struggle, adopted a new Constitution,
which replaced one that was more than 100 years old. Under the old Constitution, the judiciary consisted of some 17 classes of courts, "each separately
administered and each completely independent aside from ordinary appellate
review or judicial determinations." Practice and procedure in these courts
were governed in part "by statutes relating to specific courts"; in part "by
rules adopted by various courts"; and in part "by rules adopted by different
divisions of a court sitting in one of the twenty-one counties." In the words
of the League of Women Voters of New Jersey, this system was "characterized by a multiplicity of courts, overlapping jurisdiction of judges, and
lack of administrative direction." The "inevitable results" of this condition
were "jurisdictional confusion, delayed decisions, and excessive costs to
litigants."[11]

When the new Constitution went into effect in 1948, this complex system
was replaced by a simplified, essentially unified judicial system, made up of
seven courts, with the Supreme Court vested with the complete power to
make rules governing the administration, practice, and procedure of all courts.
The Chief Justice was made the administrative head of the new court system
and granted extensive authority to assign and reassign judges from court to
court and county to county. Since the rule-making powers of the Supreme
Court and the administrative powers of the Chief Justice could be exercised
effectively only on the basis of information about how the rules were operating and the exact status of judicial business, an administrative office was established to provide this information. The head of this office, who was given

---

[11] Woelper, *op. cit.;* Introduction to Judicial Article prepared by the League of
Women Voters of New Jersey (to present a complete judicial system) for the New
Jersey Constitutional Convention of 1947, *State of New Jersey Constitutional Conven-
tion of 1947,* Vol. IV, *Committee on the Judiciary, Record* (Bayonne, N. J.: Jersey
Printing Co.), p. 595.

the duty of collecting and analyzing statistical data on the work of the judges and on the status of judicial business, was to be appointed by and serve at the pleasure of the Chief Justice. By keeping an inventory of the case load in all of the courts and collecting other pertinent data which would show where action was necessary, it was hoped that this office would greatly assist the efficient administration of judicial business.

The net results of the constitutional change in New Jersey have been: (1) a simplified court structure which permits judges and lawyers to work more effectively; (2) simplified procedures which have worked more effectively; and (3) a system of administrative control which has permitted a more effective use of the personnel of the courts.[12] This reorganized court system has worked so exceedingly well that a number of its forms and procedures have been adopted elsewhere. Its work in meeting the problem of court congestion has proved to be especially noteworthy.[13] Although its effectiveness owes much to the creative efforts of its first Chief Justice, Arthur T. Vanderbilt, the New Jersey experience also clearly shows that a properly formulated judicial article in the state constitution can have an immense effect upon the day-by-day administration of justice in the courts.

WHAT SHOULD GO INTO THE JUDICIARY ARTICLE?

"If there is one thing to be borne in mind in [formulating] a constitution," Dean Pound advised the delegates to the New Jersey Constitutional Convention of 1947, "it is not to put in too much. Robert Louis Stevenson said that the difference between Homer and the ordinary poet was that Homer knew what to leave out." Since amending a constitution is "such a slow business" he added, do not "lay down a hard and fast series of courts, their boundaries rigidly defined." In his view, the framers of the federal Constitution "did a very good job when they provided for just one court and left the rest to

---

[12] *Ibid.*, p. 71.

[13] In 1948, when the new Constitution went into effect, there were nearly 10,000 cases awaiting trial, most of them over two years old and a considerable number eight or more years old. In 1956, in spite of increased litigation, the number of pending cases was the same, but more than half of them had been filed for less than six months. All but 15 per cent were less than one year old, and not more than one hundred were over two years old. The report of these facts was said to be the brightest spot in the first U.S. Attorney General's Conference on Congestion and Delay in 1956. Since this body considered "delay in litigation" the "most vital problem confronting the bench today" and decided to continue its work on a permanent basis the importance of the New Jersey record can be fully appreciated. "Justice delayed," 40 *Journal of the American Judicature Society* 6-11 (June, 1956).

William J. Brennan Jr., "New Jersey Tackles Court Congestion," 40 *Journal of the American Judicature Society* 44-51 (Aug., 1956); Joseph T. Karcher, "New Jersey Streamlines Her Courts; a Review of Jersey Justice," 40 *American Bar Association Journal* 759-62 (Sept., 1954).

legislation." If you incorporate "the truly fundamental things" in the judiciary article, he continued, you can "leave the rest to legislation, or as much as you can to the rules of the court."[14]

If we accept this excellent advice, how then are we to determine what constitutes "the truly fundamental things" which we want? A spokesman of the American Judicature Society provides us with one helpful approach to this question. In his view, there are two fundamental factors in a judicial system. The first has to do with the selection of judicial personnel, the second with the nature of the organization in which such personnel shall work. "Get fit men," he states, "and provide them with a simple scheme of organization, which enables every judge to work to the best of his ability. These are the fundamental principles."[15]

A brief examination of two constitutions, whose framers have worked hard to get these "fundamental principles" into the judiciary article, may provide a more precise understanding of the way in which these principles may be formulated. They are (1) the Model State Constitution, and (2) the Constitution of the Commonwealth of Puerto Rico.

THE MODEL STATE CONSTITUTION

The judicial article found in the Model State Constitution continues to be, in its revised edition of 1948, an ideal starting point for determining the fundamental principles which should go into the judiciary article of a state constitution. Since its plan of organization is based on the principle that the judicial system should be an integrated working unit, capable of coordinated and responsible effort, it provides that "the judicial power of the state shall be vested in a general court of justice which shall include a supreme court department and such other departments and subdivisions and as many judges as may be provided by law." This "general court of justice" is to "have original jurisdiction throughout the state in all causes, including claims against the state"; and the "jurisdiction" of each "department and subdivision" is to be determined "by statute or by general rules of the judicial council not inconsistent with the law, provided that the legislature shall determine the jurisdiction of the supreme court department by law." These provisions follow the federal example, in that they contain no mandate for particular courts, but permit the legislature to organize and reorganize such courts as changing needs may require.

To insure that this unified court shall work in a coordinated, purposeful

---

[14] *State of New Jersey Constitutional Convention of 1947*, Vol. IV, *Committee on the Judiciary, Record*, pp. 113-14.

[15] "Model Judicial Article and Comment Thereon," 26 *Journal of the American Judicature Society* 51 (Aug., 1942).

way, the chief justice of the state is given wide powers of direction, including the authority to (1) supervise the work of the general court of justice; (2) publish an annual report covering the business done by all parts of the general court and stating the conditions of the dockets at the close of the year; and (3) require periodic or special reports from any judicial officials or agents. To assist him in these duties the chief justice is authorized to appoint (1) an administrative director of the general court of justice to serve at his pleasure; (2) the clerk of the supreme court department; and (3) various other ministerial agents. In furtherance of a coordinated administration of the integrated judicial system, the chief justice is also given wide authority (subject to the rules of the judicial council) in assigning judges to various parts of the system as the working needs of the system require. If exercised properly, this power can make for a much more effective utilization of the judicial personnel of the state.

After providing for an integrated system, flexibly organized and administered, an effort is made to establish an effective working procedure. Where the procedure of the courts is prescribed in great detail by statute, as it is in many of the states, it adds greatly to the difficulty of judicial work. If the work of the judiciary is to be carried on in a prompt and effective manner, it should be responsible for establishing its own working procedure in an orderly way. To meet this problem, the framers of the Model State Constitution have vested in a judicial council the power of making rules of pleading, practice, and procedure. At the same time, the legislature is authorized to repeal, alter, or supplement these rules under certain circumstances. It is hoped that this provision will prevent the legislature from interfering with the details of judicial procedure, while at the same time preserving its role as the final law-making body of the state.

The judicial council, it will be noted, is made a major agency in the judicial system provided in the Model State Constitution. By its terms this body is made up of (1) the chief justice and one other member of the supreme court; (2) two judges of other departments of the general court of justice to be designated by the chief justice for four-year terms; (3) three practicing lawyers to be appointed by the governor for overlapping terms of three years, from an eligible list containing three times as many names as there are appointments to be made and presented to him by the governing board of the state bar association; (4) three laymen citizens of the state to be appointed by the governor for overlapping terms of three years; and (5) the chairman of the judiciary committee of the legislature.

In addition to the power granted to the judicial council to make or alter rules of pleading, practice, and procedure, it is authorized to (1) make rules respecting the administration of the general court of justice, including rules prescribing the duties of the administrative director and his subordinates; (2) determine the location of offices and places of sitting of the various departments and subdivisions of the general court of justice; and (3) establish or alter judicial districts for the handling of specified types of judicial business. All such rules, as indicated above, are subject to legislative modification.

Thus, the Model State Constitution continues to provide for an active role for the judicial council in rule-making and other important functions at the time when states like New Jersey, Michigan, and New York (which have had a long experience with such an agency) have seen fit to abolish it and allocate many of the functions previously performed by it to a judicial conference or to the office of the court administrator.[16] Undoubtedly, this fact will be studied closely by any state that is considering the reshaping of its judiciary article. In any event, the judiciary will probably need the assistance of some such supplementary agency in its continuing task of formulating an effective body of working rules. If experience demonstrates that a conference of the judges in the state can perform this function more effectively than a judicial council, this new body should be given the job.

Turning from the provisions for organization and procedure to those for personnel, it may be noted that the method of judicial selection proposed by the Model State Constitution is designed to make the judges responsible to the chief justice instead of to an executive officer or to a local political organization. By the terms of the article, the chief justice is to be elected by the voters of the state for an 8-year term. He, in turn, is authorized to appoint the other judges of the general court of justice (from eligible lists prepared by the judicial council containing three names for each vacancy) for a 12-year term, subject to certain conditions of recall, removal, or retirement provided by the constitution. After an appointed judge has served for four years "the qualified voters of the state or of a judicial district shall decide at the next election whether he shall be retained or recalled from office." The purpose of this provision is to insure a measure "of popular control of the judiciary with the minimum of political interference with its independence." Although there is a wide difference of opinion as to what constitutes an ideal method of judicial selection and tenure, the method proposed in the model plan has much to commend it.[17]

---

[16] See William G. Woelper, "The Judicial Conference and Its Role in the Rule-Making Process," 5 *Rutgers Law Review* 344 (Winter, 1951). For an account of the Michigan and New York action abolishing their judicial councils, see Elliott, *op. cit.*, pp. 170-71. It will be noted that by 1955, 17 states and Puerto Rico had established some form of administrative office of courts. *Ibid.*, p. 175.

[17] For an analysis of the strengths and weaknesses of the several methods in use in the states see Evan Haynes, *Selection and Tenure of Judges* (Newark, N. J.: National Conference of Judicial Councils, 1944).

Here then, in brief, are the "fundamental principles" to be found in the judiciary article of the Model State Constitution. Built laboriously over many years, it represents the collective judgment of some of the most experienced workers in the field of judicial administration as to what constitutes a proper constitutional basis for a state judiciary. Although some modifications of this model plan would seem to be in order in the light of new experience, and some changes in its provisions will probably be made in future revisions, as there have been in the past, the basic features of the plan continue to be eminently worthy of consideration by any state which is engaged in the task of reshaping its judiciary article. Certainly any attempt to bring about a major change in the organization of a judicial system will draw heavily upon the plan, as recent experiences in Hawaii, Alaska, and Puerto Rico suggest.

THE JUDICIARY ARTICLE OF PUERTO RICO

The Constitution adopted for the Commonwealth of Puerto Rico in 1952 contains a judiciary article which many students of judicial administration look upon as the best formulation of the "fundamental principles" of a judicial system that has been made up to this time. Following the pattern of the United States Constitution, the Puerto Rico article puts only the broad lines of the judiciary into the Constitution and leaves the rest to the Legislative Assembly. In conjunction with the Judiciary Act which supplements it, the judicial article provides a plan of organization which has been characterized by Judge Charles E. Clark as "the most complete realization yet known of the ideal of a modern and efficient judicial system."[18] The ideal form he refers to is that projected in the reports adopted in 1938 by the American Bar Association establishing certain "Minimum Standards of Judicial Administration" previously referred to.[19] This form, as we have seen, follows the integrated pattern advanced by Dean Pound and incorporated in all of the model plans.

In its first section the judicial article of the Puerto Rico Constitution provides that "the judicial power of Puerto Rico shall be vested in the Supreme

---

[18] Charles E. Clark and William D. Rogers, "The Judiciary Act of Puerto Rico; a Definitive Court Reorganization," 61 *Yale Law Review* 1147 (Nov., 1952); Shelden D. Elliott, "Our Faith in Justice: Puerto Rico Shows the Way to Better Courts," 42 *American Bar Association Journal* 24-28 (Jan., 1956); A. Cecil Snyder, "New Puerto Rico Judicial System is Modern and Efficient," 36 *Journal of the American Judicature Society* 134-39, 158-59 (Feb., 1953).

[19] He cites Vanderbilt, *Minimum Standards of Judicial Administration* (1949) Appendix A, pp. 495-624; and *The Improvement of the Administration of Justice; A Handbook,* prepared by the Section on Judicial Administration, American Bar Association, 3d ed. (1952); and *Model Act to Provide for an Administration for State Courts,* Handbook of the National Conference of Commissioners of Uniform State Laws (1948), pp. 167-69.

Court, and in such other courts as may be established by law" and that "the courts of Puerto Rico shall constitute a unified judicial system for the purposes of jurisdiction, operation and administration." It then provides that (1) "the Legislative Assembly may create and abolish courts, except for the Supreme Court, in a manner not inconsistent with this Constitution, and shall determine the venue and organization of the courts"; (2) "the Supreme Court shall adopt rules for the administration of the courts"; (3) "the Chief Justice shall direct the administration of the courts and shall appoint an administrative director who shall hold office at the will of the Chief Justice"; and (4) "judges shall be appointed by the Governor with the advice and consent of the Senate."

The legislature carried out the mandate of the Constitution in the Judiciary Act of 1952, which established for all of Puerto Rico a single court, known as the General Court of Justice. Within this single court is placed a Supreme Court, which is the court of last resort, and a Court of First Instance, made up of two divisions—the Superior Court and the District Courts. The Judiciary Act also provided that ". . . no case shall fail on the grounds that it has been submitted to a division without jurisdiction or authority or to a part of the court with improper venue." A case may be heard where filed if the parties agree and the judge does not object. If an objection is raised by one of the parties or the judge and it is not heard where filed, it is not dismissed; rather, it is transferred to the appropriate court and is not subject to attack, then or later, on jurisdictional grounds. This provision is looked upon as an outstanding feature of the plan.

The corollary of an integrated system of courts for purposes of jurisdiction is an integrated system of administration of the courts. The unification of the courts for purposes of administration provided for in the Constitution is reinforced by a provision of the Judiciary Act requiring the Chief Justice to assign trial judges to conduct sessions of the Court of First Instance, and to modify such assignments or make reassignments as the need arises. Thus, the Chief Justice might assign a district judge to a superior court, or vice versa. By the terms of this provision (which makes for complete mobility of judicial manpower), judicial work can be distributed in such a way that overworked judges can be given assistance and underworked judges can have their own calendars filled out or be used to help clear up backlogs of cases in other places.

To assist the Chief Justice in his task of assigning and reassigning judicial personnel on the basis of need, the Judiciary Act defines in detail the functions of the Office of Court Administration, which is under the control of the administrative director provided for in the Constitution. By the terms of the act, the functions of the administrative director are to assist the Chief Justice in his administrative duties by: (1) examining the administrative methods and efficiency of court personnel and the state of the dockets and the pending case loads of the courts; (2) collecting statistical and other data relating to the operations of the courts; (3) preparing and keeping proper books of accounting, submitting estimates and drawing the necessary requisitions upon public funds appropriated for the operation of the judicial system; (4) making recommendations to the Chief Justice for the improvement of court operations and the assignment and transfer of judges; and (5) generally performing such tasks and taking such steps as the Chief Justice shall direct for the better administration of the court.

Since it is essential to the efficient functioning of a modern judiciary system that it be integrated closely and that a single responsible individual or agency be placed at its head with full authority, adequate information, and competent assistance to make the system work effectively, and since the Chief Justice is made the top manager of the integrated judicial system of Puerto Rico, there is a real need for the Office of Court Administration, to assist him in the difficult task of directing and supervising this system. In fact, this office has been called "the vital heart of a modern judicial system."

In addition to these provisions for integrating the courts jurisdictionally and administratively, the Puerto Rico Constitution gives the Supreme Court wide rule-making authority. By its terms, this court is authorized to adopt for the courts "rules of evidence and of civil and criminal procedure," subject to legislative approval, and "rules for the administration of the courts." The Judiciary Act reaffirmed both of these grants of rule-making power, and with the assistance of various specialists in the field the Supreme Court has prepared the necessary rules of administration, procedure, and evidence.

In short, here is a plan that provides

. . . a real simplification of structure; genuine unification of agencies under a directing head with effective powers; elevation of the dignity, prestige, and consequently of the capacity of even the lowest judicial rung; a novel method for eliminating wasteful trial on appeals from minor courts; a thorough-going grant of court rule-making power; and a unique saving of jurisdiction of any case brought anywhere in the court system.

Judge Clark, who has thus described this plan, believes that it "constitutes a substantial accomplishment in law reforms" and gives to us "an example to be emulated and a model to be followed."[20] If this judgment is correct, as it would seem to be, it is only fair to say that the model which Puerto Rico has established owes a great deal to the other "model plans" which had their beginnings earlier in the century.

---

[20] *Op. cit.*, pp. 1170-1171.

Is there something else to be learned from the Puerto Rico judicial article? Judge Clark thinks there is. As he sees it "the chief lesson the Puerto Rican experience provides us is the need and value of leadership and cooperative effort in reform, so evident in the venture." Puerto Rico's judicial article, which incorporates the best features of the "model plans" so long urged for adoption in the states, was developed at a time when her new commonwealth status required action on a new constitution, and interested citizen groups took the necessary action.

When Hawaii[21] and Alaska[22] were preparing constitutions in anticipation of statehood status, there was an active interest in the formulation of a judicial article which would contain most of the best features of the "model plans," and such an article was subsequently adopted in the constitutions of the two new states.

---

[21] In 1950, the people of Hawaii drafted a Constitution which was to go into effect upon the admission of Hawaii into the Union as a state. The "Constitution of the State of Hawaii," agreed upon by the delegates to the Constitutional Convention on July 22, 1950 (to be submitted to the people of Hawaii for adoption and to the people of the United States for approval), provided that "the judicial power of the State shall be vested in one supreme court, circuit courts, and in such inferior courts as the legislature may from time to time establish" and "the several courts shall have original and appellate jurisdiction as provided by law." It made the Chief Justice of the Supreme Court the administrative head of the courts and gave him the power to assign judges from one circuit court to another for temporary service. He also was authorized to appoint an administrative director of the courts. The Supreme Court was given the power to promulgate rules and regulations relating to process, practice, procedure, and appeals, in all civil and criminal cases for all courts, which should have the force and effect of law. See H. S. Roberts, "Sound Prelude to Statehood," 39 *National Municipal Review* 377-82 (Sept., 1950). When Hawaii was admitted into the Union as a state in 1959, the succinct judicial article which was incorporated in the state Constitution was made up of six sections. The most noteworthy feature of this article was the absence of the legislative provisions that appear in so many other state constitutions. It also provides for a unified court system with a large role for the Chief Justice. J. Garner Anthony, "The Judiciary under the Constitution of the State of Hawaii," 43 *Journal of the American Judicature Society* 13-16 (June, 1959).

[22] On April 24, 1956, in preparation for a possible change in status, the people of the territory of Alaska ratified the Constitution of the State of Alaska. The judiciary article of this constitution provided for a unified judicial system made up of a Supreme Court, a superior court, and courts established by the legislature. The Supreme Court was given the rule-making power, including the power to promulgate rules of procedure. The Chief Justice was made the administrative head of all state courts and given the power to appoint an administrative director to supervise the administration of the judicial system. The Constitution also provided that all judges are to be selected by the Governor from a panel of qualified candidates submitted by the nonpartisan Judicial Council provided for by the Constitution. Three years after appointment, all judges are subject to approval or rejection by the electorate on a nonpartisan ballot. "New Alaskan Constitution Ratified," 39 *Journal of the American Judicature Society* 175 (Apr., 1956). See also, Thomas B. Stewart, "A Model Judiciary for the 49th State," 42 *ibid.* 52-59 (Aug., 1958).

LESSONS

The people of Hawaii, Alaska, and Puerto Rico were ready to make large changes in their governmental institutions to meet the responsibilities of their new status. If they had not been, it might have been more difficult to secure the adoption of the model judicial plan that has been so slow in coming to the older states. The final lesson to be drawn from this experience seems to be that, if we are to get a reorganized, modern judiciary through a re-organized judicial article, there must be a "movement firmly rooted in popular realities" to achieve it,[23] and that the success or failure of our effort will de-pend largely upon the character of the work done in getting a popular move-ment under way. This is the big job. When the public fully realizes that the success or failure of the entire constitution rests in no small degree on the effectiveness of the judicial branch[24] and that the effectiveness of that branch is closely related to the formulation of a good judiciary article, the major problem will have been solved. It is perhaps not too much to say that the precise content of the judiciary article does not present too great a difficulty today, since the provisions of the model plans which have been discussed can be adapted with good effect to the needs of any state.[25]

---

[23] Chief Justice Arthur T. Vanderbilt agreed with Judge Clark on the necessity of wide public support for judicial reforms. See "The Courts, the Public, and the Bar," text of Charles Evans Hughes Memorial Lecture Delivered at the New York County Lawyers' Association, 14 Vesey Street, New York, on February 16, 1954 (a Publication of the New York Lawyers' Association).

[24] "Of what real worth are the fundamental rights guaranteed by our Federal and state constitutions," said Chief Justice Vanderbilt, "if they cannot be enforced in a fair trial?" "The right of a fair trial," he declares, "is the most important of all rights for without it, all other rights are mere words empty and meaningless." "Anything that is necessary to secure the citizen a fair trial," he continues, "is an essential of a good ju-dicial system" and, it might be added, "a good judicial system" is hard to get without "a good judicial article." "Impasses in Justice," *Washington University Law Quarterly* 285 (No. 3, 1956).

[25] See *Judicial Articles: Selected Recent Proposals, with Explanatory Comments, op. cit.* This useful publication contains the text of recent proposed judicial articles for Illinois, Iowa, Kentucky, New Jersey, Puerto Rico, and Alaska. It also contains the text of the excellent judicial article proposed by the League of Women Voters for New Jersey (1947) with pertinent supplementary remarks. The institute publication and the League of Women Voters publication should be helpful to any group interested in the reform of its state's judicial article.

chapter XIV

taxation and finance

Frank M. Landers

The ability of a modern state government to carry on the wide range of services and activities expected by its citizens depends, in large measure, upon the provisions of the constitutional article on taxation and finance. This article cannot grant power to the state, for it already possesses all of the powers not given to the federal government.[1] To the extent that the article prohibits or limits the exercise of any of these powers, it interferes with the ability of the state to carry out the duties required by other articles and to perform services. As a consequence, the article on taxation and finance is doubly important because of its impact upon other parts of the constitution. It therefore merits the consideration of all persons, regardless of any particular interests they may have in other parts of the basic law of the state.

In its simplest form, the problem of what to include in the article on taxation and finance is a test of one's belief in our system of representative democracy. It is difficult to reconcile a position demanding a series of constitutional prohibitions or limitations upon the legislature's exercise of discretion in respect to taxation and finance with a real belief in democracy. Those who argue for constitutional checks are admitting a lack of belief in the capacity or desire of the elected representatives of the voters to estab-

---

[1] The United States Constitution contains three kinds of limitations on state taxing powers: *direct*—those specifically spelled out, such as the prohibitions against state use of customs and tonnage duties; *indirect*—such as prohibition against impairment of contracts, the "privileges and immunities" doctrine, the "equal protection of the laws" doctrine, and "due process of law"; and *implied*—such as the now considerably modified doctrine of governmental immunity. Lynn Foster Anderson and Wilson E. Williams, "Intergovernmental Fiscal Problems," chap. 26 in Committee on Public Finance, *Public Finance* (New York: Pitman Publishing Corp., 1959); see also William J. Shultz and C. Lowell Harriss, *American Public Finance,* 6th ed. (New York: Prentice-Hall, Inc., 1955), especially chap. 7.

lish and maintain an adequate and equitable system of financing public expenditures.

TABLE 10

STATE GOVERNMENT REVENUES, EXPENDITURES, AND NET DEBT,
SELECTED YEARS 1922-59
(In millions)

Year	Total Revenues	Total Expenditures	Debt Outstanding at End of Fiscal Year
1922	$ 1,360	$ 1,397	$ 1,131
1932	2,541	2,829	2,832
1942	6,870	5,343	3,257
1952	16,815	15,834	6,874
1959	29,164	31,125	16,930

Source: United States Bureau of the Census, Department of Commerce, Washington, D. C.

During recent decades the number, kind, and scope of state government activities have increased enormously. Census Bureau reports of state government revenues and expenditures clearly reflect this development.

For present purposes, it is noted that there is little likelihood this recent trend of increasing state expenditures will halt in the near future.[2] The rapid growth in the birth rate since the early years of World War II and the general increases in prices and living standards are among the factors which will continue to impose demands upon state finances that will exceed present revenue-raising capacity. In spite of efforts to cut expenditures through elimination of "unnecessary" items and more efficient provision of services, the pressure for increasing expenditures by the states will continue. This pressure has already pushed debt levels to new highs and will be a strong influence toward the modification or elimination of constitutional limits on debt and taxation.

Reflecting the great expansion in state activities have been the changes in the sources which have financed this growth. As late as 1932, when the economic depression was piling huge welfare burdens upon depleted state treasuries, the locally-administered general property tax was still a major source of state government revenue. Since then, to the keen awareness of their citizens, state governments have left few sources of revenue untouched in their seemingly endless drive for funds with which to finance the ever-growing expenditures. As a result, in 1957, property taxes amounted to only $479 million out of a total state tax revenue of $14.5 billion. The present principal

[2] Tax Foundation, *The Financial Challenge to the States* (New York: Mar., 1958).

sources of state tax revenues include general sales, motor fuels, income, motor vehicle, liquor, and tobacco taxes.

Some of the states have not been able as yet to avail themselves of all of the tax sources because their legislative bodies have been blocked by constitutional prohibitions.[3] The number of such states probably will decline as the pressure of higher expenditure requirements forces more and more of them to study and review their tax structures. The almost inevitable result of such review, in a period of increasing demands for services, and hence expenditures, is a "broadening and equalizing of the tax base." This is a polite way of justifying the removal of limitations, or of legal doubts, on the levying of taxes against protected sources or kinds of wealth and income.

THE NEED FOR SIMPLICITY AND FLEXIBILITY

There are various factors which must be considered in drafting the specific language to be included in the taxation and finance section of a constitution for a particular state. Obviously, the peculiar historical development of the state must have a prominent part in the final decision as to what to include or exclude, as well as the precise language in which the section should be couched.

Broadly, however, attention should be focused upon the need for simplicity and flexibility. Briefly stated, the longer and more complex the provisions relating to the power to tax, to incur debt, and to expend funds, the greater will be the likelihood of legal complications. Simplicity is important, without regard for the question of unlimited or limited taxing authority. It is essential as a means of removing doubts over the meaning of words and phrases, the interpretation of which frequently puts the determination of public policy in the hands of the judiciary, rather than the legislative body or the people.

The need for flexibility is and should be clearly evident. Unless state governments can, and will, adapt themselves to the changing economic and social environments, their importance in the total structure of American government will diminish. Certainly the experiences of the last three decades have demonstrated the fact that the focus of power moves to that level of government which has fiscal capacity to act, and which does act. Clearly, one of the lessons that should have been learned from the "failure" of state and local governments during the economic depression of the 1930's is that the people tend more and more to rely upon the unit of government which produces the services they need and want.

Undoubtedly, a substantial part of the inability of state and local govern-

---

[3] Commission on Intergovernmental Relations, *Report to the President for Transmittal to the Congress* (Washington: Government Printing Office, 1955), p. 98.

ments to raise large sums of money quickly is economic in character. In other words, and especially in a period of business recession or depression, it is economically unwise, as well as politically difficult, to increase taxes measurably. Interstate tax competition is allegedly an important aspect of the creation of a "favorable" climate with which to attract and hold manufacturing establishments, and hence payrolls, and their capacity to support "reasonable" governmental costs.[4] At the same time, none of the states have had the capacity to borrow large sums of money as cheaply and as easily as the federal government. It is also true that a large part of the inability of the states to move fast and successfully in these areas is the result of constitutional handicaps imposed to "protect" influential segments of the citizenry.

CONSTITUTIONAL TAX PROVISIONS AND LIMITATIONS

In spite of the fact that the Founding Fathers were keenly aware of the dangers inherent in an uncontrolled taxing power, early American constitutions did not contain much in the way of tax and finance articles. Apparently the framers of the early constitutions were content to give the legislative bodies an opportunity to develop taxation and financial systems without hindrance or guidance.

There are many who presently believe that such trust was misplaced and inevitably led—and would lead again—to abuse and disaster. In support of their position, they are able to muster impressive arguments by reference to historical developments. Certainly the careless abuse of state credit in the "public works" era of the 1830's and early 1840's, with its waste, extravagance, and thievery, led to greatly increased tax burdens and the demand for constitutional safeguards.[5]

Another example of the "need" for constitutional barriers to unlimited taxes is the development of uniformity clauses during the latter half of the nineteenth century.[6] With increasing wealth, as the country shifted from an agricultural to an industrial economy, intangible property forms became more important. The inability of the ad valorem general property tax to reach this kind of property fairly and effectively led many of the states to classify prop-

---

[4] This is a view frequently presented by business spokesmen. There are numerous publications which discuss this issue. A 1958 report to the Michigan House of Representatives' Legislative Study Committee largely discounts taxes as a controlling item (*Economic Development, Taxation and Industrial Location in Michigan*, by Wolfgang S. Stolper, chap. 2 of *Michigan Tax Study*, Staff Papers, Lansing, Michigan). Instead, the report indicates that other factors (notably labor costs) far outweigh state-local taxes as an element in locating industry.

[5] Tax Foundation, *Constitutional Debt Control in the States* (New York: 1954); B. U. Ratchford, *American State Debts* (Durham, N. C.: Duke University Press, 1941).

[6] 88 *University of Pennsylvania Law Review* 728 (1940).

erty for tax purposes. This, in turn, gave rise to fears of discrimination on the part of such owners and brought about uniformity clauses in all but a few states.

As a result of the continuing tendency to prescribe permanent cures for temporary and often nonrecurring fiscal ailments and abuses, most state constitutions today are replete with a wide variety of limitations upon the exercise of tax and finance powers. Some are detailed prescriptions of procedures governing state and local revenues; others cover minutiae of bond issues, including some that were long since issued and retired.[7] Some provisions cover such requirements as an "annual tax sufficient to defray the estimated ordinary expenses of the state," or ban the giving away of the power to tax, using it for private purposes, or the owning of stock in a private corporation. An example of detail is found in the Oregon Constitution which requires the state to do the obvious thing—namely to require ". . . all stationary [sic] required for the use of the state . . ." to be furnished by the lowest responsible bidder (Art. IX, sec. 8) These limitations may be grouped into three major headings: tax; debt; and administrative.

A recent study noted that in only seven states do the constitutions fail to impose major limitations upon the exercise of the taxing powers by the legislatures.[8] Although most of the limitations relate to specific taxes, it has been noted that in some of the states they are so numerous, so general in application, or so effective in blocking the use of specially productive revenues that the taxing powers of the legislatures are sharply restricted. The limitations include: (a) earmarking of revenues; (b) mandatory tax levies; (c) prohibitions or limitations on levying specific taxes; (d) limitations on rates; and (e) exemptions. Examples of all or most of these limitations are found in the majority of constitutions.

Earmarking of Revenues

One of the major, current weaknesses of state finances is the extensive earmarking of revenues. A 1955 study[9] reported that 51.3 per cent of total state tax collections in 1954 were earmarked for specific purposes. By individual states, earmarking of tax revenues ranged from zero in Delaware to 89 per cent in Alabama. Thus, half of state tax collections were restricted to particular functions not because of need, as such, but simply because they were designated for those purposes.

---

[7] An extreme example is the Illinois constitutional amendment adopted in 1890 authorizing the issuance of not to exceed $5,000,000 at not to exceed 5 per cent interest for the World's Columbian Exposition.

[8] Glenn D. Morrow, "State Constitutional Limitations on the Taxing Authority of State Legislatures," 9 *National Tax Journal* 126-33 (June, 1956).

[9] Tax Foundation, *Earmarked State Taxes* (New York: Nov., 1955).

There are few instances today where the collections of earmarked taxes are so greatly in excess of needs that unused surpluses pile up. What is true, however, is that many earmarked taxes are necessarily reserved for and spent upon functions or activities of relatively lesser importance than some of those inadequately financed from general purpose or unearmarked revenue.

The most frequently earmarked tax revenues are the so-called highway user levies on gasoline, motor vehicles, operators' licenses, and kindred items.[10] In fiscal 1954 only Delaware and Rhode Island failed to earmark such levies. Thirty-two states dedicated the entire proceeds to highways, and 14 designated part. Other purposes for which important taxes are earmarked are education, welfare, and the payment of debt incurred for veterans' bonuses.

Not all of this earmarking is required by constitutional provision. In 1956, only 24 of the states specifically restricted highway revenues by constitutional provisions.[11] Certainly a substantial part of the earmarking troubles could be eliminated by legislative action in repealing or modifying statutes. A major part, however, is firmly imbedded in constitutions.

The rationale for earmarking is fairly persuasive, and in no other area has it been applied more successfully than for highways. Simply stated, it is that the taxes upon gasoline and motor vehicles are devices by which motorists pay for the roads upon which they travel. Therefore, the money collected should be spent solely upon roads and to "divert" it would be to take money under false pretenses.

To a limited extent, this argument is plausible. However, if applied generally, it would be difficult to finance many state government services, especially those to clienteles less fortunate than motorists. Moreover, the earmarking principle is defective in that it completely ignores the relativity of need for public services. Because of it, there are many instances where some activities are financed on a relatively more adequate basis than are those whose support is provided from general revenues.

Mandatory Tax Levies

A frequent constitutional limitation upon the taxing power is the requirement of specific kinds of tax levies. Sometimes these provisions reflect situations that formerly appeared desirable but which have since changed to the point of becoming inequitable. The most common are requirements of general or special taxes upon property. Another common type of mandatory levy is one in lieu of property taxes in the form of specific rates on special classes of property (motor vehicles) or on income from prescribed forms of property (intangibles).

---

[10] *Ibid.*
[11] Morrow, *op. cit.*

Prohibitions or Limitations on Levying Specific Taxes

A number of state constitutions specifically prohibit the use of certain taxes for state purposes. According to Morrow,[12] property taxes are banned in Oklahoma, Texas, and Virginia, except that Virginia allows state taxation of railroad rolling stock. Florida may tax only intangible property for state purposes and Kansas prohibits state taxation of property for highway purposes. By judicial interpretation of uniformity clauses, several states are unable to levy graduated taxes on the incomes of persons or corporations. In brief, there is a wide variety of restricting provisions which limit the use of particular taxes by various states. Some of these are designed as inducements to manufacturers to locate their establishments within the state and thus "improve the tax base." A 1950 amendment to Arizona's Constitution provides that ". . . no tax shall be levied on raw or unfinished materials, unassembled parts, work in process or finished products, constituting the inventory of a manufacturer or manufacturing establishment located within the state. . . ." (Art. IX, sec. 13)

Limitations on Rates

A common type of constitutional limit on the taxing power is one that puts a ceiling on tax rates. Its most frequent use is in connection with general property taxes and the usual form is an over-all limit. About one-third of the states have such limitations.

Typical is Michigan's 15-mill rate limitation. Adopted in 1932, in the worst part of the economic depression when property tax delinquency was at an all-time high, it initially sought to limit all taxes on property to 15 mills, except where necessary to retire previously-incurred debt, or when increased to not more than 50 mills by a two-thirds vote of the electors. In the years since its adoption, Michigan has broadened its tax base by using just about every type of tax other than the general income tax. Meanwhile, and in spite of this broadening, the 15-mill limitation has been modified—by court decision and action of the Legislature and the voters—to the point that it is no longer so restrictive as originally intended.

Constitutional rate limits on other kinds of taxes are found in a number of states. Income tax rates are limited in Alabama, Arkansas, Louisiana, and North Carolina. Florida and Alabama limit death taxes to amounts that may be credited against the federal estate tax.

One of the most troublesome constitutional limitations on rates is the requirement that taxes be "uniform" or "equal." Most state constitutions have some form of this limitation, with some requiring taxes to be both equal and

---

[12] *Op. cit.*

uniform and others simply insisting on uniformity, at least within classes.[13] The existence of this requirement of uniformity has produced many legal actions and opinions. In some states it has been effective in blocking classification of property for taxation purposes. It has also prevented graduated income taxes in states where a tax on the income from property has been deemed to be a tax upon the property.[14]

Exemptions

Most states have provisions in their constitutions exempting the property of educational, religious, and eleemosynary institutions from taxation. A number also exempt homesteads. In the main, however, tax exemptions are found in the statutes rather than in the constitution.

Although a relatively minor problem in terms of state constitutions, the whole subject of exemptions is one which needs careful reexamination. The pressure for increased revenues in the decades ahead should bring the entire subject under review.

Value of Tax Limitations

Judged by the size of the state tax "burden" and its increasing trend in recent decades, it would appear that the over-all system of constitutional tax limitations has been ineffective so far as the total of state tax levies is concerned. On the other hand, there are a number of states which have been, and still are, effectively prevented from utilizing some of the more productive and, by current standards, more equitable tax sources. Notable in this connection are the 17 states which do not have individual income taxes. While not all of them are blocked by specific constitutional prohibition, the limitations in the basic law have been a major factor in maintaining their avoidance of this lucrative source.

CONSTITUTIONAL DEBT LIMITATIONS

Generally, constitutional limits on debt are designed to protect the taxpayer by preventing legislatures from mortgaging the future with expenditures in excess of current revenues. As recently as 1954, all but 5 states (Connecticut, Mississippi, New Hampshire, Tennessee, and Vermont) had some kind of constitutional limitation on the amount, kind, and purpose of debt that could be incurred.[15] Of the 43 states which had some kind of limitation,

---

[13] Shultz and Harriss, *op. cit.*

[14] *Report of the Michigan Constitutional Revision Study Commission* (Lansing: 1942). (Mimeographed.)

[15] Tax Foundation, *Constitutional Debt Control in the States, op. cit.*

20 required constitutional amendment in order to create new debt, 20 required a popular referendum, and 3 had minor procedural restrictions.

Most of the states with constitutional limitations have specific dollar amounts that cannot be exceeded without amendment or referendum. These limits range from as low as $50,000 to as high as $2,000,000. A few of the states limit this borrowing to a percentage of assessed valuations or some other factor such as a percentage of the yearly appropriations.

The 1954 study showed that in 40 states the legislatures had unlimited power to borrow for certain specific and restricted purposes, such as to repel invasion or suppress insurrection. The constitutions of 24 of the states permitted borrowing for casual deficits and 5 authorized borrowing in anticipation of taxes. In 16 states, the legislatures were authorized to refund existing indebtedness.

Fairly commonly, state constitutions contain prohibitions against the lending of the state's credit for the benefit of individuals or private enterprise. This provision was written into constitutions as a result of the experiences of the "public improvements" programs of the early 1800's.

Both the necessity for and the value of constitutional debt limitations are open to question. As in the case of constitutional tax limitations, the answers to both questions depend upon the situation in a particular state.

Broadly, though, as Ratchford[16] has noted, state governments are the only units which have imposed upon themselves constitutional limitations curbing their borrowing power. Although there have been many examples of actions by legislatures which seem to justify—even demand—constitutional limitations, there are other examples, admittedly in the minority, of states in which the legislative bodies have exercised discretion as well as or even better than have the electorates.

It can be argued that limitations do not, in fact, limit; instead, they simply make the fiscal processes more cumbersome and costly. On the other hand, it is not difficult to find situations where the existence of constitutional barriers prevented runaway borrowing and, presumably, wasteful expenditure. Overall, the evidence is not generally conclusive either way—a fact that underscores the previous assertions that each state must judge its own case primarily in the light of the facts it faces.

When a particular state has decided it will adopt a constitutional limitation upon debt, what should be its scope? Briefly, to be effective, it should include *all* obligations, whether met from general or special revenues, except for those of bona fide, self-supporting, business-type ventures such as bridge commissions. The lending or use of funds for any private purpose should be

---

[16] Ratchford, *op. cit.*

specifically prohibited. To be most easily administered and meaningful, Ratchford suggests the debt limit be set at not to exceed the average state revenue over the preceding five years.[17] He notes that such a plan has the advantages of (1) flexibility by expanding or contracting with revenues; (2) exerting a steady pressure; (3) not declining sharply in periods of depression; (4) being simple enough to be succinctly expressed in a constitution; (5) leaving little room for misinterpretation by the courts; and (6) being strong enough to keep debt within safe bounds. As in most existing constitutions, this limit would be voided in connection with indebtedness incurred for suppressing insurrection or repelling invasion and for refunding.

Constitutional Limitations on Finance Administration

Generally, state constitutions do not limit legislative action in relation to the organization and methods of fiscal administration. Although many constitutions—in prescribing the general administrative framework—establish various offices, such as treasurer and auditor, which frequently become involved in fiscal administration, it cannot be said that the discretionary powers of the legislatures are seriously limited.

Nevertheless, the number and variety of administrative provisions in the tax and finance articles are many. Assessment dates and ratios and other aspects of property tax administration are occasionally prescribed. Many state constitutions specify the name, composition, and other aspects of the administrative agencies charged with the collection of taxes, administration of debt, or supervision of local government finances.

Intergovernmental Aspects

As noted by the Kestnbaum Commission on Intergovernmental Relations the constitutional limitations on the fiscal powers of local governments are even more restrictive than those on the states.[18] In many states, the local governments are subject to constitutional as well as statutory provisions which limit their taxing and borrowing to prescribed proportions of the taxable value of property. Moreover, in most of the states they are also denied the right to levy nonproperty taxes of any real significance. On this last point, however, there seems to be an increasing tendency to give the local units the right to utilize some of the more important nonproperty taxes.[19]

---

[17] *Ibid.*

[18] *Op. cit.,* p. 98.

[19] For example, California permits municipalities to levy $\frac{1}{2}$ cent on the state-collected retail sales tax. Pennsylvania and New York also have given their local units rather wide powers in respect to nonproperty taxes.

Local governments frequently use this lack of local nonproperty taxing authority as an excuse for seeking additional state and federal grants and other forms of assistance. In many local units, it is not the constitutional limitations which prevent them from raising an adequate amount of local taxes. Instead, it is their inability or unwillingness to provide an adequate administration of the property tax. Low assessments combined with rate limits enable many local governments to satisfy local taxpayers with substandard tax burdens while clamoring for increased fiscal aid.[20]

Parenthetically, it might be noted that local governmental units are not infrequently responsible for constitutional provisions which interfere with the exercise of legislative discretion in tax and fiscal matters. It is certainly true, as any informed observer of state and local government knows, that many state legislatures are not sympathetic to urban problems.[21] Nevertheless, the fact remains that many state constitutions have been amended to provide favored treatment to local governments, usually at the expense of the state government.

A striking example is the so-called "sales tax diversion" amendment[22] to the Michigan Constitution. The Michigan retail sales tax of 3 per cent was adopted in 1933 to replace the state levy under the general property tax which, at its highest point in 1930, was about $30 million. Yielding $31.4 million its first year, the sales tax increased spectacularly to a present level of $300 million, or more. Its great yield provided the state government with adequate means to finance its own activities and also to underwrite an increasing level of financial assistance to its local units. These units were not satisfied, however, and a combination essentially of school districts and large city governments successfully campaigned to deprive the state of five-sixths of the sales tax yield.

There seems to be little doubt about the need for some constructive action in respect to local taxing powers. Certainly, any constitutional provisions which in themselves or in combination with inadequate local administration limit the taxing and debt authority of local governments to raise a reasonable amount of revenue should be removed. They should be given the authority, commensurate with their ability and needs,[23] to raise more of their revenue

---

[20] Frederick L. Bird, "Who Pays the Piper?," 47 *National Municipal Review* 6-10 (Jan., 1958).

[21] A current case in point is well presented by Florida's able Governor who describes the tendency of urban centers to seek assistance from the federal government as the "pass-the-buck" government. LeRoy Collins, "Cold War Casualties," 47 *National Municipal Review* 11-15 (Jan., 1958).

[22] Art. X, sec. 23, adopted in 1946 and amended in 1954.

[23] The determination of the "ability and needs" of local governments necessarily is a question which can be achieved only in respect to individual units and at specific times.

from local sources. To the extent that they may not, we can continue to look for local governments to turn to the state capitols or to Washington to solve their fiscal problems. Moreover, as Bird has noted, not only should the constitutional and statutory limits be eliminated, but, in developing a proper constitution, the revenue system should be planned in terms of the total state-local expenditure needs.[24] In the final analysis, the taxpayers of the several local units are, collectively, the taxpayers of the states. It is idle, therefore, to think of a state constitution which does not fairly, and adequately, provide for the proper financing of both state and local governments.

What Should a Constitution Provide?

In attempting to describe what a constitution should have in the way of an article on finance and taxation, it is clear that there is no ready, easy pattern that can be universally applied. The citizens of any state who contemplate a thorough revision or rewriting of this article should be governed mainly by the historical experience and the current and prospective needs of their state. It is always good to look at the experiences of other states for suggestions or warnings; it is dangerous, however, to borrow language or techniques without a full understanding of their meaning and significance for the local situation.

Constitutions, as the fundamental law, should be limited to matters of basic, long-term significance. The article on taxation and finance should not be cluttered with material which properly should be incorporated in statutes which are more easily changed. The argument that it is necessary to put certain limitations into the constitution because the legislature cannot be trusted is simply a way of saying that the legislature is not responsive to public opinion. If this is, in fact, the situation, then the answer is to correct it by changing the membership, and possibly the basis upon which membership is apportioned.

They may be an element of truth in the contention that the legislative body cannot be trusted. It may be that it cannot be trusted to do as some powerful minority group wishes in order to give that group a special advantage. Any constitutional limitation on the legislature's exercise of the taxing and debt powers should be carefully reviewed and scrutinized to determine whether it is, in fact, in the interest of the general public or of a special group.

The Model State Constitution

For many years, under the auspices of the National Municipal League, leading students and practitioners of state and local government have attempted to describe the kind of constitution which could serve as a model

---

[24] Bird, *op. cit.*

for the states. Originally published in 1921, this Model State Constitution
has been revised four times, with the latest version issued in 1948.

Article VII of this fifth edition, titled "Finance," contains 10 sections. The
first and only reference to taxation provides simply that "the power of taxation shall never be surrendered, suspended, or contracted away." By this
simple statement, completely devoid of references to specific kinds of taxes,
the committee expresses a faith in state legislative bodies—or, at least, in the
ability of the voters to keep them truly representative.

The next two sections relate to debt. The first prohibits the use of state or
local government credit by any individual, association, or private corporation.
The second requires the purposes for which debt is incurred to be spelled
out by law and, except by majority vote of the electors, prohibits debt for any
purpose other than repelling invasion, suppressing insurrection, defending
the state in war, meeting natural catastrophes, or redeeming debt existing at
the time of adoption of the constitution and for the temporary meeting of
appropriations during a single fiscal year.

The next four sections of the Model Constitution article relate to the
budget. In the first, the governor's authority to prepare and submit a budget
and appropriation bills is specified. The governor is required to submit a bill
or bills covering all recommended new or additional revenues or borrowings
with which to meet the proposed expenditures. The second section prescribes
legislative budget procedures. It prohibits passage of any special appropriations until the governor's budget shall have been enacted as introduced or
amended, unless so recommended by the governor. Public hearings are required. If one-fifth or more members request it, the governor must appear
before the legislature—in person or by designated representative—to answer
inquiries. The legislature is required to achieve a balanced budget and the
governor has an item veto.

Expenditure of public funds for private purposes is prohibited by the next
section. In the following section the procedure for expending public moneys
is outlined. The last three sections of Article VII relate to purchasing which,
so far as practicable, is required to be on the basis of competitive bidding;
postauditing, which is to be done by an auditor elected by the legislature and
serving at its pleasure; and excess condemnation.

The notes on this article in the fifth edition, written by A. E. Buck, explain and defend these provisions. The most significant feature of the article
is the almost complete omission of any discussion of taxation and the minimum amount of reference to debt. It must be concluded that this exclusion of
prohibitions and limitation upon the exercise of the taxing authority and the
very reasonable limitations relating to debt bespeak confidence in the ability

and intentions of legislative bodies to do a creditable job in this important area.

In contrast to this minimal statement on taxation and debt is the rather detailed description of budget, expenditure, purchasing, and audit procedures. Although the committee drafting the Model Constitution did not specify the organizational units, it did spell out and prescribe many details of the submission of the budget, and the legislature's actions thereon, as well as a series of prohibitions to govern appropriations.

Without disagreeing with the purposes and ideas behind these limitations, it may properly be asked why they should be incorporated into a constitution. It very well may be true that the ideas built into the Model Constitution represent the "best" current practices; but is there any guarantee that in the future these same concepts will not become outmoded and therefore obstructive?

New York state has long enjoyed an excellent reputation in respect to its fiscal administrative structure and budgetary procedures. Provisions relating to both were written into its Constitution in the 1920's and have played important roles in giving the state its excellent fiscal standing. But is there any reason to believe that the ideas and concepts embodied in the budgetary provisions of the New York Constitution will always be held to be the best? A recent report on New York state fiscal affairs, although studiously refraining from any overt criticism, seemed to reflect doubt when, after noting the 1925 amendment relative to administrative reorganization, stated that "these vast structural changes were followed by the adoption of another constitutional amendment in 1927 which outlined the basic requirements (*as they were understood at that time*) for an executive budget system."[25]

CONCLUSION

State constitutions today contain many provisions which handicap and limit the achievement of an effective and equitable system of revenue, debt, and financial administration. Most of these provisions were incorporated to correct existing abuses and to prevent future excesses, although some were clearly designed to provide special benefits to powerful interests and groups.

In spite of these limitations, state government receipts from taxes and borrowing have increased to such an extent that there is little to support any belief in the over-all effectiveness of the constitutional limitations. At the same time, it is clear that the tax limitations have frequently been used to protect some segments of taxpayers from particular types of taxes.

---

[25] Temporary Commission on the Fiscal Affairs of State Government, *Report* (Albany, N. Y.: Feb. 15, 1954), p. 23. (Italics added.)

The question of what constitutes a good article on taxation and finance is difficult to answer. Variations among the states make it a project of dubious value to prescribe a plan supposedly applicable to all states. Nevertheless, the National Municipal League has offered a Model State Constitution to serve, literally, as a model upon which the several states could build their own variations.

Properly, provisions relating to taxation and finance should be as reflective of the peculiar historical experience and future needs of the individual states as the framers can make them. Those which are held to a minimum, everything else being equal, should prove to be most satisfactory.

chapter XV

local government

Arthur W. Bromage

Local governments in the United States, whether urban or rural, are the legal creatures of the states. Except for limitations imposed by the respective state constitutions, the power of state legislatures to organize and control local governments within their borders is pervasive. The legislative power, in the absence of such restrictions, includes the creation of local governmental units; determination of their powers and forms of government; alteration of their boundaries; and their dissolution.

Comprehensive and detailed restrictions on legislative authority, however, have become the hallmark of state constitutions. During and after the nineteenth century, county organization, for example, in many states was prescribed constitutionally upon a uniform basis. In the Jacksonian movement, the constitution-makers fashioned systems of elective county boards and of elective administrative and judicial officers. They set up limitations against changing county boundaries or county seats without a public referendum. State constitutional conventions often established a county system which was decentralized, but was designed to provide uniform administrative agencies for the fulfillment of state policies and functions.

THE QUEST FOR FLEXIBILITY

As gaslights and buggies gave way to electricity and automobiles, local populations shifted. Cities and villages, incorporated within the framework of counties and townships, began elbowing one another. Such areas were on the way to becoming metropolitan agglomerations. Many counties became suburban, urban, or metropolitan in character. In the metropolitan areas, economic and social forces have cut out a way of living for which state constitutional articles on local government were never patterned. The metropolitan phenomenon, which is still unfolding in the United States, finds itself up against rigidity in the articles of state constitutions dealing with local government.

In a majority of states, constitutional stipulations as to local government not only barrier change in administrative organization for counties, but may actually inhibit the development of federated metropolitan governments. On the urban side, constitutional home rule has promoted incorporation of cities and villages, endowing them with organizational and administrative flexibility. Cities and villages have, by their number and diversity, fragmented public administration in metropolitan regions. Constitutional uniformity for counties and constitutional flexibility for cities and villages under home rule have produced, in some states, the governmental problem which is known today as the metropolitan complex—an admixture of units of government which even together do not always span the over-all aspects of needed functions and services. In many instances the problem of the whole (i.e., the metropolitan region) is greater than the sum of the parts (i.e., the individual units of local government).

In states deeply affected by demographic redistribution, constitutional articles pertaining to local government need redesigning. Metropolitan needs demand continuous attention. Social, economic, and political complexities in metropolitan areas outrun considerations that once were primary, like the theory of electing county administrative officers. The redevelopment of local government in these areas challenges our constitutional approach.

Legislative discretion to deal with metropolitan complexities is restricted today by state constitutional doctrines. To recapture the power of the state legislature over the whole will not be easy because of provisions fixed in constitutions. Also, in many of the legislatures the populous metropolitan areas do not have adequate representation. Overrepresentation of rural areas presents a political obstacle in many states to the reestablishment of legislative supremacy over local government.

HOME RULE UNDER TEST

For Cities

The states originally possessed plenary power to deal with the incorporation and organization of local governments by special acts dealing with specific units. As urban settlements grew, the legislatures began to develop special charters for particular municipal corporations. But the flexibility of the special act for municipal corporations cut both ways, and ultimately it was utilized to the detriment of municipal self-government.

During the nineteenth century, abuse of the special act system led to demands that constitutions require general law legislation. State constitutions in Ohio and in Indiana (1851) were the first to include prohibitions against special legislation applicable to municipal corporations. This action began a trend that spread from state to state and legislators, faced with the necessity of treating municipalities of divergent size by general law, began to classify cities by population. The so-called general law could then be applied to classes of cities. Prohibitions upon the special act for cities and villages were offset by legislative ingenuity.

Meanwhile, a demand developed for municipal home rule. Home rule first appeared in the Missouri Constitution of 1875 with reference to cities of over 100,000 population. It permitted local initiative in charter-drafting and local adoption or rejection of charters by referendum. The power doctrine for home rule cities was vague, for a municipal charter had to be consistent with the constitution and with the laws of the state. To give home rule a precise meaning, the state judiciary was forced to develop a legal distinction between municipal affairs and matters of statewide interest.

Early in its history municipal home rule came to lean heavily upon judicial review. Self-executing systems of home rule were written into state constitutions in general phrases descriptive of municipal affairs. This practice left to the respective state supreme courts the task of drawing the line between city affairs and matters of state concern which remained subject to general statutes. Non-self-executing plans allowed the legislature to spell out municipal home rule powers in detail, but even the implementing statutes often led to judicial determination of the exact home rule powers which were thereby expressed or might reasonably be implied.

Constitutional home rule systems, either self-executing or non-self-executing, have now been established in nearly half of the states, beginning with Missouri in 1875 and California in 1879 and ending with Alaska and Hawaii in 1959.[1] In addition, Georgia in 1954 adopted an amendment authorizing the Legislature to provide for self-government of municipalities by general law. Florida in 1956 established a constitutional home rule system applicable to Dade County and to the municipalities within that particular area.

Constitutional home rule, in its most comprehensive form, is self-executing as to municipal powers and procedure. Ohio municipalities, for example, are authorized to exercise all powers of local self-government and to adopt and enforce local police, sanitary, and other regulations not in conflict with general laws. The benefits of Ohio's constitutional grant of substantive powers are enjoyed by noncharter cities and may be exercised by ordinance. But American home rule doctrine, with the exception of Ohio, has made the ex-

---

[1] The others, in chronological order of their adoption, were: Washington, 1889; Minnesota, 1896; Colorado, 1902; Oregon, 1906; Oklahoma and Michigan, 1908; Arizona, Nebraska, Ohio, and Texas, 1912; Maryland, 1915 and 1954; Pennsylvania, 1922; New York, 1923; Nevada and Wisconsin, 1924; Utah, 1932; West Virginia, 1936; Rhode Island, 1951; Louisiana, 1952; Tennessee, 1953.

ercise of such constitutional power contingent upon the adoption of a charter.

Other systems have left constitutional home rule principles to legislative implementation. Non-self-executing constitutional provisions are usually classified as mandatory or permissive. The Michigan Constitution (1908) directed the enactment of general laws under which cities and villages could frame, adopt, and amend charters. Under such general laws, first enacted in 1909, local initiative has been freely exercised in home rule charter-making by more than 200 cities and villages.

In Pennsylvania, on the other hand, a constitutional amendment of 1922 which permitted the General Assembly to grant home rule remained for many years without implementation. It was not until 1949 that Philadelphia by legislative enactment was allowed to draft and adopt a charter. In Nevada, a constitutional home rule article of the permissive type has been in abeyance since 1924 for lack of an implementing statute. West Virginia has an enabling home rule act which embraces many details and has been narrowly interpreted by the state Supreme Court.

Home rule is the leading alternative to state-enacted, optional charter systems, and some authorities deem it superior to the optional charter plan whereby the state prescribes alternative forms for adoption by local referendum (New Jersey). Home rule permits local initiative in designing as well as in adopting charters. In some states, such as California, Michigan, Minnesota, Ohio, Oklahoma, Oregon, and Texas, many cities have drafted and adopted charters; in others, such as Nebraska, Pennsylvania, and Utah, home rule is actually exercised by few cities.

In addition to the home rule system and the optional charter plan, the special act system still prevails in a few states such as Delaware and New Hampshire. The general law approach also continues, as in Indiana.

Model constitutional provisions for municipal home rule have been developed by the National Municipal League and the American Municipal Association. The League's Model State Constitution defines home rule in broad terms as power to pass laws and ordinances relating to local affairs, property, and government, with specific enumeration of certain powers. Although the state legislature may enact laws of statewide concern, uniformly applicable to cities, the Model Constitution aims at a self-executing system, with exact boundaries of municipal powers to be defined by judicial review.

The American Municipal Association's Model Constitutional Provisions for Municipal Home Rule follows a different legal principle. The legislature by positive enactment may restrict home rule cities as to matters both of state-wide and of local concern. Although adoption of a home rule charter automatically makes available to a city a broad range of powers, no home rule power, except in such matters as organization and personnel, is beyond legislative control. A home rule *imperium in imperio* was deemed unwise because of the increasing difficulty in distinguishing between municipal and statewide concerns.

Home rule has long been advocated because of its values in activating local initiative, in preventing legislative meddling, and in saving legislators' time. Only in recent years has municipal home rule been seriously questioned. Some political scientists argue that a standard series of state-enacted optional charters available for local adoption will serve just as well. Others have contended municipal home rule often serves as a barrier to the creation of federated governments embracing central and satellite cities and villages in metropolitan regions. Home rule was developed in state constitutions as a limitation on the power of rural legislators to deal with municipal organization and operation. The city was deemed to be a relatively self-contained area with its own municipal affairs. The drawing of a boundary between matters of statewide concern and municipal affairs is increasingly difficult. But rural dominance in state legislature makes cities, in many states, reluctant to relinquish home rule.

For Counties

Provisions for county home rule in state constitutions, which followed belatedly those for municipal home rule, aimed at different objectives, being directed usually against "constitutional forms" of county government. State constitutional provisions requiring direct election of county administrative officers have often impeded the development of a county executive parallel to the strong mayor or city manager. County home rule was sought as the means to revamp county government and administrative organization.

California by constitutional amendment in 1911 became the first state to develop county home rule. Charters may be drafted by elected, local freeholders and submitted to a popular referendum. If adopted, the county charter is presented to the state Legislature for acceptance or rejection as a whole by resolution, as is the case with city charters in California. Some 10 out of a total of 57 counties have home rule charters in effect, including Los Angeles, San Diego, Alameda, San Mateo, and Sacramento. Organizational forms such as the county manager plan and the county administrator system have been developed. Twelve other states have since incorporated county home rule for all or some countries into their constitutions,[2] but in none of

---

[2] These are: Maryland, 1915 and 1954; Ohio, 1933 and 1957; Texas (limited to counties over 62,000), 1933; Missouri (limited to counties over 85,000), 1945; Louisiana (for East Baton Rouge Parish only), 1946 and (for Jefferson Parish only), 1956; Washington, 1948; Florida (for Dade County only), 1956; Minnesota, New York, and Oregon, 1958; Alaska (for units to be known as boroughs), 1959; and Hawaii, 1959.

them has county home rule been exercised to the extent that it has been in California.

In Ohio, three county charters were defeated in local referendums in the 1930's and a fourth, for Cuyahoga, never took effect because of a state Supreme Court decision. The justices held that the Cuyahoga charter transferred municipal powers to the county, and therefore required a constitutional four-way majority which was not achieved at the polls—specifically, a majority of those voting thereon in the county; in the largest city; in the area outside the largest city; and in each of a majority of the combined total of municipalities and townships.

Ohio, in 1957, again amended its Constitution to permit any county by home rule charter to exercise *concurrent* municipal powers and to change its form of government by a simple, countywide majority vote. In cases of conflict between county exercise of municipal powers and municipal or township exercise of power, the latter prevails. Such a home rule charter was rejected by the voters of Lucas County in 1959. In counties of more than 500,000, any charter provision for *exclusive* exercise of municipal powers subjects the charter to the requirement of a three-way majority of those voting thereon—in the county; in the largest municipality; and in the county area outside such municipality. However, in 1959, the voters of Cuyahoga County defeated a metropolitan home rule charter providing for *exclusive* exercise of municipal powers. Affirmative majorities were lacking both in Cleveland and in the county area outside the central city. For *exclusive* exercise of powers in counties of less than 500,000, a fourth majority is also required—a majority in each of a majority of the combined total of municipalities and townships. Constitutional home rule for counties in Ohio has led to various referendums without actual results in terms of charter adoptions.

Maryland's county home rule amendment of 1915 applied to counties and to the city of Baltimore. A subsequent amendment (1954) authorized home rule for cities; it was based on the model plan of the American Municipal Association. It was more than three decades after county home rule was constitutionally authorized that Montgomery County became the first to adopt a charter (1948). Baltimore County followed in 1956.

Missouri, the leader in municipal home rule (1875), provided in its revised Constitution of 1945 for home rule charters in counties of more than 85,000 population. This provision opened the way to a charter for St. Louis County in 1950.

In Texas and Washington, constitutional provisions for county home rule have not yet led to charter adoptions. An attempt to establish a home rule charter in El Paso County, Texas, failed for lack of the majorities required in the county, in incorporated areas, and in unincorporated areas. The state of Washington amended its Constitution in 1948 to permit county home rule. King County (Seattle), four years later, rejected a proposed charter, although only a countywide majority was required.

In Louisiana, a constitutional amendment of 1946 applicable only to East Baton Rouge Parish permitted the action of a charter commission in formulating a regional government for Baton Rouge—a plan adopted by the voters one year later. Likewise, in 1957, Jefferson Parish adopted a charter under specific authorization of another constitutional amendment (1956).

The action of Florida in making home rule possible for one metropolitan county resulted in adoption of the Dade County metropolitan charter in 1957.

Erie County (1959) was the first in New York to take advantage of the county home rule amendment of 1958 in that state.

Although county home rule has not led to as large-scale action as municipal home rule, its value for the future is not accurately measured by this limited use. Counties in many areas are rapidly becoming urban, a process which seems to increase demands for home rule. Many of the existing county charters reflect the utilization of home rule by metropolitan counties. For this reason, county home rule may well play a more important role in the future, especially in the federated, metropolitan pattern of the Dade County experiment in Florida.

Optional Law Plans: Trial and Error

For Counties

The optional law system for counties, a system first developed for municipalities, has been spreading in recent decades. The optional law system means the establishment by state act of alternative forms of organization (charters) which may be adopted by local referendum in a county or in a municipality. Flexible, broad state constitutional articles on local government or specific amendments have been the source of the necessary statutes.

Virginia's voters in 1928 by constitutional amendment authorized the General Assembly to enact optional county forms and to deviate from constitutional prescriptions calling for the direct election of various administrative officers. The Virginia optional plans resulting from this constitutional flexibility are described as the county executive form and the county manager system, the two plans being distinguished by the range of appointive authority vested in the county's chief administrative officer. Counties such as Albemarle, Arlington, and Henrico operate under optional law forms.

Other states in which constitutional flexibility permits optional law forms for counties are Montana, New York, North Carolina, North Dakota, and Oregon. In Montana, the Legislative Assembly, utilizing a constitutional amendment of 1922, in 1931 enacted an optional county manager law which Petroleum County later adopted. New York, by constitutional amendment of 1935, required the Legislature to provide alternative forms of county government. Laws of 1935, 1936, and 1937 permitted numerous options, and Monroe County adopted a county manager plan in 1936. In 1952, New York revised the options into four basic forms: county president, county manager, county director, and county administrator.

North Carolina, acting under a broad constitutional provision (1876), passed an optional act in 1927. It permitted the appointment of county managers, a plan which Guilford and Durham counties accepted within a few years. In North Dakota, a constitutional amendment of 1940 led to an optional county manager act in 1941. Similarly, an Oregon optional manager law for counties stemmed from a state constitutional amendment of 1944. As in the case of home rule, counties have been relatively slow to exploit opportunities offered in optional law systems.

For Cities

Optional law charters developed first in the field of municipal corporations. Iowa, as early as 1907, enacted an optional commission form charter which became the basis of the well-known Des Moines plan (1908). Since municipal corporations were not encumbered by a constitutional form, as were counties in many states, enactment of optional charters for cities has been a frequent state practice. Under optional laws a choice from among various forms of city government is permitted to most cities in approximately one-third of the states.[3] Still other states allow options to limited classes of cities.

Optional charter laws pertaining to cities have generally been sustained in the courts against any constitutional challenge concerning improper delegation of state legislative powers to municipal voters at a referendum. Even where state constitutional prohibitions against special acts exist, such statutes have been widely upheld against legal objections that optional charters constitute special or local laws regulating city affairs. Optional charter laws have also existed concurrently with municipal home rule systems as in Nebraska, New York, Ohio, and Wisconsin.

A comprehensive series of options was enacted by New Jersey in 1950, and this action has been described as achieving many of the objectives of "home rule." Although home rule as such did not appear in the revised New Jersey Constitution (1947), constitutional flexibility permitted the continuance and revision of optional plans. Three complete alternatives were presented:

---

[3] Included among these are: Idaho, Iowa, Kansas, Massachusetts, Montana, Nebraska, New Jersey, New Mexico, New York, North Carolina, North Dakota, Ohio, South Dakota, Virginia, and Wisconsin.

mayor council, council manager, and small municipality plan. The legislation permitted many sub-options pertaining to size of councils; election at large or by wards; partisan or nonpartisan balloting.

State constitutions have long been flexible enough to allow legislative enactment of optional charters for cities, and judicial interpretation has generally sustained such statutes. On the other hand, inflexibility is found in those states where prescribed constitutional forms of government have been a barrier to effective optional law forms for counties. In recent decades, some states have amended their constitutions to authorize legislative enactment of options for county government.

THE PERSISTENCE OF RIGIDITY

Constitutional Forms

Specifications as to county officers and their election so encumber some state constitutions that legislatures cannot significantly modify the "constitutional form." The persistence of rigidity is seen in constitutional prescriptions about the county governing body (board, commission, or court) and its composition. Most state constitutions, in addition, require the election in every county of a group of administrative and judicial officers. The listing varies from 3 or 4 officers to as many as 10 or more. Offices so established constitutionally may not be abolished, consolidated, or made appointive without constitutional change. About one-half of the constitutions still include so much detail relating to county officers that they may be said to establish a constitutional form.

Michigan exemplifies this problem of the constitutional form. The fixed pattern is the large county board, representative of townships and cities; no over-all executive; and direct election of the principal administrative officers by partisan ballot. Efforts to secure county home rule were defeated in four separate constitutional referendums between 1934 and 1944. In the face of the constitutional system, no major alternatives can be established by law. In terms of general organization, county government for rural, urban, and metropolitan counties is basically the same.

If the specific county officers are not spelled out in a state constitution, complications may still arise from stipulations about the election of officers or uniformity. In Nebraska, the Constitution requires the election of necessary county officers, and in the opinion of the state Supreme Court this requirement voided a county-manager law providing for an appointed manager. The fundamental law of Wisconsin calls for one system of town and county government as nearly uniform as practical. A statute which allowed counties (except Milwaukee) to establish small boards of commissioners rather than boards of supervisors representative of townships and municipalities was deemed unconstitutional.

The way to establish constitutional flexibility in county organization is now clear enough. It may be achieved either under county home rule provisions or under constitutional authorization for legislative enactment of optional charters. A few states have moved through these gateways to a small number of county home rule charters or state-enacted, locally approved, optional law charters. Yet, a majority of the states are still bound, more or less rigidly, by a constitutional form of county government or by a restriction calling for uniformity.

Other Restrictions

The most common state constitutional restriction pertaining to legislative action in dealing with local governments is the prohibition against special acts. Such restrictions are expressed in a variety of ways; approximately three-fourths of the state constitutions carry some form of reservation against special acts. One type is a prohibition against special or local laws on subject matters or in situations which can be dealt with legislatively by general laws. Another approach has been through the listing of subjects or units which may not be dealt with by special acts, such as incorporation of cities, towns, or villages; the affairs of counties, townships, or school districts; and the location or changing of a county seat.

The authority of a legislature to deal with civil divisions of a state by special act, without their consent, has been a matter of concern. Faced with a long record of special-act legislation meddling with specific subjects and situations in local units, state constitution-makers have evolved numerous constitutional prohibitions against such practices. There is wisdom in many constitutional strictures against "special acts." On the other hand, the requirement of rigid constitutional uniformity as to the governmental organization of counties and townships throughout a state, leaving the legislature no power to enact optional law forms, carries caution too far.

Although state legislative power commonly extends to the establishment of counties and the determination of their boundaries, here likewise constitutional restrictions often prevail. Many state constitutions require that a county must have a minimum area, and some prescribe a minimum population. A substantial minority of the constitutions state that the creation of a new county or any change of boundary must be submitted to a referendum of the voters. A majority of the state fundamental laws require that a change in the location of the county seat must go to a referendum vote. A more drastic type of limitation, found in about one-fourth of the states, imposes a constitutional ceiling on the county tax rate.

In the urge to prevent legislative meddling, state constitutions have been made too rigid. This conclusion is inescapable, especially with relation to counties and townships. Some states have found redress by constitutional amendments authorizing home rule or optional charter laws for counties. On the municipal side, the constitutional home rule movement was a reaction against legislative special acts, as were the general prohibitions on local legislation directed against specific units of government. The plenary power of legislatures to deal with local units of government has been circumscribed by constitutional norms for counties and by the home rule movement for cities. That some legislative flexibility is being recaptured is suggested by recent trends as to counties. On the municipal side few would argue against the values of home rule charters or would favor a return to legislative freedom in writing special charters for cities.

THE METROPOLITAN PROSPECT

The metropolitan-urban-rural conditions confronting us today were not envisaged when most state constitutional articles on local government were written. With approximately three out of five Americans living in 189 metropolitan areas, the economic, social, and political dynamics at work pose certain constitutional crises. Core cities, satellite cities, villages, boroughs, and urbanized towns and townships have all grown up within counties and clusters of counties, both intrastate and interstate. What kind of governmental model-building and state constitution-making will serve this melange? Most government articles in the state constitutions antedate the metropolitan scatteration of population.

In a publication in 1957, Luther Gulick proposed the creation of federated metropolitan councils—regional bodies acting as sublegislative instrumentalities, below the state level, that could enact metropolitan ordinances.[4] They might administer metropolitan aspects of functions or supervise service authorities already operative in, or to be set up for, specified activities. Most of the on-going functions of existing, traditional local governments could, under this proposal, continue. Of necessity, some metropolitan councils, being interstate in character, might stem from interstate compacts under the federal Constitution. In contrast to the boards appointed on a state or state-local basis for existing metropolitan service *authorities,* the proposed metropolitan councils would be representative, through direct election or constitutent-unit selection, of the metropolitan regions served.

To permit such far-reaching systems to come into operation, either intrastate or interstate, new state constitutional principles will be needed. The best view is that the respective state constitutional stipulations relative to local

---

[4] Luther H. Gulick, *Metro: Changing Problems and Lines of Attack* (Washington, D.C.: Governmental Affairs Institute, 1957), 30 pp.

government would be binding even upon metropolitan councils established by interstate compact. Thus, both for intrastate and interstate metropolitan governments, the flexibility of state constitutional articles pertaining to units of local administration is of paramount importance.

The metropolitan experiment begun in 1957 for Dade County, Florida, may be a forerunner of the future. The Miami area succeeded in establishing a representative, metropolitan government limited to one county. Under a state constitutional amendment (1956), power was allocated to Dade County to deal with metropolitan and urban problems. The procedure followed in bringing the plan into being was a county home rule charter adopted in a countywide referendum.

Broad home rule powers prepared the way for metropolitan functions and ordinance-making under the upper-tier Dade County Commission. Municipalities, as constituent units of the federated system, continue as the lower tier. Political representation is based on direct election for both upper- and lower-tiers of government. However, the Dade County experiment represents federation of the municipalities within a single county. It is not unlike the urban county doctrine in California, whereby county home rule and extensive empowerments permit metropolitan and urban county administration.

On the grand scale, a metropolitan council spanning multiple counties, exercising legislative powers, and being responsible for regional aspects of administration has yet to be achieved in the United States, either intrastate or interstate. And such a metropolitan council gives rise to complex issues both in state constitutional revision and in utilization of the interstate compact doctrine under the federal Constitution. An intermediate level of government cutting across hundreds of local units, that is substate and supralocal and either intrastate or interstate, outstrips older doctrines of home rule for individual counties and municipalities within particular states. More flexible state constitutional articles dealing with local governments must be developed if colossal metropolitan regions are to be governed and administered by federated governments. Federated, county home rule principles will suffice for lesser metropolitan areas within the confines of a limited land area, but are not far reaching enough to serve multicounty metropolitan areas.

CONCLUDING OBSERVATIONS

Constitutional home rule for municipalities remains a valid doctrine. In so far as it is self-executing, municipal home rule needs to be so designed as to allow for the ultimate emergence of federated metropolitan governments. Subject to a similar reservation, future developments in state constitutional principles should permit county home rule charters to be locally drafted and adopted. More constitutional flexibility, permitting for counties as well as for cities development of state-enacted, optional law charters, subject to adoption by local voters, is needed.

Most significant for the future, however, are constitutional trends authorizing new types of action for individual metropolitan counties. Systems of home rule, federated governments—arising from locally designed and locally adopted county charters and allocating functional aspects to upper and lower tiers of local government—call for constitutional readjustments in most states. The governmental requirements of even the smaller metropolitan areas are diverse, and the approach through home rule county charters is in the realm of definite possibility—provided many state constitutional articles are made more flexible.

For the great metropolitan regions, the constitutional problems are more complex, but by no means insurmountable. Multicounty metropolitan councils, substate and supralocal, having powers over metropolitan ordinance-making and over aspects of functions such as the delivery of water to units for retail distribution to ultimate consumers, will call for extensive revision of state constitutions. The articles dealing with local government, furthermore, must be sufficiently broad to permit participation of local units within different states in interstate metropolitan councils endowed by interstate compacts with sublegislative powers and administrative responsibilities. State constitutional principles must be reconsidered in the light of the transition taking place in many state and interstate areas from an urban-rural pattern of settlement to a metro-urban way of life. The revolution that the metropolitan regions may yet demand in state constitutions for the solution of their problems is only now becoming apparent.[5]

---

[5] The author expresses his indebtedness to the following sources: Council of State Governments, *State Local Relations* (Chicago: 1946), part 5; Jefferson B. Fordham, *Model Constitutional Provisions for Municipal Home Rule* (Chicago: American Municipal Association, 1953); W. Brooke Graves, *American State Government*, 4th ed. (Boston: D. C. Heath & Co., 1953), chaps. 21-23; Luther H. Gulick, *Metro: Changing Problems and Lines of Attack* (Washington, D. C.: Governmental Affairs Institute, 1957); National Municipal League, *A Symposium: New Look at Home Rule* (New York: 1955), *Digest of County Manager Charters and Laws* (New York: 1950), *Model County Charter* (New York: 1956), pp. xi-xxxviii, and *Model State Constitution*, 5th ed. (New York: 1948), secs. 801-806 and pp. 45-48; Clyde F. Snider, *Local Government in Rural America* (New York: Appleton-Century-Crofts, 1957), chaps. 1-4; John M. Swarthout and Ernest R. Bartley, *Principles and Problems of State and Local Government* (New York: Oxford University Press, 1958), chap. 20.

chapter XVI

intergovernmental relations

Herbert L. Wiltsee and Mitchell Wendell

The "changing environment of federalism"—as the President's Commission on Intergovernmental Relations in 1955 referred to the complex social, economic, and political changes during our national history—has resulted in vast expansion in governmental functions and far-reaching changes in governmental structure. Not the least of these has been the emergence, especially commencing with the depression of the 1930's, of close, cooperative relationships between and among the various units of American government. This cooperative approach to the provision of needed governmental services, based on inherent flexibilities in the system, has enabled the traditional units of government to adapt to changing conditions and to meet the demands put upon them.

In the elaboration of this cooperative approach, a wide variety of mechanisms and devices is being utilized: legal instruments of cooperation include compacts, contracts, and agreements; intergovernmental fiscal arrangements involve grants-in-aid, contingent expenditures, tax credits, and "in lieu" payments; interdependent legislation and administration have become widespread; joint and cooperative provision of services is increasingly common. Parties to these forms of cooperation, in various combinations, are the United States government, the states, territories, cities, counties, and other local jurisdictions.

Our traditional theory has been that states are sovereign, self-contained governments within the federal system. The few generally recognized exceptions to this proposition have been those provided by a limited number of clauses of the Constitution of the United States: the full faith and credit, privileges and immunities, extradition, and compact clauses.

The first two of these four areas appear to have only passing relevance to the subject of intergovernmental cooperation as it is dealt with here. Their importance lies in the benefits which they require each of the separate states to confer on individuals. They provide for no administrative or other joint undertakings, but merely for one state's recognition of acts or status attributable to another governmental unit. Although fundamental to the process of converting a group of separate states into a single national system, the full faith and credit and the privileges and immunities clauses merely make compulsory for application within the federal system the discretionary rules of comity as they are known in international law.

The extradition clause, on the other hand, requires direct dealing among states, but only with respect to one narrowly defined subject matter and on a limited basis. The cooperation envisaged by that clause does not extend to the trial of offenses by one state on behalf of another or to cooperative punishment of crime. Rather, it provides for the rendition of an accused person so that the demanding state, by itself, may enforce its own criminal laws.

The compact clause, unlike the others just mentioned, allows positive and wide-ranging intergovernmental cooperation, but this possibility has received significant attention only during the past few decades. Previously, the interstate compact was regarded almost entirely as a device for the settlement of disputed or uncertain boundaries, and thus it gave rise to few continuing relationships.

The principle of limited government, so familiar a part of the American political tradition, has been a source of restrictions—unintentionally, for the most part—on the scope of intergovernmental cooperation. In their nineteenth century context, such limitations were guarantees of freedom rather than obstacles to desirable governmental activity. If governmental projects were so small or simple as to be clearly within the competence of single units, the underlying premise of constitutions could safely be that authorization of such separate activities and their assignment to specific governmental units was the only fit way to proceed. In the setting of a century ago, governmental functions normally were devised for performance by *a* city, *a* county, *a* state, or *the* national government. It is doubtful that state constitution-makers often thought consciously along these lines; but their assumption that compartmentalized government was the reality to which their drafting should conform has had the effect in this century of raising numerous problems for the development of certain forms of intergovernmental cooperation.

FINANCING PROBLEMS

The carrying out of any administrative function necessitates money. While there are significant undertakings of a self-liquidating nature, such as toll bridges and roads, and a number of state functions that bring in some revenue of their own, such as state universities, the customary way of supplying such money is by appropriation. The constitutions of the states within our federal system universally give to the legislatures the power to appropriate money for the support of governmental services. The federal Constitution in very broad terms confers this power on Congress. It provides in sweeping manner that Congress shall have power to appropriate money to meet the debts of the United States. (Art. I, sec. 8, cl. 1.) There is no attempt in the federal Constitution to list the permissible sources or objects of such indebtedness. Furthermore, as the grant-in-aid cases beginning with *Massachusetts* v. *Mellon* (262 U.S. 447 [1923]) and *Frothingham* v. *Mellon (ibid.)* have demonstrated, it is almost impossible to question successfully the constitutional validity of a federal expenditure. Accordingly, the scope of undertakings to be supported by the United States government becomes a matter of congressional policy rather than a subject of constitutional mandate or prohibitions.

State constitutions, on the other hand, almost always contain provisions which limit the discretion of the legislature in appropriating money. The constitutional limitations which contain the seeds of difficulty for intergovernmental undertakings are few in number but far reaching in their effects, and they appear in numerous state constitutions.

An early post-World War II survey among the Western States revealed that 5 of the 11 state constitutions in that region contained provisions prohibiting the appropriation of any state funds to institutions or agencies— such as regional educational, penal, and charitable institutions—not under the absolute or exclusive control of "the state."[1] The constitutions of Colorado and California are typical. The former provides in Art. V, sec. 34:

No appropriation shall be made for charitable, industrial, educational or benevolent purposes to any person, corporation or community *not under the absolute control of the state,* nor to denominational or sectarian institutions or associations. (italics added)

A similar provision of the California Constitution, Art. IV, sec. 22, reads in relevant part:[2]

. . . and no money shall ever be appropriated or drawn from the State Treasury for the purpose or benefit of any corporation, association, asylum,

---

[1] "Memorandum of the Law Re: Constitutionality of Proposed Interstate Compacts for the Establishment and Maintenance of Regional Educational, Penal, and Charitable Institutions" (Chicago: Council of State Governments, n. d.), 16 pp. Not available for distribution.

[2] Similar provisions appear in the constitutions of Montana (Art. V, sec. 35); New Mexico (Art. IV, sec. 31); Wyoming (Art. III, sec. 36); Alabama (Art. IV, sec. 73); and Pennsylvania (Art. III, secs. 17 and 18).

hospital, or any other institution *not under the exclusive management and control of the State as a state institution. . . . .* (italics added)

These provisions were designed to keep public funds from being diverted to the use of private individuals or businesses, and to implement the doctrine of separation of church and state. Courts have so interpreted these "public purpose" clauses. In recent years, however, those seeking to develop interstate programs and institutions have been given pause by such categorial language, and notably by such phrases as: "not under the absolute control of the state" and "not under the exclusive management and control of the state as a state institution." Cooperative programs and institutions cannot possibly be under the complete control of "the state" in a conventional, third person, singular sense. If carried on as joint ventures, they are under the control and management of states in the plural.

It might be argued that in light of the well known purposes of these constitutional provisions, courts would hold an undertaking by "states" to be unaffected by the constitutional limitation. A certain amount of uneasiness is understandable, however, since there are no decided cases squarely in point. Uncertainty becomes especially damaging if the ownership of large public works is involved or if the selling of bonds secured by the interstate facilities is contemplated.

To date, the problems that could be caused by these provisions have only begun to arise. The Western States, for about a decade, dropped their efforts to develop a regional corrections compact, chiefly as a result of the provisions cited above; and as indicated below, their more recent efforts in this field had to be carefully tailored to avoid head-on constitutional conflicts. For somewhat similar reasons, to cite another instance—the South Central Forest Fire Protection Compact, drafted in 1953—representatives of Missouri were forced to conclude that their state could not constitutionally join with Arkansas, Louisiana, Mississippi, Oklahoma, and Texas in assuming the mutual aid obligations, including interchange of equipment, contemplated under that agreement.

The interestate activities which might have brought these restrictive provisions most prominently to light are the public works compacts providing for the joint construction and operation of bridge, tunnel, and other crossings of interstate water boundaries. These are precisely the functions, however, that can be most readily financed by user charges and, in the capital outlay stage, by revenue bonds. In the case of the New York Port Authority, various additional transport and related facilities have been built and administered and some of these, too, such as the airports and bus terminals, have proved to be revenue raisers.

Similar solutions are not available in the case of services which do not lend themselves to fee collection. The problem, and the arrangements that can be devised to meet it, are well illustrated by the water and corrections compacts.

The use of interstate compacts for the allocation of water from interstate streams is well known in the Western States. These agreements contain apportionments of stream flow, either on a specific acre-foot basis or pursuant to a formula embodied in the compact. Such apportionments must be administered; someone must monitor the flow and accomplish the necessary withdrawals or releases of water. It is possible that interstate administrative agencies supported by legislative appropriations might be used for these purposes. Each of the Western States, however, has a water engineer or similarly-named agency for intrastate purposes and is able to assign its part of the administrative burdens under the compact to that office. Such portion of the state engineer's appropriation as may be devoted to the administration of the compact is still an appropriation to the office of the state engineer, an agency of a single state and subject to its absolute management and control.

The Eastern States are more familiar with interstate cooperation for the maintenance of water quality. In that part of the country, several interstate agencies have been established with pollution control functions. If any of these agencies had found it necessary to acquire large and expensive public works, some constitutional fears might have been expressed concerning them. Such action has not proved necessary hitherto, although the future may bring such developments in response to increasing demands for water.

It is possible to consider interstate agencies as agencies of each of the party states. This would seem to be the clear implication of *Helvering* v. *Gerhardt* (304 U.S. 405 [1938]) and a supportable inference from *State ex rel. Dyer* v. *Sims* (341 U.S. 22 [1951]). Such a view might be helpful in overcoming constitutional restrictions of the type herein discussed; whether it is completely reassuring may depend on the severity of the language contained in particular constitutional provisions spelling out the degree of amenability to the control of one state.

The problem had to be faced squarely in the latter 1950's by the drafters of the Western Interstate Corrections Compact. That agreement authorizes the cooperative use of correctional institutions by groups of the compacting states. The purpose is to make unnecessary the construction and maintenance of costly, duplicate, or parallel facilities by the compacting states. As now conducted in the United States, prisons and rehabilitative programs belong to that class of state properties and services which are not normally financially self-sufficient and must therefore be supported by appropriations. Even though the result of such cooperative use of facilities might be to save money for each of the participating states in the long run, the operation of a joint prison would likely be an enterprise beyond the exclusive control of a single state.

Rather than face this constitutional problem head on, the drafters of the Western Interstate Corrections Compact cast the agreement on the assumption that individual states would construct and operate each of the correctional facilities which might ultimately be used in the cooperative program. A state which had not constructed a facility could purchase space and participation in the available correctional program of another state. Such an arrangement is a contract for services rather than a contribution to the maintenance of an institution not absolutely within the control of the state. The Western States which have enacted the compact hope and expect that the practical result of such contracts will be similar to that which could be obtained by direct appropriation to a genuinely interstate institution. At the same time, the difference in legal form should be sufficient to avoid constitutional conflicts. An additional feature of the Western Corrections Compact makes it possible for one state to make a capital contribution to a correctional institution being constructed or enlarged in another party state, provided that such a contribution secures a contractual reservation of space to be used by the contributor for its inmates upon completion of the facility. This, too, would seem to be a contract for services, but it is probably as far as one can safely go in the face of constitutional provisions such as those set forth above.

In at least two instances, states have amended their constitutions with participation in particular compacts in mind. Desirous of entering the Southern Regional Education Compact, but faced with a financial provision of the Colorado and California type quoted above, the Virginia General Assembly in 1950 approved and the electorate two years later adopted the following amendatory language to Section 141 of the state Constitution:

. . . the General Assembly may appropriate funds to an agency, or to a school or institution of learning owned or controlled by an agency, created and established by two or more States under a joint agreement to which this State is a party for the purpose of providing educational facilities for the citizens of the several States joining in such agreement. . . .

New York in 1938 amended its Constitution (Art. X, sec. 5) by relieving corporations created by interstate compact from the auditing and referendum requirements imposed on intrastate public corporations. But while these instances demonstrate that it is possible to solve individual problems of intergovernmental cooperation when they arise in specific form, such an approach is inferior to conscious recognition by drafters of state constitutions of the need for and growing significance of intergovernmental cooperation.

Conflict of Interest

Another source of constitutional difficulty for intergovernmental cooperation has appeared recently from an unexpected quarter. The problem of conflict of interest is a familiar one to our public law. Its basic point is that public officials should not be permitted to occupy two or more positions which are antagonistic to each other. From time to time this idea appears to be juxtaposed with theories of separation or division of powers within a government and between the national government and the states. In its most familiar guise, the idea has been embodied in constitutional provisions forbidding an official of one branch of government from holding an office of profit in another branch. By a kind of *a fortiori* reasoning, some state constitutions seem to have applied the same notion to service with another government within the federal system, especially for elected or high policy-making officials. While the theoretical efficacy of such constitutional prohibitions in preventing the corrupting influence of conflicts of interest may be appealing, a sweeping requirement of such abstract purity, especially when imbedded in the constitution, can have unfortunate practical consequences.

As an example of the effect of constitutional requirements of this nature, the attorney general of Texas recently found it necessary, as a result of broad prohibitions against dual office-holding contained in Article XVI of the state Constitution, to decline appointment by the President to serve as a representative of the states on a federal commission charged with the study and drafting of international rules of judicial procedure. This outcome was the more regrettable since state courts and administrative agencies are as much affected as federal courts and agencies by such rules and the federal legislation creating the commission, after strong representations from the states—including the National Association of Attorneys General—was amended to provide for two state representatives. The Texas provision appears to have allowed little room for interpretation, although it is greatly to be doubted that its framers actually intended to prevent Texas officials from contributing their knowledge and skill to the solution of joint federal-state problems.

In early 1960, a member of the New York State Senate similarly found it necessary to resign his appointment by the President to the federal Advisory Commission on Intergovernmental Relations, in light of the possible effect of Article III, section 7 of New York's Constitution in declaring his legislative office to be vacated in consequence of the appointment. Since New York has been in the van of the movement toward improved and expanded intergovernmental cooperation and was so at the time that this section was reviewed by a constitutional convention in 1938, again it may be doubted that those who framed the provision had consequences of this sort in mind.

The potential mischief which might be caused by such provisions could indeed be great, since state constitutions contain a bewildering variety and number of prohibitions against dual office-holding. In many instances, the prohibition may be neither clear nor sweeping, but the existence of doubt could obstruct close cooperation between the federal and state governments— or in light of some wordings, between different state governments. It is more than likely that the demands of a modern federal system will require increasing establishment of bodies of a joint federal-state or interstate character in order to achieve optimum coordination of governmental activities and policies. Consequently, care should be taken to see that general provisions designed to guard against corruption or dilemmas of conscience are not so constructed as to inhibit desirable undertakings of an intergovernmental nature. The conclusion is inescapable that detailed specification of these matters can best be left to statutory delineation, on the basis of broad constitutional language directing and enabling the legislature to act in this area.

WORDS OF LIMITATION

The above discussion suggests that inadvertence in the use of language by drafters of constitutional provisions and ill-advised assumptions concerning the ability to compartmentalize government are likely to present problems for intergovernmental cooperation in various ways. Many types of intergovernmental action are still relatively new or lie entirely in the future and it is not surprising, therefore, that no one has undertaken a systematic survey of state constitutions in order to discover such limiting verbiage. We can be aware only of the embarrassments that have come to light thus far, more or less by accident.

So far as the writers know, there is only one implemented venture in interstate cooperation that has come to grief because of litigation in which it was actually decided by a court that a state constitutional provision prevented the undertaking. New Mexico and Texas, with a particular geographic area in mind, in the 1930's entered into a school district compact by whose terms an interstate district consisting of a community in each state could be established. The consolidated school was placed in operation, but a suit ordered its dissolution. The difficulty was found in a provision of the Texas Constitution conferring on counties the power to establish school districts. The provision had previously been rewritten to permit a school district to "embrace parts of two or more counties." The Texas court, in setting aside the interstate district, held that the sense of the provision was that intercounty districts should be "within the state."[3] The framers of this provision presumably had

---

[3] *Parks* v. *West*, 102 Texas 11, 111 SW 726 (1908); *Texas-New Mexico School Dist. No. 1* v. *Farnwell Independent School Dist.*, 184 SW 2d 642 (1944).

no conscious intention to foreclose interstate school districts, although that became the result.

In the absence of a thorough examination of state constitutions from this point of view, that would either dispel or confirm the suspicion, one cannot help feeling that many such words or phrases of limitation may be present. Phrases like "*a* county may" or "*the* state shall have power to" are susceptible of restrictive interpretation that could limit the constitutional grants of authority to single units of government acting separately.

THE ROAD TO IMPROVEMENT

Since the growing complexities of modern life and the increasing burdens being placed on all levels of government within our federal system require a freedom to engage in intergovernmental undertakings which was not appreciated in the past, the public welfare requires a constitutional pattern that recognizes these new necessities. Such recognition can come either from the liberal interpretation of existing provisions or from the writing of new ones.

If the words do not fly directly in the face of a desired result, much can be done by friendly interpretation. The extent to which such a process has expanded the powers of the national government to meet situations not envisaged by the Founding Fathers is well known. The Supreme Court, when dealing with the role of the states in our federal system, frequently has been less generous. One recent pronouncement of the Court, however, is worth pondering for its philosophy. In *New York* v. *O'Neill* (79 S. Ct. 564, 571 [1959]), upholding the constitutionality of the Uniform Rendition of Witnesses Act, the court said:

> To hold that these and other arrangements are beyond the power of the states and federal government because there is no specific empowering provision in the U. S. Constitution would be to take an unwarrantedly constricted view of state and national powers and would hobble the effective functioning of our federalism. Diffusion of power has its corollary of diffusion of responsibilities with its stimulus to cooperative effort in devising ways and means for making the federal system work. It is an interplay of living forces of government to meet the evolving needs of a complex society.

The tradition of state constitutional interpretation usually has been much more restrictive. Consequently, the need for more suitable phraseology in the state constitutions may be greater.

The road to improvement may entail the painstaking process of removing or altering short and random phrases which, however unintentionally, inhibit intergovernmental cooperation. In any event, constitutional conventions and revision commissions, of either limited or general scope, should give

conscious consideration to correcting possible limiting effects on intergovernmental cooperation of all parts of constitutions.

The past two decades have seen the beginnings of efforts to devise constitutional provisions specifically aimed at authorizing and facilitating intergovernmental cooperation. The drafters of Missouri's Constitution, adopted
in 1945, took cognizance of the growing needs of local governments, particularly in metropolitan areas (the major ones of which, in Missouri, are
adjacent to interstate boundaries), and developed a broad concept of interlocal cooperation. Article VI, section 16, authorizes the enactment of laws to
permit Missouri municipalities or political subdivisions to contract and cooperate with other municipalities and subdivisions, in or out of the state, or
with states or the United States, for planning, development, construction,
acquisition, or operation of any public improvement or facility or for a
common service. In Florida, a proposed new constitution that was drafted a
little more than a decade later included a provision (Art. VII, sec. 14) similar
to that of Missouri, although its benefits would not have extended to cooperation across state lines.

The Model State Constitution (5th ed., 1948), contains a four-section
article (Art. XI, sec. 1100-3) which seeks to facilitate intergovernmental
cooperation by particular authorizations for specific forms of cooperation, i.e.,
federal-state relations; interstate relations; "cooperation of governmental
units" by which, in effect, is meant interlocal cooperation; and "consolidation
and cooperation of local units."

The authors are of the view that these provisions carry over to a large
extent some of the unfortunate assumptions on compartmentalization mentioned previously, and that in consequence many of the potential forms of
intergovernmental cooperation in the future (federal-state, state-local, interlocal within a state or across state lines, across international boundaries, and
others) find inadequate enablement in the article as written. Cooperation of
local jurisdictions (sec. 1102) clearly omits reference to activities across state
lines; interstate relations (sec. 1101) are anticipated in terms of joint agencies, although many cooperative interstate programs may and do take other
forms which the section apparently does not sanction; federal-state relations
(sec. 1100) are seen solely in terms of state compliance with or conformity to
federal initiative. And a further feature of dubious wisdom is the derivation
of constitutionality for any state act designed to effectuate cooperation with a
valid congressional act—other express provisions of the state constitution to
the contrary notwithstanding. The implication that political subdivisions may
make arrangements with the United States or other governments without
reference to controls or checks or review as to propriety by the state government—a concept also utilized in the new Alaska Constitution (Art. XII,

sec. 2)—presents possible serious consequences in the future for orderly and responsible state government.[4] Conditioning the exercise of this power of local cooperation on state legislative action, as is done by Hawaii's new Constitution (Art. XIV, sec. 5), appears more desirable.

Much can be said for incorporating express provisions on intergovernmental cooperation in the state constitutions of the future, although the absence of such provisions has not, of itself, been a major factor in retarding desired cooperation in the past. Any such provisions must be drafted with care and imagination to assure that the practical effects shall be to encourage rather than inhibit the widest range and flexibility of joint action. All combinations of cooperation should be authorized in the most general and all-inclusive terms possible. Any restrictive measures which may be desirable are better left to ordinary statute where they can be more flexibly designed and more readily modified as circumstances indicate.

Cooperation across international boundaries in many localities also appears to be of growing importance. Metropolitan Detroit, for one, has problems which suggest cooperation with adjoining portions of the province of Ontario; civil defense for states and localities bordering on Canada and Mexico can bring increased forms of mutual aid across these international boundaries; the control and abatement of air and water pollution in international border areas bring to mind still other opportunities for concerted action at the state and local government levels. Obviously, many such forms of cooperation will require review and sanction by the Congress pursuant to Article I, section 10, clause 3 of the United States Constitution; but in an enablement in the constitution of possible future forms of state and local cooperation, those which cross international lines should not be ignored lest the courts be forced to find that the omissions make them unconstitutional.

The authors suggest the following clause for consideration by constitutional conventions as providing a broad basis for facilitating an optimum variety of forms of intergovernmental cooperation:

The state, or any one or more of its municipal corporations and other subdivisions, may exercise any of their respective powers, or undertake any function jointly or in cooperation with any one or more other states, or municipal corporations, or other subdivisions of such states, or the United States, or with a foreign power, and may participate in the financing of any such joint or cooperative projects or undertakings; provided that any municipality or other subdivision of this state does not exercise or perform, or bind itself to exercise or perform any power or function not conferred upon it by this constitution or

---

[4] See, Frederick L. Zimmermann and Mitchell Wendell, "No Positive Barriers," 47 *National Civic Review* 522-25, 554 (Nov., 1959).

by statute; and provided further that the joint or cooperative exercise of such power or performance of such function is not contrary to statute.[5]

Before ending this discussion, a brief word of caution should be uttered to correct the possible conclusion that obstacles imbedded in state constitutions have been frequent deterrents to cooperative undertakings. The nature of the topic assigned has made it necessary to concentrate on cases in which constitutional provisions raise difficulties, actual or potential. Such a focus is desirable because improvements come by attention to weaknesses which can then be eradicated. So far as the writers know, however, very few projects of intergovernmental cooperation have been abandoned for constitutional reasons. Nevertheless, each such abandonment is a misfortune in a federal system that must depend for its strength on devising and applying new and improved techniques of coordination and cooperation. In the intergovernmental field, the task of constitution-makers should be to produce the greatest possible flexibility.

---

[5] Based on proposed language in *ibid.*, pp. 525, 554.

chapter XVII

new constitutions for a new era in state government

Charlton F. Chute

In 1935, William Bennett Munro wrote an article for *The Annals* entitled "An Ideal State Constitution," fully recognizing that the answer could not be short and simple but stating that "any man's honest answer to such an important question is entitled to a hearing." He noted that Thomas Jefferson's views on the subject had been "promptly consigned to oblivion by his contemporaries" and any revisionist might anticipate the same fate for his own views. With these provisos he listed the following specifications:

A state constitution should confine itself to fundamentals. . . . The bill of rights should be reduced to a minimum. . . . The framework of state government should be simplified. . . . The powers of the executive should be increased. . . . The judges of all the state courts should be appointed by the governor for long terms. . . . A large number of matters now incorporated in the state constitution should be transferred to an administrative code. . . . Provision should be made for direct legislation. . . . The constitution should provide alternative methods of amendment.[1]

These were offered, he said, not as matured conclusions but rather merely as a basis for discussion.

While no polling of opinion has been attempted since Munro wrote, it is likely that most of the points that be made would be supported by many, and perhaps a majority, of students of state government today.

This chapter is concerned, not with an ideal state constitution, but rather with the kind of constitution that is needed for a new era in state government. It is presented with the same qualifications about completeness and oracular wisdom that Munro expressed a quarter of a century ago.

---

[1] 181 *The Annals* 1-10 (Sept., 1935).

The subject raises, quite naturally, the important question of the nature of this "new era." Can its dimensions be measured factually, or does their definition require the occult powers of a seer? Are all states equally involved, or is the impact of its problems felt to a greater degree in some states than in others? Which states will be most importantly and quickly affected by the rise of the new era? Finally, what are the implications of the coming new era for state government, and particularly for state constitutions?

POPULATION CHANGES

A number of developments in the 25 years since Munro's essay appeared indicate the factual basis on which to build a conception of the new era on whose threshold many states now stand, and into which some are moving with great speed. Three of the main factors are growth in population, changes in the character and distribution of population, and changes in the transportation pattern.

A lowered birth rate in the mid-1930's, when Munro wrote, led many students of population at that time to believe that the nation was approaching population stability. During the past two decades, of course, both marriage and birth rates have increased sharply. Estimates of the Bureau of the Census anticipate a national population, based on current trends, of 200 million by 1967—less than 10 years hence. Actuaries indicate the possibility of a national population of 300 million by the year 2000. There are reasons to believe that most of this added population will be concentrated in certain states, as will be discussed later.

Along with population growth, drastic changes are occurring in the composition and distribution of population. The long-term decline in the rural-farm population continues. The onward movement of the agricultural revolution enables fewer farmers more than to meet the food requirements of the urban and the rural nonfarm population. Commercial agriculture now possesses many of the attributes of a modern industrial undertaking. The movement of population from farm to city continues.

The agricultural economist, John D. Black, in his presidential address to the American Economic Association in 1955, stated that it was reasonable to expect a continued decline in the number of farms in the United States until about 1975, and then a slight rise in the number until the year 2000.

The Census discloses that the proportion of the population that is urban continues to increase. More importantly, most of the population growth occurs in what the Bureau of the Census calls standard metropolitan areas (SMAs),[2]

---

[2] The term "standard metropolitan areas," used in the 1950 Census, has been changed to "standard metropolitan statistical areas," with a slightly altered definition, for use in the 1960 Census.

that is, in the large cities and their environs. Here, the large central cities are growing but slightly, if at all, whereas the rural outskirts are showing the most spectacular increase in population on a percentage basis.

The speed of the shift from rural to urban or metropolitan in some states is, perhaps, not fully appreciated. Governor LeRoy Collins recently stated that "Florida's population in my lifetime will have shifted from eight out of ten in rural to eight out of ten in urban areas."[3] When the Bureau of the Census in 1910 first counted what it then called "metropolitan districts," it found none in Texas that could meet its relatively high requirement of a central city with a population of at least 200,000 population. The 1950 Census, however, listed 15 standard metropolitan areas in Texas, more than are found in any other state, and a preliminary release for the 1960 Census shows 6 new ones in this state.

In 1935, there were no statewide toll roads and very few limited access highways. Roads and highways of that time, though given an all-weather surface, were designed primarily for horse-drawn vehicles. The opening of the Pennsylvania Turnpike in 1940 showed how much a limited-access, long-distance, multilane expressway, designed for use by motor cars, could contribute to the speed, safety, economy, enjoyment, and comfort of long automobile trips. The success of this highway, which fulfilled the promise of the Bronx River Parkway, the original limited-access automobile highway, opened in 1925, led other states to build similar toll roads where the volume of traffic seemed likely to justify the expense. Today, the states are building a national interstate highway system, largely after the pattern first revealed in the Pennsylvania Turnpike, but without the toll feature. Private automobile ownership has more than doubled, rising from 32 million in 1940 to 67 million in 1958. The truck movement of intercity freight, which was in its infancy in 1935, has had a dramatic rise. In contrast, the total mileage in the railroad network has been declining for many years.

Recent studies forecast a continuance of this trend. Among them are Dewhurst on *America's Needs and Resources,* the Rutgers study of *The Economy of New Jersey,* and Indiana University's analysis of *Indiana's Economic Resources and Potential.*[4] All anticipate little growth in passenger and freight movements on the part of railroads but considerable increase in transportation provided both by passenger cars and by trucks.

---

[3] 57 *Fortune* 30 (March, 1958).

[4] J. Frederick Dewhurst and Associates, *America's Needs and Resources, a New Survey* (New York: Twentieth Century Fund, 1955) ; Salomon J. Flink and Associates, *The Economy of New Jersey* (New Brunswick: Rutgers University Press, 1958); Schuyler F. Otteson, *Indiana's Economic Resources and Potential* (Bloomington: Bureau of Business Research, Indiana University, 1955), particularly Section III, "Transportation," by L. L. Waters and Charles Thomas Moore.

It is now known that the growth of urban population together with the rise of auto and truck transportation is building a new kind of *regional* economy that encompasses largely adjacent and near-by metropolitan areas. Many aspects of this economy are imperfectly understood at present, and more research is needed on them.

There is no reason, at this time, to anticipate a reversal in population trends. It is reasonable to expect a continued growth of population nationally, most of which will be urban in character, but located increasingly on the outskirts of our largest concentrations, the standard metropolitan statistical areas. The pattern of urban settlement will apparently be less dense than it was in the largest cities in the nineteenth century because of the dispersion permitted by the automobile, the truck, and the state highway.

The new era with which we are concerned stems, I believe, not so much from the doctrinal concerns of political science as from the tremendous increase in the number of citizens, both realized and impending, and the changes in their pattern of living, with a resultant mounting pressure on state governments of new needs, the satisfaction of some of which will require constitutional change.

Population growth since 1950, of course, has not been evenly distributed over the nation. According to preliminary reports of the 1960 Census, the leading states in absolute gain during the decade have been, in descending order: California, Florida, Texas, New York, Michigan, Illinois, and New Jersey, and the leaders in percentage of increase, again in descending order, have been: Florida, Nevada, Alaska, Arizona, and California. Three states are reported to have lost population: Arkansas, Mississippi, and West Virginia.

For convenience of analysis, the states may be divided into three classes on the basis of the extent of their metropolitan development. The first class contains the states in which more than half of the population resides in metropolitan areas. It includes, in descending order of percentage, New Jersey, Rhode Island, New York, Massachusetts, California, Pennsylvania, Maryland, Illinois, Connecticut, Delaware, Ohio, Michigan, Washington, Missouri, Utah, Colorado, Florida, and Texas.

The population of each of the first 15 was more than 50 per cent metropolitan in 1950, and Colorado, Florida, and Texas have been added because they had almost reached the 50 per cent mark at the time of the 1950 Census and are believed to have grown remarkably in that direction since then. Preliminary 1960 Census reports indicate that Nevada and Hawaii, at least, will have to be added to the list of states in this first class. Although there are only 20 states in the first class, they account for nearly two-thirds of the national population. All of these states, according to the Bureau of the

Census, are gaining in population. This class includes the 9 most populous states.

The second class consists of states that have one or more standard metropolitan areas but whose population is less than half metropolitan in character. In 1950 there were 27 states in this group, consisting of the following 24 (in descending order), plus Colorado, Florida, and Texas: Indiana, Arizona, Minnesota, Tennessee, Virginia, Oregon, Wisconsin, Louisiana, Georgia, Alabama, West Virginia, Nebraska, Iowa, Kansas, Kentucky, Oklahoma, South Carolina, North Carolina, New Mexico, New Hampshire, Maine, South Dakota, Arkansas, and Mississippi. It may well be that the 1960 Census will show that some of these states, such as Indiana and Arizona, should be added to the first class.

The third class contains states with not a single standard metropolitan area; and in 1950 there were only 6 of them: Nevada, Wyoming, Idaho, Montana, North Dakota, and Vermont. Preliminary 1960 Census data indicate metropolitan areas in Montana, North Dakota and Nevada, so these states should be transferred from the third to the second class. To the third class should be added the new state of Alaska, which to date does not appear to contain a standard metropolitan statistical area. The states in this class, in general, will feel the impact of metropolitan growth only indirectly in such matters as tourism, vacationing, hunting and fishing, winter sports, the demand for farm products, and the development of water resources.

METROPOLITAN AREA PROBLEMS

The traditional concept of a metropolitan area in political science literature is that of a large central city and its suburbs, *placed in a green rural setting*. This was a quite natural view, for when the Census first counted what it called "metropolitan districts" in 1910 each was fairly well isolated from the rest. At that time, and for many years thereafter, no two metropolitan areas were adjacent to each other. This fact, together with the slight use of automobiles for commuting and trucks for intercity freight moving, led political scientists to regard each metropolitan area as "a social and economic unit"; hence, the literature has tended to deal with each metropolitan area on an individual basis. There is almost no mention of the fact that two or more metropolitan areas that are contiguous may have common governmental problems much more complex than they would have if each were physically separate. For example, it is only within the past five years that we have come to realize that three adjacent metropolitan areas, each having a population of, say, half a million, are likely to have important economic interrelationships and greater problems relating to water supply, sewage disposal, air pollution, traffic congestion, parks, and so forth than if each was surrounded by open country and quite separate from the others. The realists of the world of business tend to view the three areas as one consumer market with a population of a million and a half.

It is therefore important to recognize here that many of the largest metropolitan areas are contiguous (as defined by the Bureau of the Census), that the places where the fringe areas touch frequently show the greatest current growth in population and industry, and that the governmental problems of such urban regions are often much more complicated than would be those of the like metropolitan areas located separately. They become so difficult, in point of fact, that state government is increasingly being called upon, in one way or another, to find a solution for them. The paragraphs that follow will, it is hoped, make clear the importance of the urban region—group of contiguous metropolitan areas—in the new era.[5] A few specific examples, rather than generalized statements, may best illustrate the nature of the new problems which the growth of population in contiguous metropolitan areas is bringing to state government.

The first two examples involve New Jersey on the East Coast and California on the West. In humid New Jersey, the eighth most populous state, 9 out of every 10 inhabitants in 1950 lived in metropolitan areas. In semiarid California, the second largest state in population, better than 4 out of 5 inhabitants lived in metropolitan areas in 1950. In both, serious plans have been in the making for some time to put the state government squarely into the middle of the water business—building dams and aqueducts, impounding water in reservoirs, and transporting and selling it to local water utilities for distribution to consumers. Until very recently, the development of water sources has been almost exclusively a function of *local* government in this country, but here are examples of state governments preparing to enter the field, largely because of the geography of rainfall and water need, financial requirements, and the pressure of mounting metropolitan populations. It is important to note that this is not simply a question of the state enacting some laws, or undertaking a study, or regulating use, or giving some free advice or financial aid; it will involve the planning, design, and building of huge public works by the state, the spending of immense sums of money, and the continuing storage, supply, and selling of water in wholesale quantities far into the future. It looks to *state administration* helping to meet metropolitan area problems on the grand scale.

New Jersey entered the water business in a relatively small, but significant, way a number of years ago. Water consumption in the highly urbanized

---

[5] The definition and identification of such groups is discussed in greater detail in Charlton F. Chute, "Today's Urban Regions," 45 *National Municipal Review* 274-80, 334-39 (June, July 1956).

northern part of the state in recent years has exceeded the average annual yield. Dry years have caused hardship for water users in many areas in this section.

At the suggestion of industries needing water, the state in 1937 acquired the unused Delaware and Raritan Canal, built over 100 years ago, which carries water from the Delaware River through Trenton (one SMA) into New Brunswick (part of another SMA). The canal was repaired to the extent necessary, and raw water was conveyed and sold to industries along its route, the statute requiring that contracts for sale be signed by the Governor. A few years later the statute was amended to permit the sale of raw water by the state to units of local government. It is worth noting that it took these actions, not for reasons of political doctrine, as, for example, a belief that the function of providing raw water for domestic and industrial uses was more properly a state function than a local function, or for partisan reasons of wanting to "meddle," but rather because there was a water shortage, the canal was there standing idle, and it would cost very little to meet an urgent human need in this way. In brief, it was a practical solution to a practical problem.

The water needs of northern New Jersey increase, however, as the population and industry of the state continue to grow. Engineering studies made for the state indicate that there is sufficient rainfall, but that reservoirs and other works must be built if the future growth of the state is not to be curtailed for lack of an adequate water supply.

In 1955 the voters defeated a $100,000,000 state bond issue to build a reservoir, perhaps in part because a complete engineering report on the project had not been finished prior to the election. In November, 1958, however, a $45,000,000 state bond issue to build a reservoir was approved by the voters of New Jersey.

This state has also helped to protect the ground water sources of southern New Jersey by purchasing the 100,000-acre Wharton Tract which lies about half way between the Atlantic City and Camden areas in 1954.

Political scientists may well ask, why should the state be doing these things, or, to put it differently, why shouldn't metropolitan area governments be created to develop adequate water sources? One answer is that it is difficult to delimit metropolitan areas in this state satisfactorily. How many metropolitan areas are there in North Jersey? Is Mercer County (containing Trenton) a part of North Jersey, or not? Is Monmouth County part of a metropolitan area? From a practical point of view, water is needed in many parts of North Jersey, whether these be included within the boundaries of a metropolitan area or not; or, to put it another way, the definition of a metropolitan area as framed at the local level may be too restrictive to meet the needs of the problem. Finally, many people in this state have a greater confidence in state government than in some possible alternatives.

California has long had a water problem, and its state government has recently spent an estimated $10,000,000 to analyze its present dimensions and to prepare a long-range state water plan. To quote from the official *Preview of the California Water Plan:* "Well over 70 percent of the stream flow occurs north of a line drawn roughly through Sacramento. In contrast, an estimated 77 percent of the present consumptive water requirement and 80 percent of the forecast ultimate are found south of the same line."[6]

The metropolitan area that probably is most in need of additional water is San Diego. The near-by water sources are virtually completely developed. The water needed by San Diego in the future will have to be impounded in Northern California and transported about 600 miles south. Some appreciation of the magnitude of this undertaking is afforded when we remember that on the Atlantic Coast this would mean transporting water a distance greater than that from Boston, Massachusetts, to Richmond, Virginia.

Unless additional water sources are developed, the growth of population and industry in Southern California will be severely limited in a few years' time. In this area people are accustomed to bringing water considerable distances. The city of Los Angeles developed the water source in the Owens Valley, 240 miles distant, about 1910, and the Metropolitan Water District of Southern California brought its share of the water 300 miles from the Colorado River in the 1930's. Now the major local water sources are fully developed and the one remaining practical addition seems to be the water in the northern counties of the state. Making fresh water from salt water is out of the question as a practical matter at this time because of costs.

Here again it may be asked, why look to the state government? Why not rely on a metropolitan district, or a new metropolitan area government? The answer seems to be that it is not politically feasible to have a metropolitan district actively developing a water source in a remote part of the state, when intervening metropolitan areas are in need of water, unless these areas are included in the program in some manner acceptable to them. What this means, in a practical way, is that the outcome will depend on the politics of power *at the state level,* because state legislation is almost sure to be required. In such a situation it is only natural for many interests involved, and they greatly exceed the few metropolitan areas that have been referred to in this brief account, to prefer state government administration to that of any one of the parties at interest. Another reason for state action often is that the

[6] California. State Water Resources Board, *Preview of the California Water Plan* (Sacramento: the Board, 1956), p. 4.

cost of a project will greatly exceed the financial capacity of a single metropolitan area.

In short, water in California has outgrown being a *local* problem, or a *metropolitan area* problem, and is now a *state* problem. At the general election in November, 1960, the voters of the state are being asked to approve a state bond issue of $1.75 billion to start construction based on the California Water Plan.

From the foregoing discussion it can be assumed that the continued increase in the populations of existing metropolitan areas and the emergence of new metropolitan areas will, in many states, collectively tend to exhaust the natural resources in the immediate environments. Water will become increasingly scarce, the nearby air, streams, and lakes will tend to become polluted, and adjacent open space for parks and recreation will be more and more difficult to find. This situation already prevails in several of the states in the first class, but it has not occurred in many of the states in the second and third classes.

STATE CONSTITUTIONS AND METROPOLITAN PROBLEMS

What do these developments mean from the point of view of state constitutions? In the first place, the nature of this new era into which we are moving is not sufficiently well understood by the general public, and more particularly by enough of those leaders who shape and write new constitutions or constitutional amendments. Second, many present-day state constitutions were designed to meet nineteenth-century rural problems; they were adopted at a time when the development of a single metropolitan area, not to speak of a chain or cluster of contiguous metropolitan areas, was unforeseen. Such constitutions contain provisions that hamper or prevent action at the state or local level needed to meet the problems of the new era. Relatively few state constitutions have provisions that deal specifically with metropolitan areas, and these are based on concepts of an earlier time. They tend to name a particular metropolitan area, or to assume that the metropolitan problems occur in widely separated counties. They do not sufficiently anticipate the emerging pattern.

The Missouri Constitution of 1945, for example, in Article VI, section 30, provides alternative means by which an over-all government for the St. Louis metropolitan area that lies within the state of Missouri can be achieved. Unfortunately, by its terms, it applies only to the city of St. Louis and St. Louis County. Today, metropolitan St. Louis is growing southward into Jefferson County and westward into St. Charles County but, under the terms of the Constitution, these areas may not be included. Nor does this Constitution make available to other metropolitan areas in the state, such as Kansas City, the alternatives provided for St. Louis.

A second example is afforded by a proposed amendment to the Ohio Constitution which was defeated by the voters in November, 1958. It proposed to establish a method by which metropolitan federations of local governments could be formed in any county in which the largest city had a population of more than 50,000. This had the merit of being general in form, but apparently would not permit the local governmental units in two or more contiguous counties to form one metropolitan federation. This proposal would be easier to explain if all metropolitan areas in Ohio were far apart and if each were contained within a single county. This is not the case, however, for the Bureau of the Census recognizes Lorain and Cuyahoga counties (Cleveland) as one SMA, and many SMAs are clearly adjacent to one another in the rapidly growing northeastern corner of the state.

A third example comes from the series of proposed constitutional amendments developed in Florida in 1957. They would have retained the existing constitutional provisions relating to metropolitan government for Dade County (Miami) and would have provided for city governments in Jacksonville and Key West to be coextensive with their respective county boundaries, under certain conditions. They failed, however, to recognize that Palm Beach County had achieved the status of a standard metropolitan area in 1956 and that the Bureau of the Census had later found Fort Lauderdale, the largest city in Broward County, to have a population in excess of 50,000. Recently it has been declared a standard metropolitan statistical area in the preliminary releases of the 1960 Census. The counties of Dade, Broward, and Palm Beach form a contiguous group of what are apparently now metropolitan counties on Florida's "Gold Coast." By this omission there was a failure to recognize the emerging problem of metropolitan area government in Florida. It is perhaps fortunate that these proposed amendments were not submitted to the voters for adoption.

CONSTITUTIONAL OBSTACLES IN THE NEW ERA

The trends of recent decades seem to indicate a role of ever greater importance for county government, particularly in metropolitan areas. In many states, functions once exercised by townships and cities have been assumed by the county. Relatively few county functions have passed on to state government. The future role of the county in the government of metropolitan areas appears to be great—not that it necessarily represents the ultimate solution of the problem, but rather that it may constitute a convenient building block. The main asset of the county is that it is usually larger in area than the other units of local government and, hence, more likely to comprehend the metropolitan area. Its chief drawbacks, generally, are a weak governmental structure, a lack of appropriate governmental powers, and too many officials with insufficient vision. The fact that county governments almost always lack a chief executive, which is a major defect in an urban situation, is often due to constitutional provisions requiring a county board or its equivalent under another name, plus the reasoning that put such provisions in constitutions in the first place, and that keeps them there today.

A few constitutions have been amended to permit home rule charters, or optional forms of government, for counties, and a small number of appointed or elected county executives are found here and there. Many populous counties in metropolitan areas, however, continue to operate, after a fashion, with no chief executive. The difficulty of making a change is shown by the fact that two attempts to amend the Michigan Constitution to permit home rule county charters generally, and two attempts to permit such a charter for Wayne County (Detroit) alone, have failed at the polls.

Another type of constitutional difficulty is illustrated by the New York Constitution, Article VIII, section 1, which states that no county, city, town, village, or school district shall "give or loan its credit to or in aid of any individual, or public or private corporation or association. . . ." This provision has been held to forbid two or more cities or counties from selling bonds to finance the construction of an otherwise proper, jointly owned facility. The Constitution was amended in 1953 to permit such units of local government, by law, to contract indebtedness to finance joint undertakings for three stated purposes: (1) a supply of water, (2) the conveyance, treatment, and disposal of sewage, and (3) drainage. A later constitutional amendment has removed the constitutional prohibition on joint financing of otherwise lawful undertakings.

Yet another example of a constitutional provision which limits municipal cooperation is the curious Article XVIII, section 6 of the Ohio Constitution, which reads:

Any municipality, owning or operating a public utility for the purpose of supplying the service or product thereof to the municipality or its inhabitants, may also sell and deliver to others any transportation service of such utility and the surplus product of any other utility in an amount not exceeding in either case fifty per centum of the total service or product supplied by such utility within the municipality.

This provision was adopted by amendment in 1912.

If we turn from local to state government, some new obstacles to meeting modern problems appear in certain commonwealths. New Jersey and California, in attempting to solve their water problems, have not encountered the kind of constitutional obstacles that loom ahead in many states.

A constitutional prohibition in many states, traceable to certain well-known nineteenth century events, states that "the state shall never contract any debts for works of internal improvement." Sometimes the prohibition is broader, applying to "engaging in works of internal improvement." Just what is a "work of internal improvement" is frequently decided by a court.

When the state highway systems were being developed in the early years of the present century several states found it necessary to amend such provisions in their constitutions. Thus, the Michigan provision reading "the state shall not be a party to nor interested in any work of internal improvement, nor engaged in carrying on such work," was amended in 1905 by adding "except in the improvement of or aiding in the improvement of the public wagon roads and in the expenditure of grants to the state of land or other property. . . ."

This was often the pattern—a general prohibition was amended to create a specific exception, thus leaving a very broad prohibition still in effect.

Another example is afforded by Alabama, whose constitutional language forbidding the state to "engage in work of internal improvement" was amended in 1922 to enable the state "when authorized by appropriate laws passed by the Legislature to engage in the work of internal improvements, of promoting, developing, constructing, maintaining and operating all harbors and seaports within the state or its jurisdiction at a cost not exceeding ten million dollars." The result was the construction of the Alabama State Docks at Mobile, an asset of considerable value to the metropolitan areas of Mobile and Birmingham.

The full extent, and the present legal interpretation, of these constitutional restrictions on the states' interest in works of internal improvement are not known, but it was recently reported that the constitutions of Maryland, Minnesota, Ohio, and Wisconsin contain such general prohibitions on the contracting of state debt. A news dispatch of October 12, 1958, from Virginia states that "the chief question raised is whether state aid (to expand the port of Hampton Roads) would violate a section of the state constitution that prohibits Virginia from becoming a party to 'any work of internal improvement except public roads and public parks.' " In a decision dated March 16, 1959 (Harrison v. Day), the Supreme Court of Appeals solved the problem by taking a narrow definition of the term "internal improvement."

The Michigan Constitution (1955) indicates the logical next stage of development. Article X, section 14, reads:

The state shall not be a party to, nor be interested in, any work of internal improvement, nor engage in carrying on any such work, except:

1. In the development, improvement and control of or aiding in the development, improvement and control of public roads, harbors of refuge, waterways, airways, airports, landing fields and aeronautical facilities;

2. In the development, improvement and control of or aiding in the development, improvement and control of rivers, streams, lakes and water levels, for purposes of drainage, public health, control of flood waters and soil erosion;

3. In reforestation, protection and improvement of lands in the state of Michigan;

4. In the expenditure of grants to the state of land or other property.

This section would seemingly prohibit the state of Michigan from developing a water source, as New Jersey plans to do, unless it could be justified under the term "public health." The California plan clearly involves "control of flood waters" and "control of water levels." At any rate, the above language does not specifically say that the state may engage in a work of internal improvement to provide water for domestic, industrial, and agricultural purposes. It is interesting to compare this omission with the inclusion of the four terms "airways, airports, landing fields and aeronautical facilities" to describe one kind of permitted public works. The section illustrates the difficulty, if not the impossibility, of trying to list all activities that are to be permitted. Doubtless it would be better to remove the prohibition on works of internal improvement entirely and rely on the legislature, the referendum on legislation, and the popular approval of state bond issues for the proper degree of public control.

There are, in addition, a few states, such as Indiana, Nebraska, and Florida, whose constitutions forbid state debt generally, except to meet a casual deficit, repel invasion, or finance other fairly limited purposes. This kind of restriction may constitute one of the most serious constitutional obstacles to the provision of needed public works at the state level to solve some of the governmental problems of the new era.

Several political scientists, noting the procedure by which Metropolitan Toronto was created by legislative act without the approval of a popular referendum, have questioned the widespread procedure in this country of requiring the consent of those proposed to be annexed into a metropolitan government. Lee S. Greene has written, "annexation has been frozen in many instances because of mistaken insistence on asking the consent of those to be annexed. We don't ask people whether they wish to belong to the United States, or to a state. The national government somewhat resolutely declined to allow the seceding states to depart. But cities are treated differently by our state legislatures."[7] Those who are of this opinion will be interested to note that the state Legislature in New York, unlike the provincial legislature of

---

[7] "Thoughts on Metropolitan Areas," 9 GRA Reporter 25 (Second Quarter, 1957).

Ontario, is powerless to require annexation because of the restriction in Article IX, Section 14, of the state Constitution which says "no territory shall be annexed to any city until the people of the territory proposed to be annexed shall have consented to such annexation by a majority vote on a referendum called for that purpose." This provision was adopted as an amendment as recently as 1927.

In Delaware, extension of the jurisdiction of Wilmington by annexation has proved practically impossible because of a constitutional provision requiring a two-thirds vote of all the members elected to each house of the legislature.

Most realistic students of state government have long been concerned about the lack of statewide planning in nearly all of our commonwealths. The kind of new era that has been sketched, with mounting urban populations and physically limited natural resources, requires much more careful planning than was needed when states were mainly rural and agricultural.

While comprehensive state planning is conspicuous by its absence, individual state departments here and there do a creditable job of planning in particular fields. Mention has already been made of the very important California Water Plan developed so carefully over a number of years. Texas is now proceeding to develop a state water plan, following the adoption of a constitutional amendment in 1957 which authorizes the issuance of $200,-000,000 in state bonds to provide a fund for the state to lend to its units of local government for water development purposes. The amendment also provides for the creation of a Water Development Board. New Jersey is another state that has given much time and money to the development of a state water plan. These are steps in the right direction, but they fall considerably short of the well-balanced over-all planning needed by heavily metropolitan states such as Texas and California.

In the years to come more thought must be given to the means of developing sound state-level planning. Perhaps such action can be achieved through legislation, but it may be that a brief constitutional provision making the governor, as chief executive, responsible for the planning function will prove the stronger and sounder approach. Consideration must also be given to developing procedures that will guarantee to spokesmen of local units a hearing of their views before administrative and legislative agencies prior to decision and action by state governments on plans that will affect them.

about our authors

FRANCIS R. AUMANN, Professor of Political Science, Ohio State University. A.B., Ohio Wesleyan University, 1921; A.M., Ohio State University, 1925; Ph.D., State University of Iowa, 1928. Author or coauthor of six books, the latest of which are *The Instrumentalities of Justice* (1956) and *The Government and Administration of Ohio* (with Harvey Walker, 1956). Author of over 60 articles for journals in the fields of public law and public administration.

ERNEST R. BARTLEY, Professor of Political Science, University of Florida. A.B., Nebraska Wesleyan University, 1940; M.A., University of Nebraska, 1941; Ph.D., University of California, Berkeley, 1948. Consultant on city planning, submerged land matters, and constitutional revision; author of books and monographs relating to these subjects and of college textbooks in American government.

JOHN E. BEBOUT, Assistant Director, National Municipal League, and Director, Temporary Commission on the Revision and Simplification of the [New York State] Constitution. A.B., Rutgers University, 1923; M.A., 1938. Actively engaged in civic work for many years; consultant to the Alaska Constitutional Convention and to various official bodies on problems of state and local government; author of numerous studies and articles in these fields.

ARTHUR W. BROMAGE, Professor of Political Science, University of Michigan. B.S., Wesleyan University, 1925; M.A., Harvard University, 1926; Ph.D., 1928. Former member of official study commissions concerned with state, local, and metropolitan problems in Michigan. Author of books on state, county, and municipal government and administration. Member of the Council of the National Municipal League; honorary member of the International City Managers' Association.

CHARLTON F. CHUTE, Director, Institute of Public Administration. A.B., University of California, Los Angeles, 1929; Ph.D., University of Chicago, 1935. Consultant and researcher for various governmental agencies—federal, state, and local—including the President's Commission on Social Trends, the

Missouri Constitutional Convention, and the Philadelphia Charter Commission. Author of two books and numerous articles in the state and local government field.

DAVID FELLMAN, Professor of Political Science, University of Wisconsin. A.B., University of Nebraska, 1929, A.M., 1930; Ph.D., Yale University, 1934. Taught at the University of Nebraska, 1934-47. Former editor of the *Midwest Journal of Political Science;* author of *The Defendant's Rights* (1958) and *The Limits of Freedom* (1959). Member of the Governor's Commission on Human Rights of the State of Wisconsin and of the national council of the American Association of University Professors.

W. BROOKE GRAVES, Adjunct Professor of Political Science, The American University. A.B., Cornell University, 1921; M.A., University of Pennsylvania, 1923, and Ph.D., 1936. Entered government work after 20 years in the teaching profession. Author of *American State Government* (1936, fifth edition in preparation) and *Public Administration in a Democratic Society* (1950), among others, and of numerous articles in professional journals and law reviews. Editor of the American Commonwealths Series.

JOHN P. KEITH, Executive Director, Regional Plan Association, Inc., New York. Formerly Assistant Director, American Society for Public Administration; Senior Associate, National Municipal League; Staff Member, Citizens Research Council of Michigan and Institute of Public Affairs, The University of Texas. Author of several books and of articles in professional journals.

LOUIS E. LAMBERT, Assistant Professor of Government, Indiana University. A.B., University of Iowa, 1932, M.A., 1936; Ph.D., Indiana University, 1950. Director of introductory course in American Government; author of a number of studies on Indiana state government.

FRANK M. LANDERS, Director, since 1949, Budget Division, Michigan State Department of Administration. A.B., University of Michigan, 1935, A.M., 1938. Has held positions as Secretary of the Michigan Tax Commission, Research Director of the Michigan Department of Revenue, and examiner in the United States Bureau of the Budget. President, National Association of State Budget Officers, 1954-55; consultant on budget administration in the Philippines (1954) and in Vietnam (1956).

ROBERT S. RANKIN, Professor of Political Science and Chairman of the Department of Political Science, Duke University; member, City Council, Durham, North Carolina. A.B., Tusculum College, 1920; A.M., Princeton

University, 1922, Ph.D., 1924. President, Southern Political Science Association (1930); author of several books and numerous articles in professional journals in the fields of constitutional law and American government. Member, United States Commission on Civil Rights.

BENNETT M. RICH, Professor of Political Science, Rutgers University. A.B., Waynesburg College, 1930; A.M., University of Michigan, 1932, Ph.D., 1941. Author, *The Presidents and Civil Disorder* (1941) and *The Government and Administration of New Jersey* (1957).

EMIL J. SADY, Senior Programme Officer, United Nations Division for Public Administration. B.S. and M.S., University of Southern California, 1938; M.A., Columbia University, 1945. Formerly a member of the senior staff in governmental studies, Brookings Institution; consultant to the Planning Board of Puerto Rico and to the Alaska Constitutional Convention; and Chief, Pacific Division, Office of Territories, United States Department of the Interior. Recipient of the Department's Distinguished Service Award (1952) and the Rockefeller Public Service Award (1953). Author of *The United Nations and Dependent Peoples* (1956).

CHARLES W. SHULL, Professor of Political Science, Wayne State University. A.B., Ohio Wesleyan University, 1926; M.A., Ohio State University, 1927, Ph.D., 1929. Associated with the Department of Political Science at Wayne University since 1930; has written extensively in the fields of legislative apportionment, unicameralism, and legislative investigations. President of Pi Sigma Alpha, 1941-47. Vice President of the Midwest Conference of Political Scientists (1953); Book Review Editor of *Social Science* and Managing Editor of the *Midwest Journal of Political Science.*

HARVEY WALKER, Professor of Political Science, Ohio State University. A.B., University of Kansas, 1923; M.A., University of Minnesota, 1927, Ph.D., 1928; LL.B., Ohio State University, 1948. Secretary-Treasurer, American Political Science Association, 1942-50; National Secretary-Treasurer, National President, Pi Sigma Alpha; Budget Director, State of Ohio, 1929-31; Expert, UN TAA, Brazil and Central America. Author of *Public Administration in the United States* (1937); *The Legislative Process* (1948); *Government and Administration of Ohio* (with Francis R. Aumann, 1956), and numerous articles in professional journals and law reviews.

O. DOUGLAS WEEKS, Professor of Government, The University of Texas. B.A., Ohio Wesleyan University, 1918; M.A., University of Wisconsin,

1919, Ph.D., 1924. Was a member of the Committee on American Legislatures of the American Political Science Association; consultant in the revision of the Model State Constitution. Author of numerous monographs and articles on American and Texas politics and elections and on the American legislative process.

HENRY WELLS, Associate Professor of Political Science, University of Pennsylvania. A.B., University of Illinois, 1937; M.A., Louisiana State University, 1939; Ph.D., Yale University, 1947. Member of the research staff, Puerto Rico Constitutional Convention, 1951-52. Publications include articles on developments toward self-government in American territories.

MITCHELL WENDELL, Professor of Political Science, American International College; member of the staff of the New York Joint Legislative Committee on Interstate Cooperation. A.B., Brooklyn College, 1943; LL.B., Columbia University, 1945, Ph.D., 1949. Author of *Relations between the Federal and State Courts* and (with Frederick L. Zimmermann) of *The Interstate Compact since 1925* and *Congress: A Second Umpire of the Federal System.*

HERBERT L. WILTSEE, Director, Southern Office, Council of State Governments; Secretary, National Legislative Conference; Secretary, National Association of Attorneys General. B.A., Ohio Wesleyan University, 1935; M.A., University of Chicago, 1950. Former Director of Research and Publications, Council of State Governments; Lecturer in Political Science, University of Chicago.

selected bibliography

W. Brooke Graves, compiler

GENERAL WORKS

Books and Monographs

Bartley, Ernest R., ed. Criteria of Constitution Drafting, *and* What a State Constitution Should Contain. Florida Constitution Advisory Commission, n. p., n. d. Pp. 25. Research Report No. 5.

Bebout, John E. "The Constitution as a Plan for Government." In Model State Constitution, with Explanatory Articles, 5th ed., pp. 23-25. New York: National Municipal League, 1948.

————. "Schedule: Launching a New Constitution." In *ibid.,* pp. 51-52.

Bondy, William. The Separation of Governmental Powers. New York: Columbia University, 1896. In Studies in History, Economics and Public Law.

Brennan, Ellen E. Plural Office-Holding in Massachusetts, 1760-1780; a Study in the Separation of Powers. Chapel Hill: University of North Carolina Press, 1944.

Dealey, James Q. Growth of American State Constitutions from 1776 to the End of the Year 1914. Boston: Ginn & Co., 1915. Pp. 308. Bibliography, pp. 297-301.

Dishman, Robert B. The Constitutional Document as a Constitutional Problem. New York: National Municipal League, 1960.

Edwards, Richard A., and others. Index Digest of State Constitutions, 2d ed. New York: Oceana Press, 1959. Pp. 1132. First prepared by the Legislative Drafting Fund, Columbia University, for the New York State Constitutional Convention Committee. Albany: J. B. Lyon Company, 1915.

Graves, W. Brooke. "State Constitutions and Constitutional Conventions, 1939-1940." In The Book of the States, 1941-1942, pp. 45-55. Chicago: Council of State Governments, 1941. The first of a series of articles which have appeared in each succeeding issue of The Book of the States.

————. What Should a State Constitution Contain? New York: National Municipal League, 1938. Reprinted and reproduced in many places, as in Governor's Committee on Preparatory Research for the New Jersey Constitutional Convention. Trenton, 1947; also in Convention Proceedings, Vol. II, pp. 1329-35.

Green, Fletcher M. Constitutional Development in the South Atlantic States, 1776-1860; a Study in the Evolution of Democracy. Chapel Hill: University of North Carolina Press, 1930. Pp. 328. Bibliography, pp. 305-24.

NOTE: Much of the work on this bibliography was done in 1957-58 in connection with the National Municipal League's project on State Constitutions and Constitutional Revision.

Harris, Roy V. "Separation of the Branches of Government." Georgia Bar Association, Proceedings, 1944, pp. 191-98.

Hawaii. Legislature. Legislative Reference Bureau. Manual of State Constitutional Provisions. Honolulu: University of Hawaii, 1950. Pp. 396.

Hicks, John D. The Constitutions of the Northwest States. Lincoln: University of Nebraska Press, 1923. Pp. 162. Bibliography, pp. 155-62. Covers states of Idaho, Montana, North Dakota, South Dakota, Washington, and Wyoming.

Kettleborough, Charles, ed. The State Constitutions and the Federal Constitution and Organic Laws of the Territories and Other Colonial Dependencies of the United States of America, 3 vols. Indianapolis: B. F. Bowen & Co., 1918; reissued, Indianapolis: Bobbs-Merrill Co., 1928.

McCarthy, M. Barbara. The Widening Scope of American Constitutions. Washington, D. C.: Catholic University of America, 1928. Pp. 135.

McIlwain, Charles H. Constitutionalism, Ancient and Modern, rev. ed. Ithaca: Cornell University Press, 1958. A Gold Seal Book. Pp. 180.

McLaughlin, Andrew C. Foundations of American Constitutionalism. New York: New York University Press, 1932. Pp. 176.

Moore, Russell F., ed. Modern Constitutions; with Brief Commentaries. Ames, Iowa: Littlefield, Adams, 1957. Pp. 305.

Mott, Rodney L., and Hindman, Wilbert L., eds. Constitutions of the States and the United States. New York State Constitutional Convention Committee, Report, Vol. III. Albany: 1938. Pp. 1845.

National Municipal League. Model State Constitution, with Explanatory Articles, 5th ed. New York: 1948. Pp. 57. Prepared by State Government Committee, W. Brooke Graves, chairman.

Ohio. State Library. A Digest of State Constitutions. Columbus: F. J. Heer Co., 1912.

Oklahoma. Legislature. Legislative Council. Oklahoma Constitutional Studies. Oklahoma City: 1950. Pp. 604.

Owen, J. Kimbrough, ed. Papers Delivered at the panel on State Constitutional Developments. Forty-fourth Annual Meeting, American Political Science Association, Chicago, December 1948. Baton Rouge: Louisiana State University, 1949. Mimeographed.

Poore, Benjamin P., ed. The Federal and State Constitutions, Colonial Charters, and Other Organic Laws of the United States, 2 vols. Washington, D. C.: Government Printing Office, 1877.

Public Administration Service. Constitutional Studies Prepared . . . for the Alaska Constitutional Convention, 3 vols. Chicago: 1955. Mimeographed.

Spiro, Herbert J. Government by Constitution; the Political Systems of Democracy. New York: Random House, 1959. Pp. 496.

Stimson, Frederic J. The Law of the Federal and State Constitutions of the United States. Boston: Boston Book Co., 1908. Pp. 386.

Thornton, Hershel V. What a State Constitution Should Contain. Oklahoma City: Oklahoma Legislative Council, November 1947. Pp. 7, mimeographed.

Thorpe, Francis N., ed. The Federal and State Constitutions, Colonial Charters, and Other Organic Laws of the States, Territories, and Colonies Now or Heretofore Forming the United States of America, 7 vols. Washington, D. C.: Government Printing Office, 1909.

Wheeler, John P., and Bebout, John E. Recent Thinking about State Constitutions. Washington, D. C.: American Political Science Association, 1959. Pp. 24, mimeographed.

Willbern, York Y. Suggestions Concerning a Study of the Historical Development of State Constitutions. Prepared for a conference at the National Municipal League, New York, September 7, 1957. Pp. 9, mimeographed.

Articles

Aikin, Charles. "State Constitutional Law, 1939-1940." American Political Science Review, August 1940, pp. 700-18.

————. "————, 1940-1941." American Political Science Review, August 1941, pp. 683-700.

————. "————, 1941-1942." American Political Science Review, August 1942, pp. 667-88.

Bates, Frank G. "Constitutional Amendments." American Political Science Review, August 1914, pp. 445-51.

Beale, Howard K. "On Rewriting Reconstruction History." American Historical Review, July 1940, pp. 807-27.

Benson, George C. S. "State Constitutional Development in 1935." American Political Science Review, April 1936, pp. 275-79.

————. "————, 1936." American Political Science Review, April 1937, pp. 280-85.

Boudin, Louis B. "Majority Rule and Constitutional Limitations." Lawyers Guild Review, March-April 1944, pp. 1-11.

Braden, George D. "Search for Objectivity in Constitutional Law." Yale Law Journal, February 1948, pp. 571-94.

Burdine, J. Alton. "Basic Materials for the Study of State Constitutions and State Constitutional Development." American Political Science Review, December 1954, pp. 1140-52.

Callender, Clarence N., and others, eds. "The State Constitution of the Future." Annals, September 1935, entire issue.

Carpenter, William S. "Separation of Powers in the Eighteenth Century." American Political Science Review, February 1928, pp. 32-44.

Cassinelli, C. W. "The 'Consent' of the Governed." Western Political Quarterly, June 1959, pp. 391-409.

Coil, H. W. "Remarks on Separation of Powers: a Reply to Professor Kinnane." American Bar Association Journal, May 1952, pp. 365-68, 441.

Cole, Kenneth C. " 'Government,' 'Law,' and the Separation of Powers." American Political Science Review, June 1939, pp. 424-40.

Connors, Arthur. "Constitutional Amendments and Referred Measures." American Political Science Review, February 1936, pp. 104-109.

Cushman, Robert E. "Constitutional Law in 1930-1931." American Political Science Review, April 1932, pp. 256-84. For questions of state power, see pp. 270-84, and similarly in subsequent articles in this annual series.

Dealey, James Q. "General Tendencies in State Constitutions." American Political Science Review, February 1907, pp. 200-12.

————. "Our State Constitutions." Annals, Supplement, 1907.

————. "The Trend of Recent Constitutional Changes." American Political Science Review, February 1912, pp. 53-60.

De Grazia, Alfred. "State Constitutions—Are They Growing Longer?" State Government, April 1954, pp. 82-83.

Dionisopoulos, P. Allen. "Indiana, 1851, Alaska, 1956: a Century of Difference in State Constitutions." Indiana Law Journal, Fall 1958, pp. 34-55.

Dodd, Walter F. "Defense of Our Constitutional System." American Bar Association Journal, May 1937, pp. 344-46.

————. "Judicial Function in Construing a Written Constitution." Illinois Law Quarterly, June 1922, pp. 219-32.

————. "Judicially Non-enforcible Provisions of Constitutions." University of Pennsylvania Law Review, September 1931, pp. 54-93.

————. "Problem of State Constitutional Construction." Columbia Law Review, June 1920, pp. 635-56.

Enslow, Harold R. "State Constitutional Development through Amendment in 1931." American Political Science Review, February 1932, pp. 96-98.

————. "————, 1932." American Political Science Review, May 1933, pp. 227-36.

————. "————, 1933." American Political Science Review, May 1934, pp. 245-50.

————. "————, 1934." American Political Science Review, June 1935, pp. 432-37.

Fairlie, John A. "The Separation of Powers." Michigan Law Review, February 1923, pp. 393-436.

Fellman, David. "Constitutional Law in 1958-1959: II." American Political Science Review, June 1960, pp. 474-93. Deals with state questions.

Field, Oliver P. "State Constitutional Law in 1928-1929." American Political Science Review, August 1929, pp. 688-717.

————. "————, 1929-1930." American Political Science Review, August 1930, pp. 666-86.

————. "————, 1930-1931." American Political Science Review, August 1931, pp. 650-70.

Gallagher, Hubert R. "State Constitutional Development in 1938-1939." American Political Science Review, June 1940, pp. 506-12.

Gardner, Dillard S. "The Continuous Revision of Our State Constitution." North Carolina Law Review, April 1958, pp. 297-313.

Gilmore, Eugene A. "Changing Constitutional Concepts." Oregon Law Review, December 1934, pp. 131-38; discussion, pp. 148-52.

————. "Constitutional Integrity—Changing Concepts." Nebraska Law Bulletin, May 1936, pp. 403-16.

Godshall, W. Leon. "State Constitutional Development through Amendment in 1927." American Political Science Review, February 1929, pp. 102-105.

————. "————, 1928." American Political Science Review, May 1929, pp. 404-409.

————. "————, 1929." American Political Science Review, May 1930, pp. 367-70.

————. "————, 1930." American Political Science Review, May 1931, pp. 327-36.

————. "————, 1933." American Political Science Review, April 1934, pp. 245-50.

————. "————, 1934." American Political Science Review, April 1935, pp. 432-37.

Grant, James A. C. "State Constitutional Law, 1935-1936." American Political Science Review, August 1936, pp. 692-712.

————. "————, 1936-1937." American Political Science Review, August 1937, pp. 659-79.

————. "————, 1937-1938." American Political Science Review, August 1938, pp. 670-93.

————. "————, 1938-1939." American Political Science Review, August 1939, pp. 615-33.

Graves, W. Brooke. "The Fourth Edition of the Model State Constitution." American Political Science Review, October 1941, pp. 916-19.

————. "Writing a New Constitution. National Municipal League's Committee on State Government Reports to the St. Louis Conference." National Municipal Review, February 1942, pp. 92-99.

Green, Thomas F., Jr. "A Malapropian Provision of State Constitutions." Washington University Law Quarterly, April 1939, pp. 359-81.

Guild, Frederick H. "Amendments to State Constitutions, 1923-1924." American Political Science Review, August 1925, pp. 541-44.

Haines, Charles G. "State Constitutional Law in 1931-1932." American Political Science Review, August 1932, pp. 660-82.

————. "————, 1932-1933." American Political Science Review, October 1933, pp. 752-68.

————. "————, 1933-1934." American Political Science Review, August 1934, pp. 611-27.

————. "————, 1934-1935." American Political Science Review, August 1935, pp. 610-30.

Harris, Robert J. "Constitutional Law in 1949-1950." American Political Science Review, March 1951, pp. 86-109.

Havard, William C. "Notes on a Theory of State Constitutional Change: the Florida Experience." Journal of Politics, February 1959, pp. 80-104.

Huff, W. H. "New Charter of Slavery." National Bar Journal, June 1944, pp. 65-69.

————. "Peonage or Debt Slavery in the Land of the Free." National Bar Journal, March 1945, pp. 43-49.

Humphrey, J. P. "The Theory of the Separation of Functions." University of Toronto Law Journal, Lent Term 1946, pp. 331-60.

Jefferson, B. S. "Supreme Court and State Separation and Delegation of Powers." Columbia Law Review, January 1944, pp. 1-33.

Kerwin, Jerome G. "The State Constitution and Our Local Government." Illinois Law Review, May 1938, pp. 32-41.

Kettleborough, Charles. "Amendments to State Constitutions, 1919-1921." American Political Science Review, May 1922, pp. 245-76.

Lardner, Lynford A. "How Far Does the Constitution Separate Church and State?" American Political Science Review, March 1951, pp. 110-32.

Laughlin, C. V. "A Study in Constitutional Rigidity." University of Chicago Law Review, January 1943, pp. 142-76.

Llewellyn, Karl L. "The Constitution as an Institution." Oregon Law Review, December 1934, pp. 108-18; discussion, pp. 118-30.

Lyon, C. S. "Old Statutes and New Constitution." Columbia Law Review, September 1944, pp. 599-638.

McClain, Emlin. "Written and Unwritten Constitutions in the United States." Columbia Law Review, February 1906, pp. 69-81.

McMurray, O. K. "Some Tendencies in Constitution Making." California Law Review, March 1914, pp. 203-24.

Morey, William C. "The First State Constitutions." Annals, September 1893, pp. 201-32.

Munro, William B. "An Ideal State Constitution." Annals, September 1935, pp. 1-10.

Neuberger, Richard L. "States in Straitjackets." American Magazine, April 1951, pp. 34-35, 121-24.

"On State Constitutions." Washington University Law Quarterly, April 1942, entire issue.

Parker, Reginald. "The Historic Basis of Administrative Law: Separation of Powers and Judicial Supremacy." Rutgers Law Review, Spring 1958, pp. 449-81.

————. "Separation of Powers Revisited—Its Meaning in Administrative Law." Michigan Law Review, May 1951, pp. 1009-38.

Rossman, George. "Spirit of Laws: the Doctrine of Separation of Powers." American Bar Association Journal, February 1949, pp. 93-96.

Sherman, Gordon E. "Early Suggestions of the Modern Written Constitution." Yale Law Journal, February 1906, pp. 172-77.

Sherwood, Foster H. "State Constitutional Law in 1946-1947." American Political Science Review, August 1947, pp. 723-30.

————. "————, 1947-1948." American Political Science Review, August 1948, pp. 694-729.

————. "————, 1948-1949." American Political Science Review, August 1949, pp. 735-65.

"Some Notes on Constitution Making in the States." Constitution Review, April 1922, pp. 114-19. Covers Illinois, Louisiana, and Pennsylvania.

Ten Broek, Jacobus. "State Constitutional Law in 1942-1943." American Political Science Review, August 1943, pp. 642-60.

————, and Graham, Howard J. "————, 1943-1944." American Political Science Review, August 1944, pp. 670-92.

————, ————. "————, 1944-1945." American Political Science Review, August 1945, pp. 685-719.

————, ————. "————, 1945-1946." American Political Science Review, August 1946, pp. 703-28.

Warp, George. "Independent Regulatory Commissions and the Separation of Powers Doctrine." Notre Dame Lawyer, March 1941, pp. 183-93.

Webster, William C. "A Comparative Study of the State Constitutions of the American Revolution." Annals, May 1897, pp. 64-104.

Wickersham, George W. "New States and Constitutions." Yale Law Journal, November 1911, pp. 1-31. Criticizing the initiative, referendum, and recall.

Wilson, Francis G. "The Mixed Constitution and the Separation of Powers." Southwestern Social Science Quarterly, June 1934, pp. 14-28.

Woods, Charles A. "On Making Constitutions." American Bar Association Journal, January 1925, pp. 47-51.

CONSTITUTIONAL REVISION—GENERAL

Books and Monographs

Bebout, John E. "Making a New Constitution." In Papers Delivered at the Panel on State Constitutional Developments, Forty-fourth Annual Meeting, American Political Science Association, December 1948. Baton Rouge: Louisiana State University, 1949. Mimeographed.

Bromage, Arthur W. "New Patterns in Constitution Making." In *ibid.*

Cape, William H. Constitutional Revision in Kansas. Lawrence: Governmental Research Center, University of Kansas, 1958. Pp. 76.

Citizens Research Council of Michigan. Michigan Constitutional Issues. Detroit, June 1960. Pp. 42.

Dauer, Manning J. The Proposed New Florida Constitution: an Analysis. Gainesville: Public Administration Clearing Service, University of Florida, 1958. Pp. 20.

Dodd, Walter F. The Revision and Amendment of State Constitutions. Baltimore: Johns Hopkins Press, 1910. Pp. 350.

————. "Revision of State Constitutions." In Academy of Political Science, Proceedings, 1914-1915, pp. 54-72.

Duvell, J. E. Modernizing State Constitutions. Gainesville: Public Administration Clearing Service, University of Florida, 1950. Pp. 11.

George, John J. Amendment and Revision of State Constitutions. Governor's Committee on Preparatory Research for the New Jersey Constitutional Convention, Trenton, 1947. Also in Convention Proceedings, Vol. II, pp. 1759-66.

Glosser, Lauren A. Constitutional Revision in the States of the Union, rev. ed. Columbus: Ohio Program Commission, January 1951.

Graves, W. Brooke. "Procedural Changes in State Constitutions." In Papers Delivered at the Panel on State Constitutional Developments, Forty-fourth Annual Meeting, American Political Science Association, December 1948. Baton Rouge: Louisiana State University, 1949. Mimeographed.

————. Salient Issues in Constitutional Revision. A discussion outline prepared for a conference at the National Municipal League, New York, September 4, 1957. Pp. 5, mimeographed.

————. "State Reorganization and Constitutional Revision in the Twentieth Century." In National Conference on Government, Proceedings, 1953, pp. 1-4. New York: National Municipal League, 1954. Panel on More Responsible States at Richmond meeting, November 1953.

Greene, Lee S., ed. Papers on Constitutional Revision, 2 vols. Knoxville: University of Tennessee Record, 1947.

Hobbs, Edward H., ed. Yesterday's Constitution Today. University: Bureau of Public Administration, University of Mississippi, 1960. Pp. 151.

Keith, John P. Methods of Constitutional Revision. Austin: Bureau of Municipal Research, University of Texas, 1949.

————. Public Relations Program for a Citizen Committee. Austin: Bureau of Municipal Research, University of Texas, 1950.

League of Women Voters of the United States. The League and State Constitutional Revision. Washington, D. C., n. d.

Modernizing State Constitutions. New York: National Municipal League, March 1948. Pp. 21. Reprint of a series of articles appearing in the National Municipal Review.

Mussey, Henry R., ed. Revision of the State Constitution, 2 parts. Academy of Political Science, Proceedings, 1914-1915, pp. 1-215.

Nelson, Frances F. Constitutional Change in Kansas. Lawrence: Governmental Research Center, University of Kansas, 1958. Pp. 41.

New York. Temporary Commission on the Revision and Simplification of the Constitution. First Steps Toward a Modern Constitution. Legislative Document No. 58. Albany: 1959. Pp. 104.

New York Chamber of Commerce. Modernizing the State Constitution. New York: 1960. Pp. 14.

Sanders, John L. Constitutional Revision and Court Reform: A Legislative History, 1959. Chapel Hill: Institute of Government, University of North Carolina, 1959. Pp. 39, mimeographed.

Short, Lloyd M. Substantive Changes in State Constitutions. In Papers Delivered at the Panel on State Constitutional Developments, Forty-fourth Annual Meeting, American Political Science Association, December 1948. Baton Rouge: Louisiana State University, 1949. Mimeographed.

Sturm, Albert L. Methods of State Constitutional Reform. Ann Arbor: University of Michigan Press, 1954. Pp. 175.

Vandenbosch, Amry. The Constitution of Kentucky: Suggestions for Revision. Lexington: Bureau of Government Research, University of Kentucky, 1948.

White, John P. Voting Machines and the 1958 Defeat of Constitutional Revision in Michigan. Ann Arbor: Institute of Public Administration, University of Michigan, 1960. Pp. 50.

Articles

Bebout, John E. "Recent Constitution Writing." Texas Law Review, October 1957, pp. 1071-89.

Braden, George D. "A New Constitution for Connecticut." Connecticut Bar Journal, June 1950, pp. 121-81; September 1950, pp. 265-323.

Chute, Charlton F. "How to Get a New Constitution." National Municipal Review, March 1947, pp. 124-30.

"Constitutional Revision Concerns Women Voters." National Municipal Review, October 1949, p. 470.

Dodd, Walter F. "Constitutional Convention or Amending Clause?" Illinois Law Review, April 1915, pp. 612-19.

Edison, Charles. "How to Wake up an Old State." National Municipal Review, December 1951, pp. 574-79.

"Governors Speak Up for Constitutional Revision." National Municipal Review, March 1955, pp. 145-46.

Graves, W. Brooke. "Fourth Edition of the Model State Constitution." American Political Science Review, October 1941, pp. 916-19.

————. "Writing a New Constitution." National Municipal Review, February 1942, pp. 92-99.

Hindman, Wilbert L. "A 'Working Model' State Constitution." State Government, April 1942, pp. 83-84, 92.

Kerney, James, Jr. "Price of a New Constitution." National Municipal Review, January 1952, pp. 14-17, 63.

Lambert, Louis E., and McPheron, E. B. "Modernizing Indiana's Constitution." Indiana Law Journal, Winter 1951, pp. 185-206.

Lavery, Urban A. "Revising a Constitution." Illinois Law Review, February 1921, pp. 437-46.

Lockard, W. Duane. "Constitutional Revision in Connecticut." Connecticut Bar Journal, January 1953, pp. 163-69.

McDemott, Edward J. "Making a Constitution." American Law Review, November-December 1919, pp. 853-78.

Owen, J. Kimbrough. "Blazing the Constitution Trail." National Municipal Review, March 1948, pp. 140-44.

————. "Constitutional Revision by the Research Method." National Municipal Review, May 1948, pp. 267-70. On work of Louisiana Law Institute.

Powell, Alden L. "Constitutional Growth and Revision in the South." Journal of Politics, May 1948, pp. 354-84.

Reed, Harry. "Constitutional Reform in the States." North American Review, July 1875, pp. 1-36.

Reeves, John E. "The Constitution Making Process." Kentucky Law Journal, November 1947, pp. 63-80.

————, and Vanlandingham, Kenneth S. "Amending and Revising State Constitutions." Kentucky Law Journal, January 1947, pp. 119-28.

"Remaking the States' Constitutions." World's Work, August 1917, pp. 363-64.

"Renovating Used Constitutions." State Government, March 1931, pp. 8-9.

Ridgeway, Marian, and Drury, James W. "Constitutional Revision." Your Government, December 15, 1948, entire issue. Published at University of Kansas.

Rohlfing, Charles C. "Amendment and Revision of State Constitutions." Annals, September 1935, pp. 180-87.

Rosewater, Victor. "A Curious Chapter in Constitution Making." Political Science Quarterly, September 1921, pp. 409-19.

Satterfield, Millard H. "County Government and Constitutional Revision in Tennessee." Tennessee Law Review, February 1947, pp. 707-17.

Sears, Kenneth C. "Constitutional Revision and the Party Circle Bills." University of Chicago Law Review, February 1947, pp. 200-14.

————. "Voting on Constitutional Conventions and Amendments." University of Chicago Law Review, June 1935, pp. 612-18.

————, and Laughlin, C. V. "A Study in Constitutional Rigidity." University of Chicago Law Review, January 1943, pp. 142-76.

Seymour, Charles B. "The Nature and Effect of Changes in Constitutions." Kentucky Law Journal, November 1924, pp. 51-61.

"State Constitutions Subject of Studies." National Municipal Review, November 1949, p. 524.

Stubbs, W. B. "Constitution Making in Georgia." Georgia Bar Journal, February 1944, pp. 207-13.

"A Time to Try Men's Constitutions." National Municipal Review, June 1943, pp. 282-83.

White, Thomas R. "Amendment and Revision of State Constitutions." University of Pennsylvania Law Review, June 1952, pp. 1132-52.

Witherspoon, John H. "Urges Bar Leadership in Obtaining Revision of State Constitution." Detroit Lawyer, March 1948, pp. 55-63.

PRINCIPAL METHODS OF REVISION

Constitutional Conventions

Bebout, John E. Recent Developments in the Use of the Constitutional Convention in the States. New York: National Municipal League, 1955. Pp. 21, mimeographed. Paper presented at the Annual Meeting, American Political Science Association, Boulder, Colorado, September 8, 1955.

Faust, Martin L. Organization Manual. Missouri Constitutional Convention of 1943. Columbia: 1943.

Hoar, Roger S. Constitutional Conventions, Their Nature, Powers, and Limitations. Boston: Little, Brown & Co., 1917. Pp. 240.

Illinois. General Assembly. Legislative Reference Bureau. The Procedure and Problems of the Constitutional Convention. Springfield: 1920. Illinois Constitutional Convention Bulletin No. 1.

Jameson, John A. A Treatise on Constitutional Conventions; Their History, Powers, and Modes of Proceeding. New York: Scribners, 1867. Fourth Edition, revised and enlarged. Chicago: Callaghan & Co., 1887. Pp. 684.

Kuhlman, Arthur F., comp. Official Publications Relating to American State Constitutional Conventions. New York: H. W. Wilson Co., 1935.

O'Rourke, Vernon A., and Campbell, D. W. Constitution Making in a Democracy. Baltimore: Johns Hopkins Press, 1943. Deals mainly with New York Convention of 1938.

Sady, Emil J. Manual on the Administration of a State Constitutional Convention. New York: National Municipal League, September 1957. Pp. 5, mimeographed. A discussion outline prepared for a conference at the League offices.

Uhl, Raymond, and others. Constitutional Conventions; Organization, Powers, Functions and Procedures. Columbia: Bureau of Public Administration, University of South Carolina, 1951. Pp. 34. Constitution Bulletin No. 1.

Walker, Harvey. The Legislative Process; Law Making in the United States. New York: Ronald Press, 1948. Pp. 482. Includes discussion of conventions.

* * *

Almand, B. "The States Should Call a Constitutional Convention." Georgia Bar Journal, May 1948, pp. 437-46.

Bebout, John E., and Kass, Julius. "The Status of Constitutional Convention in New Jersey." University of Newark Law Review, Summer 1938, pp. 146-72.

Braxton, A. Caperston. "Powers of Conventions." Virginia Law Register, June 1901, pp. 79-100.

Bromage, Arthur W. "Michigan Con Con Fails; Non-voters Help Kill Move to Secure Convention to Produce Needed Revision of State Constitution." National Civic Review, January 1959, pp. 12-14, 28.

Connor, James T. "Call for a Constitutional Convention." Loyola Law Review, June 1945, pp. 72-73.

Connors, Arthur. "Constitutional Conventions." American Political Science Review, May 1918, pp. 270-71.

"Constitution Making." New Republic, November 20, 1915, pp. 59-60.

"Constitutional Revision by a Restricted Convention." Minnesota Law Review, February 1951, pp. 283-97.

Dodd, Walter F. "The First State Constitutional Convention, 1776-1783." American Political Science Review, November 1908, pp. 545-61.

————. "State Constitutional Conventions and State Legislative Power." Vanderbilt Law Review, December 1948, pp. 27-34.

Dorr, Harold M. "The Myth of the Constitutional Convention." Michigan Alumnus Quarterly Review, December 6, 1947, pp. 22-33.

Haines, Charles G. "Can a State Legislature Call a Constitutional Convention without First Submitting the Question to the Electorate?" Texas Law Review, April 1923, pp. 329-35.

Hendricks, Homer. "Some Legal Aspects of Constitutional Conventions." Texas Law Review, February 1924, pp. 195-219.

Hindman, Wilbert L. "Road-Blocks to Conventions." National Municipal Review, March 1948, pp. 129-32, 144. Discusses three: legal, political, psychological.

Hoar, Roger S. "Invention of Constitutional Conventions." Constitution Review, April 1918, pp. 97-100.

Keasby, E. O. "Legislature—to Call a Constitutional Convention." New Jersey Law Journal, May 1895, pp. 152-58.

Lavery, Urban A. "Constitutional Convention or Super-Legislature?" Illinois Law Review, November 1919, pp. 269-71.

Loeb, Isadore. "Constitutions and Constitutional Conventions." Missouri Historical Review, January 1922, pp. 189-238.

Poletti, Charles. "First Steps in Streamlining a Constitution." State Government, August 1938, pp. 148-49, 157.

Rich, Bennett M. "Convention or Commission?" National Municipal Review, March 1948, pp. 133-39.

Seabury, Samuel. "Property Representation and the Constitutional Convention." National Municipal Review, December 1937, pp. 567-71.

Sears, Kenneth C. "Voting on Constitutional Conventions and Amendments." University of Chicago Law Review, June 1935, pp. 612-18.

Shenton, Clarence G. "Can the Legislature Alone Call a Constitutional Convention?" Temple Law Quarterly, November 1935, pp. 25-40.

Sims, Cecil. "Limited Constitutional Convention in Tennessee." Tennessee Law Review, December 1949, pp. 1-8.

Thornton, W. W. "Power of the Legislature to Call a Constitutional Convention." Central Law Journal, November 8, 1924, pp. 368-72.

Williams, Henry N. "Calling a Limited Constitutional Convention." Tennessee Law Review, April 1950, pp. 249-56.

Constitutional Commissions

Florida. Constitution Advisory Commission. Recommended Constitution for Florida. n. p., n. d.

Gosnell, Cullen B., and Anderson, C. David. The Government and Administration of Georgia, Chapter 3. New York: Thomas Y. Crowell Co., 1956. Vol. 9 in American Commonwealths Series.

Kentucky. Constitution Review Commission. 1954 Report. Frankfort: 1954.

New York. Legislature. Temporary State Commission on the Constitutional Convention. First Interim Report. Legislative Document No. 8. Albany: February 1957. Pp. 17.

————. ————. ————. Second Interim Report. Legislative Document No. 57. Albany: September 1957. Pp. 58.

————. ————. Special Legislative Committee on the Revision and Simplification of the State Constitution. Inter-Law School Committee Report on the Problem of Simplification of the Constitution. Legislative Document No. 57. Albany: May 1958. Pp. 225.

North Carolina. Constitutional Commission. Report of the . . . to the Governor and Members of the General Assembly of the State of North Carolina. Raleigh: 1959. Pp. 146.

Oregon. Governor's and Legislative Constitutional Committee. Report. Salem: 1955.

Rich, Bennett M. The Government and Administration of New Jersey, Chapter 2. New York: Thomas Y. Crowell Co., 1957. Vol. 28 in American Commonwealths Series.

Saye, Albert B., ed. Records of the Commission of 1943-1944 to Revise the Constitution of Georgia, 2 vols. Atlanta: By authority of the State, 1946.

Sturm, Albert L. Methods of State Constitutional Reform. Ann Arbor: University of Michigan Press, 1954. Especially pp. 121-47.

* * *

Aikin, Charles. "The Movement for Revision of the California Constitution: the State Constitutional Commission." American Political Science Review, May 1931, pp. 337-42.

Arnall, Ellis. "25 Study Georgia Basic Law." National Municipal Review, January 1944, pp. 11-13.

Bebout, John E. "New Jersey Commission on Constitutional Revision Reports." National Municipal Review, June 1942, pp. 343-45.

Hendrickson, Robert C. "New Jersey Considers a New Constitution." State Government, December 1942, pp. 231-32, 249-71.

Hindman, Wilbert L. "Constitutional Research for California Revision Project." National Municipal Review, May 1948, pp. 270-71.

Lewis, William D. "Constitutional Revision in Pennsylvania." American Political Science Review, November 1921, pp. 558-65.

Logan, Bell. "Constitution Revision for Oklahoma." State Government, June 1949, pp. 155-56, 161-62.

Miller, William. "The Report of New Jersey's Constitutional Commission." American Political Science Review, October 1942, pp. 900-906.

Mowrer, Edmund C. "Constitutional Amendments in Vermont." American Political Science Review, February 1923, pp. 70-79.

Owen, J. Kimbrough. "Constitutional Revision in Louisiana: the Preliminary Stage." State Government, December 1947, pp. 304-306, 320.

————. "Constitutional Revision by the Research Method." National Municipal Review, May 1949, pp. 267-70.

"Renovating Used Constitutions." State Government, March 1931, pp. 8-9. Compares California and West Virginia Commissions.

Rich, Bennett M. "Convention or Commission?" National Municipal Review, March 1948, pp. 133-39.

————. "Revision by Commission." National Municipal Review, April 1951, pp. 201-206.

Saye, Albert B. "Georgia's Proposed New Constitution." American Political Science
Review, June 1945, pp. 459-63.

Short, Lloyd M. "Constitutional Revision for Minnesota." State Government, May
1950, pp. 97-99.

Constitutional Initiative and Referendum

Council of State Governments. Constitutional Amendments and Direct Legislation.
Chicago: 1940.

New York. State Constitutional Convention Committee. Problems Relating to Legislative Organization and Procedure, Chapter 9. Albany: 1938.

Spencer, Richard C. Proposals Voted on in 1944: Elections 1944. Washington, D. C.:
U. S. Bureau of the Census, 1945. One of a series of annual publications.

Steinbicker, Paul G., and Faust, Martin L. Manual on the Amending Procedure and
the Initiative and Referendum. Missouri Constitutional Convention of 1943.
Columbia: 1943.

*   *   *

"Amending and Revising the Constitution by Initiative." Southern California Law
Review, December 1948, pp. 54-56.

"Constitutional Amendments—Direct Legislation."State Government, January 1957,
inside front cover.

Crouch, Winston W. "The Constitutional Initiative in Operation." American Political
Science Review, August 1939, pp. 634-45.

————. "Direct Legislation Laboratory." National Municipal Review, February 1951,
pp. 634-45.

Foxcroft, F. "Constitution Making and the Initiative." Atlantic Monthly, June 1906,
pp. 792-96.

Hallett, George H., Jr. "The Constitutional Initiative Starts a New Advance." National
Municipal Review, May 1935, pp. 254-57.

Lewis, William D. "A New Method of Constitutional Amendment by Popular Vote."
Annals, September 1912, pp. 311-25.

The Role of the Legislature

Weeks, O. Douglas. Research in the American State Legislative Process. Ann Arbor:
J. W. Edwards, 1947.

*   *   *

Bebout, John E. "New Task for a Legislature." National Municipal Review, January
1944, pp. 17-21.

Shenton, Clarence G. "Can the Legislature Alone Call a Constitutional Convention?"
Temple Law Quarterly, November 1935, pp. 25-40.

Thornton, W. W. "Power of the Legislature to Call a Constitutional Convention."
Central Law Journal, November 8, 1924, pp. 368-72.

AMENDING PROCEDURES

Council of State Governments. Constitutional Amendments and Direct Legislation—
1936. Chicago: December 1936. Pp. 31. Additions and corrections issued,
March 1937.

————. ————, 1937. Chicago: January 1938. Pp. 18, mimeographed.

————. ————, 1940. Chicago: December 1940. Pp. 27, mimeographed. A
Digest of Constitutional Amendments, Initiated and Referred Statutes Voted
upon in the Several States during 1940.

Dodd, Walter F. Revision and Amendment of State Constitutions. Baltimore: Johns
Hopkins Press, 1922. Pp. 350.

Graves, W. Brooke. Procedural Changes in State Constitutions. In Papers Delivered
at the Panel on State Constitutional Developments, Forty-fourth Annual Meeting,
American Political Science Association, December 1948. Baton Rouge: Louisiana
State University, 1949. Mimeographed.

Gray, Edward R. State Proposals Voted on in 1943. Washington, D. C.: U. S. Bureau
of the Census, January 1944. Pp. 7.

————, and Kellner, Clarence A. State Proposals Voted upon in Elections of
1939. Washington, D. C.: U. S. Bureau of the Census, December 1939.

Hudson, Irby R. The Amending Process in State Constitutions. In Papers on Constitutional Revision, pp. 1-13. Knoxville: Bureau of Public Administration,
University of Tennessee, 1947.

Illinois. General Assembly. Legislative Reference Bureau. The Amending Article of
the Constitution. Springfield: 1919. Pp. 33. Constitutional Convention Bulletin
No. 3.

Juergensmeyer, John E., and Sokolow, Alvin D. The Campaign for the Illinois
Reapportionment Amendment. Urbana: Institute of Government and Public
Affairs, University of Illinois, 1957. Pp. 63, mimeographed.

Ross, Carl A. Report on Amendments and Changes in the Constitutions of the Thirteen
Original States before and after the Adoption of the U. S. Constitution. Albion,
Michigan: the Author, April 1947. Pp. 4, mimeographed.

Saye, Albert B. A Constitutional History of Georgia, Chapter 15. Athens: University
of Georgia Press, 1948. On amendments and more amendments.

Spencer, Richard C. Proposals Voted on in 1944. Washington, D. C.: U. S. Bureau
of the Census, April 1945.

————, and Meck, Anna A. State Proposals Voted on in 1946. Washington, D. C.:
U. S. Bureau of the Census, May 1947.

State Proposals Voted upon in the 1938 Elections. Washington, D. C.: U. S. Bureau
of the Census, December 1938.

————, 1939. Washington, D. C.: U. S. Bureau of the Census, December 1939.

————, 1940. Washington, D. C.: U. S. Bureau of the Census, December 1941.

Steinbicker, Paul G., and Faust, Martin L. Manual on the Amending Procedure and
the Initiative and Referendum. Missouri Constitutional Convention of 1943.
Columbia: 1943.

Tennessee. University. Bureau of Public Administration. The Amending Process in
State Constitutions. Knoxville: 1946.

*　　*　　*

Benson, George C. S. "State Constitutional Development through Amendment in 1935." American Political Science Review, April 1936, pp. 275-79.

————. "————, 1936." American Political Science Review, April 1937, pp. 280-85.

"California's Constitutional Amendomania." Stanford Law Review, January 1949, pp. 279-88.

Connors, Arthur. "Constitutional Amendments and Referred Measures, 1915." American Political Science Review, February 1916, pp. 104-109.

————. "————, 1917." American Political Science Review, May 1918, pp. 268-71.

"Constitutional Amendments." State Government, January 1954, p. 1.

"Constitutional Amendments—Direct Legislation." State Government, January 1953, pp. 1-2.

"————." State Government, January 1957, inside front cover. List adopted in November 1956.

Cummins, Damian L. "Amending the Constitution." Commonweal, April 16, 1936, pp. 709-11.

Dodd, Walter F. "Judicial Control over the Amendment of State Constitutions: Courts' Control over Form, Process, and Substance of Amendments." Columbia Law Review, November 1910, pp. 618-38.

"First Steps Toward a Modern Constitution." National Civic Review, February 1960, pp. 64-65, 82.

Garner, James W. "The Amendment of State Constitutions." American Political Science Review, February 1907, pp. 213-47.

Garrison, Lloyd K. "The Form of a Constitutional Amendment." American Labor Legislation Review, March 1937, pp. 11-16.

Ireland, Gordon. "Constitutional Amendments—Power of Conventions." Tulane Law Review, December 1931, pp. 75-82.

McKinney, Madge M. "Constitutional Amendment in a Democracy." Public Opinion Quarterly, October 1939, pp. 635-45.

"Many Amendments Submitted to Voters." National Municipal Review, December 1956, pp. 541-44. Georgia, 58; Louisiana, 48.

"Note on Amending Procedure." Minnesota Municipalities, December 1940, pp. 478-79.

Owen, J. Kimbrough. "Constitutional Revision by the Research Method: Louisiana Law Institute Sets Pattern for Others." National Municipal Review, May 1948, pp. 267-70.

"People Vote on Constitutional Amendments in Nine States in 1938." National Municipal Review, February 1938, pp. 109-10.

Reeves, John E., and Vanlandingham, Kenneth E. "Amending and Revising State Constitutions." Kentucky Law Journal, January 1947, pp. 119-28.

Rider, Harry A. "Amendments to State Constitutions." American Political Science Review, August 1919, pp. 429-50.

Rohlfing, Charles C. "Amendment and Revision of State Constitutions." Annals, September 1935, pp. 180-87.

Sears, Kenneth C. "Voting on Constitutional Convention and Amendments." University of Chicago Law Review, June 1935, pp. 612-18.

Thomas, David Y. "Amending a State Constitution by Custom." American Political Science Review, November 1929, pp. 920-21.

Tichenor, C. O. "The Amendment of Constitutions." American Law Review, July-August 1901, pp. 495-509.

Todd, H. S. "Legislation by Constitutional Amendment." Constitution Review, July 1921, pp. 217-23.

Trewhitt, H. L. "Tennessee Amends Her Constitution." State Government, June 1954, pp. 119-22, 128.

Vose, Clement E. "Conservatism by Amendment." Yale Review, December 1956, pp. 176-90.

White, Thomas R. "Amendment and Revision of State Constitutions." University of Pennsylvania Law Review, June 1952, pp. 1132-52.

Whitfield, J. B. "Amending State Constitutions." Michigan Law Review, February 1913, pp. 302-307.

Wigmore, John H. "A Program for Legislative Efficiency by Constitutional Amendment." Illinois Law Review, November 1929, pp. 315-18.

index